Pragmatic Asset Protection

A Guide

Robert L. Sommers

Sommers-Taxapedia.com

ISBN-10: 0983791910
ISBN-13: 978-0-9837919-1-1

Cover art and layout by Crawshaw Design

Sommers-Taxapedia.com

Prnted in the United States of America

About the Author

Robert L. Sommers provides sophisticated legal advice concerning complex tax, business and estate planning issues.

As an acknowledged expert in the field of tax law, Bob has written hundreds of articles, columns, and action guides and spoken at dozens of events.

Bob Sommers is The Tax Prophet. He has created and written The Tax Prophet website, a vital resource to those seeking solid U.S. tax information, issue spotting and analysis.

As a full-time practicing attorney in the heart of San Francisco's Financial District, Bob owns and operates a general tax law firm.

He focuses on U.S. and foreign individuals and small companies in the areas of

- Estate planning (wills, trusts and family-based entities)
- Foreign tax
- Business start-ups and funding
- Employee stock options
- Probate and trust administration
- Federal and California tax controversies (audits, appeals and litigation)

Certified as a Tax Specialist by the California Board of Legal Specialization of the State Bar of California (a distinction earned by less than .05% of all attorneys licensed to practice law in California,) Bob also received a postgraduate legal degree (LL.M.) in taxation from New York University School of Law in 1985, the premier graduate tax program in the U.S.

Bob has testified before the US Senate's Finance Committee regarding tax scams on the Internet. He is in demand as an expert witness in both criminal and civil cases involving Tax and Trust Law, Tax Fraud, Busted Tax Shelters, and Bogus Trust Arrangements.

The Wall Street Journal, New York Times, Forbes, CNN to Money magazine and the Best of the Web have all reviewed Bob's work and his contributions to legal education. Reviews online.

You can sign up to receive his Free Newsletter, a monthly update on current tax issues.

Contents

1. INTRODUCTION

- "I want to protect my assets from frivolous lawsuits and runaway jury verdicts."

- "I don't want my spouse or her family to get my assets if we get divorced."

- "I don't trust my business partners, if things go wrong, they'll sue me for everything I have."

- "My tenant is claiming that her baby will have life-long health problems because of toxic mold found in my rental unit."

- "I'm a doctor and am concerned that I'll be sued into the poorhouse, no matter how much I pay for malpractice insurance."

These examples echo the complaints and frustrations of individuals concerned about losing their assets. Unfortunately, because there is a demand for asset protection, a supply of so-called asset protection experts has emerged, many of them unsavory and out to make a quick buck. But for those who want to protect their assets against lawsuits and creditors, there are solid methods to accomplish this, if you know the rules and understand that careful planning and attention to detail is required.

Simply stated, asset protection generally involves the creation of, and transfer of debtor's assets to, one or more business entities that legally limit creditors from seizing and selling the transferred assets in satisfaction of a current or future debt.

INTRODUCTION

In general, an asset protection plan shifts ownership and control of assets from the debtor, thereby converting assets that otherwise can be easily seized and sold by a creditor, into assets beyond the creditor's reach. By transferring assets into certain types of trusts or limited liability entities (corporations, limited partnerships and limited liability companies), in which the debtor owns an interest in the entity but not the actual asset, the creditor is restricted to the debtor's potential economic interest in the entity. The creditor is thwarted from seizing and selling the entity's assets. For example, if a debtor properly transfers assets to a partnership or limited liability company (LLC), in general, a creditor is limited to the debtor's rights to distributions from the partnership or LLC.

As discussed below, from a practical standpoint the debtor's interest in an entity is often worthless to a creditor, especially when the creditor is not entitled to voting or management rights. Thus, by creating entities with effective restrictions, a legal barrier is imposed between a creditor's attempt to seize and sell a debtor's assets in satisfaction of a legal judgment or other claim, and the assets themselves.

There are two general types of asset protection:

1. Using off-shore jurisdictions to place assets outside the reach of creditors and the U.S. court system; and

2. Using entities formed within the U.S. in states with favorable debtor protection laws. Usually, these jurisdictions protect the limited liability nature of the entity as a barrier against a direct judgment against the debtor

INTRODUCTION

and thus, indirectly, protect the debtor against creditors who attempt to "disregard" the entity in hopes of seizing the assets held within the entity.

Note: Another asset protection scheme utilizes sham trusts or entities to hide assets from creditors, a method so transparently phony that it will not be discussed in this Guide.

Domestic asset protection is expressly sanctioned under the law. Public policy allows owners to operate businesses without personal liability beyond the capital invested in the business. Virtually all major business operations are conducted with limited liability entities, such as corporations, limited partnerships and LLCs.

The test of any asset protection plan is whether it will pass muster before a skeptical judge or jury and success depends on marshaling the law and arguments that support the plan. In general, this requires using the limited liability laws to structure a valid business or investment entity and has true economic substance and avoiding the fraudulent transfer pitfalls (discussed at length below).

In contrast, an offshore asset protection entity will invariably fail both the legitimacy and fraudulent transfer tests. More importantly, it raises a huge red flag to a judge or jury, because outside of hiding assets from creditors, the plan will have no genuine economic substance.

2 OFF-SHORE ASSET PROTECTION

Off-shore asset protection has been hyped by various professionals and foreign countries as the exclusive method to protect assets against potential creditors. As I have written in several articles, off-shore asset protection is mostly an illusion designed to scare off unsophisticated creditors. It is expensive and does not accomplish true asset protection because U.S. courts, once the scam has been presented to them, have rejected the argument that a person can successfully place his assets outside the jurisdiction of the court.

In the celebrated case of <u>Federal Trade Commission v. Affordable Media</u>, 179 F. 3d 1228 (9th Cir, 1999), the U.S. federal district court judge tossed the defendant in jail for contempt of court for violating the court's order to return assets secreted in an off-shore jurisdiction to the U.S., even though the defendant claimed it was "impossible" for him to do so under his asset protection structure. The judge's actions were upheld on appeal to the 9th Circuit Court of Appeals. The court ridiculed the notion (and the theories of several well-known off-shore asset protection promoters) that a debtor could voluntarily place his assets outside the reach of the U.S. and then claim it was "impossible" for him to retrieve those assets. The court rejected self-imposed impossibility as a defense to compliance with a court order to return assets to the U.S.

The Lesson: The court may not have jurisdiction over the assets, but it does have jurisdiction over the person. Thus, debtor's assets might be protected but his liberty is not and expect him to spend months in jail for contempt of court if he attempts to place assets beyond the jurisdiction of the U.S. courts.

3. DOMESTIC ASSET PROTECTION

In contrast to the failed and useless off-shore asset protection schemes, domestic asset protection does not hide assets or interfere with a creditor's right to enforce a judgment. Instead, it uses the laws of a favorable jurisdiction (such as Delaware or Nevada) to limit the creditor's rights to such a degree that a prudent creditor would be discouraged from pursing a judgment. Under domestic asset protection, it is possible to limit the creditor's right to a "charging order" against a debtor's "economic interest" in an entity. A charging order carries no right to vote, manage, liquidate or control the entity or the assets held by the entity.

3.1. Charging Order

Understanding how a charging order works is key for those seeking legally-sanctioned protection of their assets. A charging order is the exclusive creditor remedy when a debtor holds an interest in a general partnership, limited partnership or limited liability company. Of the three, the limited liability company (LLC) is usually the preferred choice since its members are not personally liable for the debts of the entity. A charging order permits a judgment creditor to receive future distributions that otherwise would have been received by the debtor, if and when such distributions are made, until the judgment is satisfied. The debtor retains all other ownership rights, such as the right to vote and make managerial decisions — rights the debtor had prior to the charging order. In fact, the creditor's interest under a charging order is subordinate to future entity liens and encumbrances.

Domestic Asset Protection

By placing a client's assets in one or more LLCs, creditors are limited to obtaining a charging order, and if the LLC's Operating Agreement is properly drafted, the creditor cannot compel distributions of income or sales of assets held by the LLC. The creditor receives an "economic interest" only (the right to distributions if and when they are made) but no right to vote or control the LLC, or to reach the assets of the LLC in satisfaction of a judgment.

An economic interest subject to the charging order could be liable for income taxes, whether or not any money is actually distributed to the creditor. An LLC's manager may have no interest in arbitrating issues between the creditor and debtor, and if the LLC agreement directs the manager to send a K-1 (information return sent to partners and LLC members) to the economic interest holder, the creditor could receive the K-1 for income that was not actually distributed. The possibility of paying taxes on distributions never received should deter most creditors from seeking a charging order.

3.2. Additional Protections

A partnership or LLC interest may be bifurcated into a voting interest and an economic interest. A charging order pertains to an economic interest only. The voting and management rights are retained by the debtor. With a properly drafted partnership or LLC agreement, the holder of an economic interest has no voting or management rights, no right to information such as tax returns or the books and records of the entity and no right to the partnership or LLC agreement itself. The partnership or LLC agreement may require the holder of an economic interest to pay a pro-rata share

Domestic Asset Protection

of any additional capital contributions mandated by the management and the failure to pay up could cause the termination of the interest. Consequently, a creditor seeking a charging order could be flying blind without any access to the information needed to make an informed decision whether to obtain a charging order in the first place.

3.3. Case Law

Evans v. Galardi, 546 P.2d 313, 16 Cal. 3d 300 (1976) is a California Supreme Court decision defining a charging order's scope as applied to a limited partner's interest in a limited partnership. The Court's reasoning applies to general partnerships and LLCs as well. The court, in Footnote 15, quotes Taylor v. S & M Lamp, Co., (1961), 190 Cal. App. 2d 700 as follows:

> "'Charging orders on partnership interests have replaced levies of execution as the remedy for reaching such interests."
>
> "This is a correct statement of the law as applied to the ordinary case, i.e., (1) where the partnership continues a bona fide existence and (2) where there is no transfer of partnership assets without a fair and adequate consideration or in fraud of creditors of either the partnership or of individual partners.

Not all attempts to limit creditors to the charging order remedy have been successful. In re Ehmann, 319 B.R. 200 (Bankr. D. Ariz.1995) is a strange case involving an LLC (Fiesta) where the members had no affirmative obligations or duties under the operating agreement. A bankruptcy trustee successfully asserted

Domestic Asset Protection

that a state law charging order did not limit the trustee to merely a debtor's distributive economic interest in an LLC, but the trustee could have a receiver appointed to operate (or dissolve and liquidate) the LLC. In a subsequent order dated December 7, 2005, the court stated:

> "Utilizing a legitimate business structure for the sole purpose of shielding assets from creditors borders on a fraud on creditors."

> The conduct of Fiesta and its manager since the Trustee's appointment demonstrates an unequivocal intent to operate Fiesta as if it were a revocable living spendthrift trust.

Note: This court order was withdrawn as part of a settlement payment to the Trustees.

Thus, a partnership or limited liability company engaging in valid business operations is critical to obtaining charging order protection and since the purpose of the protection is for the benefit of the innocent partner or member, it is strongly recommended that an LLC has at least two members, one of whom should own at least 2%, preferably at least 5%. Of course, in addition the entity must have proper documentation and function as a true business entity.

4. FRAUDULENT TRANSFERS

4.1. Introduction

Most attempts at asset protection fail because of fraudulent transfer laws. These are state laws, generally uniform throughout the U.S.. that protect creditors against unsophisticated debtors attempting to transfer assets out of their names when a creditor is breathing down their necks, although the scope of the fraudulent transfer laws covers much more than just last-minute transfers.

The rights of existing creditors are determined under applicable state law. Asset protection does not work when there is an existing creditor or if a claim arises within a period of years (determined by state law) after the asset protection plan is placed into service. Too often, debtors engaging in asset protection run afoul of applicable state fraudulent transfer laws.

Thus, a fundamental aspect to asset protection is understanding how the fraudulent transfer laws work and designing a plan to avoid them. In general terms, a transfer is fraudulent if it is made with: (i) actual intent to hinder, delay or defraud any creditor, present or future, or (ii) the transfer is made for less than full and adequate consideration and as a result, the debtor does not have sufficient assets to satisfy the creditor's claim. Thus, by not deliberately engaging in a transaction to hinder, delay or defraud a creditor and making sure that a transfer is for full value (for if less than full value, the debtor retains sufficient assets to satisfy claims), the debtor can sidestep the fraudulent transfer barrier.

Fraudulent Transfers

4.2. Examples – Good and Bad

The classic example of what not to do involves the transfer of real estate, usually a resident, from the debtor to the debtor's spouse, brother or sister while in the middle of a lawsuit. This will never be successful. What does work is having the debtor's brother purchase a home in the brother's name and lease it to the debtor, because the property was never in the debtor's name in the first place.

One of the most interesting examples of crude, but evidently successful, asset protection involved the late Attorney Roy Cohn of New York. Mr. Cohn was infamous for being Joseph McCarthy's right-hand man during the communist witch-hunt Senate hearings in the 1050s. He later became a successful New York attorney and political powerbroker, representing entertainers and mobsters alike.

Mr. Cohn filed tax returns but never paid taxes. IRS audited him for 20 years and then finally sued him for $7.0 million in back taxes. How did he get away from the IRS for 20 years? Mr. Cohn made sure never to have a bank account or assets in his own name. Assets were owned by others, including his mother, whom he treated as a business associate. Evidently, his salary from his law firm was a dollar a year. The firm, however, paid for his expenses. Thus, there was nothing for the IRS to grab, even though Mr. Cohn led an extravagant life.

The lesson: Own nothing in your name and do not have a bank or financial account. Stating the Cohn principle differently, "Own nothing, control everything."

Fraudulent Transfers

4.3. Fraudulent Transfers

If the settlor has already committed an act that could give rise to a legal claim against him, it is usually too late to transfer assets out of his name. There are two basic types of fraudulent transfers that creditors may challenge: actual intent and constructive intent transfers. **Note:** References in this Guide are to California's version of the Fraudulent Transfers Act.

1. Actual Intent Transfers: A transfer is deemed fraudulent and may be set aside if it is made with an "actual intent to hinder, delay or defraud any creditor" of the transferor, whether present or future.

2. Constructive Intent Transfers: Generally, a constructive fraudulent transfer occurs when property is transferred for "less than reasonable value," if any of the following three requirements are met:

a. The debtor is left with "unreasonably small" assets for carrying out the business in which the debtor is engaged or about to engage;

b. The debtor intended to incur, or reasonably believed or reasonably should have believed, that he or she would incur debts beyond his or her ability to pay as they became due; or

c. The debtor was insolvent or became insolvent as a result of the transfer..

Generally, there is a four-year statute of limitations for "constructive" fraudulent transfers, but this varies from state to state. For "actual intent" fraudulent transfers, legal action can be

Fraudulent Transfers

brought at any time before the later of (1) four years after the transfer was made; or (2) within seven years of when the transfer was made, as long as the action is brought within one year after the transfer or obligation could reasonably have been discovered by the claimant. Again, this could vary from state to state.

4.4. Defining a Fraudulent Transfer

California Civil Code Sec. 3439.04(a) [which is almost identical to the Uniform Fraudulent Transfers Act – reproduced in full in the research section] defines a fraudulent transfer as follows:

(a) A transfer made or obligation incurred by a debtor is fraudulent as to a creditor, whether the creditor's claim arose before or after the transfer was made or the obligation was incurred, if the debtor made the transfer or incurred the obligation as follows:

(1) With actual intent to hinder, delay, or defraud any creditor of the debtor.

(2) Without receiving a reasonably equivalent value in exchange for the transfer or obligation, and the debtor either:

(A) Was engaged or was about to engage in a business or a transaction for which the remaining assets of the debtor were unreasonably small in relation to the business or transaction; or

(B) Intended to incur, or believed or reasonably should have believed that he or she would incur, debts beyond his or

Fraudulent Transfers

her ability to pay as they became due.

In essence, the Act prevents debtors from placing assets outside the reach of creditors. In <u>Mejia v. Reed</u>, 31 Cal 4th 657, 664 (2003), the California Supreme Court made the following general observations concerning the Act:

> The UFTA [Uniform Fraudulent Transfers Act] was enacted in 1986; it is the most recent in a line of statutes dating to the reign of Queen Elizabeth I. "This Act, like its predecessor and the Statute of 13 Elizabeth, declares rights and provides remedies for unsecured creditors against transfers that impede them in the collection of their claims." ...Under the UFTA, a transfer is fraudulent, both as to present and future creditors, if it is made "[w]ith actual intent to hinder, delay, or defraud any creditor of the debtor." ... Even without actual fraudulent intent, a transfer may be fraudulent as to present creditors if the debtor did not receive "a reasonably equivalent value in exchange for the transfer" and "the debtor was insolvent at that time or the debtor became insolvent as a result of the transfer or obligation." ...On its face, the UFTA applies to all transfers.

4.5. Actual Intent

In <u>Reddy v. Gonzalez</u>, 8 Cal. App 4th 118, 123-124, Mr. Gilbert, a debtor, transferred his interest in his personal residence to his spouse to stymie the efforts of a creditor to satisfy a judgment against Mr. Gilbert. In finding that the transfer amounted to actual fraud, the court noted:

> Gilbert testified that he conveyed his interest in the Milpitas property to defendant to protect it from his

Fraudulent Transfers

creditors. This testimony clearly and convincingly evidenced Gilbert's intent to prevent his creditors from obtaining satisfaction of their claims from Gilbert's interest in the Milpitas property. This is actual fraud.

United States v. Townley, E.D.Wash. No. CV-02-00384-RHW, July 29, 2004, affirmed, 2006 WL 1345248 (9th Cir. 05/17/2006 – unpublished opinion) involved a situation where a debtor placed his personal assets beyond the reach of the legal process. In Townley, taxpayers, who were residents of Washington State, engaged in an asset protection plan involving transfers to the Beaver Valley Trust. At the time of the transfer, 1995, taxpayers had no current creditors, however, the stated purpose for the transfers was to shield their assets against the claims of future unknown creditors. Washington State has adopted the Uniform Fraudulent Transfer Act.

According to Mr. Townley, he formed the Beaver Valley Trust out of concern over "lawsuits from the exposure we had from liability from troubled boys in the State of Washington." Five years later, in 2000, taxpayers incurred a federal tax liability. IRS then filed suit in U.S. District Court to reduce the federal tax assessments to judgment, set aside the transfers to the Beaver Valley Trust as fraudulent, and to foreclose on the federal tax liens.

The district court held that the fact that taxpayers engaged in asset protection for the express purpose of defeating the claims of future creditors violated the actual intent provisions of the Washington state fraudulent transfer act. The court found the

Fraudulent Transfers

admission that the Townleys made the transfers to protect against unknown future creditors was a veritable confession of their actual intent to hinder, delay or defraud all creditors, including the IRS:

> "[The Townleys] assert that no 'hypothetical future judgment creditor' exists, nor did one ever exist. * * * [The Townleys fail] to realize that the IRS is such a creditor. Under [the Townleys'] reasoning, the Washington Uniform Fraudulent Transfer Act would never protect future creditors. A close reading of §19.40.041, however, demonstrates that this section provides protections to both present and future creditors." ...

> "If this statute is read by inserting the players in this case, it would read as follows: A transfer made or obligation incurred by the Townleys (debtor) is fraudulent as to the United States (a creditor), if the Townleys made the transfer or incurred the obligation with actual intent to hinder, delay, or defraud any potential plaintiffs who may have a cause of action (any creditor) against the Townleys (debtor). Mr. Townley's statement that he wanted to protect his assets from any potential 'lawsuits from the exposure we had liability from troubled boys in the State of Washington' represents direct evidence of his intent to defraud one of his potential future creditors..."

The lessons in <u>Reddy</u> and <u>Townley</u> are clear: If the sole and stated purpose of engaging in a transaction is to shield assets from creditors, the plan may be successfully attacked under the "actual intent" clause of the fraudulent transfers act. In the <u>Townley</u> case, gift transfers were made to a trust, ostensibly for Townley's children, but Townley himself retained control over the trust and used its assets without compensation paid to the trust;

Fraudulent Transfers

thus, the trust was considered a sham and the alter ego of Townley.

In contrast, the asset protection described in this Guide involves the formation of legitimate business entities that do not hide or shield assets from creditors, but provide for legal creditor remedies (the charging order) that protects an entity against a creditor of one of the owners from seizing and selling an entity's assets – a vital distinction. (See the LLC Memo in Section 7; also see In Re Turner, below, "Asset protection is not illegal and is honored by the law if done for a legitimate purpose.")

4.5. Circumstantial Evidence of Actual Intent.

In addition to the direct evidence of actual intent, actual intent may be established through circumstantial evidence under CCP §3439.04 (b), which enumerates a list of 11 factors (badges of fraud), any or all of which may be considered. The list of factors is not meant to be exclusive. The following are the most prevalent fraud factors:

1. Whether the transfer or obligation was to an insider.

2. Whether debtor retained possession or control of the property transferred after the transfer.

3. Whether the transfer or obligation was disclosed or concealed.

4. Whether before the transfer was made or obligation was incurred, debtor had been sued or threatened with suit.

5. Whether the transfer was of substantially all debtor's assets.

Fraudulent Transfers

6. Whether debtor removed or concealed assets.

7. Whether the value of the consideration received by debtor was reasonably equivalent to the value of the asset transferred or the amount of the obligation incurred.

8. Whether debtor was insolvent or became insolvent shortly after the transfer was made or the obligation was incurred.

4.6. The "Friendly Lender" Transaction

Outside of transferring a home or property outright to a spouse or relative, a friendly "phony" loan transaction, in which the home is retained by the debtor, but a mortgage or lien is placed on the home for a debt owed to a friend who will not foreclose on the property, is another form of crude asset protection that will not work. Example: Debtor is in the middle of a lawsuit and owns a home with $500,000 in equity. Debtor's brother (or a corporation owned by debtor's brother) provides debtor with a line of credit worth $500,000 and places a mortgage on debtor's home. All of a sudden, debtor has no equity in the home because of the mortgage and the creditor cannot seize and sell the property.

Incurring debt obligations, however, may constitute fraudulent transfers. The Act provides that either a transfer of assets or an obligation incurred by a debtor falls within the ambit of a fraudulent transfer:

> (a) A transfer made <u>or obligation incurred</u> by a debtor is fraudulent as to a creditor, whether the
>
> creditor's claim arose before or after the transfer was made or the obligation was incurred, ... [emphasis added]

Fraudulent Transfers

C.F. Trust, Inc v. DEP, Inc. Nos. 95-14438-SSM, 97-1017 Oct. 31, 1997, United States Bankruptcy Court, E.D. Virginia, involved a series of transactions, including a friendly creditor, J.P. Development, which held a judgment against Barrie Peterson to prevent other creditors from attaching his assets. The court concluded the arrangement was tantamount to a fraudulent conveyance and J.P. Development was the *alter ego* of the debtor Barrie Peterson:

> The conclusion is inescapable that J.P. Development was nothing but Barrie Peterson's straw in the transaction and holds the assignment of judgment for his benefit. [FN18]
>
> FN18. In particular, it would appear that a primary purpose of having J.P. Development hold the judgment was in order to obtain friendly liens against Barrie Peterson's assets that could be used to shield those assets from his creditors. ...[Emphasis added]

In Wu v. Tseng, Slip Copy, 2007 WL 201087 (E.D.Va.), January 24, 2007, The U.S. District Court in Virginia held against a defendant who sought to protect his assets by placing a friendly creditor lien on a parcel of valuable real property.

Defendant, Mr. Tseng, obtained various sham loans from related entities and secured the repayment of the loans with a parcel of valuable real estate to prevent a judgment creditor from selling the real estate. The creditor, Mr. Wu, claimed that the various loan transfers were accomplished with the intent to hinder, defraud or delay his creditors. Mr. Wu also contended that Mr. Tseng, by obtaining a loan which could never be repaid except by

Fraudulent Transfers

a sale of the real property serving as collateral for the loan, insured that Mr. Tseng retained equitable title to the real property while protecting it from Mr. Wu's eventual judgment lien. The court found that such a transfer, if proven, would violate Virginia's fraudulent conveyance statutes.

In Fleet Credit Corporation v. TML Bus Sales, Inc., 65 F.3d 119 (9th Cir. 1995), a debtor (Berthold) owned a corporation (Taylor Bus Service) and placed the corporation into Chapter 11 Bankruptcy. Two of debtor's friends formed a new Nevada corporation (Victory Enterprises). The Taylor Bus Service then transferred Victory Enterprises the sum of $1.9 million through a bogus loan. The court found the transfer from Taylor Bus Service to Victory Enterprise amounted to a fraudulent transfer under California law since the transfer was made with actual intent to hinder, delay or defraud the creditors of Taylor Bus Service and Berthold.

The court also found that Berthold operated Taylor Bus Service as an extension of himself and used the funds in Taylor Bus Service for personal expenses having nothing to do with the operation of the corporation's business. The court then concluded there was a double-layer of fraud:

> Berthold hid $1.9 million in an account at Charles Schwab. His alter ego corporation loaned the money to another corporation in a fraudulent conveyance designed to keep the money away from creditors....so for Berthold's creditors to get it [the $1.9 million], they had to penetrate two layers of fraud, the alter ego corporation and the fraudulent conveyance.

Fraudulent Transfers

4.7. Invalid Asset Protection – No Independent Business Purpose

In Re Turner, 335 B.R. 140 (Bankr. N.D. Cal. 2005). involved the transfer by a husband and wife of their residence (Home), while a lawsuit was pending against the husband, to a Nevada LLC (RICH, LLC), 99% owned by a Bahamas Trust (GG Trust) and 1% owned by another Nevada corporation (Proset) formed by the husband and wife. The court found that the LLC structure was merely the alter ego of the husband and wife and the transfer to the trust was fraudulent under California law. The court described two types of asset protection, one that is legal and permitted under state law and the other which is invalid and will be disregarded and noted the following:

> The evidence presented persuaded the Court that RICH, LLC and Proset were Debtor's alter egos. The Debtor admitted that these entities were created and their relationship structured to maximize the protection of his assets: i.e., the Home. "Asset protection is not illegal and is honored by the law if done for a legitimate purpose. For example, an individual may do business through a corporation or limited liability company and will not be held personally liable for the debts of the entity. The assets of the corporation or limited liability company will not be considered assets of the individual interest holder. However, an entity or series of entities may not be created with no business purpose and personal assets transferred to them with no relationship to any business purpose, simply as a means of shielding them from creditors. Under such circumstances, the law views the entity as the alter ego of the

Fraudulent Transfers

individual debtor and will disregard it to prevent injustice.

The Court in <u>Turner</u> recognized that individuals cannot avail themselves of state-enacted limited liability laws that protect investors engaged in legitimate, bona fide business activities, to shield their personal assets from creditors. See <u>Fleet Credit Corporation</u> (discussed above) for another example of using a alter ego for improper fraudulent conveyance purposes.

4.8. Invalid Asset Protection – Alter Ego Doctrine

In <u>Associated Vendors, Inc. v. Oakland Meat Co., Inc et al.</u>, 210 Cal. App. 2d 825 (1962), the appellant brought an action against the respondents, (Meat Co. and Packing Co.) and other individuals to collect, inter alia, unpaid rental on property leased by appellant to Packing Co. Appellant sought to impose liability upon Meat Co. and the other individual defendants on the theory that Packing Co. was the *alter ego* (second self) of the other respondents. The court analyzed the *alter ego* doctrine as follows:

> ... the 2 requirements are: "1) that there be such unity of interest and ownership that the separate personalities of the corporation and the individual no longer exist, and 2) that, if the acts are treated as those of the corporation alone, an inequitable result will follow." The general rule is stated as follows:
>
> "Before a corporation's acts and obligations can be legally recognized as those of a particular person, and vice versa, it must be made to appear

Fraudulent Transfers

> that the corporation is not only influenced and governed by that person, but that there is such a unity of interest and ownership that the individuality, or separateness, of such person and corporation has ceased, and that the facts are such that an adherence to the fiction of the separate existence of the corporation would, under the particular circumstances, sanction a fraud or promote injustice."

The court listed a variety of factors that other courts have considered in analyzing the particular circumstances of each case:

1. The treatment by an individual of the assets of the corporation as his own;

2. The identical equitable ownership in the two entities;

3. The identification of the equitable owners thereof with the domination and control of the two entities;

4. The identification of the directors and officers of the two entities in the responsible supervision and management;

5. Sole ownership of all of the stock in a corporation by one individual or the members of a family;

6. The use of the same office or business location;

7. The employment of the same employees and/or attorney;

8. The use of a corporation as a mere shell, instrumentality or conduit for a single venture or the business of an individual or

Fraudulent Transfers

another corporation;

9. Concealment and misrepresentation of the identity of the responsible ownership, management and financial interest, or concealment of personal business activities;

10. The disregard of legal formalities and the failure to maintain arm's length relationships among related entities;

11. The diversion of assets from a corporation by or to a stockholder or other person or entity, to the detriment of creditors, or the manipulation of assets and liabilities between entities so as to concentrate the assets in one and the liabilities in another;

12. The use of a corporation as a subterfuge of illegal transactions.

4.8. Fraudulent Transfers and Domestic Asset Protection

Formation of a domestic LLC to operate an ongoing business or real estate portfolio should avoid the application of fraudulent transfer laws. First, a transfer to an LLC does not render the client insolvent, since it is a tax-free exchange in which assets are transferred to an entity in exchange for an interest in the entity which is equal in value to the assets transferred. Second, the creditor has the remedy of a charging order, as mandated under state law, so there is no interference with the creditor's rights to satisfy a claim under state law and the debtor is not rendered judgment-proof.

Instead of acting outside the law, the debtor is using the state law protections afforded those operating a business This is

Fraudulent Transfers

a superior position to defend in court, if required, compared to sending assets to some far-flung foreign jurisdiction, then thumbing your nose at the judge, claiming his has no jurisdiction over the assets.

Under the LLC structure, the rights of a creditor are altered and, depending on how the LLC is structured, a charging order, as discussed above, may be little practice value to a creditor.

In the typical case, the actual intent portion of the Act arises when a debtor transfers title to property to a relative or sham trust, or engages in a friendly lender transaction, usually during a lawsuit or after a creditor commences efforts to collect a debt. By making sure there are independent business reasons for forming an LLC, such as limited liability for the members, stable management and facilitating estate and gift planning, the transfer should avoid the "actual intent to hinder, delay or defraud any creditor" portion of the statute. The reasons should be well-documented (See the LLC Memo in Section 7) and, of course, all legal requirements, such as state filings and reporting the income and expenses in accordance with the entity's ownership, should be scrupulously followed. As the California Supreme Court in Evans, noted:

> Where, as in the instant case, the partnership is a viable business organization and plaintiff does not show that he will be unable to secure satisfaction of his judgment by use of a charging order or by levy of execution against the debtors' other personally owned property, there is no reason to permit deviation from the prescribed statutory process [of a charging order].

5. DOMESTIC ASSET PROTECTION

This is a simple plan that uses LLCs to protect assets. **Example:** Assume a client who owns several real estate properties or one or more businesses, is concerned about potential lawsuits and wants a business and investment structure that maximizes estate planning and gifting opportunities as well as provides for centralized management and continuity in the event of the client's death. The client should consider either the simplified or complex approaches described below.

5.1. Basic Structure:

1. Form a Delaware Series, LLC, under the laws of the State of Delaware ("Holding") A series LLC permits the formation of one or more subsidiaries (called "series" or "cells") owned by Holding, but which operate as independent LLCs for liability purposes.

> **Note:** This structure is similar to a parent-subsidiary relationship under corporate law, where each subsidiary is owned by the parent corporation.

> **Note:** In some states, the series will need to qualify as an independent LLC. Also, for bankruptcy protection, a series may want to be treated as an independent LLC.

2. Place each real estate property or business in a separate series to maximize liability protection under Delaware law. Once again, there may be reasons to have the series registered as an independent LLC in the state where the real estate is owned or the business is operated.

Domestic Asset Protection

3. Holding should be owned by at least two owners, perhaps the client as to 90% and, perhaps, a trust for the client's children as to 10%.

> **Note:** Holding, LLC will be a manager-managed LLC, and the manager (Client) should be given the power under the Operating Agreement to purchase, sell, exchange and finance properties.

In this example, client owns three real estate properties, one in California, one in Hawaii and one in Nevada. Assume that Nevada does not require an independent LLC to operate the real estate there. The following is a diagram of the basic LLC structure using Holding and three series.

Domestic Asset Protection

Asset Protection Using LLCs - Basic Structure

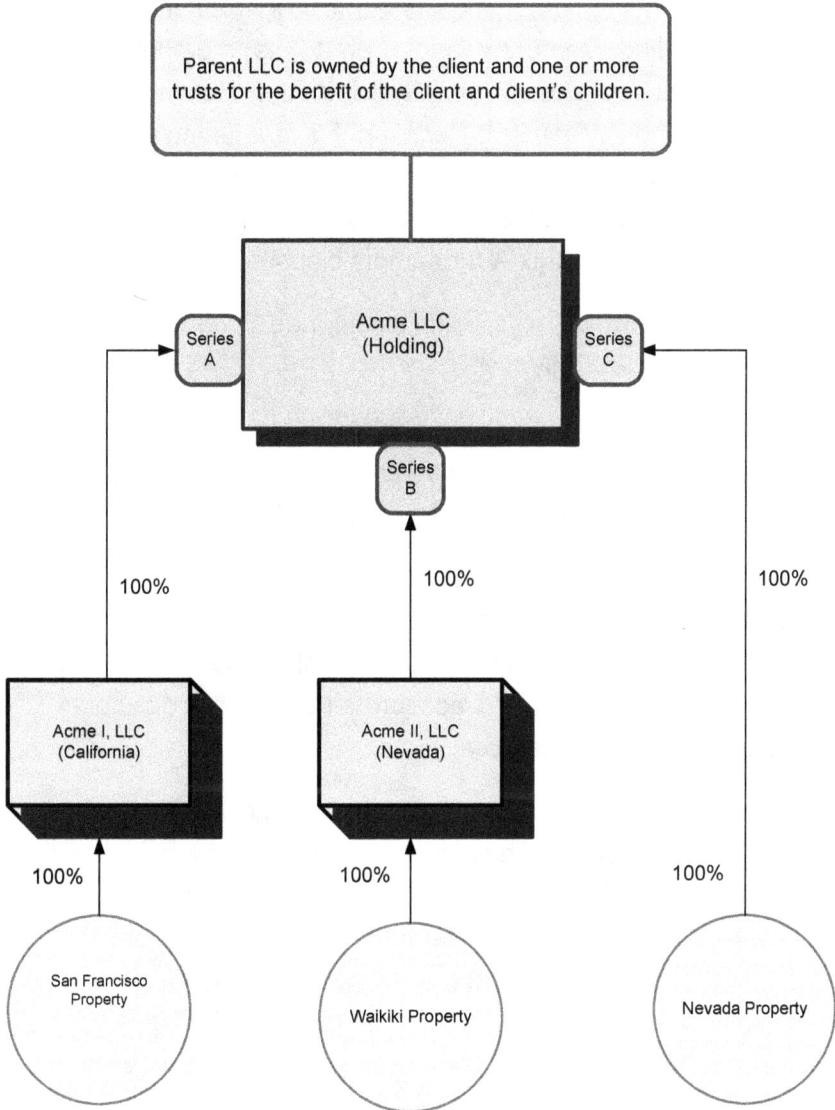

Parent LLC is owned by the client and one or more trusts for the benefit of the client and client's children.

Acme LLC
(Holding)

Series A

Series B

Series C

100%

100%

100%

Acme I, LLC
(California)

Acme II, LLC
(Nevada)

100%

100%

100%

San Francisco Property

Waikiki Property

Nevada Property

Domestic Asset Protection

5.2. Operating Agreement Provisions

Basically, the income and loss will flow from the Operating LLCs to Holding Company and then to its members. Asset protection clauses should be placed in the Holding Company LLC's Operating Agreement. Because this is a Delaware LLC, the favorable provisions under Delaware law would apply. The operating agreement should have some or all of the following provisions (See Appendix A for sample clauses):

1. Restriction of a creditor's/assignee's remedy to a "charging order" only;

2. No liquidation in whole or in part without the unanimous consent of all members and no member has the right to withdraw capital or property from the LLC;

3. In the event of an assignment or charging order, the other members may elect, at their sole option, to "buy" the interest subject to the charging order at its then-current fair market value, taking into account all applicable discounts, as determined by appraisal;

4. Manager has discretion as to income received and expenses incurred. Thus, income can flow from Holding Company to Management LLC and then to the Children's Trust, even if Client's interest in Holding Company is subject to a charging order. Manager has the discretion to permit or deny an IRC Sec. 754 election (to step-up or down the basis in partnership assets under certain circumstances);

5. Provisions appointing new managers by the Members;

Domestic Asset Protection

6. Manager has discretion to retain income regardless of tax consequences to members and to issue K-1 forms to a creditor as the person liable for payment of taxes on income (regardless of whether or not income is distributed); and

7. Provisions for additional capital calls with rights of forfeiture if the creditor fails to make the additional capital call payments.

8. Provisions for charging a member the costs of defending a third party claim against a member's interest, including attorney's fees and a reasonable fees incurred by the manager, and securing these costs and fees by the member's interest in the LLC. In other words, a creditor would need to pay, in full, the total costs and fees incurred by the LLC to obtain a charging order on the member's economic interest.

5.3. Reasons For This Approach

Each real property asset or business is isolated in a separate series so that if one of the properties or businesses is subjected to a lawsuit, the other properties will be insulated from the claim. Holding LLC is a Delaware LLC. There are valid business reasons for its formation, i.e. the implementation of business, financial and estate planning.

Since Client does not have a direct interest in each of the series (but has an indirect interest through ownership in Holding LLC) and only functions as manager of Holding (a position that can be resigned), Client's potential creditors should be unable to

Domestic Asset Protection

claim against assets held in the operating businesses or interests held by Holding LLC.

> **Note:** A lawsuit by a creditor against client's interest in Holding occurs in Delaware, since the client owns an interest in a Delaware series LLC, and Delaware's legal system generally favors debtors over creditors, the opposite of other notoriously business unfriendly jurisdictions.

5.4. Complex Structure

The complex structure builds on the basic structure. In essence, the manager of Holding and any independent LLCs or series is another LLC ("Management") that is owned by a trust for the children. Management has no ownership, economic or voting rights in Holding or the series created by Holding. Thus, client has no direct management rights over the entity, he is the manager of the Management, LLC, but can resign from that position, if necessary. Thus, even if the charging order protection is somehow defeated by a creditor, this structure makes it difficult, if not impossible, for a court to order Management LLC (a non-member manager) to turn over assets, because of a creditor's claim against one of the individual members of Holding, LLC. Also, if the non-member manager takes actions under the LLC's operating agreement, such as making additional capital calls, the potential claim of the debtor's directly self-dealing in the entity is defeated.

The owner of Management LLC is a trust for the benefit of Client's children. The trustee will be Client and an independent trustee. The trust appoints Client as manager of Management LLC.

Domestic Asset Protection

If need be, Client can resign as manager and another person appointed. In addition, client's interest in Holding may be transferred to a special spendthrift trust, described in Section 5.5.

Management fees will be earned by the trust which will benefit the Client's children (i.e. income will flow to the children and be taxed at their tax brackets, a distinct benefit if the children are over age 18 and pay taxes at their own rates). The following diagram illustrates the complex LLC approach:

Domestic Asset Protection

Asset Protection Using LLCs – Complex Structure

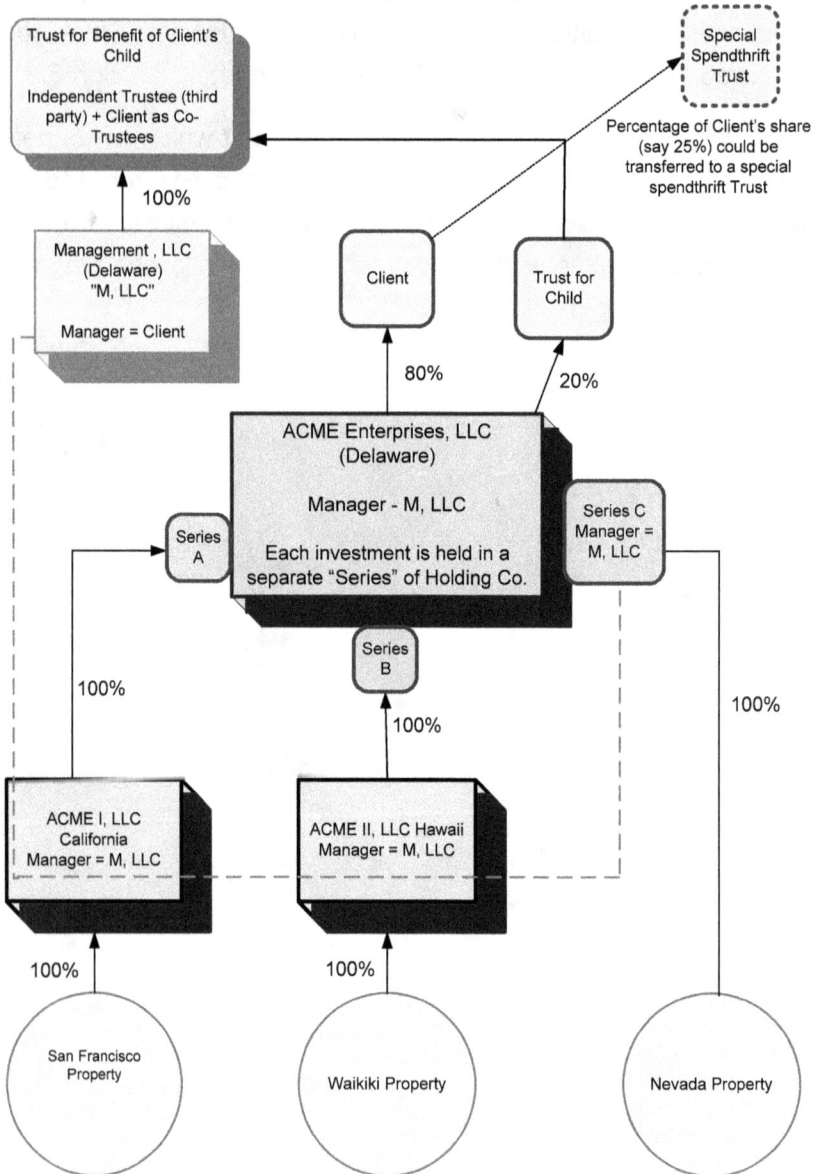

Trust for Benefit of Client's Child

Independent Trustee (third party) + Client as Co-Trustees

Special Spendthrift Trust

Percentage of Client's share (say 25%) could be transferred to a special spendthrift Trust

100%

Management , LLC (Delaware) "M, LLC"

Manager = Client

Client

Trust for Child

80%

20%

ACME Enterprises, LLC (Delaware)

Manager - M, LLC

Each investment is held in a separate "Series" of Holding Co.

Series A

Series B

Series C Manager = M, LLC

100%

100%

100%

ACME I, LLC California Manager = M, LLC

ACME II, LLC Hawaii Manager = M, LLC

100%

100%

San Francisco Property

Waikiki Property

Nevada Property

Domestic Asset Protection

5.5 Special Spendthrift Trusts

The general rule for trusts is that a person cannot create a trust to protect himself against his creditors. Such a trust is considered void against public policy; otherwise, everyone would form a trust, name themselves as beneficiaries and then hold their assets in trust free of creditor claims. However, some states, notably Nevada, have enacted legislation that allows a client to place assets in a special trust in which the client is the beneficiary, and the assets held in the trust are not subject to creditor's claims.

Of course, the fraudulent transfer rules apply to the funding of the trust, but the Nevada statute of limitations is merely two years, not the traditional four to seven years.

> **Note**: The term, "spendthrift" refers to a beneficiary that may spend money imprudently and is in need of protection against his or her improvident spending habits. A spendthrift provision is common in trusts and states that a beneficiary cannot sell or assign his or her rights in the trust to a third party, which effective prevents a creditor from obtaining any of the income or assets of the trust. Thus, the protection of a spendthrift clause is absolute and is superior to the charging order protection permitted in the partnership and LLC context.

In the complex structure, a portion of client's ownership interest may be held by a spendthrift trust. Thus, assuming the interest was acquired by the trust more than two years before a creditor's claim arose, the trust provides protection against any creditors claims. The client, however, cannot have control over the assets held in the trust or over the timing or amount of distributions made by the trustees to the client as the trust's beneficiary. Obviously, once the trust distributes money to the client, there is no longer any asset protection and, assuming the client places the money in a bank account, the creditor may grab the funds.

However, as long as the LLC interest and any earnings on the LLC interest are retained by the trust, the client's creditors are held at bay. Also, the trustee could pay funds to third parties for the benefit of the beneficiary, rather than to the beneficiary directly, thereby eliminating the chance that a beneficiary's bank account may be flush with funds.

5.6. Equity Stripping

Equity stripping reduces the value of an asset by placing a lien or encumbrance on the asset, such as a mortgage. The lien or encumbrance secures the repayment of a debt. For example, if you borrow $100,000 from a bank, you sign a promissory note for repayment. The promissory note is then secured with a mortgage on your property so if you fail to repay the loan, the bank can foreclose (seize and sell) your home. As a result, the equity in the home is stripped by $100,000, thereby reducing its value to a creditor by $100,000.

Equity stripping will likely fail under the friendly lender situations described in section 4.6., therefore, it is important that the lender is an independent third party, a bank or lending institution and that the transaction be respected as a real deal. This means that the paperwork must be in order and that timely payments must be made on the loan in accordance with the documents.

Domestic Asset Protection

A transaction in which a debtor's economic interest in a partnership or LLC is pledged as part of the collateral supplied to an independent third party lender should effectively block a creditor from obtaining a charging order, since the debtor's economic interest in the partnership or LLC has been encumbered. The security agreement between the lender and debtor should state that a charging order will constitute a default under the loan agreement.

There are several variations of equity stripping, including accounts receivable financing with a lender, which removes a company's accounts receivable and cash flow as a target for creditors. Another variation involves cross-collateralization, such as a pledge of debtor's economic interest in a partnership or LLC as collateral for a loan, guarantee or as security for some other type of financial transaction.

6. CASE STUDY: TRUST DISTRIBUTION AND A PENDING LAWSUIT

6.1. Facts

John Smith, as settlor, formed the Smith Revocable Trust dated May, 1, 2000 ("Trust'). Mr. Smith died on October 10, 2008 and pursuant to the Trust instrument, John Jones and Sam Taylor became the successor co-trustees ("Trustees"). Under the Trust instrument, upon the death of Mr. Smith, the Trustees are to administer the Trust and distribute the assets to the Trust's beneficiaries.

6.2. Acme Lawsuit

The Trust is currently a defendant in a civil lawsuit, Acme v. Smth, Superior Court of California, County of Anycounty (hereafter "Acme Lawsuit") filed on February 10, 2005 and involving the sale of a principal residence by Mr. Smith to the Plaintiff, Mr. Acme. The claims in the Acme Lawsuit are contingent (uncertain), unliquidated (the value is undetermined) and disputed. Thus far, the Plaintiffs have not provided any evidence suggesting that Mr. Smith is legally liable for the damages claimed in the Acme Lawsuit. Allegations of fraud and misrepresentations have been raised by the Plaintiff regarding damage to the residence and its contents. In addition, there is a claim for personal injury based on exposure to mold. There are multiple additional defendants in the case, including two real estate brokerage firms. Discovery in the case has proceeded and the Trustees' attorney, Troy Allstar, is in a position to evaluate the likelihood of damages being awarded against the Trust.

Case Study – Trust Distribution

6.3. Allstar Analysis

On February 1 2009, Mr. Allstar rendered an opinion as to the likelihood of damages and the probability the Plaintiff will recover from the Trust. According to Mr. Allstar's opinion:

1. The cost of repair to the residence is $250,000

2. The loss to personal property is $90,000

3. The claim of personal injuries is $60,000.

4. The probability that damages would be awarded against the Trust is 25%.

5. The cost of future attorney's fees and expert's fees through trial is $50,000.

Based on the foregoing analysis, the likely damage amount is: $400,000, which, for purposes of making an insolvency analysis under CC §3439.02 (a), is then multiplied by the probability the Trust would be found liable for the damages; 25%, resulting in the valuation of the Plaintiff's claim of $100,000. Add the additional attorney's and expert's fees to the cost of the litigation, and the amount needed to reserve for the claim in the Acme Lawsuit, including future attorney and expert fees is $150,000. To provide a cushion against any unexpected expenses or costs involved with the Acme Lawsuit, the trust proposes to reserve the sum of $250,000, which is 200% of the value of the Plaintiff's claim in the Acme Lawsuit. **Note:** Settlements with other defendants would reduce the likely damage amount, dollar-for-dollar, thereby reducing the Trust's potential liability accordingly.

Case Study – Trust Distribution

6.3. Issue

Whether the Trustees may reserve the sum of $250,000 for legal fees and damages and then distribute the balance of the Trust estate to the beneficiaries, without running afoul of the insolvency tests under California's Fraudulent Conveyance Act,?

6.4. Conclusion

Under California law, the Trust will not be rendered insolvent by the transfer of Trust assets to its beneficiaries, since the Trust has adequately reserved the funds to pay any reasonable judgment of damages (as well as future attorney and expert fees) stemming from the contingent, unliquidated and disputed claims against Mr. Smith in the Acme Lawsuit. Hence, the Trust will not be rendered insolvent by proposed distributions. In addition —

1. There is no evidence that the Trustees' have actual intent to hinder, delay or defraud a current or future creditor under CC §3439.04 (a)(1).

2. There is no circumstantial evidence that the Trustees intended to hinder, delay or defraud a current or future creditor under "badges of fraud" tests, because the trustees of the Trust prudently and rationally reserved a sum of money that was double the reasonable amount of potential damages under the Acme Lawsuit.

6.4. Analysis

Trustees obtained a Declaration form their trial attorney setting forth the reasonable amount of potential damages the Trustees could expect to pay with respect to the Acme Lawsuit (including

Case Study – Trust Distribution

future attorney and expert fees). Trustees propose to reserve an amount that doubles the reasonable estimate of supplied provided by their litigation attorney. The Trustees propose to distribute the balance of the Trust estate to the rightful beneficiaries, while reserving $250,000 in case of a future settlement or judgment against the decedent in the Acme Lawsuit.

6.5. No Direct Evidence of Actual Intent

The purpose of the Trust's distributions to the beneficiaries is to carry out the Trustees' fiduciary duties under the Trust instrument. As such, the distributions are not made with any actual intent to interfere with a creditor's rights under §3439.04(a)(1) – a transfer of property made with actual intent to hinder, delay or defraud any creditor.

Actual intent was found in the case of Reddy v. Gonzalez, 8 Cal. App 4th 118, 123-124, in which Mr. Gilbert, a debtor, transferred his interest in his personal residence to his spouse in order to stymie the efforts of a judgment creditor to satisfy her judgment against Mr. Gilbert. Applying Reddy to the purpose of the distributions, there is no actual intent to defraud a creditor or to prevent creditors from obtaining satisfaction of their claims. There is a large amount of money reserved for the payment of the creditor's claim — twice the amount determined to be the reasonable amount of damages that could be awarded. There is lacking the motivation needed to find actual intent under the fraudulent transfer provisions of CC §3439.04(a)(1).

6.6. Circumstantial Evidence of Actual Intent.

The enumerated badges of fraud factors contained in the Act

Case Study – Trust Distribution

that could impact the Trust distributions are the following:

1. Whether the transfer or obligation was to an insider.

    Analysis: No – trust distributions will be made to the beneficiaries pursuant to the trust agreement.

2. Whether the debtor retained possession or control of the property transferred after the transfer.

    Analysis: No, the beneficiaries received the property.

3. Whether the transfer or obligation was disclosed or concealed.

    Analysis: The trust distributions will be disclosed since the beneficiaries receiving them will need to sign documents that they received the distributions.

4. Whether before the transfer was made or obligation was incurred, the debtor had been sued or threatened with suit.

    Analysis: Yes, the Trust has been sued, but has taken appropriate and reasonable steps to pay any reasonable damage award stemming from the lawsuit.

5. Whether the transfer was of substantially all the debtor's assets.

    Analysis: No, the Trustees will reserve funds in excess of the reasonable value of Plaintiff's damage claim.

Case Study – Trust Distribution

6. Whether the debtor removed or concealed assets.

Analysis: No.

7. Whether the value of the consideration received by the debtor was reasonably equivalent to the value of the asset transferred or the amount of the obligation incurred.

Analysis: Not applicable since this is a Trust distribution and the beneficiaries have the right to receive the distributions.

8. Whether the debtor was insolvent or became insolvent shortly after the transfer was made or the obligation was incurred.

Analysis: No. The Trust is not insolvent. It retained funds substantially in excess of the reasonable recovery amount.

6.7. The Reasonably Equivalent Value Test

A fraudulent transfer can be shown either through the Act's actual intent section or the reasonable equivalent value test which reads as follows:

(2) Without receiving a reasonably equivalent value in exchange for the transfer or obligation, and the debtor either:

(A) Was engaged or was about to engage in a business or a transaction for which the remaining assets of the debtor were unreasonably small in relation to the business or transaction; or

Case Study – Trust Distribution

       (B) Intended to incur, or believed or reasonably should have believed that he or she would incur, debts beyond his or her ability to pay as they became due.

The trust distributions did not render the Trust's assets unreasonably small in relation to the transaction and the transfers were not beyond the Trust's ability to pay debts when they became due. **Note:** The focus is whether the remaining assets were <u>unreasonably small</u> in relation to the transaction. The statute takes into account the <u>reasonableness</u> in valuing assets and debts, which is what the trustees of the Trust did when they obtained an opinion of counsel as to the reasonable likelihood of paying potential damages and the likely amount of those damages.

In essence, the Act prevents debtors from placing assets outside the reach of creditors and rendering themselves insolvent in the process. In <u>Mejia v. Reed</u>, 31 Cal 4th 657, 664 (2003), the California Supreme Court made the following general observations concerning the Act:

> The UFTA was enacted in 1986; it is the most recent in a line of statutes dating to the reign of Queen Elizabeth I. ... Even without actual fraudulent intent, a transfer may be fraudulent as to present creditors if the debtor did not receive "a reasonably equivalent value in exchange for the transfer" and "<u>the debtor was insolvent at that time or the debtor became insolvent as a result of the transfer or obligation.</u>" (Civ. Code, § 3439.05.) [emphasis added].

Case Study – Trust Distribution

Applying Mejia to the current situation, inquiry is whether the Trust will become insolvent if the Trustees first reserves an adequate amount to pay a disputed, unliquidated and contingent liability, and then distribute the balance of the Trust assets to the beneficiaries as required under the Trust instrument. As a related

matter, the determination of insolvency involves the proper valuation of the Trust's assets and debts. In this case, a potential claim that is contingent, unliquidated and disputed must be valued.

6.7. Definition of Insolvency

CC §3439.02 (a) defines insolvency as follows:

> A debtor is insolvent if, at fair valuations, the sum of the debtor's debts is greater than all of the debtor's assets.

Thus, the definition of insolvency involves the "fair valuation" of both debts and assets. **Note:** the statute uses the plural term, "fair valuations," making it clear that both debts and assets must be appropriately adjusted to fair market value. **Note:** The term, "claim" includes contingent, unliquidated and disputed liabilities, such as Plaintiff's claim in the Acme Lawsuit.

In In re Bay Plastics, Inc., 187 B.R. 315, 328 n.22 (Bankr. C.D. Cal. 1995), the court defined the balance sheet test as follows:

> Insolvency is defined in California Civil Code § 3439.02(a): "A debtor is insolvent if, at fair valuations, the sum of the debtor's debts is greater than all of the debtor's assets." UFTA § 2(a) is

Case Study – Trust Distribution

essentially the same. These statutes adopt the balance sheet test for insolvency: a debtor is insolvent if the liabilities exceed the assets.

The usual starting point for determining the sufficiency of assets is the balance sheet, particularly if the balance sheet is prepared according to generally accepted accounting principles consistently applied. ...However, these principles do not control a court's decision regarding the solvency of an entity...

The valuation of assets for insolvency purposes is based on "a fair valuation." ... The values of assets must be updated in light of subsequent use and market conditions: in accounting parlance, they must be "marked to market."

In addition, a balance sheet may include intangible assets such as goodwill that may have no liquidation or going concern value, and which thus must be deleted in evaluating the solvency of an entity. Goodwill cannot be sold to satisfy a creditor's claim.

This is the same approach to determining fair valuation used in the U.S. bankruptcy code (discussed below). For the purposes of the balance sheet insolvency test, a contingent debt must be reduced to its present, or estimated, value. <u>In re Xonics Photochemical, Inc.</u>, 841 F.2d 198, 200 (7th Cir. 1988).

6.8. Concept of "Fair Valuation"

The U.S. bankruptcy code uses "fair valuation" concept to determine insolvency. Simply put, if the sum of an entity's debts is

Case Study – Trust Distribution

greater than the sum of its assets at a "fair valuation," the entity is insolvent. This test is referred to as the "balance sheet" insolvency test. Contingent debts must be included in the computation of overall indebtedness.

In In re Xonics Photochemical, Inc., the 7th Circuit Court of Appeals made it clear that for bankruptcy purposes, both assets

and liabilities must be discounted to its present or expected value as part of the insolvency determination:

> The principle ... has long been recognized in cases dealing with the question whether a firm is insolvent .... It makes no difference whether the firm has a contingent asset or a contingent liability; the asset or liability must be reduced to its present, or expected, value before a determination can be made whether the firm's assets exceed its liabilities. (emphasis added).

In Baldi v. Samuel Son & Co., 548 F.3d 579, 582 (7th Cir. Ill. 2008), the court quoted In re Xonics Photochemical, Inc. for the following:

> Contingent liabilities are--contingent. "By definition,
>
> a contingent liability is not certain--and often is highly unlikely--ever to become an actual liability. To value the contingent liability it is necessary to discount it by the probability that the contingency will occur and the liability become real." In re Xonics Photochemical, Inc., 841 F.2d 198, 199 (7th Cir. 1988); see, e.g., Freeland v. Enodis Corp., 540 F.3d 721, 730 (7th Cir. 2008); In re Chase & Sanborn Corp., 904 F.2d 588, 594 (11th Cir. 1990. (emphasis added).

Case Study – Trust Distribution

In <u>Freeland v. Enodis Corp.</u>, 540 F.3d 721, 730 (7th Cir. Ind. 2008), the court, once again, quoted <u>In re Xonics Photochemical, Inc.</u> for the following:

> Because an entity's liability on a contingent debt may never come into being, a contingent liability is not valued at its full amount when assessing the entity's solvency. Rather, a contingent liability is <u>valued at its face amount multiplied by the probability that it will become due</u>. In re <u>Xonics Photochemical, Inc.</u>, 841 F.2d 198, 200 (7th Cir. 1988). (emphasis added)

In the current case, under the balance sheet insolvency test, Trustees need to determine the fair valuation of the trust's assets and liabilities. For the Acme Lawsuit, a contingent, unliquidated and disputed liability, the fair valuation must discount the liability by the probability that the contingency will occur and the liability will become real. In this regard, a trustee will typically rely on the testimony of an accountant, an appraiser, or a business valuation expert. "Whenever possible, a determination of insolvency should be based on reasonable appraisals or expert testimony." <u>Roblin Indus., Inc.</u>, 78 F.3d at 38. See also, <u>Klein v. Tabatchnick</u>, 610 F.2d 1043, 1048 (2d Cir. 1979) ("[A] finding on the issue of insolvency often depends upon the factual inferences and conclusions of expert witnesses....").

In the current matter, Trustees have obtained an expert's opinion from Troy Allstar, the trial attorney handling the case, as to the amount and likelihood of damages stemming from the claim in the lawsuit. There has been extensive discovery in the case and the damages involve determinations of actual damages to the residence and contents. Mr. Allstar is familiar with these types of cases and would qualify as an expert witness under federal or state rules. Mr. Allstar computed the reasonable likelihood of damages and likely percentage that Plaintiffs would prevail against the trust. Thus, the valuation of the claim in the Acme Lawsuit has been evaluated in accordance with In re Xonics Photochemical, Inc.

In conclusion, if the Trustees reserve the sum of $250,000, which is twice the likely value of the claim in the Acme Lawsuit, plus the projected future attorney's fees and expert's fees should the case proceed to trial, the Trust will not be insolvent, since the amount reserved exceeds the value of the potential claim by 200%.

7. MEMO - USING AN LLC

The following is a short memo that illustrates the advantages of using an LLC to hold real estate. Note the business reasons for using the LLC. Asset Protection is just one of many issues involved and the emphasis is on protecting the innocent (non-debtor) members.

MEMORANDUM

To: Client
From: Attorney
Re: Operating Commercial Real Estate Through an LLC

I.   EXAMPLE

The following individuals (A, B and C) own two commercial buildings in the following percentages as tenants in common:

Real Estate:	A	B	C
Last Ave. – 6 units.	35%	45%	20%
First Street - 8 units	60%	20%	20%

II.   RECOMMENDATION

The owners should place their tenant in common interests in the real estate into a Limited Liability Company ("LLC") and receive membership interests in proportion to the value of the real estate contributed to the LLC. The current property manager should be the "manager" of the LLC. This will allow the LLC to manage the real estate assets in one entity.

Using an LLC

III.   DISCUSSION

A. The Perils of Individual Ownership of Undivided Real Estate Interests as Tenants in Common.

Absent an LLC (or similar structure), each beneficiary will own an undivided pro-rata share of each asset in his or her individual name as tenant in common.

1. Tenants in common have the right to partition and sell property by filing a lawsuit.

2. Creditors of a tenant in common (including tax authorities) may seize and sell (or become the owner of) the property interest held by an owner as tenant in common.

3. A tenant in common may become personally liable for any tort claims occurring with respect to the property (including hazardous waste claims).

4. If a tenant in common dies, a probate in the county in which the property is located may be necessary.

5. There is no continuity of management or control with respect to property held by tenants in common absent an express agreement among all tenants in common.

6. No ability to make special allocations or income gain or loss, or other adjustments permitted with an LLC.

Using an LLC

B.   The Advantages to Using an LLC to Manage Real Estate

In contrast to a distribution of an interest directly to each beneficiary as tenant in common, placing the real estate into a Limited Liability Company ("LLC") offers the following advantages:

1. Continuity of management and professional management. Essentially the same management will continue. Income and expenses will be distributed to the members on a pro-rata basis or special allocations can be made, subject to the applicable rules regarding "substantial economic effect" of special allocations.

2. Rights of members to sell, encumber or assign their respective interests may be restricted by agreement.

3. Rights of members to partition and sell the properties or to receive an undivided interest in the properties may be eliminated.

4. Individuals will not own the properties directly, therefore, they will not have personal liability for any potential hazardous substance or contract or tort claims with respect to the properties.

5. Lower value of interest for estate tax purposes since a greater minority discount will apply if property is owned in an LLC rather than as individuals.

Using an LLC

6. Use of agreements to purchase each other's interests, such as a first right of refusal or repurchase agreement at a substantial discount, are available to members. Ability to sell the interest or pass it to members' heirs.

7. Broader ownership: An LLC, unlike an S corporation, may have foreign members, corporations, other partnerships and LLCs, and irrevocable trusts as members.

8. Creditors of a member may not seize and sell LLC assets. A creditor is limited to a charging order against a debtor-member's interest; therefore, a creditor cannot disrupt the LLC operations and the non-debtor members are protected.

8. *(California Concern)* Advantageous Proposition 13 rules. If an individual owning an undivided interest in land sells that interest, Proposition 13 will apply. There must be a change in ownership (50+%) in an LLC for Proposition 13 to apply.

9. No probate on property. Undivided interests in land held individually are subject to probate in the county in which the land is located.

10. For non-resident aliens, there could be advantages to owning land in an LLC if the LLC interest, in turn, is owned by a foreign corporation. Land held individually by a foreign person which is then transferred to a foreign country requires

that a tax return be filed and any gain on the transaction reported.

IV.   OTHER ISSUE

(California Concern) Proposition 13 reappraisals: Property taxes are reassessed to fair market value when a change in ownership occurs.   Although a change in ownership usually occurs when a property is sold, in some circumstances, there can be a change in ownership when interests in a corporation, partnership or LLC shift.

> **NOTE:** If the ownership interests remain exactly the same when the LLC is formed, there will be no Proposition 13 reappraisal at that time. Properties will be reassessed when 50+% of the interests are transferred by the original owners to other members or third parties.

8. CONCLUSION

If properly structured, domestic asset protection provides far superior protection against creditors than the off-shore asset protection schemes touted by certain estate planners and off-shore banks and trust companies, many of whom have dubious credibility. The off-shore asset protection route generally consists of a meaningless paper transaction that attempts to thwart U.S. jurisdictions by pretending assets are held off-shore and outside debtor's control. U.S. courts have consistently rejected this illusion in all the reported cases dealing with this issue.

In contrast, domestic asset protection uses laws enacted by the legislature with respect to LLCs and that are consistent with U.S. court decisions and judgment remedies. The debtor does not interfere with the charging order process; he merely informs the creditor that obtaining a charging order may become very costly.

In other words, the creditor is free to choose the charging order remedy, but at a potential cost which makes the remedy not worth pursuing.

The key to successful asset protection is understanding the fraudulent transfer rules and limiting creditors to the remedy of a charging order. Use of special spendthrift trusts may eliminate potential creditor's claims entirely. By using the complex structure, along with a special spendthrift trust described in this Guide, a client may retain indirect control over the management of his assets, while greatly reducing the risk of creditor claims.

Even the simplified structure described in this Guide will provide substantial asset protection. The simplified structure can be combined with a special spendthrift trust and equity stripping

Conclusion

concepts to achieve greater protection.

Successful asset protection requires careful thought and document drafting. Just as important, the plan must be implemented through action, meaning that the agreements must be followed and payments must be made according to the documentation. Sham documents and transactions will not protect a debtor against a determined creditor.

9. APPENDIX A – SAMPLE LLC CLAUSES

NOTE: THE FOLLOWING ARE EXAMPLES FOR ILLUSTRATION PURPOSES ONLY.

LLC Operating Agreement – Sample Provisions

1. Definitions

"Assignee" means the Person who has acquired an Economic Interest in the Company but is not a Member. An Assignee's interest is subject to, and the Assignee, by virtue of receiving an Economic Interest in the Company becomes bound by, the terms and conditions of this Agreement, including, but not limited to, liens and indemnifications, additional Capital Contributions and restrictions on ownership and Transfer. An Assignee is not entitled to any has no right to review or inspect the Company's documents, tax returns or business or financial books and records as defined in paragraph [Financial Records] (collectively "Company records") and is not entitled to any of the information contained in or considered part of the Company records.

"Economic Interest" means a Person's right to share in and to receive distributions of the income, gains, losses, deductions, credit, or similar items from the Company, but does not include any other rights of a Member including, without limitation, the right to vote or to participate in management, or any right to information concerning the business and affairs of the Company. The assignee of an Economic Interest will be considered the owner for tax purposes and will receive all tax information reporting forms consistent therewith.

Appendix A – Sample LLC Clauses

"Interest Holder" means any Person who holds an Economic Interest, whether as a Member or as an Assignee of a Member. With respect to non-Members, the term "Interest Holder" is strictly limited to the rights, obligations and limitations under this Agreement pertaining to an Assignee of a Member.

"Membership Interest" means a Member's rights in the Company, collectively, including the Member's Economic Interest, any right to Vote or participate in management, and any right to information concerning the business and affairs of the Company.

2. Additional Capital Contributions

In addition to the Capital Contributions set forth in paragraph [capital contributions] each Interest Holder shall be required to make additional contributions of capital to this Company, in proportion to that Interest Holder's Percentage of Economic Interest in the Company, from time to time, upon a capital call made by the Manager.   If an Interest Holder fails to make an additional capital contribution within 20 business days of a written demand by the Manager, that Interest Holder's economic interest and any voting interest, will be automatically forfeited to the Company and the Interest Holder will not be entitled to any compensation or payment for the forfeited interest.

3. Withdrawals and Interest; No Priority of Return

A Member shall not be entitled to withdraw any part of the Member's Capital Contribution or to receive any distributions,

Appendix A – Sample LLC Clauses

whether of money, assets, liabilities or property of any type or description, from the Company, except as provided in this Agreement. No interest shall be paid on funds or property contributed to the capital of the Company or on the balance of the Member's Capital Account. No Member shall have priority over any other Member, with respect to the return of a Capital Contribution, or distributions or allocations of income, gains, losses, deductions, credits, or items thereof.

4. Transfers

Except as provided in this Agreement, no Member may Transfer all, or any portion of, or any interest or rights in, the Membership Interest owned by the Member. Each Member hereby acknowledges the reasonableness of this prohibition in view of the purposes of the Company and the relationship of the Members. The attempted Transfer of any portion or all of a Membership Interest in violation of the prohibition contained in this paragraph 5.1 shall be deemed invalid, null and void, and of no force or effect, except any Transfer mandated by operation of law and then only to the extent necessary to give effect to such Transfer by operation of law.

5. Restrictions on Transfer

Except as provided in this Agreement, a Member shall not Transfer any part of the Member's Membership Interest in the Company, whether now owned or hereafter acquired, unless (i) the Manager and, in addition, 75% of the Members Vote to

Appendix A – Sample LLC Clauses

approve the transferee's admission to the Company as a Member upon such Transfer; (ii) the proposed transferee agrees to be bound by all the terms and conditions of this Agreement as then in effect; (ii) the proposed transferee provides a legal opinion of counsel, satisfactory to the Manager that the transfer of the Membership Interest does not violate any federal or state securities laws; and (iv) the Transfer of the Membership Interest, when added to the total of all other Membership Interests transferred in the preceding twelve (12) months, will not cause the termination of the Company under the Internal Revenue Code. No Member may encumber or permit or suffer any lien, charge or encumbrance of all or any part of the Member's Membership Interest in the Company unless such lien, charge or encumbrance has been approved in writing by the Manager. Any Transfer or lien, charge or encumbrance of a Membership Interest without such approval shall be null and void.

Should it be determined that any of the foregoing provisions of this paragraph [transfer restrictions] are unenforceable, then a Transfer in violation of this Agreement shall be strictly limited to the remedies provided by a charging order under state law. A charging order will constitute a full and complete assignment of transferor's entire Economic Interest in the Company, the transferee will become an Assignee under this Agreement and the Involuntary Withdrawal provisions of Article [involuntary withdrawal] will apply. This paragraph does not deprive any Member of the benefit of any exemption from legal process applicable to that Member's interest.

Appendix A – Sample LLC Clauses

5. Involuntary Withdrawal

Definition of Involuntary Withdrawal

"Involuntary Withdrawal" means, with respect to any Member, the occurrence of any of the following events:

(1)   the Member makes an assignment or Transfer for the benefit of creditors, or is subject to a court order (including but not limited to a charging order), agreement or property settlement or division involving the Transfer of all or a portion of a Membership or Economic Interest to a third party, including, but not limited to, a spouse, former spouse, or a domestic partner.

(2)   the Member is bankrupt;

(3)   the Member files a petition seeking for the Member any reorganization, arrangement, composition, readjustment, liquidation, dissolution, or similar relief under any state law;

(4)   the Member seeks, consents to, or acquiesces in the appointment of a trustee for, receiver for, or liquidation of the Member or of all or any substantial part of the Member's properties;

(5)   if the Member is an individual, the Member's death or adjudication by a court of competent jurisdiction as incompetent to manage the Member's person or property;

(6)   if the Member is acting as a Member by virtue

Appendix A – Sample LLC Clauses

of being a trustee of a trust, the termination of the trust;

(7)   if the Member is a partnership or limited liability company, the dissolution and commencement of winding up of the partnership or limited liability company;

(8)   if the Member is a corporation, the dissolution of the corporation or the revocation of its charter;

(9)   if the Member is a partnership, limited liability company or corporation, a change in control of such entity;

(10)   if the Member is an estate, the distribution by the fiduciary of the estate's entire interest in the Company;

(11)   if the Member files an action seeking a decree of judicial dissolution pursuant to the Act;

(12)   if the Member breaches this Agreement, or any other agreement, contact, declaration, representation or warranty with the Company, and does not cure such breach within 15 days of receipt of written notice thereof signed by the Manager after the Members entitled to Vote holding not less than Sixty Percent (60%) of the Membership Interests decided to issue the notice; Or

(13)   upon the affirmative Vote of Members, including the Member whose Withdrawal is being Voted upon, holding not less than Eighty Percent (80%) of the Membership Interests to terminate such Member's Membership Interest.

Appendix A – Sample LLC Clauses

6. Successor of Withdrawn Member Continues as Unadmitted Assignee

Immediately upon the occurrence of an Involuntary Withdrawal, the successor of the withdrawn Member shall thereupon become an Interest Holder but shall not become a Member. If the Company is continued, the successor Interest Holder shall have all the rights of an Interest Holder but shall not have the right to exercise any other rights of a Member.

In addition, if the Involuntary Withdrawal occurred under paragraph (12) or (13), the Company shall have a lien on the Withdrawal Interest (defined below) for any and all costs, expenses and fees incurred by the Company arising from or out of the actions or conduct of the Member subject to the Involuntary Withdrawal.

7. Optional Buy-out in Event of Involuntary Withdrawal.

(1)   If the Members elect to continue the Company after an Involuntary Withdrawal, the withdrawn Member or the successor in interest to such Member (collectively "Withdrawn Member") shall be deemed to offer for sale to the Company (the "Withdrawal Offer") all of the Membership or Economic Interest of the Withdrawn Member (the "Withdrawal Interest").

(2)   The Withdrawal Offer shall be and remain irrevocable for a period (the "Withdrawal Offer Period") ending at 11:59 P.M. local time at the Company's principal

Appendix A – Sample LLC Clauses

office on the one-hundred eightieth (180th) day following the date the Members elect to continue the Company. At any time during the Withdrawal Offer Period, the Company may accept the Withdrawal Offer by notifying the Withdrawn Member of its acceptance (the "Withdrawal Notice"). The Withdrawn Member shall not be deemed a Member or Manager for the purpose of the Vote on whether the Company shall accept the Withdrawal Offer.

(3).   If the Company accepts the Withdrawal Offer, the Withdrawal Notice shall fix a closing date (the "Withdrawal Closing Date") for the purchase which shall be not earlier than ten (10) or later than ninety (90) days after the expiration of the Withdrawal Period.

(4)   If the Company accepts the Withdrawal Offer, the Company shall purchase the Withdrawal Interest for a price equal to 75% of the amount the Withdrawn Member would receive if the Company were liquidated and an amount equal to the Book Value (defined below) if it were available for distribution to the Members pursuant to paragraph [modified book value], less any liens or encumbrances on the Withdrawal Interest or other amounts owed by the Withdrawn Member to the Company. The Withdrawal Purchase Price shall be paid on an installment basis, such payments shall be in equal monthly installments of principal over a period that shall expire no later than two years from the Withdrawal Closing Date, with simple interest on the unpaid balance of 5% per annum.

Appendix A – Sample LLC Clauses

(5)   If the Company fails to accept the Withdrawal Offer, then the Withdrawn Member, upon the expiration of the Withdrawal Offer Period, shall thereafter be treated as an Assignee of a Member.

Modified Book Value

(1)   The term "Book Value" means the book value of the Company as of the end of the last full calendar quarter immediately preceding the month in which the event giving rise to the purchase and sale of the Membership or Economic Interest occurred, as determined in accordance with the terms of this paragraph. Notwithstanding anything contained in this Agreement to the contrary, the computation of Book Value shall be subject to the following provisions:

(a)   Book Value shall not include any proceeds collected or collectible by the Company under any policy or policies of life or disability insurance insuring the life or disability of a Member.

(b)   No additional allowance of any kind shall be made for the goodwill, trade names, or any other intangible asset or assets (the "Intangible Assets") of the Company other than the aggregate dollar amount for any of those Intangible Assets appearing on the most recent balance sheet of the Company prior to the date on which Book Value is to be determined.

Appendix A – Sample LLC Clauses

(c) Reserves for contingent liabilities shall not be treated as a liability for purposes of determining Book Value.

(d) No adjustment shall be made to Book Value as a result of any event occurring subsequent to the date as of which Book Value is to be determined.

(e) Anything contained in this Agreement to the contrary notwithstanding, Book Value shall be calculated for the purposes of this Agreement on an accrual basis even if the Company shall have used a different accounting method for that or any prior period.

(2) Book Value shall be determined by the accountants regularly employed by the Company. For the purposes of this Agreement, the determination of such accountants shall be binding and conclusive upon all parties.

8. Indemnification -- Claims Against or Valuations of an Interest Holder

For purposes of this paragraph, "Debtor" refers to an Interest Holder holding Economic Interest or a Member holding a Membership Interest in the Company and the term "Debtor's Interest" refers to the interest held by the Debtor in the Company. If a Debtor causes the Company, its Manager(s) or Member(s) to expend any time, money or other financial resources with respect to any claims, demands or liens against, or valuations of, the Debtor's Interest in the Company (collectively "Claims"), including,

9.   Appendix A – Sample LLC Clauses

but not limited to, Claims involving creditors, spouses, successors, assigns or tax authorities, then, in addition to any and all other remedies provided under this Agreement, the Debtor hereby fully and unconditionally indemnifies and holds harmless the Company from any and all costs, fees, payments and compensation associated with, or arising from, such Claims, including, but not limited to, all out-of-pocket costs and professional fees (including fees paid to accountants, attorneys, appraisers, and financial advisors) incurred by the Company, as well as compensation paid, at the rate of $200.00 per hour, to any other Member or Manager for his or her time spent in connection with any Claims, including all travel time (hereafter "Indemnification").

Upon written notice from the Company, the Debtor agrees to secure the Indemnification by assigning or pledging such Person's Economic Interest and Membership Interest (if the Debtor has a Membership Interest) and any proceeds therefrom to the Company, and, in addition, will deposit with the Company the sum of $15,000 to cover the initial fees, costs and compensation that may be incurred by the Company under the Indemnification (hereafter "Deposit"). The Deposit will be held in a separate account and the Debtor will replenish the Deposit to the sum of $15,000 on a monthly basis on or before the 15th day of each month. The Company will have the right to transfer any distributions, payments or proceeds payable or due to the Debtor to fund the Deposit. The portion of the Deposit not expended by the Company under the Indemnification will be returned to the Debtor after the final conclusion of the matter or matters that gave rise to the Indemnification.

Appendix A – Sample LLC Clauses

The failure of a Debtor to comply fully with the terms and conditions of this paragraph shall be considered a default. If the Debtor fails to cure the default within 15 days after receipt of written notice of the default, the Company will be entitled to exercise the remedies available under this Agreement against a defaulting Debtor without further notice. Upon a default in the payment of the Deposit, the Company will have the right to raise the Deposit to a maximum of $30,000 per month, whether or not the default has been cured. This Indemnification shall expressly survive the Voluntary Termination or Involuntary Termination of the Debtor's Economic Interest and Membership Interest in the Company. If upon a default that is not timely cured, the Company forecloses on its security interest in Debtor's Economic Interest and thereafter there remains an amount owed under the Indemnification that is unpaid, the Company shall have full recourse against the Debtor for the unpaid portion of the amounts owed under the Indemnification.

10. RESOURCE MATERIAL

TABLE OF AUTHORITIES AND RESOURCES

Item   Description   **Page**

RESOURCE MATERIAL

TABLE OF AUTHORITIES AND RESOURCES (cont.)

On-Line Resources

http://www.irs.gov/pub/irs-utl/emporind.pdf

1: FTC V AFFORDABLE MEDIA, LLC

179 F.3d 1228 (1999) FEDERAL TRADE COMMISSION, Plaintiff-Appellee, v. AFFORDABLE MEDIA, LLC, Defendant, and Denyse Lindaalyce Anderson; Michael K. Anderson, Defendants-Appellants.

No. 98-16378. United States Court of Appeals, Ninth Circuit.

Argued and Submitted January 13, 1999.

Decided June 15, 1999.

1229*1229 1230*1230 Pamela J. Naughton and Michael P. McCloskey, Baker & McKenzie, San

Diego, California, for the defendants-appellants.

Michael S. Fried, Federal Trade Commission, Washington, D.C., for the plaintiff-appellee.

1231*1231 Before: WIGGINS, TASHIMA, and SILVERMAN, Circuit Judges.

WIGGINS, Circuit Judge:

A husband and wife, Denyse and Michael Anderson, were involved in a telemarketing venture that offered investors the chance to participate in a project that sold such modern marvels as talking pet tags and water-filled barbells by means of late-night television. Although the promoters promised that an investment in the project would return 50 per cent in a mere 60 to 90 days, the venture in fact was a Ponzi scheme, which eventually unraveled and left thousands of investors with tremendous losses. When the Federal Trade Commission brought a complaint against the telemarketing duo, they claimed that they were simply innocent dupes rather than a modern day telephonic Bonnie and Clyde.

While the investors' money was lost in the fraudulent scheme, the Andersons' profits from their commissions remained safely tucked away across the sea in a Cook Islands trust. When the Commission brought a civil action to recover as much money as possible for the defrauded investors, the Andersons advanced two incredible propositions. First, they claimed that they should retain the 45 percent commissions they received for their role in the fraud, even though they acknowledged that the investors were defrauded. They claimed this entitlement because they merely sold the toxic investments that fueled the scheme and propped up the duplicitous house of cards. Second, the Andersons claimed that they were unable to repatriate the assets in the Cook Islands trust because they had willingly relinquished all control over the millions of dollars of commissions in order to place

1: FTC V AFFORDABLE MEDIA, LLC

this money overseas in the benevolent hands of unaccountable overseers, just on the off chance that a law suit might result from their business activities. The learned district court was skeptical of both arguments and choose to grant the Commission its requested preliminary relief.

An old adage warns that a fool and his money are easily parted. This case shows that the same is not true of a district court judge and his common sense. After the Andersons refused to comply with the preliminary injunction by refusing to return their illicit proceeds, the district court ound the Andersons in civil contempt of court. The Andersons appealed. We have jurisdiction

under 28 U.S.C. § 1292(a)(1) and we affirm.[1] I

Sometime after April 1997, Denyse and Michael Anderson became involved with The Sterling Group ("Sterling"). Sterling sold such imaginative products as the "Aquabell," a water-filled dumbbell, the "Talking Pet Tag," and a plastic wrap dispenser known as "KenKut" by means of late-night television commercials broadcast between the hours of 11:00 p.m. and 4:00 a.m. The Andersons formed Financial Growth Consultants, LLC ("Financial") to serve as the primary telemarketer of media units, an investment that afforded purchasers the opportunity to receive a portion of the profits generated from the sales of Sterling's outlandish products. Financial's telemarketers thereupon set about locating prospective investors in the media unit scheme.

The media units sold for $5,000. Each media unit entitled the investor to participate in the sale of Sterling's products from 201 of the late-night commercials. Each 1232*1232 product sold for $20.00. The investor would receive $7.50 for each product sold during his 201 commercials, up to a maximum of five products per commercial. According to Financial's telemarketers, the investors would likely receive $37.50 per commercial (from five products sold during each commercial) for a total of $7,537.50-an astronomical fifty percent return in sixty to ninety days. Financial, for its part, would receive forty-five percent of the investor's $5,000.00 investment, an amount that the Andersons assert is the industry standard. It appears that Financial's telemarketers were especially skilled at marketing the media units. Financial may have raised at least $13,000,000 from investors in the media-unit scheme, retaining an estimated $6,300,000 in commissions for itself. Perhaps unsurprisingly to those not involved in the media-unit project, it turned out that Sterling could not sell enough Talking Pet Tags and Aquabells to return the promised yields to the media-unit investors. Instead, it appears that Sterling used later investors' investments to pay the promised yields to earlier investors-a classic Ponzi scheme.

1: FTC V AFFORDABLE MEDIA, LLC

On April 23, 1998, the Federal Trade Commission (the "Commission") filed a complaint in the United States District Court for the District of Nevada, charging the Andersons, Financial, and others with violations of the Federal Trade Commission Act (the "Act") and the Telemarketing Sales Rule for their participation in a scheme to telemarket fraudulent investments to consumers. Upon motion by the Commission, the district court issued an ex parte temporary restraining order against the defendants.[2] After hearings on April 30 and May 8, 1998, the district court entered a preliminary injunction against the defendants, which incorporated the provisions of the temporary restraining order. Both the temporary restraining order and the preliminary injunction required the Andersons to repatriate any assets held for their benefit outside of the United States.

In July, 1995, the Andersons had created an irrevocable trust under the law of the Cook Islands. The Andersons were named as co-trustees of the trust, together with AsiaCiti Trust Limited ("AsiaCiti"), a company licensed to conduct trustee services under Cook Islands law. Apparently, the Andersons created the trust in an effort to protect their assets from business risks and liabilities by placing the assets beyond the jurisdiction of the United States courts. As discussed more fully below, the provisions of the trust were intended to frustrate the operation of domestic courts, by removing the Andersons as trustees and preventing AsiaCiti from repatriating any of the trust assets to the United States if a so-called "event of duress" occurred.

In response to the preliminary injunction, the Andersons faxed a letter to AsiaCiti on May 12, 1998, instructing AsiaCiti to provide an accounting of the assets held in the trust and to repatriate the assets to the United States to be held under the control of the district court. AsiaCiti thereupon notified the Andersons that the temporary restraining order was an event of duress under the trust, removed the Andersons as co-trustees under the trust because of the event of duress, and refused to provide an accounting or repatriation of the assets. The trust assets were therefore not repatriated to the United States and the Andersons have provided only limited 1233*1233 information to the district court and the Commission regarding the trust assets.

On May 7, 1998, the Commission moved the district court to find the Andersons in civil contempt for their failure to comply with the temporary restraining order's requirements that they submit an accounting of their foreign assets to the Commission and to repatriate all assets located abroad. At a hearing on June 4, 1998, the district court found the Andersons in civil contempt of court for failing to repatriate the trust assets to the United States and failing to provide an accounting of the trust's assets. The district court, however, continued the hearing

1: FTC V AFFORDABLE MEDIA, LLC

until June 9, then until June 11, and finally until June 17, in an effort to allow the Andersons to purge themselves of their contempt. In attempting to purge themselves of their contempt, the Andersons attempted to appoint their children as trustees of the trust, but AsiaCiti removed them from acting as trustees because the event of duress was continuing. At the June 17 hearing, the district court indicated that it believed that the Andersons remained in control of the trust and rejected their assertion that compliance with the repatriation provisions of the trust was impossible. At the close of the June 17 hearing, the district judge ordered the Andersons taken into custody because they had not purged themselves of their contempt. The Andersons timely appealed the district court's issuance of the preliminary injunction and finding them in contempt. We affirm the district court.[3]

II

The first issue in the Anderson's appeal concerns the district court's issuance of the preliminary injunction. This court only subjects a district court's order regarding preliminary injunctive relief to "limited review." Does 1-5 v. Chandler, 83 F.3d 1150, 1152 (9th Cir.1996). We will reverse a district court's issuance of a preliminary injunction only if the district court abused its discretion by basing its decision on an erroneous legal standard or on clearly erroneous factual findings. See id. Based on the record, we find that the district court did not abuse its discretion in issuing the preliminary injunction.

Section 13(b) of the Act allows a district court to grant the Commission a preliminary injunction "[u]pon a proper showing that, weighing the equities and considering the Commission's likelihood of ultimate success, such action would be in the public interest." 15 U.S.C. § 53(b). Section 13(b), therefore, "places a lighter burden on the Commission than that imposed on private litigants by the traditional equity standard; the Commission need not show irreparable harm to obtain a preliminary injunction." FTC v. Warner Communications, Inc., 742 F.2d 1156, 1159 (9th Cir.1984). Under this more lenient standard, "a court must 1) determine the likelihood that the Commission will ultimately succeed on the merits and 2) balance the equities." Id. at 1160.

A. Likelihood of Success on the Merits

In its complaint, the Commission alleged that: (1) the Andersons and Financial violated Section 5(a) of the Act by representing that consumers were highly likely to earn returns of 25 percent or more on their investments within a period of 90 days even though these consumers were not likely to earn such returns; and (2)

1: FTC V AFFORDABLE MEDIA, LLC

the Andersons and Financial violated Section 310.3 of the Telemarketing Sales Rule, 16 C.F.R. § 310.3(a)(2)(vi), by misrepresenting a material aspect of the investors' investment opportunity by misrepresenting the return the investors were likely to earn. In granting the preliminary 1234*1234 injunction, the district court found a "substantial likelihood that the Commission will ultimately succeed" in establishing that the Andersons and their company had violated these provisions and were likely to violate these provisions in the future. Preliminary Injunction, entered and served May 22, 1998, at 2. The Andersons do not deny that the Sterling enterprise was a Ponzi scheme. Instead, the Andersons challenge the district court's order by claiming that the Commission will not succeed in holding them personally liable for their involvement in the scheme. This contention lacks merit; the Commission has made a sufficient showing to justify preliminary injunctive relief.

The Andersons claim that the Commission will not succeed on the merits in holding them personally liable for restitution for any deceptive practices of Financial. Their contention reveals a crucial misunderstanding regarding the requisite factual showing in order to obtain preliminary, as compared to permanent, injunctive relief. Once the correct standard is applied, it becomes abundantly clear that the district court did not abuse its discretion in finding that the Commission had made a sufficient showing that it will likely succeed in holding the Andersons personally liable for Financial's misconduct.

Individuals are personally liable for restitution for corporate misconduct if they "had knowledge that the corporation or one of its agents engaged in dishonest or fraudulent conduct, that the misrepresentations were the type upon which a reasonable and prudent person would rely, and that consumer injury resulted." FTC v. Publishing Clearing House, Inc., 104 F.3d 1168, 1171 (9th Cir.1997). The knowledge requirement can be satisfied by showing that the individuals had actual knowledge of material misrepresentations, [were] recklessly indifferent to the truth or falsity of a misrepresentation, or had an awareness of a high probability of fraud along with an intentional avoidance of the truth. Id.[4] The Commission, however, "is not required to show that a defendant intended to defraud consumers in order to hold that individual personally liable." Id.

The Andersons concede that reckless indifference is legally sufficient to impose personal liability on principals for corporate wrongdoing. Instead of challenging the legal standard applied by the district court, they challenge the court's factual findings. In its preliminary injunction, the district court found "substantial evidence that [the Andersons] were at least recklessly indifferent to the deceptive profit representations of the telemarketers" who worked for Financial and its

1: FTC V AFFORDABLE MEDIA, LLC

independent sales offices. Preliminary Injunction, entered and served May 22, 1998, at 2. The Andersons assert that the district court's "finding of reckless indifference is based on clearly erroneous findings of fact." Appellants' Opening Brief at 27. In making this assertion, the Andersons reveal a fundamental misunderstanding of the factual showing necessary to support a district court's preliminary injunction (as compared to a permanent injunction) as well as confusion regarding the appropriate legal standards for imposing personal liability on principals for corporate misconduct.

In reviewing a preliminary injunction, our review is significantly constrained because of the state of the record available for our review. This constraint is especially limiting when we are asked to review the district court's factual findings that serve as the basis for a preliminary injunction. 1235*1235 We have explained these limitations in another case in which we had to review a district court's issuance of a preliminary injunction:

We begin by identifying how little we can assist in the final resolution of the critical issues before the district court. Until a permanent injunction is granted or denied, we are foreclosed from fully reviewing the important questions presented. ... Review of factual findings at the preliminary injunction stage is, of course, restricted to the limited and often nontestimonial record available to the district court when it granted or denied the injunction motion. The district court's findings supporting its order granting or denying a permanent injunction may differ from its findings at the preliminary injunction stage because by then presentation of all the evidence has been completed. Then too, our determination whether its subsequent findings are clearly erroneous may differ from our view taken at the preliminary stage.

Zepeda v. INS, 753 F.2d 719, 723-724 (9th Cir.1985) (emphasis added). Recognizing the limitations we face, and applying the appropriately deferential level of scrutiny to the district court's findings, the Andersons' contentions can be dealt with without any difficulty.

The Andersons claim that the district court's finding of reckless indifference was clearly erroneous because they had conducted extensive due diligence before becoming involved with Sterling. The district court was skeptical of the Andersons' claim because extensive due diligence likely would have brought to light the scheme's fraudulent nature.[5] More importantly, the Andersons' assertion evidences a clear misunderstanding of the relevant standard for personal liability on the part of corporate principals for corporate misconduct. The extent of an individual's involvement in a fraudulent scheme alone is sufficient to establish

1: FTC V AFFORDABLE MEDIA, LLC

the requisite knowledge for personal restitutionary liability. See FTC v. Sharp, 782 F.Supp. 1445, 1450 (D.Nev.1991); FTC v. Amy Travel Service, Inc., 875 F.2d 564, 574 (7th Cir.1989) ("Also, the degree of participation in business affairs is probative of knowledge.") The Andersons' control of Financial, the chief telemarketer of Sterling and the media units, establishes strong evidence of the Andersons' knowledge. See Sharp, 782 F.Supp. at 1450 ("Here, Hall was a principal in, and president of MEHA, the chief broker of White Rock mines. Hall was deeply involved in the marketing of White Rock for around two and a half years. Thus, there is strong evidence that Hall knew his representations were false.").

Even though the Andersons claim to have relied on their due diligence efforts, ample evidence, at least for preliminary injunctive relief, supports the district court's conclusion that in light of their central involvement in the media unit scheme the Andersons were at a minimum recklessly indifferent to the truth of the representations Financial was making regarding the profit potential of the media unit investments. See id; see also Pantron I Corporation, 33 F.3d at 1104 ("Given the overwhelming evidence that no scientific support existed for the product's efficacy claims, Lederman could not have 1236*1236 failed to know that the scientific support claims were false unless he intentionally avoided the truth.").

The district court found that the promised yields on the media unit investments were so extraordinary that the Andersons should have been suspicious of the investment scheme. The Andersons claim that the district court miscalculated the promised yield on the media units. Instead of the 1000% annualized yield that the district court found would be necessary to earn the promised returns to the investors, they claim that under a profit-margin peritem analysis, the media units only had to yield a more modest 50% return in 60 to 90 days in order to deliver the promised yields-an annualized return of 200% to 300%. The Andersons seem to believe that these more modest returns on the media unit investments were so reasonable that they were not required to conduct more extensive due diligence. Perhaps the Andersons' telemarketers were able to convince their victims that Sterling could sell enough water-filled barbells and talking pet name tags to deliver 50% returns on their investments in 60 to 90 days, but the Andersons have failed to convince us that the district court erred in finding that experienced business persons like the Andersons should have conducted greater due diligence efforts before representing to potential investors that the investment would yield 50% returns in a mere 60 to 90 days. Consequently, we cannot conclude, at least at this preliminary stage of the proceeding, that the district court clearly erred when it found that "[t]he Andersons had experience in the investment business, and should have been highly suspect of promises of such yields [on the media unit investments]. Yet they fell woefully short in verifying the legitimacy of the venture

1: FTC V AFFORDABLE MEDIA, LLC

they were promoting." Opinion and Order, entered and served May 22, 1998, at 2. Therefore, we find that the Commission has shown a sufficient likelihood of succeeding in holding the Andersons personally liable for the actions of Financial to warrant preliminary relief.

B. Balance of the Equities

The Andersons also argue that the district court ignored the hardships borne by the Andersons and Financial because of the issuance of the preliminary injunction. This argument ignores the fact that the district court released monies to pay Inter Com's operating expenses,[6] to pay Inter Com's employees, and to pay for the Andersons' living expenses and attorneys' fees. Therefore the burden of the preliminary injunction, although not insubstantial, is not as great as the Andersons claim. We find that the district court did not clearly err in balancing the equities involved in this case.

Under this Circuit's precedents, "when a district court balances the hardships of the public interest against a private interest, the public interest should receive greater weight." FTC v. World Wide Factors, Ltd., 882 F.2d 344, 347 (9th Cir.1989); see also Warner Communications, Inc., 742 F.2d at 1165. Obviously, the public interest in preserving the illicit proceeds of the media unit-scheme for restitution to the victims is great.

Incredibly, the Andersons assert that "the district court did not find that there was a likelihood of asset dissipation." Appellants' Reply Brief at 7. This astounding assertion is made even in light of the clear finding of the district court that "[t]here is a substantial likelihood that, absent the continuation of the asset freeze, the Enjoined Defendants will conceal, dissipate, or otherwise divert their assets, thereby defeating the possibility of the Court granting effective final relief in the form of equitable monetary relief for consumers." Preliminary Injunction, entered and served May 22, 1998, at 2. Given the Andersons' history of spiriting their commissions away to a Cook Islands trust, which was intentionally designed to frustrate 1237*1237 United States courts' powers to grant effective relief to prevailing parties, the district court's finding regarding the likelihood of dissipation is far from clearly erroneous.

Based on our review of the record, the district court did not clearly err in balancing the equities in this case simply because the court concluded that the important public interest in preserving the Andersons' steep commissions from the Ponzi scheme was more important than the private interests, the harm to which was minimized by the district court's release of monies to pay particular expenses.

1: FTC V AFFORDABLE MEDIA, LLC

Therefore, we find that the Commission has adequately shown that the balance of the equities warrants preliminary injunctive relief.

C. Mootness

The Andersons also contend that their cessation of sales for Sterling mooted the need for injunctive relief. In making this contention, the Andersons exhibit a startling misunderstanding of the nature of the preliminary relief that the district court actually granted. At a minimum, the Andersons' cessation of sales has no bearing on the need to repatriate the assets they have secreted off to the Cook Islands. More importantly, however, their argument mischaracterizes the law to such a degree that they are advocating a legal proposition that is precisely opposite the rule established by our precedents. As such, we conclude that the Commission's need for injunctive relief has not become moot.

The Andersons' first difficulty arises from their misunderstanding of the preliminary relief that the district court actually granted the Commission. The preliminary injunction contains both a prohibitory component and a mandatory component. In relevant part, the prohibitory component prohibited the Andersons from (1) engaging in certain types of business practices, (2) destroying any of their financial records, or (3) dissipating any of their assets. In relevant part, the mandatory component of the preliminary injunction required the Andersons to (1) prepare and deliver financial reports to the Commission's counsel, and (2) transfer to the United States all funds and assets held in foreign countries. While the Andersons' cessation of sales might possibly effect the need to restrain them from engaging in prohibited business practices, it could in no way affect the need to have the Andersons repatriate their assets from the Cook Islands. Therefore, the Andersons' cessation of sales for Sterling has not rendered moot the Commission's need for the mandatory component of the preliminary injunction. The Andersons also appear to misunderstand the legal significance of their voluntary cessation of sales for Sterling in terms of the prohibitory aspect of the preliminary injunction. The Andersons contend that "[v]oluntary cessation of an unlawful course of conduct precludes the issuance of an injunction if there is no cognizable danger of recurrent violations." Appellants' Opening Brief at 28. Contrary to the Andersons' assertion, however, it is actually well-settled "that an action for an injunction does not become moot merely because the conduct complained of was terminated, if there is a possibility of recurrence, since otherwise the defendant's would be free to return to [their] old ways." FTC v. American Standard Credit Systems, Inc. 874 F.Supp. 1080, 1087 (C.D.Cal.1994) (quoting Allee v. Medrano, 416 U.S. 802, 811, 94 S.Ct. 2191, 40 L.Ed.2d 566 (1974)) (internal citations omitted) (emphasis added).

1: FTC V AFFORDABLE MEDIA, LLC

In part, the Andersons' misunderstanding may involve a misunderstanding of the difference between the effect of the perpetrator's conduct, as compared to the victim's conduct, on the need for injunctive relief. The difference is that the victim can moot her need for injunctive relief by her own conduct, but the alleged wrongdoer can not moot the need for injunctive relief as easily. This confusion becomes apparent from the cases upon which the Andersons rely. If an employee leaves the employ of an employer, she can not obtain injunctive relief to prevent her former employer 1238*1238 from engaging in future retaliation in the workplace. See Taylor v. Resolution Trust Corp., 56 F.3d 1497, 1502 (D.C.Cir.1995). It would obviously be a different case if an employer claimed that an injunction to prevent future retaliation against current employees was no longer necessary because the employer had stopped retaliating against its employees in the workplace.

It is possible, of course, that a defendant's conduct can moot the need for injunctive relief, but the "test for mootness in cases such as this is a stringent one." United States v. Concentrated Phosphate Export Ass'n., Inc., 393 U.S. 199, 203, 89 S.Ct. 361, 21 L.Ed.2d 344 (1968). The reason that the defendant's conduct, in choosing to voluntarily cease some wrongdoing, is unlikely to moot the need for injunctive relief is that the defendant could simply begin the wrongful activity again: "Mere voluntary cessation of allegedly illegal conduct does not moot a case; if it did, the courts would be compelled to leave `[t]he defendant ... free to return to his old ways.'" Id. (quoting United States v. W.T. Grant Co., 345 U.S. 629, 632, 73 S.Ct. 894, 97 L.Ed. 1303 (1953)).

The Andersons contend that they have satisfied their burden because "[t]he FTC did not offer any admissible evidence that the Andersons were likely to repeat any wrongful conduct." Appellants' Opening Brief at 28. This asserted failure on the part of the Commission, however, is not sufficient to satisfy the Andersons' burden of establishing that the need for injunctive relief has become moot as a result of their own conduct.[7] The standard for the voluntary cessation exception to mootness is "whether the defendant is free to return to its illegal action at any time." Public Utilities Comm'n of California v. Federal Energy Regulatory Comm'n, 100 F.3d 1451, 1460 (9th Cir. 1996). In order to meet their burden, the Andersons must show that "subsequent events [have] made it absolutely clear that the allegedly wrongful behavior cannot reasonably be expected to recur." Norman-Bloodsaw v. Lawrence Berkeley Laboratory, 135 F.3d 1260, 1274 (9th Cir.1998) (internal quotation omitted); cf. Lindquist v. Idaho State Bd. of Corrections, 776 F.2d 851, 854 (9th Cir.1985) (A case may become moot as a result of voluntary cessation of wrongful conduct only if "interim relief or events have completely and irrevocably eradicated the effects of the alleged violation.").

1: FTC V AFFORDABLE MEDIA, LLC

The Andersons allege nothing that would suggest that it is "absolutely clear" that their wrongful activities are not reasonably likely to recur. Because they have failed to satisfy their burden, we can not conclude that the need for injunctive relief is moot solely because of the Andersons' cessation of their unlawful conduct.

In light of our conclusions regarding the Andersons' various challenges to the propriety of the district court's granting the Commission preliminary injunctive relief, we conclude that the district court did not abuse its discretion in issuing the preliminary injunction, based on the factual record available at such a preliminary stage of the proceeding.

III

The next issue on appeal is the district court's finding the Andersons in 1239*1239 contempt for refusing to repatriate the assets in their Cook Islands trust.[8] We review a district court's civil contempt order for an abuse of discretion. Hilao v. Estate of Marcos, 103 F.3d 762, 764 (9th Cir.1996). We review the district court's findings of fact in connection with the civil contempt adjudication for clear error. Reliance Ins. Co. v. Mast Constr. Co., 84 F.3d 372, 375 (10th Cir.1996). We review a district court's findings in connection with rejecting an impossibility defense for clear error. See Fortin v. Commissioner of Mass. Dep't of Pub. Welfare, 692 F.2d 790, 797 (1st Cir.1982) (affirming contempt order when district court's finding that compliance was not impossible was not clearly erroneous). Based on the record before us, we find that the district court did not abuse its discretion in holding the Andersons in contempt.

The standard for finding a party in civil contempt is well settled:

The moving party has the burden of showing by clear and convincing evidence that the contemnors violated a specific and definite order of the court. The burden then shifts to the contemnors to demonstrate why they were unable to comply.

Stone v. City and County of San Francisco, 968 F.2d 850, 856 n. 9 (9th Cir.1992) (citations omitted).

The temporary restraining order required the Andersons, in relevant part, to "transfer to the territory of the United States all funds, documents and assets in foreign countries held either: (1) by them; (2) for their benefit; or (3) under their direct or indirect control, jointly or singly." Temporary Restraining Order, entered and served April 23, 1998, at 8. These provisions were continued in the prelimi-

1: FTC V AFFORDABLE MEDIA, LLC

nary injunction. See Preliminary Injunction, entered and served May 22, 1998, at 9. It is undisputed that the Andersons are beneficiaries of an irrevocable trust established under the laws of the Cook Islands. The Andersons do not dispute that the trust assets have not been repatriated to the United States. Instead, the Andersons claim that compliance with the temporary restraining order is impossible because the trustee, in accordance with the terms of the trust, will not repatriate the trust assets to the United States.

A party's inability to comply with a judicial order constitutes a defense to a charge of civil contempt. See United States v. Rylander, 460 U.S. 752, 757, 103 S.Ct. 1548, 75 L.Ed.2d 521 (1983) ("While the court is bound by the enforcement order, it will not be blind to evidence that compliance is now factually impossible. Where compliance is impossible, neither the moving party nor the court has any reason to proceed with the civil contempt action."). The Andersons claim that the refusal of the foreign trustee to repatriate the trust assets to the United States, which apparently was the goal of the trust, makes their compliance with the preliminary injunction impossible.

Although the Andersons assert that their "inability to comply with a judicial decree is a complete defense to a charge of civil contempt, regardless of whether the inability to comply is selfinduced," Appellants' Reply Brief at 12 (emphasis added), we are not certain that the Andersons' inability to comply in this case would be a defense to a finding of contempt. It is readily apparent that the Andersons' inability to comply with the district court's repatriation order is the intended result of their own conduct-their inability to comply and the foreign trustee's refusal to comply appears to be the precise goal of the Andersons' trust.[9] The Andersons claim 1240*1240 that they created their trust as part of an "asset protection plan." See Appellant's Opening Brief at 36. These "[s]o-called asset protection trusts are designed to shield wealth by moving it to a foreign jurisdiction that does not recognize U.S. judgments or other legal processes, such as asset freezes." Debra Baker, Island Castaway, ABA Journal, October 1998, at 55. The "asset protection" aspect of these foreign trusts arises from the ability of people, such as the Andersons, to frustrate and impede the United States courts by moving their assets beyond those courts' jurisdictions:

Perhaps most importantly, situs courts typically ignore United States courts' demands to repatriate trust assets to the United States. A situs court will not enforce a United States order from a state court compelling the turnover of trust assets to a creditor that was defrauded under United States law, or assets that were placed into a self-settled spendthrift trust.

1: FTC V AFFORDABLE MEDIA, LLC

James T. Lorenzetti, The Offshore Trust: A Contemporary Asset Protection Scheme, 102 Com. L.J. 138, 143-144 (1997). Because these asset protection trusts move the trust assets beyond the jurisdiction of domestic courts, often times all that remains within the jurisdiction is the physical person of the defendant. Because the physical person of the defendant remains subject to domestic courts' jurisdictions, courts could normally utilize their contempt powers to force a defendant to return the assets to their jurisdictions. Recognizing this risk, asset protection trusts typically are designed so that a defendant can assert that compliance with a court's order to repatriate the trust assets is impossible:

Another common issue is whether the client may someday be in the awkward position of either having to repatriate assets or else be held in contempt of court. A well-drafted [asset protection trust] would, under such a circumstance, make it impossible for the client to repatriate assets held by the trust. Impossibility of performance is a complete defense to a civil contempt charge.

Barry S. Engel, Using Foreign Situs Trusts For Asset Protection Planning, 20 Est. Plan. 212, 218 (1993).

Given that these offshore trusts operate by means of frustrating domestic courts' jurisdiction, we are unsure that we would find that the Andersons' inability to comply with the district court's order is a defense to a civil contempt charge. We leave for another day the resolution of this more difficult question because we find that the Andersons have not satisfied their burden of proving that compliance with the district court's repatriation order was impossible. It is well established that a party petitioning for an adjudication that another party is in civil contempt does not have the burden of showing that the other 1241*1241 party has the capacity to comply with the court's order. See NLRB v. Trans Ocean Export Packing, Inc., 473 F.2d 612, 616 (9th Cir.1973). Instead, the party asserting the impossibility defense must show "categorically and in detail" why he is unable to comply. Id.; See also Rylander, 460 U.S. at 757, 103 S.Ct. 1548 ("It is settled, however, that in raising this defense, the defendant has a burden of production.").

In the asset protection trust context, moreover, the burden on the party asserting an impossibility defense will be particularly high because of the likelihood that any attempted compliance with the court's orders will be merely a charade rather than a good faith effort to comply. Foreign trusts are often designed to assist the settlor in avoiding being held in contempt of a domestic court while only feigning compliance with the court's orders:

1: FTC V AFFORDABLE MEDIA, LLC

Finally, the settlor should be aware that, although his trust will probably prove unassailable by domestic creditors, he may face minor hassles while defending his trust in court. In particular, if a creditor attacks an offshore trust in United States court, the settlor may face contempt of court orders during the proceedings. . . . [T]here is a possibility that the court will . . . order the settlor to collect his assets from the trust and turn them over to the court. If the settlor does not comply with these orders, a court may hold him in contempt. However, there are ways around such a conflict. . . . [T]he settlor could comply with the court order and `order' his trustee to turn over the funds, knowing full well that the trustee will not comply with his request. Thereby, the settlor would technically comply with the court's orders, escape contempt of court charges, and still rest assured that his assets will remain protected.

James T. Lorenzetti, The Offshore Trust: A Contemporary Asset Protection Scheme, 102 Com. L.J. 138, 158 (1997). With foreign laws designed to frustrate the operation of domestic courts and foreign trustees acting in concert with domestic persons to thwart the United States courts, the domestic courts will have to be especially chary of accepting a defendant's assertions that repatriation or other compliance with a court's order concerning a foreign trust is impossible.

Consequently, the burden on the defendant of proving impossibility as a defense to a contempt charge will be especially high.

Given these considerations, we cannot find that the district court clearly erred in finding that the Andersons' compliance with the repatriation order was not impossible because the Andersons remain in control of their Cook Islands trust. In finding the Andersons in civil contempt, the district court rejected the Andersons' impossibility defense, specifically finding that the Andersons "in the judgment of the Court [and] from the evidence that I've heard are in control of this trust." Transcript of June 17, 1998 Hearing Regarding Plaintiff's Motion for Civil Contempt, p. 30. Because we only review a district court's findings in con-nection with rejecting an impossibility defense for clear error, we will treat the district court's finding that the Andersons were in control of their trust as a find-ing of fact, subject only to the clearly erroneous standard of review. Based upon the record before us, we find that the district court's finding that compliance with the repatriation order was possible because the Andersons remain in control of their trust was not clearly erroneous.

The Andersons claim that they have "demonstrated to the district court `categori-cally and in detail' that they can not comply with the repatriation section of the preliminary injunction." Appellants' Reply Brief at 13. The district court was not

1: FTC V AFFORDABLE MEDIA, LLC

convinced and neither are we. While it is possible that a rational person would send millions of dollars overseas and retain absolutely no control over the assets, we share the district court's skepticism. The 1242*1242 district court found, notwithstanding the Andersons' protestations, that

As I look at the totality of the scheme of what I see before me at this time, I have no doubt that the Andersons can if they wish to correct this problem and provide the means of putting these funds in a position that they can be accountable if the final determination of the Court is that the funds should be returned to those who made these payments.

Transcript of June 9, 1998 Hearing Regarding Plaintiff's Motion for Civil Contempt, p. 18.

We cannot say that this finding was clearly erroneous. The Andersons had previously been able to obtain in excess of $1 million from the trust in order to pay their taxes. Given their ability to obtain, with ease, such large sums from the trust, we share the district court's skepticism regarding the Andersons' claim that they cannot make the trust assets subject to the court's jurisdiction.

Moreover, beyond this general skepticism concerning the Andersons' lack of control over their trust, the specifics of the Andersons' trust indicate that they retained control over the trust assets. These offshore trusts allow settlors, such as the Andersons, significant control over the trust assets by allowing the settlor to act as a cotrustee or "protector" of the trust. See Debra Baker, Island Castaway, ABA Journal, October 1998, at 56 ("Further, an offshore trust, may allow settlors to maintain significant control over their assets. Trusts can include cotrustees in the United States to watch over the actions of the foreign trustees, and settlors can name anyone, including themselves, as `protectors' to oversee the trustees and veto their actions if necessary."). When the settlors retain this type of control, however, they can jeopardize the asset protection scheme because they will be subject to a U.S. court's personal jurisdiction and be forced to exercise their control to repatriate the assets. See id. ("If litigation is threatened, the protector and the co-trustee can resign so that no one within the personal jurisdiction of a federal or state court has control over the assets of the trust.").

The district court's finding that the Andersons were in control of their trust is well supported by the record given that the Andersons were the protectors of their trust. A protector has significant powers to control an offshore trust. See Gideon Rothschild, "Establishing and Drafting Offshore Asset Protection Trusts," 23 Est. Plan. 65, 70 (1996) ("The use of a trust protector or advisor is common

1: FTC V AFFORDABLE MEDIA, LLC

among foreign trusts. This person . . . has the power to replace trustees and veto certain actions by the trustees."). A protector can be compelled to exercise control over a trust to repatriate assets if the protector's powers are not drafted solely as the negative powers to veto trustee decisions or if the protector's powers are not subject to the anti-duress provisions of the trust. See id. ("The protector's powers should generally be drafted as negative powers and subject to the anti-duress provisions to protect against an order compelling the protector to exercise control over the trust."). The Andersons' trust gives them affirmative powers to appoint new trustees and makes the anti-duress provisions subject to the protectors' powers,[10] therefore, they can force the foreign trustee to repatriate the trust assets to the United States.

Perhaps the most telling evidence of the Andersons' control over the trust was their conduct after the district court issued its temporary restraining order ordering the repatriation of the trust funds. The Andersons sent a notice to the foreign 1243*1243 trustee, ordering it to repatriate the trust assets because the district court had issued a temporary restraining order. The foreign trustee removed the Andersons from their positions as co-trustees and refused to comply with the repatriation order. After the Andersons claimed that compliance with the repatriation provisions of the temporary restraining order was impossible, the Commission revealed to the court that the Andersons were the protectors of the trust. The Andersons immediately attempted to resign as protectors of the trust. This attempted resignation indicates that the Andersons knew that, as the protectors of the trust, they remained in control of the trust and could force the foreign trustee to repatriate the assets.[11]

The Andersons contend that even though they are the protectors of the trust, it is impossible for them to repatriate the trust assets. The Andersons' argument, that "[t]here is a misstep in the FTC's logic," Appellants' Reply Brief at 17, ignores the fact that they bear the burden of proving impossibility, not the Commission. Their pointing to a few provisions of the trust, alone,[12] is insufficient to carry their burden or to establish that the district court's finding that they remain in control of their trust was clearly erroneous.[13]

Because we see no clear error in the district court's finding that the Andersons remain in control of their trust and could repatriate the trust assets, the district court did not abuse its discretion in holding them in contempt. We, therefore, affirm the district court's finding the Andersons in contempt. Given the nature of the Andersons' so-called "asset protection" trust, which was designed to frustrate the power of United States' courts to enforce judgments, there may be little else that a district court judge can do besides exercise its contempt powers to coerce

1: FTC V AFFORDABLE MEDIA, LLC

people like the Andersons into removing the obstacles they placed in the way of a 1244*1244 court. Given that the Andersons' trust is operating precisely as they intended, we are not overly sympathetic to their claims and would be hesitant to overly-restrict the district court's discretion, and thus legitimize what the Andersons have done.

AFFIRMED.

[1] We also grant the Commission's motion to strike the materials contained in the first tab of Appellants' Supplemental Excerpts of Record. These materials are declarations, executed in September 1998, months after the district court issued the preliminary injunction and found the Andersons in contempt of court. We, therefore, order these materials stricken. See Kirshner v. Uniden Corp. of Am., 842 F.2d 1074, 1078 (9th Cir.1988) (striking portions of excerpts of record that were "neither filed with the district court, considered by the court, nor even before the court when it entered the order that [appellant] now challenges on appeal").

[2] The temporary restraining order prohibited the Andersons, the other defendants, and their agents from making false or misleading statements in connection with the marketing of investments or destroying or otherwise failing to maintain their business records. It also froze the defendants' assets and required the defendants to provide a financial statement to the Commission's counsel. In addition, it required any financial institutions in possession of the defendants' assets to preserve the assets and provide the Commission's counsel information about the assets. Finally, it required the defendants to repatriate all assets outside of the United States to the territory of the United States.

[3] Subsequent to the Andersons' appeal to this court, but prior to oral argument, the district court ordered the Andersons released from custody. In its Release Order, filed December 22, 1998, the district court ordered the Andersons released but found that they remain in contempt of court. Because they remain in contempt, their appeal of the court's order finding them in contempt has not been rendered moot, even though they are no longer in custody.

[4] The Commission claims that knowledge or reckless indifference is not necessary for disgorgement, as compared to restitution. The Commission bases this claim upon cases dealing with the Commodity Futures Trading Commission. This argument has been proffered by the Commission before and this Circuit has declined to reach the issue. See, e.g., FTC v. Pantron I Corporation, 33 F.3d 1088, 1103 (9th Cir.1994). We will not decide today whether the Act allows the

1: FTC V AFFORDABLE MEDIA, LLC

Commission to obtain disgorgement, without regard to the defendant's mental state, because we believe that the Commission has made a sufficient showing of reckless indifference to obtain preliminary injunctive relief.

[5] The district court found the Andersons' due diligence efforts to be extremely deficient. See Opinion and Order, entered and served May 22, 1998, at 2-3. The only reliable information concerning actual sales by Sterling was obtained five months after the Andersons began selling the media units for Sterling. Nor did the Andersons conduct continuing diligence efforts to ensure that the media units were profitable investments rather than the Ponzi scheme that they proved to be. Id. Although the Andersons emphasize what they feel were adequate due diligence efforts, they fail to respond in any way to the specific deficiencies noted by the district court. Our review of the record indicates that there is more than sufficient evidence to support the district court's findings and nothing approaching what would be necessary for us to conclude that the district court's findings were clearly erroneous, given the level of deference afforded a district court's findings in connection with a preliminary injunction.

[6] When the temporary restraining order was granted, the Andersons had already discontinued their involvement with Sterling. They were operating a new telemarketing company, Inter Com, in the same office in which they had operated Financial.

[7] Because the Andersons have failed to satisfy their burden of proving that they are not likely to resume engaging in illegal telemarketing activities, we do not decide today the merits of the Andersons' assertion that the Commission has failed to "offer any admissible evidence that the Andersons were likely to repeat any wrongful conduct." Nevertheless, we do note that one of the Andersons' complaints about the preliminary injunction is that it disrupted the operations of the Andersons' new telemarketing project, Inter Com. According to the Andersons, Inter Com is involved with pre-paid residential telephone service rather than the sale of media units. Inter Com apparently is involved with Tel Com Plus, which was subject to at least one state cease and desist order. At this point, the factual record is insufficient for us to decide whether the Andersons' involvement in another fraudulent telemarketing scheme could provide a sufficient independent basis for the prohibitory aspect of the preliminary injunction.

[8] We have interlocutory appellate jurisdiction over the district court's adjudication of civil contempt where it is incident to an appeal from a preliminary injunction. See Diamontiney v. Borg, 918 F.2d 793, 796-97 (9th Cir. 1990).

1: FTC V AFFORDABLE MEDIA, LLC

[9] The Andersons' trust created the circumstances in which a foreign trustee would refuse to repatriate assets to the United States by means of so-called duress provisions. Under the trust agreement, an event of duress includes "[t]he issuance of any order, decree or judgment of any court or tribunal in any part of the world which in the opinion of the protector will or may directly or indirectly, expropriate, sequester, levy, lien or in any way control, restrict or prevent the free disposal by a trustee of any monies, investments or property which may from time to time be included in or form part of this trust and any distributions therefrom." Trust Agreement at 3. Upon the happening of an event of duress, the trust agreement provides that the Andersons would be terminated as co-trustees, so that control over the trust assets would appear to be exclusively in the hands of a foreign trustee, beyond the jurisdiction of a United States court:

Notwithstanding any other provision contained in this deed any trustee hereof shall automatically cease to be a trustee upon the happening of an event of duress within the territory where such trustee is ... resident (in the case of an individual) and upon ceasing to be a trustee pursuant to this clause such trustee shall be divested of title to the property of this trust which shall automatically vest in the remaining or continuing trustee (if any) located in a territory not having an event of duress and the form for administration of this trust shall notwithstanding any other provision in this deed be deemed to be the place of residence or incorporation (if a corporation) of such continuing trustee.

Trust Agreement at 17 (emphasis added).

[10] For example, the trust provides the protectors with discretion to conclusively determine that an event of duress has not occurred: "For the purpose of determining whether an Event of Duress has occurred pursuant to paragraph (c) and paragraph (d) of this clause (1)(a)(vi) of this Deed, the written certificate of the Protector to that effect shall be conclusive." Trust Agreement at 3 (emphasis added).

[11] Although we have concentrated on the Andersons' capacity as protectors of the trust to support the district court's finding that the Andersons remain in control of the trust, we have not considered whether other facts might support the Andersons' continuing control over the trust, regardless of who is the protector of the trust. The Andersons attempted to resign their position as protectors and that attempt appears to have failed. If the Andersons have in fact resigned their position as protectors, they may still remain in control of the trust. We have not resolved this issue at this time because the Andersons have conceded that they are the protectors of the trust.

1: FTC V AFFORDABLE MEDIA, LLC

[12] The district court excluded evidence that the Andersons claimed supported their impossibility defense. The Andersons did not challenge this evidentiary ruling at all until their Reply Brief. Accordingly, we will not consider the propriety of the district court's exclusion of the Andersons' evidence concerning impossibility. See All Pacific Trading, Inc. v. Vessel M/V Hanjin Yosu, 7 F.3d 1427, 1434 (9th Cir.1993). Moreover, what little the Andersons say in their Reply Brief cannot be considered an adequate argument challenging the district court's evidentiary ruling. From the Andersons' meager assertions, it is unclear what their challenge to the district court's ruling would be.

[13] The provisions of the trust also make clear that the Andersons' position as protectors gives them control over the trust. In provisions of the trust agreement that the Andersons conveniently fail to reference, the trust agreement makes clear that the Andersons, as protectors, have the power to determine whether or not an event of duress has occurred: "For the purpose of determining whether an Event of Duress has occurred pursuant to paragraph (c) and paragraph (d) of this clause (1)(a)(vi) of this Deed, the written certificate of the Protector to that effect shall be conclusive." Trust Agreement at 3 (emphasis added). Moreover, the very definition of an event of duress that the Andersons assert has occurred makes clear that whether or not an event of duress has occurred depends upon the opinion of the protector: "The issuance of any order, decree or judgement of any court or tribunal in any part of the world which in the opinion of the Protector will or may directly or indirectly, expropriate. . . ." Trust Agreement at 3 (emphasis added). Therefore, notwithstanding the provisions of the trust agreement that the Andersons point to, it is clear that the Andersons could have ordered the trust assets repatriated simply by certifying to the foreign trustee that in their opinion, as protectors, no event of duress had occurred.

2: EVANS V GALARDI

LEWIS W. EVANS, Plaintiff and Appellant,
v. JOHN N. GALARDI et al., Defendants; EL DORADO IMPROVEMENT CO.,
Third Party Claimant and Respondent.

Docket No. L.A. 30470.

Supreme Court of California. In Bank.

March 2, 1976.

302*302 COUNSEL

Robert S. Sturges for Plaintiff and Appellant.

No appearance for Defendants.

Hodge & Hodges, Hodge, Hodges & Martin and John R. Skoog for Third Party
Claimant and Respondent.

OPINION

SULLIVAN, J.

El Dorado Improvement Co. (El Dorado), a limited partnership, made and delivered pursuant to Code of Civil Procedure section 689[1] its verified third party claim to certain personal property upon which a writ of execution had been levied to enforce a judgment for money in favor of plaintiff Lewis W. Evans and against defendants John N. Galardi and Richard E. Hodge. After a hearing, the court sustained the claim and entered a judgment on third party claim declaring that at the time of levy of the writ the title to the property in 303*303 question was vested in the third party claimant. Plaintiff appeals from the judgment. The facts are not in dispute. El Dorado is a limited partnership formed for the purpose of owning and managing certain real property in the City of South Lake Tahoe, California, and of constructing, owning and managing a motel on the premises. Eventually, a motel known as the Rodeway Inn was built. When the partnership was formed in June 1969, plaintiff and defendants were the limited partners and entitled to receive all of the partnership net profits. The general partner at all times material herein was a California corporation known as El Dorado Improvement Corporation which operated the motel and whose stock initially was owned entirely by plaintiff and defendants. Raymond Haley was the president of the corporate general partner and in this position was charged with the over-all management of the business and with the supervision of its large number of employees.

ǀ

2: EVANS V GALARDI

About September 15, 1970, plaintiff, defendants and El Dorado Improvement Corporation entered into a written contract whereby plaintiff agreed to sell and defendants agreed to purchase for the sum of $50,000 all of plaintiff's right, title and interest in the limited partnership and all of plaintiff's stock in the corporate general partner. Defendants executed and delivered to plaintiff their promissory note for the full amount of the purchase price. The respective obligations were undertaken by the parties as individuals, and not in their status as limited partners or shareholders of the corporate general partner. El Dorado was not a party to the agreement of purchase and sale and did not sign either the agreement or the promissory note. As a result of this transaction, defendants as limited partners in El Dorado each became entitled to 50 304*304 percent of its net profits, if any, and became the owners of all of the stock of the corporate general partner.

Defendants defaulted on the promissory note and about April 2, 1971, plaintiff brought an action against them in their individual capacity to recover on it. Ultimately judgment was entered in favor of plaintiff and against defendants individually in the sum of $60,008.15.[2]

On May 9, 1973, plaintiff obtained a writ of execution for the full amount of the judgment,[3] and instructed the Sheriff of El Dorado County to levy execution upon the Rodeway Inn and to place a keeper there to collect the receipts of the business until the judgment was satisfied.

El Dorado filed a third party claim (see fn. 1, ante) to the property and business receipts alleging that it was the sole owner of the Rodeway Inn and its receipts and that defendants had no interest in the property upon which a writ of execution could properly be levied to enforce plaintiff's judgment. It further alleged that plaintiff could have reached defendants' partnership interests to satisfy his judgment only by means of a charging order, which had not been utilized in the instant case. As previously stated, the claim was sustained.

(1a) Plaintiff does not dispute that the legal title to the Rodeway Inn and to the money receipts generated by the motel is vested in El Dorado. Rather, he asserts that since defendants in their capacities as limited partners are each entitled to one-half of the net profits, they together in fact own the entire equitable and beneficial interest in El Dorado's assets.[4] On this basis, he contends: First, that he should be permitted to reach the partnership assets in satisfaction of his judgment against these defendants as individuals; and second that El Dorado is not a bona fide third party and hence may not assert a claim under Code of Civil Procedure section 689.

2: EVANS V GALARDI

We begin our analysis by observing that as a general rule "[a]ll goods, chattels, moneys or other property, both real and personal, or any 305*305 interest therein, of the judgment debtor, not exempt by law ... are liable to execution." (Code Civ. Proc., § 688.) Thus, the initial and most important question confronting us is whether defendants, in their capacities as limited partners, have any interest in the assets of El Dorado as such which renders these assets potentially subject to execution in satisfaction of a personal judgment against defendants. In answering this question, we find it helpful to discuss briefly some of the basic principles underlying the law governing limited partnerships.

(2) The form of business association known as a "limited partnership" was not recognized at common law and is strictly a creature of statute. (2 Rowley on Partnership (2d ed. 1960) Limited Partnerships, § 53.0, pp. 549-550; 2 Barrett & Seago, Partners and Partnerships, Law and Taxation (1956) Limited Partnerships, § 1, p. 483; Alley v. Clark (E.D.N.Y. 1947) 71 F. Supp. 521, 524; Skolny v. Richter (1910) 139 App.Div. 534 [124 N.Y.S. 152, 154].)[5] It can generally be described as a type of partnership comprised of one or more general partners who manage the business and who are personally liable for partnership debts, and one or more limited partners who contribute capital and share in the profits, but who take no part in running the business and incur no liability with respect to partnership obligations beyond their capital contribution. (Corp. Code, § 15501[6]; 2 Barrett & Seago, Partners and 306*306 Partnerships, Law and Taxation, supra, Limited Partnerships, § 1, p. 482; 2 Rowley on Partnership, supra, Limited Partnerships, § 53.0, p. 549.) The obvious purpose underlying legislative recognition of this type of business entity was to encourage trade by permitting "a person possessing capital to invest in business and to reap a share of the profits of the business, without becoming liable generally for the debts of the firm, or risking in the venture more than the capital contributed, provided he does not hold himself out as a general partner, or participate actively in the conduct of the business." (Skolny v. Richter, supra, 124 N.Y.S. 152, 155; see also Clapp v. Lacey (1868) 35 Conn. 463, 466.)

The California Legislature first legitimated limited partnerships in this state in 1870 by enacting a "special partnership" statute (Stats. 1869-1870, ch. 129, p. 123). These provisions were subsequently repealed in 1929, when the Legislature adopted the Uniform Limited Partnership Act.[7] Among other things, this act sets forth with considerable specificity the rights and obligations of the general and the limited partners, including a detailed description of their proprietary interests in the business. With certain specified limitations, the general partner has all of the rights and powers enjoyed by partners in "non-limited" partnerships. (§ 15509.) Thus, by reference to the Uniform Partnership Act (§ 15001 et seq.), his

2: EVANS V GALARDI

property rights include: "(1) his rights in specific partnership property, (2) his interest in the partnership, and (3) his right to participate in the management." (§ 15024, italics added.)[8] In sharp contrast, the limited partner is given no property interest in the specific partnership 307*307 assets as such. Rather, he is entitled, among other things,[9] "to receive a share of the profits or other compensation by way of income, and to the return of his contribution as provided in Sections 15515 and 15516." (§ 15510, subd. (2).)[10]

(1b) This unwillingness on the part of the Legislature to grant the limited partner a property interest in the specific assets owned by the partnership, while at the same time providing for such an interest in the general partner, compels the conclusion that the limited partner has no interest in the partnership property by virtue of his status as a limited partner. Thus, such assets are not available to satisfy a judgment against the limited partner in his individual capacity. (Code Civ. Proc., § 688.)

While our research has disclosed no reported California decision which has considered this question, we note that our conclusion in this regard finds ample support in the decisions of our sister states and of the federal courts as well as in various treatises and other legal authorities. (See, e.g., Reiter v. Greenberg (1968) 21 N.Y.2d 388 [288 N.Y.S.2d 57, 60, 235 N.E.2d 118]; In re Panitz & Co. (D.Md. 1967) 270 F. Supp. 448, 453, affirmed sub nom. Hammerman v. Arlington Federal Sav. & Loan Assoc., 308*308 385 F.2d 835; Alley v. Clark, supra, 71 F. Supp. 521, 526-527; Sanderson v. Cooke (1931) 256 N.Y. 73 [175 N.E. 518, 521-522]; Appeal of Silberman (1926) 105 Conn. 192 [134 A. 778, 785], reversed in part on other grounds sub nom. Blodgett v. Silberman (1927) 277 U.S. 1 [72 L.Ed. 749, 48 S.Ct. 410]; Harris v. Murray (1864) 28 N.Y. 574 [86 Am.Dec. 268, 269, 270]; 2 Barrett & Seago, Partners and Partnerships, Law and Taxation, supra, Limited Partnerships, § 1, p. 485; 2 Rowley on Partnership, supra, Limited Partnerships, §§ 53.18, 53.26, pp. 582, 594; Comment, The Limited Partnership (1954) 2 U.C.L.A.L.Rev. 105, 118-119.)

Thus, in a case substantially identical to the one at bench, the New York Court of Appeal held that a sheriff lacked the power and jurisdiction to sell property owned by a limited partnership in execution of a judgment against a limited partner. In so holding, the court reasoned: "The interest of Harris [the limited partner] in the property of a limited partnership can hardly be said to be an interest in the property of the firm. He advanced to the firm a sum of money, which he is entitled to receive back, with interest, at the termination of the partnership; he is also entitled to a share in the profits; but he is to no further extent the owner of the property. Upon payment of these claims, the property would belong to the

2: EVANS V GALARDI

general partners." (Harris v. Murray, supra, 28 N.Y. 574 [86 Am. Dec. 268, 270].)[11]

Quite apart from the lucid statutory language and the overwhelming weight of authority, the very nature of the limited partner's relationship with the business organization indicates that he has no property interest in the specific partnership assets which would render them available to his personal creditors. The limited partner is, primarily, an investor, who contributes capital and thereby acquires the right to share in the business 309*309 profits. (See Uniform Limited Partnership Act, Official Comment, § 1.) His contribution must be in the form of cash or other property, may not consist of services (§ 15504), and must be specified as to amount in the partnership certificate. (§ 15502.) His surname may not be used as part of the firm name. (§ 15505.) He may not actively participate in the conduct of the business. (§ 15507.) Assuming that he complies with these conditions, he is not liable as a general partner on business debts and obligations, except to the extent of his capital contribution. (§§ 15501, 15507.) His death or withdrawal will not dissolve the partnership (§§ 15519, 15520, 15521), and he is not a proper party to proceedings by or against the firm. (§ 15526.) In sum, "[t]he most striking feature of the relation of a special partner to the copartnership is its detached and impersonal character which accentuates sharply its dissimilarity from the relations of a general partner." (Skolny v. Richter, supra, 124 N.Y.S. at p. 155.)

In the instant case, it is undisputed that plaintiff's action on the promissory note and the ensuing judgment were against defendants as individuals, and that El Dorado was not named as a party to the action or as a judgment debtor. Furthermore, there is no question but that the cash receipts of the Rodeway Inn constitute an asset owned by El Dorado. Therefore, under the principles heretofore discussed, defendants in their capacities as limited partners had no property interest in these receipts; accordingly, the receipts were improperly levied upon in execution of plaintiff's judgment against defendants. (Code Civ. Proc., § 688.)[12]

We are not persuaded by plaintiff's argument that a contrary conclusion is compelled simply because defendants were entitled to 100 percent of the net partnership profits in their capacity as limited partners. The Uniform Limited Partnership Act does not distinguish between the rights and obligations of limited partners or their relationship with the firm depending upon the extent of their ownership interest. Nor does plaintiff suggest any grounds for ignoring the result mandated by the act in the instant case.

310*310 Plaintiff does not claim and certainly did not establish at the hearing

2: EVANS V GALARDI

before the trial court, that there is any basis for finding that El Dorado is not, in fact, a bona fide limited partnership or that defendants' relationship with the firm indicates that they should be treated as general partners.[13] Nor does he allege that defendants used this form of business to defraud plaintiff or anyone else or that they treated the business assets as their own. (See, e.g., Minton v. Cavaney (1961) 56 Cal.2d 576, 579 [15 Cal. Rptr. 641, 364 P.2d 473].) In short, plaintiff provides no legal basis for the rule he would have us adopt and accordingly we reject it.

(3) We wish to point out that our decision in this regard does not leave plaintiff remediless. Section 15522, subdivision (1), establishes a method by which a creditor of a limited partner may satisfy his claim from the debtor's partnership interest through the use of a so-called charging order.[14] In construing a virtually identical statute applicable to "non-limited" partnerships (§ 15028, subd. (1)), this court stated that "charging orders on partnership interests have replaced levies of execution as the remedy for reaching such interests." (Baum v. Baum (1959) 51 Cal.2d 610, 612-613 [335 P.2d 481].)

Plaintiff would have us adopt an exception to this statutory prohibition against execution (§§ 15028, 15522) to cover those cases in which the partnership is owned entirely by the judgment debtors.[15] He argues that 311*311 the purpose underlying the enactment of these statutes is to protect innocent partners from the injustice and hardship they may suffer when partnership property is sold in execution of a judgment against an individual partner. (Taylor v. S & M Lamp Co., supra, 190 Cal. App.2d 700, 708.) This purpose, so the argument goes, is not furthered by disallowing execution against specific partnership assets in cases when the judgment debtors own the entire proprietary interest in the business.

We decline plaintiff's invitation to recognize such an implied exception to the required use of the statutory charge procedure. Where, as in the instant case, the partnership is a viable business organization and plaintiff does not show that he will be unable to secure satisfaction of his judgment by use of a charging order or by levy of execution against the debtors' other personally owned property, there is no reason to permit deviation from the prescribed statutory process.

(1c) Finally, plaintiff argues that since El Dorado was owned entirely by defendants, it was not a bona fide third party claimant for purposes of Code of Civil Procedure section 689 and therefore could not properly assert a third party claim under this statute. In making this argument, plaintiff relies upon various authorities which state that a partnership is not necessarily viewed as a separate legal entity for all purposes. (See, e.g., 1 Barrett & Seago, Partners and Partnerships,

2: EVANS V GALARDI

Law and Taxation, supra, Characteristics of a Partnership, § 1.2, pp. 151-156; 1 Rowley on Partnership, supra, Historical and Preliminary, § 1.3, pp. 22-23.)

In answering plaintiff's contention, we need only point out that a limited partnership is viewed as an entity separate and apart from the limited partners for purposes of suing and being sued. (Code Civ. Proc., § 388, subd. (a); § 15526.)[16] The limited partner is not a proper party to proceedings by or against the limited partnership (§ 15526), and the limited partnership is not involved in suits against the limited partners in their individual capacity. (2 Rowley on Partnership, supra, Limited Partnerships, § 53.26, p. 594.)

312*312 In the instant case, El Dorado was not named or in any way involved in plaintiff's suit against defendants. Nor did the judgment entered in the action purport to hold the limited partnership liable. Rather, the suit was based upon plaintiff's personal claim against defendants as individuals and the judgment was rendered accordingly. Thus, El Dorado may be viewed as an entity separate and apart from the limited partners for purposes of this action.

Furthermore, we have previously determined that defendants had no interest in the property seized in execution of plaintiff's judgment, and that El Dorado was the legal owner of this property. Under these circumstances, El Dorado could properly assert its right to these assets by filing a third party claim under Code of Civil Procedure section 689.[17]

The judgment is affirmed.

Wright, C.J., McComb, J., Tobriner, J., Mosk, J., Clark, J., and Richardson, J., concurred.

[1] Section 689 provides in relevant part: "If tangible or intangible personal property levied on, whether or not it be in the actual possession of the levying officer, is claimed by a third person as his property by a written claim verified by his oath or that of his agent, setting out the reasonable value thereof, his title and right to the possession thereof and delivered, together with a copy thereof, to the officer making the levy, such officer must release the property and the levy unless the plaintiff, or the person in whose favor the writ runs, within five days after written demand by such officer, made by registered or certified mail within five days after being served with such verified claim, gives such officer an undertaking executed by at least two good and sufficient sureties, in a sum equal to double the value of the property levied upon.

".... ....

2: EVANS V GALARDI

"Whenever a verified third party claim is delivered to the officer as herein provided, upon levy of execution or attachment (whether any undertaking hereinabove mentioned be given or not), the plaintiff, or the person in whose favor the writ runs, the third party claimant, or any one or more joint third party claimants, shall be entitled to a hearing in the court in which the action is pending or from which the writ issued for the purpose of determining title to the property in question.... At the conclusion of the hearing the court shall give judgment determining the title to the property in question, which shall be conclusive as to the right of the plaintiff, or other person in whose favor the writ runs, to have said property levied upon, taken, or held, by the officer and to subject said property to payment or other satisfaction of his judgment. In such judgment the court may make all proper orders for the disposition of such property or the proceeds thereof."

[2] The judgment was thereafter modified and affirmed on appeal and has become final.

[3] Plaintiff concedes that he had received a payment of $18,000 in partial satisfaction of the judgment and hence that the writ of execution was improperly issued with respect to this amount.

[4] Plaintiff points out that the corporate general partner has no equity ownership in El Dorado, and in any event, its stock is owned entirely and equally by the two judgment debtors.

[5] The origin, history and purpose of this type of business organization was described by the New York court in Ames v. Downing (1850) 1 Bradf. 321, 329-330: "The system of limited partnerships, which was introduced by statute into this State, and subsequently very generally adopted in many other States of the Union, was borrowed from the French Code. (3 Kent, 36; Code de Commerce, 19, 23, 24.) Under the name of la Societe en commandite, it has existed in France from the time of the middle ages; mention being made of it in the most ancient commercial records, and in the early mercantile regulations of Marseilles and Montpelier. In the vulgar Latinity of the middle ages it was styled commenda, and in Italy accomenda. In the statutes of Pisa and Florence, it is recognized so far back as the year 1160: also in the ordinance of Louis-le-Hutin, of 1315; the statutes of Marseilles, 1253; of Geneva, of 1588. In the middle ages it was one of the most frequent combinations of trade, and was the basis of the active and widely-extended commerce of the opulent maritime cities of Italy. It contributed largely to the support of the great and prosperous trade carried on along the shores of the Mediterranean, was known in Languedoc, Provence, and Lombardy, entered into most of the industrial occupations and pursuits of the age, and even

2: EVANS V GALARDI

travelled under the protection of the arms of the Crusaders to the city of Jerusalem. At a period when capital was in the hands of nobles and clergy, who, from pride of caste, or canonical regulations, could not engage directly in trade, it afforded the means of secretly embarking in commercial enterprises, and reaping the profits of such lucrative pursuits, without personal risk; and thus the vast wealth, which otherwise would have lain dormant in the coffers of the rich, became the foundation, by means of this ingenious idea, of that great commerce which made princes of the merchants, elevated the trading classes, and brought the Commons into position as an influential estate in the Commonwealth."

[6] Hereafter, unless otherwise indicated, all section references are to the Corporations Code.

[7] See Statutes 1929, chapter 865, pages 1912, 1913. This act was subsequently reenacted into sections 15501-15531 (Stats. 1949, ch. 383, pp. 674, 688). As of 1974, the act had been adopted in 48 states as well as in the District of Columbia and the Virgin Islands.

[8] Section 15025 defines the nature of and the limitations upon a partner's interest in specific partnership property:

"(1) A partner is co-owner with his partners of specific partnership property holding as a tenant in partnership.

"(2) The incidents of this tenancy are such that:

"(a) A partner, subject to the provisions of this chapter and to any agreement between the partners, has an equal right with his partners to possess specific partnership property for partnership purposes; but he has no right to possess such property for any other purpose without the consent of his partners.

"(b) A partner's right in specific partnership property is not assignable except in connection with the assignment of rights of all the partners in the same property.

"(c) A partner's right in specific partnership property is not subject to attachment, or execution, except on a claim against the partnership. When partnership property is attached for a partnership debt the partners, or any of them, or the representatives of a deceased partner, cannot claim any right under the homestead or exemption laws.

"(d) On the death of a partner his right in specific partnership property vests in the surviving partner or partners, except where the deceased was the last surviving partner, when his right in such property vests in his legal representative. Such

2: EVANS V GALARDI

surviving partner or partners, or the legal representative of the last surviving partner, has no right to possess the partnership property for any but a partnership purpose.

"(e) A partner's right in specific partnership property is not subject to dower, curtesy, or allowances to widows, heirs, or next of kin, and is not community property."

The general partner's interest in specific partnership property is in addition to his interest in his share of the profits and surplus. (§ 15026.)

[9] The limited partner is also given "the same rights as a general partner to "

(a) Have the partnership books kept at the principal place of business of the partnership, and at all times to inspect and copy any of them.

"(b) Have on demand true and full information of all things affecting the partnership, and a formal account of partnership affairs whenever circumstances render it just and reasonable, and

"(c) Have dissolution and winding up by decree of court." (§ 15510, subd. (1).)

[10] Section 15515 states: "A limited partner may receive from the partnership the share of the profits or the compensation by way of income stipulated for in the certificate; provided, that after such payment is made, whether from the property of the partnership or that of a general partner, the partnership assets are in excess of all liabilities of the partnership except liabilities to limited partners on account of their contributions and to general partners."

Section 15516 defines and circumscribes the limited partner's right to withdraw his contribution and to dissolve the partnership.

Section 15502 provides that the certificate which must be filed to form a limited partnership must specify "[t]he share of the profits or the other compensation by way of income which each limited partner shall receive by reason of his contribution." In the instant case, the partnership agreement in effect at the time of these proceedings apparently gave each defendant the right to 50 percent of the net partnership profits.

Section 15518 states that "[a] limited partner's interest in the partnership is personal property."

[11] Courts have similarly concluded that a limited partner has no right, title or

2: EVANS V GALARDI

interest in specific partnership property which would enable him to maintain an action to recover such property under the Trading with the Enemy Act (Alley v. Clark, supra, 71 F. Supp. 521, 526-527), which would permit a court to assume jurisdiction over such property when a limited partner undergoes bankruptcy (In re Panitz & Co., supra, 270 F. Supp. 448, 453) or which would subject a person selling limited partnership interests in a company formed to purchase, operate and manage real property to statutes governing real estate brokers (Reiter v. Greenberg, supra, 288 N.Y.S.2d 57, 60-61).

We are aware that the decision of the Ninth Circuit Court of Appeals in Donroy, Ltd. v. United States (9th Cir.1962) 301 F.2d 200, contains language supportive of a contrary position. In holding that a Canadian corporation, which was a limited partner in a California limited partnership, had a "permanent establishment" in the United States for purposes of a tax convention with Canada, the court stated that "each partner, whether general or limited has an interest as such in the assets and profits of the partnership, including the physical plant or offices at which the partnership conducts its business...." (Id., at p. 207.) However, the court's finding of such an interest for purposes of a tax convention is not persuasive authority in regard to the question at bar.

[12] It is possible that a portion of these cash receipts may, eventually, constitute "net profits" of El Dorado to which defendants will be entitled as limited partners. However, there is absolutely no evidence in the record as to the financial status of El Dorado which indicates what, if any, part of the receipts may find their way into defendant's hands in the form of distributed net profits. Furthermore, plaintiff did not purport to limit the scope of execution accordingly. Finally, section 15522 indicates that plaintiff must obtain a charging order, rather than a writ of execution, to reach defendants' interests in the limited partnership. (See discussion in text accompanying fn. 14, infra.)

3: IN RE EHMANN

In re Gregory Leo EHMANN, Debtor. Louis A. Movitz, Trustee, Plaintiff, v. Fiesta Investments, LLC, Defendant.

Bankruptcy No. 2-00-05708-RJH. Adversary No. 04-00956.

United States Bankruptcy Court, D. Arizona.

January 13, 2005.

201*201 John J. Hebert, Phoenix, AZ, for Debtor.

OPINION DENYING DEFENDANT'S MOTION TO DISMISS COUNT I

RANDOLPH J. HAINES, Bankruptcy Judge.

The Court here concludes that because the operating agreement of a limited liability company imposes no obligations on its members, it is not an executory contract. Consequently when a member who is not the manager files a Chapter 7 case, his trustee acquires all of the member's lights and interests pursuant to Bankruptcy Code[1] §§ 541(a) and (c)(1), and the limitations of §§ 365(c) and (e) do not apply.

PageProcedural Background

Plaintiff Louis A. Movitz ("Trustee") is the Chapter 7 Trustee for the estate of Debtor Gregory L. Ehmann ("Debtor"). The Trustee has sued Defendant Fiesta Investments, LLC ("Defendant" or "Fiesta"), an Arizona limited liability company of which the Debtor was a member when his bankruptcy case was filed. The Trustee's suit seeks a declaration that the Trustee has the status of a member in Fiesta, a determination that the assets of Fiesta are being wasted, misapplied or diverted for improper purposes, and an order for dissolution and liquidation of Fiesta or the appointment of a receiver for Fiesta.

202*202 Fiesta has moved to dismiss the complaint. The Court understood Fiesta's motion as directed to Count II of the complaint to be based solely on an argument that the Court lacks subject matter jurisdiction, which this Court has already denied. The motion to dismiss Count I rests more on substantive law, arguing essentially that the Trustee has no rights with respect to Fiesta other than the right to receive a distribution that might have been made to the Debtor if and when Fiesta decides to make such a distribution. Such a motion to dismiss should be granted only if the Court concludes that the Trustee could prove no set of facts that would entitle him to any remedy other than simply waiting to see if Fiesta should ever decide to make a distribution.

3: IN RE EHMANN

Background Facts

The Trustee's complaint identifies Fiesta as an Arizona limited liability company that was formed in approximately 1998 by the Debtor's parents, Anthony and Alice Ehmann. At the time it was formed, it had two assets, a 17% interest in City Leasing Co. Ltd. and 25% interest in Desert Farms LLC. Shortly after this bankruptcy case was filed, however, City Leasing was liquidated and as a result of that liquidation Fiesta received cash distributions in the amount of approximately $837,000 in the summer of 2000. Fiesta is still receiving regular quarterly distributions of cash from its other asset, Desert Farms.

The Trustee's complaint stems from the fact that although no formal distributions have been declared or paid to members, and certainly not to the Debtor, substantial amounts of cash have flowed out of Fiesta to or for the benefit of other members, including $374,500 in loans to members or to corporations owned or controlled by members, a $42,500 payment to one member, and $124,000 paid to another member to redeem his interest. In response to the Trustee's demand for information and distributions, the managing member of Fiesta, the Debtor's father, responded that he had created "Fiesta a few years ago to remove assets from our estate for estate tax purposes, and to accumulate investments for the benefit of our children after our deaths .... [W]e see no reason to accede to the wishes of any member or assignee of any member which runs contrary to our original goals." Yet the outflow of over half a million dollars does not seem to be consistent with the original goal "to accumulate investments for the benefit of our children after our deaths."

The Parties' Arguments

While the parties disagree on several relevant legal principles, a dispute that is absolutely central to the motion to dismiss is whether the Trustee's rights are governed by Bankruptcy Code § 541(c)(1) or by § 365(e)(2). In a very general sense, the latter provision, if applicable, permits the enforcement of state and contract law restrictions on the Trustee's rights and powers, whereas the former provision, if applicable, would render such restrictions and conditions unenforceable as against the Trustee. Because § 541 applies generally to all property and rights that the Trustee acquires, whereas § 365 applies more specifically to executory contract rights, the answer to this question hinges on whether the Trustee is asserting a property right or an executory contract right.

The Trustee's complaint does not expressly seek to exercise any rights under an executory contract, nor does it identify the Fiesta Operating Agreement as being

3: IN RE EHMANN

an executory contract, but merely attaches it as an exhibit. Indeed, as Fiesta notes, the deadline for the Trustee to have assumed or rejected an executory contract 203*203 has long since passed.[2] In its motion to dismiss, Fiesta relies heavily on various provisions of the Fiesta Operating Agreement which provide that in the event a trustee acquires a member's interests, such action shall not dissolve the company or entitle "any such assignee to participate in the management of the business and affairs of the company or to exercise the right of a Member unless such assignee is admitted as a Member ...." Operating Agreement ¶ 17.2. "Such an assignee that has not become a Member is only entitled to receive to the extent assigned the share of distributions ... to which such Member would otherwise be entitled with respect to the assigned interest." Id. Fiesta further notes that such limitations on the rights of assignees of members' interests in LLCs are specifically authorized by state law, Arizona Revised Statutes ("A.R.S.") § 29-732(A). Fiesta also argues that the Trustee is akin to a judgment creditor, and that A.R.S. § 29-655(c) provides that a charging order is the exclusive remedy by which a judgment creditor of a member may satisfy a judgment out of the member's interest in an LLC. Nowhere in its motion to dismiss, however, does Fiesta argue that the Operating Agreement creates an executory contract between Members and the LLC, that § 365(e)(2) renders such provisions on which Fiesta relies enforceable against the Trustee, or that § 541(c)(1) is for some other reason inapplicable.

In response, the Trustee argues that he is not a mere assignee of the Debtor's membership interest, but rather acquired all of the Debtor's right, title and interest pursuant to § 541(a). He argues, further, that the Trustee took the Debtor's rights free of certain conditions and restrictions that would otherwise devalue the asset in the hands of any other assignee, pursuant to § 541(c)(1).

In reply, Fiesta relies on § 365(e) to maintain that the state and contract law restrictions are enforceable against the Trustee notwithstanding § 541(c)(1). Nowhere, however, does Fiesta ever establish, much less even attempt to demonstrate, that the Trustee's complaint seeks to enforce rights under an executory contract. To the contrary, Fiesta simply assumes or flatly asserts that the Trustee's rights hinge entirely on an executory contract: "In the case at bar, there is no dispute that if the Operating Agreement is considered as a partnership agreement it is an executory contract." Fiesta Reply at 6. And yet the very case that Fiesta cites after making that assertion itself concluded that a partnership relationship may include both an executory contract and a nonexecutory property interest in the profits and surplus. Cutler v. Cutler (In re Cutler), 165 B.R. 275, 280 (Bankr.D.Ariz. 1994)(Case, B.J.).

3: IN RE EHMANN

If a partnership relation entails both executory contract rights and nonexecutory property rights, then it would seem to necessitate a threshold determination of which kind of rights are at issue for the particular kind of relief a Trustee seeks with respect to a partnership or LLC. Before reaching that issue, however, it may be fruitful first to examine whether the Fiesta Operating Agreement even includes any executory contract rights.

Legal Analysis

Although the Bankruptcy Code contains no definition of an executory contract, the Ninth Circuit has adopted the "Countryman Test": "[A] contract is exec 204*204 utory if 'the obligations of both parties are so far unperformed that the failure of either party to complete performance would constitute a material breach and thus excuse the performance of the other.' "[3]

While Fiesta undoubtedly owes many obligations to its members pursuant to the Operating Agreement, for the contract to be executory there would also have to be some material obligation owing to the company by the member. Moreover, such member's obligation must be so material that if the member did not perform it, Fiesta would owe no further obligations to that member.

As noted above, in its briefing on the motion to dismiss Fiesta has not attempted to demonstrate that the Operating Agreement is in fact an executory contract, much less to demonstrate exactly what material obligation is owed to the company by its members. Moreover, the founding member's statement of the purposes for which the company was formed suggests that it is very likely there are no such obligations. The purpose was twofold: to remove assets from the parents' estates for estate tax purposes, and to accumulate investments for the benefit of their children after their deaths. One would certainly not expect the children-members to have any obligations with respect to satisfaction of that first goal, which was a unilateral act by the parents, and it is highly unlikely the children-members undertook any obligations with respect to the second goal, any more than would an ordinary prospective heir.

This suspicion is borne out by a close reading of the Operating Agreement itself. It imposes many obligations on the managers, but as noted above the manager is the Debtor's father, not the Debtor. Article V is entitled "Rights and Obligations of Members," but in fact it identifies only rights and no obligations. It (1) limits members' liability for company debts, (2) grants members the right to obtain a list of other members, grants members the right to approve by majority vote the sale, exchange or other disposition of all or substantially all of the company's

3: IN RE EHMANN

assets, (4) grants the members rights to inspect and copy any documents, (5) grants members the same priority as to return of capital contributions or to profits and losses, and (6) grants the permissible transferee of a member's interests the right to require the company to adjust the basis of the company's property and the capital account of the affected member. In short, the Article of the Operating Agreement that is partially titled "Obligations of Members" reveals that members have no obligations to the company.

In the entire Agreement, the only provision where members, who are not managers, agree to do anything is Article 7.4, which provides in part that "Each member agrees not to voluntarily withdraw from the company as a member ...." It is now questionable in the Ninth Circuit whether such an agreement merely to refrain from acting is sufficient, standing alone, to create an executory contract.[4] But we need not go that far to resolve this issue, bethe 205*205 sentence in which each member agrees not to voluntarily withdraw goes on to say: "[A]nd each Member further agrees that if he attempts to withdraw from the Company in violation of the provisions of this paragraph, he shall receive One Dollar ($1.00) in payment of his interest in the Company and the remaining portion of such Member's interest shall be retained by the Company as liquidated damages." This reveals that what at first may have appeared as a mandatory obligation is in fact merely an option, which gives each member the option of withdrawing if he is willing to accept $1.00 for his interest. But under Helms, such an unexercised option is not an executory contract.[5]

As demonstrated by the excellent analysis in Smith,[6] it is facile to assume that all partnership agreements are executory contracts. Closer analysis reveals that if there are no material obligations that must be performed by the members of a limited liability company or the limited partners in a limited partnership, then the contract is not executory and is not governed by Code § 365.[7] This case is therefore unlike others that have expressly found "an obligation to contribute capital" and other "continuing fiduciary obligations among the partners that make this [Partnership] Agreement an executory contract." [8]

In the absence of any obligation on the part of the member, it is difficult to see 206*206 where an executory contract lies. This is consistent with the whole purpose of Fiesta. It was created simply as a way to reduce the estate tax liabilities that might otherwise have been incurred upon the death of the parents and the distribution of their estate to their heirs. Indeed, as King Lear suggests, the irrevocable transfer of the parents' assets to Fiesta and the irrevocable gift of membership interests in Fiesta to their children probably creates even less obligations on the children than the ordinary filial obligations morally felt by most expectant

3: IN RE EHMANN

heirs.

Moreover, not only do there not appear to be any obligations imposed upon members by the Fiesta Operating Agreement, but there are certainly none with respect to either receipt of a distribution or proper management of the company by its managers. Members do not have to do anything to be entitled to proper management of the company by the managers. The Trustee's complaint does not involve the Debtor's lone arguable obligation not to voluntarily withdraw.

Because there are no obligations imposed on members that bear on the rights the Trustee seeks to assert here, the Trustee's rights are not controlled by the law of executory contracts and Bankruptcy Code § 365. Consequently the Trustee's rights are controlled by the more general provision governing property of the estate, which is Bankruptcy Code § 541.

Code § 541(c)(1) expressly provides that an interest of the debtor becomes property of the estate notwithstanding any agreement or applicable law that would otherwise restrict or condition transfer of such interest by the debtor. All of the limitations in the Operating Agreement, and all of the provisions of Arizona law on which Fiesta relies, constitute conditions and restrictions upon the member's transfer of his interest. Code § 541(c)(1) renders those restrictions inapplicable. This necessarily implies the Trustee has all of the rights and powers with respect to Fiesta that the Debtor held as of the commencement of the case.

It therefore appears that the Trustee may be able to prove a set of facts that would entitle the Trustee to some remedy. The appropriate remedy might include a declaration of the Trustee's rights, redemption of the Debtor's interest,[9] appointment of a receiver to operate the partnership in accordance with its purposes and the members' rights,[10] or dissolution, wind up and liquidation. Consequently 207*207 Fiesta's motion to dismiss must be denied.

[1] Unless otherwise indicated, all chapter, section, and rule references are to the Bankruptcy Code, 11 U.S.C. §§ 101-1330, and to the Federal Rules of Bankruptcy Procedure, Rules XXXXXXXX.

[2] The bankruptcy case was filed as a voluntary Chapter 7 on May 26, 2000. Bankruptcy Code § 365(d)(1) provides that in a Chapter 7 case,an executory contract is deemed rejected unless assumed or rejected by the Trustee within 60 days after the filing of the case.

[3] Unsecured Creditors' Comm. v. Southmark Corp. (In re Robert L. Helms Constr. and Dev. Co., Inc.), 139 F.3d 702, 705 (9th Cir.1998), quoting Griffel v.

3: IN RE EHMANN

Murphy (In re Wegner), 839 F.2d 533, 536 (9th Cir.1988), and citing Vern Countryman, Executory Contracts in Bankruptcy: Part I, 57 MINN. L.REV. 439, 460 (1973).

[4] In the case where the Ninth Circuit first expressly adopted the Countryman test, it held that such an agreement to refrain from acting may be sufficient to make a contract executory: "Because of the exclusive nature of the license which Fenix received, Select-Seat was under a continuing obligation not to sell its software packages to other parties. Violation of this obligation would be a materi-cause al breach of the licensing agreement." Fenix Cattle Co. v. Silver (In re Select-A-Seat Corp.), 625 F.2d 290, 292 (9th Cir.1980)(decided under the prior Bankruptcy Act). That decision was legislatively repealed in 1984 by the adoption of § 365(n). More recently, the en banc decision in Helms, supra note 3, reformulated the test in a way that focuses only on affirmative performance: "The question thus becomes: At the time of filing, does each party have something it must do to avoid materially breaching the contract?" 139 F.3d at 706. And the Andrews/Westbrook analysis, as thoroughly explained in In re Bergt, 241 B.R. 17, 21-36 (Bankr.D.Alaska 1999), demonstrates that it makes no sense to determine the "executoriness" of a contract if its assumption would impose no administrative liability on the estate, because the avoidance of such administrative liability when it exceeds the contractual benefits is the sole reason for executory contract law.

[5] Helms, supra note 3, at 705.

[6] Samson v. Prokopf (In re Smith), 185 B.R. 285, 292-93 (Bankr.S.D.I11.1995) (a majority of courts that have found limited partnership agreements to be executory contracts "have either accepted the executory contract characterization summarily or have dealt with limited partnership agreements under which the limited partner has continuing financial obligations to the partnership.").

[7] See, e.g., In re Garrison-Ashburn, L.C., 253 B.R. 700, 708-09 (Bankr.E.D.Va.2000)(there is no executory contract and § 365 does not apply to an operating agreement that imposes no duties or responsibilities on its members, but merely provides for the structure of the management of the entity); Smith, supra note 6, at 291-95 (limited partnership agreement was not executory as to a limited partner/debtor who had no material obligations to perform; the Chapter 7 trustee steps into the shoes of the debtor and may exercise debtor's right to dissolve the partnership).

[8] Calvin v. Siegal (In re Siegal), 190 B.R. 639, 643 (Bankr.D.Ariz.l996)(Case, J.),

3: IN RE EHMANN

citing In re Sunset Developers, 69 B.R. 710, 712 (Bankr.D.Idaho 1987). See also Summit Invest, and Dew Corp. v. Leroux, 69 F.3d 608 (1st Cir. 1995)(§ 365 applies to general partner debtors who have duties and obligations to limited partnership); Broyhill v. DeLuca (In re DeLuca), 194 B.R. 65 (Bankr.E.D.Va. 1996)(§ 365 applies to debtors who were managers of limited liability company with ongoing duties and responsibilities; because debtors' personal identity and participation were material to the development project, the § 365(e)(2) exception to assumption applies); In re Daugherty Constr., Inc., 188 B.R. 607, 612 (Bankr.D.Neb.l995)(operating agreements are executory contracts because there are material unperformed and continuing obligations among the members, including participation in management and contributions of capital).

[9] As noted above, Fiesta has already redeemed one member's interest for $124,000. That suggests that it has the power to do so, that redemption of a member's interest is not contrary to Fiesta's interests or purposes, and that $124,000 might be an appropriate value for the Debtor's interest. Because the schedules filed in this case reflect priority and unsecured debts of less than $70,000, such a remedy might entirely satisfy the Trustee while simultaneously avoiding any disruption of the partnership or any conflict with the purposes for which it was created.

[10] Although § 105(b) provides that "a court may not appoint a receiver in a case under this title," the precise language of that provision and case law make clear that it applies only to the administrative bankruptcy "case," not to an adversary proceeding. A "case" is what is commenced by the filing of a petition, e.g., § 301, whereas a "proceeding" is commenced by a summons and complaint, Bankruptcy Rules 7001 & 7004. The provision was added simply because the Code "has ample provision for the appointment of a trustee when needed." S.Rep. No. 989, 95th Cong.2d Sess. 29 (1978), U.S.Code Cong. & Admin.News 1978, 5787, 5815. Consequently § 105(b) "does not prohibit the appointment of a receiver in a related adversary proceeding if otherwise authorized and appropriate." 2 LAWRENCE P. KING, COLLIER ON BANKRUPTCY ¶ 105.06, at 105-84.7 (15th Ed.2004). Accord, Craig v. McCarty Ranch Trust (In re Cassidy Land and Cattle Co.), 836 F.2d 1130, 1133 (8th Cir.1988); In re Memorial Estates, Inc., 797 F.2d 516, 520 (7th Cir. 1986)("The power cut off by section 105(b) of the Bankruptcy Code is the power to appoint a receiver for the bankrupt estate, that is, a receiver in lieu of a trustee.").

NOTE: SKIPS 11 - 12 ?????

[13] We note that even if plaintiff were able to show that defendants should be

3: IN RE EHMANN

viewed and treated as general partners, he could not reach the partnership assets by reason of this fact alone. Section 15025, subdivision (2)(c) provides that "[a] partner's right in specific partnership property is not subject to attachment, or execution, except on a claim against the partnership." Section 15509 makes the same rule applicable to general partners in a limited partnership.

[14] Section 15522 provides in relevant part as follows: "On due application to a court of competent jurisdiction by any creditor of a limited partner, the court may charge the interest of the indebted limited partner with payment of the unsatisfied amount of such claim: and may appoint a receiver, and make all other orders, directions, and inquiries which the circumstances of the case may require."

[15] In urging that we recognize this exception plaintiff relies upon the case of Taylor v. S & M Lamp Co. (1961) 190 Cal. App.2d 700 [12 Cal. Rptr. 323]. However, the specific holding of that case indicates that plaintiff's reliance thereon is misplaced. We quote the relevant portion of that opinion: "`Charging orders on partnership interests have replaced levies of execution as the remedy for reaching such interests.'

"This is a correct statement of the law as applied to the ordinary case, i.e., (1) where the partnership continues a bona fide existence and (2) where there is no transfer of partnership assets without a fair and adequate consideration or in fraud of creditors of either the partnership or of individual partners. But, if as alleged. (a) dissolution occurred (see Corp. Code, §§ 15029 and 15031 as to definition and causes of dissolution), or (b) there was a transfer of partnership assets to one or more of the remaining partners, or to a third party, without a fair and adequate consideration or for the purpose of defrauding creditors of the partnership or of individual partners, then we do not have the ordinary and usual situation which Corporations Code, sections 15025 and 15028, are designed to protect. To apply the general rule as a shield to such a situation is contrary to reason and would violate public policy." (Id., at pp. 710-711.)

[16] Code of Civil Procedure section 388 provides in relevant part that "[a]ny partnership or other unincorporated association, whether organized for profit or not, may sue and be sued in the name which it has assumed or by which it is known." While a general partner may be joined as a party to proceedings by or against the firm, the limited partner may not. (Code Civ. Proc., § 388, subd. (b); § 15526; see also Uniform Limited Partnership Act, § 26: Riviera Congress Associates v. Yassky (1966) 18 N.Y.2d 540 [277 N.Y.S.2d 386, 391, 223 N.E.2d 876]; 2 Rowley on Partnership, supra, Limited Partnerships, § 53.26, p. 594; 68 C.J.S., Partnership, § 486, subd. (a), pp. 1037-1038.)

3: IN RE EHMANN

[17] It is noteworthy that plaintiff states in his brief on appeal that "[t]he purpose of the third party claim procedure is to ascertain whether the debtor has any right, title, or interest in the property levied upon." This is exactly the purpose served by the proceedings in the instant case.

4: UNIFORM FRAUDULENT TRANSFERS ACT

Drafted by the

NATIONAL CONFERENCE OF COMMISSIONERS
ON UNIFORM STATE LAWS

and by it

APPROVED AND RECOMMENDED FOR ENACTMENT
IN ALL THE STATES

at its

ANNUAL CONFERENCE
MEETING IN ITS NINETY-THIRD YEAR
IN KEYSTONE, COLORADO
JULY 27 – AUGUST 3, 1984

WITH PREFATORY NOTE AND COMMENTS

**DRAFTING COMMITTEE ON
UNIFORM FRAUDULENT TRANSFER ACT**

MORRIS W. MACEY, Suite 900, 133 Carnegie Way, N.W., Atlanta, GA 30303,
Chairman

GERALD L. BEPKO, Indiana University, School of Law, 735 West New York
Street, Indianapolis, IN 46202

WILLIAM D. HAWKLAND, Louisiana State University Law Center, Baton
Rouge, LA 70803

GRANT S. NELSON, University of Missouri-Columbia, School of Law,
Columbia, MO 65211

NEAL OSSEN, Room 611, 410 Asylum Street, Hartford, CT 06103

GEORGE R. RICHTER, JR., Suite 500, 4000 MacArthur Boulevard, Newport
Beach, CA 92660

BRYCE E. ROE, 340 East 400 South, Salt Lake City, UT 84111

FRANK R. KENNEDY, University of Michigan, School of Law, Ann Arbor, MI
48109, Reporter

4: UNIFORM FRAUDULENT TRANSFERS ACT

CARLYLE C. RING, JR., 710 Ring Building, Washington, DC 20036, President (Member Ex Officio)

PHILLIP CARROLL, 120 East Fourth Street, Little Rock, AR 72201, Chairman, Executive Committee

WILLIAM J. PIERCE, University of Michigan, School of Law, Ann Arbor, MI 48109, Executive Director

SIDNEY S. EAGLES, JR., P.O. Box 888, Raleigh, NC 27602, Chairman, Division E (Member Ex Officio)

REVIEW COMMITTEE

RALPH A. COLE, 1224 Bannock Street, Denver, CO 80204, Chairman
FRANCISCO L. ACEVEDO NOGUERAS, GPO Box CH, San Juan, PR 00936
HARRY M. WALSH, 3 State Capitol, St. Paul, MN 55155

NATIONAL CONFERENCE OF COMMISSIONERS
ON UNIFORM STATE LAWS
645 North Michigan Avenue, Suite 510
Chicago, Illinois 60611

UNIFORM FRAUDULENT TRANSFER ACT

PREFATORY NOTE

The Uniform Fraudulent Conveyance Act was promulgated by the Conference of Commissioners on Uniform State Laws in 1918. The Act has been adopted in 25 jurisdictions, including the Virgin Islands. it has also been adopted in the sections of the Bankruptcy Act of 1938 and the Bankruptcy Reform Act of 1978 that deal with fraudulent transfers and obligations.

The Uniform Act was a codification of the "better" decisions applying the Statute of 13 Elizabeth. See Analysis of H.R. 12339, 74th Cong., 2d Sess. 213 (1936). The English statute was enacted in some form in many states, but, whether or not so enacted, the voidability of fraudulent transfer was part of the law of every American jurisdiction. Since the intent to hinder, delay, or defraud creditors is seldom susceptible of direct proof, courts have relied on badges of fraud. The weight given these badges varied greatly from jurisdiction, and the Conference sought to minimize or eliminate the diversity by providing that proof of certain fact combinations would conclusively establish fraud. In the absence of evidence of the existence of such facts, proof of a fraudulent transfer was to depend on evidence of

4: UNIFORM FRAUDULENT TRANSFERS ACT

actual intent. An important reform effected by the Uniform Act was the elimination of any requirement that a creditor have obtained a judgment or execution returned unsatisfied before bringing an action to avoid a transfer as fraudulent. See American Surety Co. v. Conner, 251 N.Y. 1, 166 N.E. 783, 67 A.L.R. 244 (1929) (per C.J. Cardozo).

The Conference was persuaded in 1979 to appoint a committee to undertake a study of the Uniform Act with a view to preparing the draft of a revision. The Conference was influenced by the following considerations:

(1) The Bankruptcy Reform Act of 1978 has made numerous changes in the section of that Act dealing with fraudulent transfers and obligations, thereby substantially reducing the correspondence of the provisions of the federal bankruptcy law on fraudulent transfers with the Uniform Act.

(2) The Committee on Corporate Laws of the Section of Corporations, Banking & Business Law of the American Bar Association, engaged in revising the Model Corporation Act, suggested that the Conference review provisions of the Uniform Act with a view to determining whether the Acts are consistent in respect to the treatment of dividend distributions.

(3) The Uniform Commercial Code, enacted at least in part by all 50 states, had substantially modified related rules of law regulating transfers of personal property, notably by facilitating the making and perfection of security transfers against attack by unsecured creditors.

(4) Debtors and trustees in a number of cases have avoided foreclosure of security interests by invoking the fraudulent transfer section of the Bankruptcy Reform Act.

(5) The Model Rules of Professional Conduct adopted by the House of Delegates of the American Bar Association on August 2, 1983, forbid a lawyer to counsel or to assist a client in conduct that the lawyer knows is fraudulent.

The Drafting Committee appointed by the Conference held its first meeting in January of 1983. A first reading of a draft of the revision of the Uniform Fraudulent Conveyance Act was had at the Conference's meeting in Boca Raton, Florida, on July 27, 1983. The Committee held four meetings in addition to a meeting held in connection with the Conference meeting in Boca Raton. Meetings were also attended by the following representatives of interested organizations:

Robert Rosenberg, Esq., of the American Bar Association;

4: UNIFORM FRAUDULENT TRANSFERS ACT

Richard Cherin, Esq., of the Commercial Financial Services Committee of the Corporation, Banking and Business Law Section of the American Bar Association;

Robert Zinman, Esq., of the American College of Real Estate Lawyers;

Bruce Bernstein, Esq., of the National Commercial Finance Association;

Ernest E. Specks, Esq., of the Real Property, Probate and Trust Law Section of the American Bar Association.

The Committee determined to rename the Act the Uniform Fraudulent Transfer Act in recognition of its applicability to transfers of personal property as well as real property, "conveyance" having a connotation restricting it to a transfer of personal property. As noted in Comment (2) accompanying § 1(2) and Comment (8) accompanying § 4, however, this Act, like the original Uniform Act, does not purport to cover the whole law of voidable transfers and obligations. The limited scope of the original Act did not impair its effectiveness in achieving uniformity in the areas covered. See McLaughlin, Application of the Uniform Fraudulent Conveyance Act, 46 Harv.L.Rev. 404, 405 (1933).

The basic structure and approach of the Uniform Fraudulent Conveyance Act are preserved in the Uniform Fraudulent Transfer Act. There are two sections in the new Act delineating what transfers and obligations are fraudulent. Section 4(a) is an adaptation of three sections of the U.F.C.A.; § 5(a) is an adaptation of another section of the U.F.C.A.; and § 5(b) is new. One section of the U.F.C.A. (§ 8) is not carried forward into the new Act because deemed to be redundant in part and in part susceptible of inequitable application. Both Acts declare a transfer made or an obligation incurred with actual intent to hinder, delay, or defraud creditors to be fraudulent. Both Acts render a transfer made or obligation incurred without adequate consideration to be constructively fraudulent – i.e., without regard to the actual intent of the parties – under one of the following conditions:

(1) the debtor was left by the transfer or obligation with unreasonably small assets for a transaction or the business in which he was engaged;

(2) the debtor intended to incur, or believed that he would incur, more debts than he would be able to pay; or

(3) the debtor was insolvent at the time or as a result of the transfer or obligation.

As under the original Uniform Fraudulent Conveyance Act a transfer or obligation that is constructively fraudulent because insolvency concurs with or follows failure to receive adequate consideration is voidable only by a creditor in exis-

4: UNIFORM FRAUDULENT TRANSFERS ACT

tence at the time the transfer occurs or the obligation is incurred. Either an existing or subsequent creditor may avoid a transfer or obligation for inadequate consideration when accompanied by the financial condition specified in § 4(a)(2)(i) or the mental state specified in § 4(a)(2)(ii).

Reasonably equivalent value is required in order to constitute adequate consideration under the revised Act. The revision follows the Bankruptcy Code in eliminating good faith on the part of the transferee or obligee as an issue in the determination of whether adequate consideration is given by a transferee or obligee. The new Act, like the Bankruptcy Act, allows the transferee or obligee to show good faith in defense after a creditor establishes that a fraudulent transfer has been made or a fraudulent obligation has been incurred. Thus a showing by a defendant that a reasonable equivalent has been given in good faith for a transfer or obligation is a complete defense although the debtor is shown to have intended to hinder, delay, or defraud creditors.

A good faith transferee or obligee who has given less than a reasonable equivalent is nevertheless allowed a reduction in liability to the extent of the value given. The new Act, like the Bankruptcy Code, eliminates the provision of the Uniform Fraudulent Conveyance Act that enables a creditor to attack a security transfer on the ground that the value of the property transferred is disproportionate to the debt secured. The premise of the new Act is that the value of the interest transferred for security is measured by and thus corresponds exactly to the debt secured. Foreclosure of a debtor's interest by a regularly conducted, noncollusive sale on default under a mortgage or other security agreement may not be avoided under the Act as a transfer for less than a reasonably equivalent value.

The definition of insolvency under the Act is adapted from the definition of the term in the Bankruptcy Code. Insolvency is presumed from proof of a failure generally to pay debts as they become due.

The new Act adds a new category of fraudulent transfer, namely, a preferential transfer by an insolvent insider to a creditor who had reasonable cause to believe the debtor to be insolvent. An insider is defined in much the same way as in the Bankruptcy Code and includes a relative, also defined as in the Bankruptcy Code, a director or officer of a corporate debtor, a partner, or a person in control of a debtor. This provision is available only to an existing creditor. Its premise is that an insolvent debtor is obliged to pay debts to creditors not related to him before paying those who are insiders.

The new Act omits any provision directed particularly at transfers or obligations

4: UNIFORM FRAUDULENT TRANSFERS ACT

of insolvent partnership debtors. Under § 8 of the Uniform Fraudulent Conveyance Act any transfer made or obligation incurred by an insolvent partnership to a partner is fraudulent without regard to intent or adequacy of consideration. So categorical a condemnation of a partnership transaction with a partner may unfairly prejudice the interests of a partner's separate creditors. The new Act also omits as redundant a provision in the original Act that makes fraudulent a transfer made or obligation incurred by an insolvent partnership for less than a fair consideration to the partnership.

Section 7 lists the remedies available to creditors under the new Act. It eliminates as unnecessary and confusing a differentiation made in the original Act between the remedies available to holders of matured claims and those holding unmatured claims. Since promulgation of the Uniform Fraudulent Conveyance Act the Supreme Court has imposed restrictions on the availability and use of prejudgment remedies. As a result many states have amended their statutes and rules applicable to such remedies, and it is frequently unclear whether a state's procedures include a prejudgment remedy against a fraudulent transfer or obligation. A bracketed paragraph is included in Section 7 for adoption by those states that elect to make such a remedy available.

Section 8 prescribes the measure of liability of a transferee or obligee under the Act and enumerates defenses. Defenses against avoidance of a preferential transfer to an insider under § 5(b) include an adaptation of defenses available under § 547(c)(2) and (4) of the Bankruptcy Code when such a transfer is sought to be avoided as a preference by the trustee in bankruptcy. In addition a preferential transfer may be justified when shown to be made pursuant to a good faith effort to stave off forced liquidation and rehabilitate the debtor. Section 8 also precludes avoidance, as a constructively fraudulent transfer, of the termination of a lease on default or the enforcement of a security interest in compliance with Article 9 of the Uniform Commercial Code.

The new Act includes a new section specifying when a transfer is made or an obligation is incurred. The section specifying the time when a transfer occurs is adapted from Section 548(d) of the Bankruptcy Code. Its premise is that if the law prescribes a mode for making the transfer a matter of public record or notice, it is not deemed to be made for any purpose under the Act until it has become such a matter of record or notice.

The new Act also includes a statute of limitations that bars the right rather than the remedy on expiration of the statutory periods prescribed. The law governing limitations on actions to avoid fraudulent transfers among the states is unclear

4: UNIFORM FRAUDULENT TRANSFERS ACT

and full of diversity. The Act recognizes that laches and estoppel may operate to preclude a particular creditor from pursuing a remedy against a fraudulent transfer or obligation even though the statutory period of limitations has not run.

SECTION 1. DEFINITIONS. As used in this [Act]:

(1) "Affiliate" means:

(i) a person who directly or indirectly owns, controls, or holds with power to vote, 20 percent or more of the outstanding voting securities of the debtor, other than a person who holds the securities,

(A) as a fiduciary or agent without sole discretionary power to vote the securities; or

(B) solely to secure a debt, if the person has not exercised the power to vote;

(ii) a corporation 20 percent or more of whose outstanding voting securities are directly or indirectly owned, controlled, or held with power to vote, by the debtor or a person who directly or indirectly owns, controls, or holds with power to vote, 20 percent or more of the outstanding voting securities of the debtor, other than a person who holds the securities,

(A) as a fiduciary or agent without sole power to vote the securities;

or

(B) solely to secure a debt, if the person has not in fact exercised the

power to vote;

(iii) a person whose business is operated by the debtor under a lease or other agreement, or a person substantially all of whose assets are controlled by the debtor; or

(iv) a person who operates the debtor's business under a lease or other agreement or controls substantially all of the debtor's assets.

(2) "Asset" means property of a debtor, but the term does not include:

(i) property to the extent it is encumbered by a valid lien;

(ii) property to the extent it is generally exempt under nonbankruptcy law; or

(iii) an interest in property held in tenancy by the entireties to the extent it is not

4: UNIFORM FRAUDULENT TRANSFERS ACT

subject to process by a creditor holding a claim against only one tenant.

(3) "Claim" means a right to payment, whether or not the right is reduced to judgment, liquidated, unliquidated, fixed, contingent, matured, unmatured, disputed, undisputed, legal, equitable, secured, or unsecured.

(4) "Creditor" means a person who has a claim.

(5) "Debt" means liability on a claim.

(6) "Debtor" means a person who is liable on a claim.

(7) "Insider" includes:

(i) if the debtor is an individual,

(A) a relative of the debtor or of a general partner of the debtor;

(B) a partnership in which the debtor is a general partner;

(C) a general partner in a partnership described in clause (B); or

(D) a corporation of which the debtor is a director, officer, or person

in control;

(ii) if the debtor is a corporation,

(A) a director of the debtor;

(B) an officer of the debtor;

(C) a person in control of the debtor;

(D) a partnership in which the debtor is a general partner;

(E) a general partner in a partnership described in clause (D); or

(F) a relative of a general partner, director, officer, or person in control of the debtor;

(iii) if the debtor is a partnership,

(A) a general partner in the debtor;

(B) a relative of a general partner in, or a general partner of, or a person in con-

4: UNIFORM FRAUDULENT TRANSFERS ACT

trol of the debtor;

(C) another partnership in which the debtor is a general partner;

(D) a general partner in a partnership described in clause (C); or

(E) a person in control of the debtor;

(iv) an affiliate, or an insider of an affiliate as if the affiliate were the debtor; and

(v) a managing agent of the debtor.

(8) "Lien" means a charge against or an interest in property to secure payment of a debt or performance of an obligation, and includes a security interest created by agreement, a judicial lien obtained by legal or equitable process or proceedings, a common-law lien, or a statutory lien.

(9) "Person" means an individual, partnership, corporation, association, organization, government or governmental subdivision or agency, business trust, estate, trust, or any other legal or commercial entity.

(10) "Property" means anything that may be the subject of ownership.

(11) "Relative" means an individual related by consanguinity within the third degree as determined by the common law, a spouse, or an individual related to a spouse within the third degree as so determined, and includes an individual in an adoptive relationship within the third degree.

(12) "Transfer" means every mode, direct or indirect, absolute or conditional, voluntary or involuntary, of disposing of or parting with an asset or an interest in an asset, and includes payment of money, release, lease, and creation of a lien or other encumbrance.

(13) "Valid lien" means a lien that is effective against the holder of a judicial lien subsequently obtained by legal or equitable process or proceedings.

Comment

(1) The definition of "affiliate" is derived from § 101(2) of the Bankruptcy Code.

(2) The definition of "asset" is substantially to the same effect as the definition of "assets" in § 1 of the Uniform Fraudulent Conveyance Act. The definition in this Act, unlike that in the earlier Act, does not, however require a determination that the property is liable for the debts of the debtor. Thus, an unliquidated claim for

4: UNIFORM FRAUDULENT TRANSFERS ACT

damages resulting from personal injury or a contingent claim of a surety for reimbursement, contribution, or subrogation may be counted as an asset for the purpose of determining whether the holder of the claim is solvent as a debtor under § 2 of this Act, although applicable law may not allow such an asset to be levied on and sold by a creditor. Cf. Manufacturers & Traders Trust Co. v. Goldman (In re Ollag Construction Equipment Corp.), 578 F.2d 904, 907-09 (2d Cir. 1978).

Subparagraphs (i), (ii), and (iii) provide clarification by excluding from the term not only generally exempt property but also an interest in a tenancy by the entirety in many states and an interest that is generally beyond reach by unsecured creditors because subject to a valid lien. This Act, like its predecessor and the Statute of 13 Elizabeth, declares rights and provides remedies for unsecured creditors against transfers that impede them in the collection of their claims. The laws protecting valid liens against impairment by levying creditors, exemption statutes, and the rules restricting levyability of interest in entireties property are limitations on the rights and remedies of unsecured creditors, and it is therefore appropriate to exclude property interests that are beyond the reach of unsecured creditors from the definition of "asset" for the purposes of this Act.

A creditor of a joint tenant or tenant in common may ordinarily collect a judgment by process against the tenant's interest, and in some states a creditor of a tenant by the entirety may likewise collect a judgment by process against the tenant's interest. See 2 American Law of Property 10, 22, 28-32 (1952); Craig, An Analysis of Estates by the Entirety in Bankruptcy, 48 Am.Bankr.L.J. 255, 258-59 (1974). The levyable interest of such a tenant is included as an asset under this Act.

The definition of "assets" in the Uniform Fraudulent Conveyance Act excluded property that is exempt from liability for debts. The definition did not, however, exclude all property that cannot be reached by a creditor through judicial proceedings to collect a debt. Thus, it included the interest of a tenant by the entirety although in nearly half the states such an interest cannot be subjected to liability for a debt unless it is an obligation owed jointly by the debtor with his or her cotenant by the entirety. See 2 American Law of Property 29 (1952); Craig, An Analysis of Estates by the Entirety in Bankruptcy, 48 Am.Bankr.L.J. 255, 258 (1974). The definition in this Act requires exclusion of interests in property held by tenants by the entirety that are not subject to collection process by a creditor without a right to proceed against both tenants by the entirety as joint debtors.

The reference to "generally exempt" property in § 1(2)(ii) recognizes that all exemptions are subject to exceptions. Creditors having special rights against gen-

4: UNIFORM FRAUDULENT TRANSFERS ACT

erally exempt property typically include claimants for alimony, taxes, wages, the purchase price of the property, and labor or materials that improve the property. See Uniform Exemptions Act § 10 and the accompanying Comment. The fact that a particular creditor may reach generally exempt property by resorting to judicial process does not warrant its inclusion as an asset in determining whether the debtor is insolvent.

Since this Act is not an exclusive law on the subject of voidable transfers and obligations (see Comment (8) to § 4 infra), it does not preclude the holder of a claim that may be collected by process against property generally exempt as to other creditors from obtaining relief from a transfer of such property that hinders, delays, or defrauds the holder of such a claim. Likewise the holder of an unsecured claim enforceable against tenants by the entirety is not precluded by the Act from pursuing a remedy against a transfer of property held by the entirety that hinders, delays, or defrauds the holder of such a claim.

Nonbankruptcy law is the law of a state or federal law that is not part of the Bankruptcy Code, Title 11 of the United States Code. The definition of an "asset" thus does not include property that would be subject to administration for the benefit of creditors under the Bankruptcy Code unless it is subject under other applicable law, state or federal, to process for the collection of a creditor's claim against a single debtor.

(3) The definition of "claim" is derived from § 101(4) of the Bankruptcy Code. Since the purpose of this Act is primarily to protect unsecured creditors against transfers and obligations injurious to their rights, the words "claim" and "debt" as used in the Act generally have reference to an unsecured claim and debt. As the context may indicate, however, usage of the terms is not so restricted. See, e.g. §§ 1(1)(i)(B) and 1(8).

(4) The definition of "creditor" in combination with the definition of "claim" has substantially the same effect as the definition of "creditor" under § 1 of the Uniform Fraudulent Conveyance Act. As under that Act, the holder of an unliquidated tort claim or a contingent claim may be a creditor protected by this Act.

(5) The definition of "debt" is derived from § 101(11) of the Bankruptcy Code.

(6) The definition of "debtor" is new.

(7) The definition of "insider" is derived from § 101(28) of the Bankruptcy Code. The definition has been restricted in clauses (i)(C), (ii)(E), and (iii)(D) to make clear that a partner is not an insider of an individual, corporation, or partnership

4: UNIFORM FRAUDULENT TRANSFERS ACT

if any of these latter three persons is only a limited partner. The definition of "insider" in the Bankruptcy Code does not purport to make a limited partner an insider of the partners or of the partnership with which the limited partner is associated, but it is susceptible of a contrary interpretation and one which would extend unduly the scope of the defined relationship when the limited partner is not a person in control of the partnership. The definition of "insider" in this Act also differs from the definition in the Bankruptcy Code in omitting the reference in 11 U.S.C. § 101(28)(D) to an elected official or relative of such an official as an insider of a municipality. As in the Bankruptcy Code (see 11 U.S.C. § 102(3)), the word "includes" is not limiting, however. Thus, a court may find a person living with an individual for an extended time in the same household or as a permanent companion to have the kind of close relationship intended to be covered by the term "insider." Likewise, a trust may be found to be an insider of a beneficiary.

(8) The definition of "lien" is derived from paragraphs (30), (31), (43), and (45) of § 101 of the Bankruptcy Code, which define "judicial lien," "lien," "security interest," and "statutory lien" respectively.

(9) The definition of "person" is adapted from paragraphs (28) and (30) of § 1-201 of the Uniform Commercial Code, defining "organization" and "person" respectively.

(10) The definition of "property" is derived from § 1-201(33) of the Uniform Probate Code. Property includes both real and personal property, whether tangible or intangible, and any interest in property, whether legal or equitable.

(11) The definition of "relative" is derived from § 101(37) of the Bankruptcy Code but is explicit in its references to the spouse of a debtor in view of uncertainty as to whether the common law determines degrees of relationship by affinity.

(12) The definition of "transfer" is derived principally from § 101(48) of the Bankruptcy Code. The definition of "conveyance" in § 1 of the Uniform Fraudulent Conveyance Act was similarly comprehensive, and the references in this Act to "payment of money, release, lease, and the creation of a lien or incumbrance" are derived from the Uniform Fraudulent Conveyance Act. While the definition in the Uniform Fraudulent Conveyance Act did not explicitly refer to an involuntary transfer, the decisions under that Act were generally consistent with an interpretation that covered such a transfer. See, e.g., Hearn 45 St. Corp. v. Jano, 283 N.Y. 139, 27 N.E.2d 814, 128 A.L.R. 1285 (1940) (execution and

4: UNIFORM FRAUDULENT TRANSFERS ACT

foreclosure sales); Lefkowitz v. Finkelstein Trading Corp., 14 F.Supp. 898, 899 (S.D.N.Y. 1936) (execution sale); Langan v. First Trust & Deposit Co., 277 App.Div. 1090, 101 N.Y.S.2d 36 (4th Dept. 1950), aff'd, 302 N.Y. 932, 100 N.E.2d 189 (1951) (mortgage foreclosure); Catabene v. Wallner, 16 N.J.Super. 597, 602, 85 A.2d 300, 302 (1951) (mortgage foreclosure).

(13) The definition of "valid lien" is new. A valid lien includes an equitable lien that may not be defeated by a judicial lien creditor. See, e.g., Pearlman v. Reliance Insurance Co., 371 U.S. 132, 136 (1962) (upholding a surety's equitable lien in respect to a fund owing a bankrupt contractor).

SECTION 2. INSOLVENCY.

(a) A debtor is insolvent if the sum of the debtor's debts is greater than all of the debtor's assets, at a fair valuation.

(b) A debtor who is generally not paying his [or her] debts as they become due is presumed to be insolvent.

(c) A partnership is insolvent under subsection (a) if the sum of the partnership's debts is greater than the aggregate of all of the partnership's assets, at a fair valuation, and the sum of the excess of the value of each general partner's nonpartnership assets over the partner's nonpartnership debts.

(d) Assets under this section do not include property that has been transferred, concealed, or removed with intent to hinder, delay, or defraud creditors or that has been transferred in a manner making the transfer voidable under this [Act].

(e) Debts under this section do not include an obligation to the extent it is secured by a valid lien on property of the debtor not included as an asset.

Comment

(1) Subsection (a) is derived from the definition of "insolvent" in § 101(29)(A) of the Bankruptcy Code. The definition in subsection (a) and the correlated definition of partnership insolvency in subsection (c) contemplate a fair valuation of the debts as well as the assets of the debtor. As under the definition of the same term in § 2 of the Uniform Fraudulent Conveyance Act exempt property is excluded from the computation of the value of the assets. See § 1(2) supra. For similar reasons interests in valid spendthrift trusts and interests in tenancies by the entireties that cannot be severed by a creditor of only one tenant are not included. See the Comment to § 1(2) supra. Since a valid lien also precludes an unsecured creditor from collecting the creditor's claim from the encumbered interest in a debtor's

4: UNIFORM FRAUDULENT TRANSFERS ACT

property, both the encumbered interest and the debt secured thereby are excluded from the computation of insolvency under this Act. See § 1(2) supra and subsection (e) of this section.

The requirement of § 550(b)(1) of the Bankruptcy Code that a transferee be "without knowledge of the voidability of the transfer" in order to be protected has been omitted as inappropriate. Knowledge of the facts rendering the transfer voidable would be inconsistent with the good faith that is required of a protected transferee. Knowledge of the voidability of a transfer would seem to involve a legal conclusion. Determination of the voidability of the transfer ought not to require the court to inquire into the legal sophistication of the transferee.

(2) Section 2(b) establishes a rebuttable presumption of insolvency from the fact of general nonpayment of debts as they become due. Such general nonpayment is a ground for the filing of an involuntary petition under § 303(h)(1) of the Bankruptcy Code. See also U.C.C. § 1-201(23), which declares a person to be "insolvent" who "has ceased to pay his debts in the ordinary course of business." The presumption imposes on the party against whom the presumption is directed the burden of proving that the nonexistence of insolvency as defined in § 2(a) is more probable than its existence. See Uniform Rules of Evidence (1974 Act), Rule 301(a). The 1974 Uniform Rule 301(a) conforms to the Final Draft of Federal Rule 301 as submitted to the United States Supreme Court by the Advisory Committee on Federal Rules of Evidence. "The so-called 'bursting bubble' theory, under which a presumption vanishes upon the introduction of evidence which would support a finding of the nonexistence of the presumed fact, even though not believed, is rejected as according presumptions too 'slight and evanescent' an effect." Advisory Committee's Note to Rule 301. See also 1 J.Weinstein & M.Berger, Evidence ¶ 301 [01] (1982).

The presumption is established in recognition of the difficulties typically imposed on a creditor in proving insolvency in the bankruptcy sense, as provided in subsection (a). See generally Levit, The Archaic Concept of Balance-Sheet Insolvency, 47 Am.Bankr.L.J. 215 (1973). Not only is the relevant information in the possession of a noncooperative debtor but the debtor's records are more often than not incomplete and inaccurate. As a practical matter, insolvency is most cogently evidenced by a general cessation of payment of debts, as has long been recognized by the laws of other countries and is now reflected in the Bankruptcy Code. See Honsberger, Failure to Pay One's Debts Generally as They Become Due: The Experience of France and Canada, 54 Am.Bankr.L.J. 153 (1980); J. MacLachlan, Bankruptcy 13, 63-64, 436 (1956). In determining whether a debtor is paying its debts generally as they become due, the court should look at more than the

4: UNIFORM FRAUDULENT TRANSFERS ACT

amount and due dates of the indebtedness. The court should also take into account such factors as the number of the debtor's debts, the proportion of those debts not being paid, the duration of the nonpayment, and the existence of bona fide disputes or other special circumstances alleged to constitute an explanation for the stoppage of payments. The court's determination may be affected by a consideration of the debtor's payment practices prior to the period of alleged non-payment and the payment practices of the trade or industry in which the debtor is engaged. The case law that has developed under § 303(h)(1) of the Bankruptcy Code has not required a showing that a debtor has failed or refused to pay a majority in number and amount of his or her debts in order to prove general non-payment of debts as they become due. See, e.g., Hill v. Cargill, Inc. (In re Hill), 8 B.R. 779, 3 C.B.C.2d 920 (Bk.D.Minn. 1981) (nonpayment of three largest debts held to constitute general nonpayment, although small debts were being paid); In re All Media Properties, Inc., 5 B.R. 126, 6 B.C.D. 586, 2 C.B.C.2d 449 (Bk.S.D.Tex. 1980) (missing significant number of payments or regularly missing payments significant in amount said to constitute general nonpayment; missing payments on more than 50% of aggregate of claims said not to be required to show general nonpayment; nonpayment for more than 30 days after billing held to establish nonpayment of a debt when it is due); In re Kreidler Import Corp., 4 B.R. 256, 6 B.C.D. 608, 2 C.B.C.2d 159 (Bk.D.Md. 1980) (nonpayment of one debt constituting 97% of debtor's total indebtedness held to constitute general nonpayment). A presumption of insolvency does not arise from nonpayment of a debt as to which there is a genuine bona fide dispute, even though the debt is a substantial part of the debtor's indebtedness. Cf. 11 U.S.C. § 303(h)(1), as amended by § 426(b) of Public Law No. 98-882, the Bankruptcy Amendments and Federal Judgeship Act of 1984.

(3) Subsection (c) is derived from the definition of partnership insolvency in § 101(29)(B) of the Bankruptcy Code. The definition conforms generally to the definition of the same term in § 2(2) of the Uniform Fraudulent Conveyance Act.

(4) Subsection (d) follows the approach of the definition of "insolvency" in § 101(29) of the Bankruptcy Code by excluding from the computation of the value of the debtor's assets any value that can be realized only by avoiding a transfer of an interest formerly held by the debtor or by discovery or pursuit of property that has been fraudulently concealed or removed.

(5) Subsection (e) is new. It makes clear the purpose not to render a person insolvent under this section by counting as a debt an obligation secured by property of the debtor that is not counted as an asset. See also Comments to §§ 1(2) and 2(a) supra.

4: UNIFORM FRAUDULENT TRANSFERS ACT

SECTION 3. VALUE.

(a) Value is given for a transfer or an obligation if, in exchange for the transfer or obligation, property is transferred or an antecedent debt is secured or satisfied, but value does not include an unperformed promise made otherwise than in the ordinary course of the promisor's business to furnish support to the debtor or another person.

(b) For the purposes of Sections 4(a)(2) and 5, a person gives a reasonably equivalent value if the person acquires an interest of the debtor in an asset pursuant to a regularly conducted, noncollusive foreclosure sale or execution of a power of sale for the acquisition or disposition of the interest of the debtor upon default under a mortgage, deed of trust, or security agreement.

(c) A transfer is made for present value if the exchange between the debtor and the transferee is intended by them to be contemporaneous and is in fact substantially contemporaneous.

Comment

(1) This section defines "value" as used in various contexts in this Act, frequently with a qualifying adjective. The word appears in the following sections:

4(a)(2) ("reasonably equivalent value");
4(b)(8) ("value ... reasonably equivalent);
5(a) ("reasonably equivalent value");
5(b) ("present, reasonably equivalent value");
8(a) ("reasonably equivalent value");
8(b), (c), (d), and (e) ("value");
8(f)(1) ("new value"); and
8(f)(3) ("present value").

(2) Section 3(a) is adapted from § 548(d)(2)(A) of the Bankruptcy Code. See also § 3(a) of the Uniform Fraudulent Conveyance Act. The definition in Section 3 is not exclusive. "Value" is to be determined in light of the purpose of the Act to protect a debtor's estate from being depleted to the prejudice of the debtor's unsecured creditors. Consideration having no utility from a creditor's viewpoint does not satisfy the statutory definition. The definition does not specify all the kinds of consideration that do not constitute value for the purposes of this Act – e.g., love and affection. See, e.g., United States v. West, 299 F.Supp. 661, 666 (D.Del. 1969).

4: UNIFORM FRAUDULENT TRANSFERS ACT

(3) Section 3(a) does not indicate what is "reasonably equivalent value" for a transfer or obligation. Under this Act, as under § 548(a)(2) of the Bankruptcy Code, a transfer for security is ordinarily for a reasonably equivalent value notwithstanding a discrepancy between the value of the asset transferred and the debt secured, since the amount of the debt is the measure of the value of the interest in the asset that is transferred. See, e.g., Peoples-Pittsburgh Trust Co. v. Holy Family Polish Nat'l Catholic Church, Carnegie, Pa., 341 Pa. 390, 19 A.2d 360 (1941). If, however, a transfer purports to secure more than the debt actually incurred or to be incurred, it may be found to be for less than a reasonably equivalent value. See e.g., In re Peoria Braumeister Co., 138 F.2d 520, 523 (7th Cir. 1943) (chattel mortgage securing a $3,000 note held to be fraudulent when the debt secured was only $2,500); Hartford Acc. & Indemnity Co. v. Jirasek, 254 Mich. 131, 140, 235 N.W. 836, 839 (1931) (quitclaim deed given as mortgage held to be fraudulent to the extent the value of the property transferred exceeded the indebtedness secured). If the debt is a fraudulent obligation under this Act, a transfer to secure it as well as the obligation would be vulnerable to attack as fraudulent. A transfer to satisfy or secure an antecedent debt owed an insider is also subject to avoidance under the conditions specified in Section 5(b).

(4) Section 3(a) of the Uniform Fraudulent Conveyance Act has been thought not to recognize that an unperformed promise could constitute fair consideration. See McLaughlin, Application of the Uniform Fraudulent Conveyance Act, 46 Harv.L.Rev. 404, 414 (1933). Courts construing these provisions of the prior law nevertheless have held unperformed promises to constitute value in a variety of circumstances. See, e.g., Harper v. Lloyd's Factors, Inc., 214 F.2d 662 (2d Cir. 1954) (transfer of money for promise of factor to discount transferor's purchase-money notes given to fur dealer); Schlecht v. Schlecht, 168 Minn. 168, 176-77, 209 N.W. 883, 886-87 (1926) (transfer for promise to make repairs and improvements on transferor's homestead); Farmer's Exchange Bank v. Oneida Motor Truck Co., 202 Wis. 266, 232 N.W. 536 (1930) (transfer in consideration of assumption of certain of transferor's liabilities); see also Hummel v. Cernocky, 161 F.2d 685 (7th Cir. 1947) (transfer in consideration of cash, assumption of a mortgage, payment of certain debts, and agreement to pay other debts). Likewise a transfer in consideration of a negotiable note discountable at a commercial bank, or the purchase from an established, solvent institution of an insurance policy, annuity, or contract to provide care and accommodations clearly appears to be for value. On the other hand, a transfer for an unperformed promise by an individual to support a parent or other transferor has generally been held voidable as a fraud on creditors of the transferor. See, e.g., Springfield Ins. Co. v. Fry, 267 F.Supp. 693 (N.D.Okla. 1967); Sandler v. Parlapiano, 236 App.Div. 70, 258

4: UNIFORM FRAUDULENT TRANSFERS ACT

N.Y.Supp. 88 (1st Dep't 1932); Warwick Municipal Employees Credit Union v. Higham, 106 R.E. 363, 259 A.2d 852 (1969); Hulsether v. Sanders, 54 S.D. 412, 223 N.W. 335 (1929); Cooper v. Cooper, 22 Tenn.App. 473, 477, 124 S.W.2d 264, 267 (1939); Note, Rights of Creditors in Property Conveyed in Consideration of Future Support, 45 Iowa L.Rev. 546, 550-62 (1960). This Act adopts the view taken in the cases cited in determining whether an unperformed promise is value.

(5) Subsection (b) rejects the rule of such cases as Durrett v. Washington Nat. Ins. Co., 621 F.2d 201 (5th Cir. 1980) (nonjudicial foreclosure of a mortgage avoided as a fraudulent transfer when the property of an insolvent mortgagor was sold for less than 70% of its fair value); and Abramson v. Lakewood Bank & Trust Co., 647 F.2d 547 (5th Cir. 1981), cert. denied, 454 U.S. 1164 (1982) (nonjudicial foreclosure held to be fraudulent transfer if made without fair consideration). Subsection (b) adopts the view taken in Lawyers Title Ins. Corp. v. Madrid (In re Madrid), 21 B.R. 424 (B.A.P. 9th Cir. 1982), aff'd on another ground, 725 F.2d 1197 (9th Cir. 1984), that the price bid at a public foreclosure sale determines the fair value of the property sold. Subsection (b) prescribes the effect of a sale meeting its requirements, whether the asset sold is personal or real property. The rule of this subsection applies to a foreclosure by sale of the interest of a vendee under an installment land contract in accordance with applicable law that requires or permits the foreclosure to be effected by a sale in the same manner as the foreclosure of a mortgage. See G.Osborne, G.Nelson, & D.Whitman, Real Estate Finance Law 83-84, 95-97 (1979). The premise of the subsection is that "a sale of the collateral by the secured party as the normal consequence of default . . . [is] the safest way of establishing the fair value of the collateral . . .." 2 G.Gilmore, Security Interests in Personal Property, 1227 (1965).

If a lien given an insider for a present consideration is not perfected as against a subsequent bona fide purchaser or is so perfected after a delay following an extension of credit secured by the lien, foreclosure of the lien may result in a transfer for an antecedent debt that is voidable under Section 5(b) infra. Subsection (b) does not apply to an action under Section 4(a)(1) to avoid a transfer or obligation because made or incurred with actual intent to hinder, delay, or defraud any creditor.

(6) Subsection (c) is an adaptation of § 547(c)(1) of the Bankruptcy Code. A transfer to an insider for an antecedent debt may be voidable under § 5(b) infra.

SECTION 4. TRANSFERS FRAUDULENT AS TO PRESENT AND FUTURE CREDITORS.

4: UNIFORM FRAUDULENT TRANSFERS ACT

(a) A transfer made or obligation incurred by a debtor is fraudulent as to a creditor, whether the creditor's claim arose before or after the transfer was made or the obligation was incurred, if the debtor made the transfer or incurred the obligation:

(1) with actual intent to hinder, delay, or defraud any creditor of the debtor; or

(2) without receiving a reasonably equivalent value in exchange for the transfer or obligation, and the debtor:

(i) was engaged or was about to engage in a business or a transaction for which the remaining assets of the debtor were unreasonably small in relation to the business or transaction; or

(ii) intended to incur, or believed or reasonably should have believed that he [or she] would incur, debts beyond his [or her] ability to pay as they became due.

(b) In determining actual intent under subsection (a)(1), consideration may be given, among other factors, to whether:

(1) the transfer or obligation was to an insider;

(2) the debtor retained possession or control of the property transferred after the transfer;

(3) the transfer or obligation was disclosed or concealed;

(4) before the transfer was made or obligation was incurred, the debtor had been sued or threatened with suit;

(5) the transfer was of substantially all the debtor's assets;

(6) the debtor absconded;

(7) the debtor removed or concealed assets;

(8) the value of the consideration received by the debtor was reasonably equivalent to the value of the asset transferred or the amount of the obligation incurred;

(9) the debtor was insolvent or became insolvent shortly after the transfer was made or the obligation was incurred;

(10) the transfer occurred shortly before or shortly after a substantial debt was incurred; and

4: UNIFORM FRAUDULENT TRANSFERS ACT

(11) the debtor transferred the essential assets of the business to a lienor who transferred the assets to an insider of the debtor.

Comment

(1) Section 4(a)(1) is derived from § 7 of the Uniform Fraudulent Conveyance Act. Factors appropriate for consideration in determining actual intent under paragraph (1) are specified in subsection (b).

(2) Section 4(a)(2) is derived from §§ 5 and 6 of the Uniform Fraudulent Conveyance Act but substitutes "reasonably equivalent value" for "fair consideration." The transferee's good faith was an element of "fair consideration" as defined in § 3 of the Uniform Fraudulent Conveyance Act, and lack of fair consideration was one of the elements of a fraudulent transfer as defined in four sections of the Uniform Act. The transferee's good faith is irrelevant to a determination of the adequacy of the consideration under this Act, but lack of good faith may be a basis for withholding protection of a transferee or obligee under § 8 infra.

(3) Unlike the Uniform Fraudulent Conveyance Act as originally promulgated, this Act does not prescribe different tests when a transfer is made for the purpose of security and when it is intended to be absolute. The premise of this Act is that when a transfer is for security only, the equity or value of the asset that exceeds the amount of the debt secured remains available to unsecured creditors and thus cannot be regarded as the subject of a fraudulent transfer merely because of the encumbrance resulting from an otherwise valid security transfer. Disproportion between the value of the asset securing the debt and the size of the debt secured does not, in the absence of circumstances indicating a purpose to hinder, delay, or defraud creditors, constitute an impermissible hindrance to the enforcement of other creditors' rights against the debtor-transferor. Cf. U.C.C. § 9-311.

(4) Subparagraph (i) of § 4(a)(2) is an adaptation of § 5 of the Uniform Fraudulent Conveyance Act but substitutes "unreasonably small [assets] in relation to the business or transaction" for "unreasonably small capital." The reference to "capital" in the Uniform Act is ambiguous in that it may refer to net worth or to the par value of stock or to the consideration received for stock issued. The special meanings of "capital" in corporation law have no relevance in the law of fraudulent transfers. The subparagraph focuses attention on whether the amount of all the assets retained by the debtor was inadequate, i.e., unreasonably small, in light of the needs of the business or transaction in which the debtor was engaged or about to engage.

4: UNIFORM FRAUDULENT TRANSFERS ACT

(5) Subsection (b) is a nonexclusive catalogue of factors appropriate for consideration by the court in determining whether the debtor had an actual intent to hinder, delay, or defraud one or more creditors. Proof of the existence of any one or more of the factors enumerated in subsection (b) may be relevant evidence as to the debtor's actual intent but does not create a presumption that the debtor has made a fraudulent transfer or incurred a fraudulent obligation. The list of factors includes most of the badges of fraud that have been recognized by the courts in construing and applying the Statute of 13 Elizabeth and § 7 of the Uniform Fraudulent Conveyance Act. Proof of the presence of certain badges in combination establishes fraud conclusively – i.e., without regard to the actual intent of the parties – when they concur as provided in § 4(a)(2) or in § 5. The fact that a transfer has been made to a relative or to an affiliated corporation has not been regarded as a badge of fraud sufficient to warrant avoidance when unaccompanied by any other evidence of fraud. The courts have uniformly recognized, however, that a transfer to a closely related person warrants close scrutiny of the other circumstances, including the nature and extent of the consideration exchanged. See 1 G. Glenn, Fraudulent Conveyances and Preferences § 307 (Rev. ed. 1940). The second, third, fourth, and fifth factors listed are all adapted from the classic catalogue of badges of fraud provided by Lord Coke in Twyne's Case, 3 Coke 80b, 76 Eng.Rep. 809 (Star Chamber 1601). Lord Coke also included the use of a trust and the recitation in the instrument of transfer that it "was made honestly, truly, and bona fide," but the use of the trust is fraudulent only when accompanied by elements or badges specified in this Act, and recitals of "good faith" can no longer be regarded as significant evidence of a fraudulent intent.

(6) In considering the factors listed in § 4(b) a court should evaluate all the relevant circumstances involving a challenged transfer or obligation. Thus the court may appropriately take into account all indicia negativing as well as those suggesting fraud, as illustrated in the following reported cases:

(a) Whether the transfer or obligation was to an insider: Salomon v. Kaiser (In re Kaiser), 722 F.2d 1574, 1582-83 (2d Cir. 1983) (insolvent debtor's purchase of two residences in the name of his spouse and the creation of a dummy corporation for the purpose of concealing assets held to evidence fraudulent intent); Banner Construction Corp. v. Arnold, 128 So.2d 893 (Fla.Dist.App. 1961) (assignment by one corporation to another having identical directors and stockholders constituted a badge of fraud); Travelers Indemnity Co. v. Cormaney, 258 Iowa 237, 138 N.W.2d 50 (1965) (transfer between spouses said to be a circumstance that shed suspicion on the transfer and that with other circumstances warranted avoidance); Hatheway v. Hanson, 230 Iowa 386, 297 N.W. 824 (1941) (transfer from parent to child said to require a critical examination of surround-

4: UNIFORM FRAUDULENT TRANSFERS ACT

ing circumstances, which, together with other indicia of fraud, warranted avoidance); Lumpkins v. McPhee, 59 N.M. 442, 286 P.2d 299 (1955) (transfer from daughter to mother said to be indicative of fraud but transfer held not to be fraudulent due to adequacy of consideration and delivery of possession by transferor).

(b) Whether the transferor retained possession or control of the property after the transfer: Harris v. Shaw, 224 Ark. 150, 272 S.W.2d 53 (1954) (retention of property by transferor said to be a badge of fraud and, together with other badges, to warrant avoidance of transfer); Stephens v. Reginstein, 89 Ala. 561, 8 So. 68 (1890) (transferor's retention of control and management of property and business after transfer held material in determining transfer to be fraudulent); Allen v. Massey, 84 U.S. (17 Wall.) 351 (1872) (joint possession of furniture by transferor and transferee considered in holding transfer to be fraudulent); Warner v. Norton, 61 U.S. (20 How.) 448 (1857) (surrender of possession by transferor deemed to negate allegations of fraud).

(c) Whether the transfer or obligation was concealed or disclosed: Walton v. First National Bank, 13 Colo. 265, 22 P. 440 (1889) (agreement between parties to conceal the transfer from the public said to be one of the strongest badges of fraud); Warner v. Norton, 61 U.S. (20 How.) 448 (1857) (although secrecy said to be a circumstance from which, when coupled with other badges, fraud may be inferred, transfer was held not to be fraudulent when made in good faith and transferor surrendered possession); W.T. Raleigh Co. v. Barnett, 253 Ala. 433, 44 So.2d 585 (1950) (failure to record a deed in itself said not to evidence fraud, and transfer held not to be fraudulent).

(d) Whether, before the transfer was made or obligation was incurred, a creditor sued or threatened to sue the debtor: Harris v. Shaw, 224 Ark. 150, 272 S.W. 2d 53 (1954) (transfer held to be fraudulent when causally connected to pendency of litigation and accompanied by other badges of fraud); Pergrem v. Smith, 255 S.W.2d 42 (Ky.App. 1953) (transfer in anticipation of suit deemed to be a badge of fraud; transfer held fraudulent when accompanied by insolvency of transferor who was related to transferee); Bank of Sun Prairie v. Hovig, 218 F.Supp. 769 (W.D.Ark. 1963) (although threat or pendency of litigation said to be an indicator of fraud, transfer was held not to be fraudulent when adequate consideration and good faith were shown).

(e) Whether the transfer was of substantially all the debtor's assets: Walbrun v. Babbitt, 83 U.S. (16 Wall.) 577 (1872) (sale by insolvent retail shop owner of all of his inventory in a single transaction held to be fraudulent); Cole v. Mercantile

4: UNIFORM FRAUDULENT TRANSFERS ACT

Trust Co., 133 N.Y. 164, 30 N.E. 847 (1892) (transfer of all property before plaintiff could obtain a judgment held to be fraudulent); Lumpkins v. McPhee, 59 N.M. 442, 286 P.2d 299 (1955) (although transfer of all assets said to indicate fraud, transfer held not to be fraudulent because full consideration was paid and transferor surrendered possession).

(f) Whether the debtor had absconded: In re Thomas, 199 F. 214 (N.D.N.Y. 1912) (when debtor collected all of his money and property with the intent to abscond, fraudulent intent was held to be shown).

(g) Whether the debtor had removed or concealed assets: Bentley v. Young, 210 F. 202 (S.D.N.Y 1914), aff'd, 223 F. 536 (2d Cir. 1915) (debtor's removal of goods from store to conceal their whereabouts and to sell them held to render sale fraudulent); Cioli v. Kenourgios, 59 Cal.App. 690, 211 P. 838 (1922) (debtor's sale of all assets and shipment of proceeds out of the country held to be fraudulent notwithstanding adequacy of consideration).

(h) Whether the value of the consideration received by the debtor was reasonably equivalent to the value of the asset transferred or the amount of the obligation incurred: Toomay v. Graham, 151 S.W.2d 119 (Mo.App. 1941) (although mere inadequacy of consideration said not to be a badge of fraud, transfer held to be fraudulent when accompanied by badges of fraud); Texas Sand Co. v. Shield, 381 S.W.2d 48 (Tex. 1964) (inadequate consideration said to be an indicator of fraud, and transfer held to be fraudulent because of inadequate consideration, pendency of suit, family relationship of transferee, and fact that all nonexempt property was transferred); Weigel v. Wood, 355 Mo. 11, 194 S.W.2d 40 (1946) (although inadequate consideration said to be a badge of fraud, transfer held not to be fraudulent when inadequacy not gross and not accompanied by any other badge; fact that transfer was from father to son held not sufficient to establish fraud).

(i) Whether the debtor was insolvent or became insolvent shortly after the transfer was made or obligation was incurred: Harris v. Shaw, 224 Ark. 150, 272 S.W. 2d 53 (1954) (insolvency of transferor said to be a badge of fraud and transfer held fraudulent when accompanied by other badges of fraud); Bank of Sun Prairie v. Hovig, 218 F.Supp. 769 (W.D. Ark. 1963) (although the insolvency of the debtor said to be a badge of fraud, transfer held not fraudulent when debtor was shown to be solvent, adequate consideration was paid, and good faith was shown, despite the pendency of suit); Wareheim v. Bayliss, 149 Md. 103, 131 A. 27 (1925) (although insolvency of debtor acknowledged to be an indicator of fraud, transfer held not to be fraudulent when adequate consideration was paid and whether debtor was insolvent in fact was doubtful).

4: UNIFORM FRAUDULENT TRANSFERS ACT

(j) Whether the transfer occurred shortly before or shortly after a substantial debt was incurred: Commerce Bank of Lebanon v. Halladale A Corp., 618 S.W. 2d 288, 292 (Mo.App. 1981) (when transferors incurred substantial debts near in time to the transfer, transfer was held to be fraudulent due to inadequate consideration, close family relationship, the debtor's retention of possession, and the fact that almost all the debtor's property was transferred).

(7) The effect of the two transfers described in § 4(b)(11), if not avoided, may be to permit a debtor and a lienor to deprive the debtor's unsecured creditors of access to the debtor's assets for the purpose of collecting their claims while the debtor, the debtor's affiliate or insider, and the lienor arrange for the beneficial use or disposition of the assets in accordance with their interests. The kind of disposition sought to be reached here is exemplified by that found in Northern Pacific Co. v. Boyd, 228 U.S. 482 (1913), the leading case in establishing the absolute priority doctrine in reorganization law. There the Court held that a reorganization whereby the secured creditors and the management-owners retained their economic interests in a railroad through a foreclosure that cut off claims of unsecured creditors against its assets was in effect a fraudulent disposition (id. at 502-05). See Frank, Some Realistic Reflections on Some Aspects of Corporate Reorganization, 19 Va. L.Rev. 541, 693 (1933). For cases in which an analogous injury to unsecured creditors was inflicted by a lienor and a debtor, see Jackson v. Star Sprinkler Corp. of Florida, 575 F.2d 1223, 1231-34 (8th Cir. 1978); Heath v. Helmick, 173 F.2d 157, 161-62 (9th Cir. 1949); Toner v. Nuss, 234 F.S. 457, 461-62 (E.D.Pa. 1964); and see In re Spotless Tavern Co., Inc., 4 F.Supp. 752, 753, 755 (D.Md. 1933).

(8) Nothing in § 4(b) is intended to affect the application of § 2-402(2), 9-205, 9-301, or 6-105 of the Uniform Commercial Code. Section 2-402(2) recognizes the generally prevailing rule that retention of possession of goods by a seller may be fraudulent but limits the application of the rule by negating any imputation of fraud from "retention of possession in good faith and current course of trade by a merchant-seller for a commercially reasonable time after a sale or identification." Section 9-205 explicitly negates any imputation of fraud from the grant of liberty by a secured creditor to a debtor to use, commingle, or dispose of personal property collateral or to account for its proceeds. The section recognizes that it does not relax prevailing requirements for delivery of possession by a pledgor. Moreover, the section does not mitigate the general requirement of § 9-301(1)(b) that a nonpossessory security interest in personal property must be accompanied by notice-filing to be effective against a levying creditor. Finally, like the Uniform Fraudulent Conveyance Act this Act does not pre-empt the statutes governing bulk transfers, such as Article 6 of the Uniform Commercial Code. Compliance

4: UNIFORM FRAUDULENT TRANSFERS ACT

with the cited sections of the Uniform Commercial Code does not, however, insulate a transfer or obligation from avoidance. Thus a sale by an insolvent debtor for less than a reasonably equivalent value would be voidable under this Act notwithstanding compliance with the Uniform Commercial Code.

SECTION 5. TRANSFERS FRAUDULENT AS TO PRESENT CREDITORS.

(a) A transfer made or obligation incurred by a debtor is fraudulent as to a creditor whose claim arose before the transfer was made or the obligation was incurred if the debtor made the transfer or incurred the obligation without receiving a reasonably equivalent value in exchange for the transfer or obligation and the debtor was insolvent at that time or the debtor became insolvent as a result of the transfer or obligation.

(b) A transfer made by a debtor is fraudulent as to a creditor whose claim arose before the transfer was made if the transfer was made to an insider for an antecedent debt, the debtor was insolvent at that time, and the insider had reasonable cause to believe that the debtor was insolvent.

Comment

(1) Subsection (a) is derived from § 4 of the Uniform Fraudulent Conveyance Act. It adheres to the limitation of the protection of that section to a creditor who extended credit before the transfer or obligation described. As pointed out in Comment (2) accompanying § 4, this Act substitutes "reasonably equivalent value" for "fair consideration."

(2) Subsection (b) renders a preferential transfer – i.e., a transfer by an insolvent debtor for or on account of an antecedent debt – to an insider vulnerable as a fraudulent transfer when the insider had reasonable cause to believe that the debtor was insolvent. This subsection adopts for general application the rule of such cases as Jackson Sound Studios, Inc. v. Travis, 473 F.2d 503 (5th Cir. 1973) (security transfer of corporation's equipment to corporate principal's mother perfected on eve of bankruptcy of corporation held to be fraudulent); In re Lamie Chemical Co., 296 F. 24 (4th Cir. 1924) (corporate preference to corporate officers and directors held voidable by receiver when corporation was insolvent or nearly so and directors had already voted for liquidation); Stuart v. Larson, 298 F. 223 (8th Cir. 1924), noted 38 Harv.L.Rev. 521 (1925) (corporate preference to director held voidable). See generally 2 G. Glenn, Fraudulent Conveyances and Preferences 386 (rev. ed. 1940). Subsection (b) overrules such cases as Epstein v. Goldstein, 107 F.2d 755, 757 (2d Cir. 1939) (transfer by insolvent husband to wife to secure his debt to her sustained against attack by husband's trustee);

4: UNIFORM FRAUDULENT TRANSFERS ACT

Hartford Accident & Indemnity Co. v. Jirasek, 254 Mich. 131, 139, 235 N.W. 836, 389 (1931) (mortgage given by debtor to his brother to secure an antecedent debt owed the brother sustained as not fraudulent).

(3) Subsection (b) does not extend as far as § 8(a) of the Uniform Fraudulent Conveyance Act and § 548(b) of the Bankruptcy Code in rendering voidable a transfer or obligation incurred by an insolvent partnership to a partner, who is an insider of the partnership. The transfer to the partner is not vulnerable to avoidance under § 4(b) unless the transfer was for an antecedent debt and the partner had reasonable cause to believe that the partnership was insolvent. The cited provisions of the Uniform Fraudulent Conveyance Act and the Bankruptcy Act make any transfer by an insolvent partnership to a partner voidable. Avoidance of the partnership transfer without reference to the partner's state of mind and the nature of the consideration exchanged would be unduly harsh treatment of the creditors of the partner and unduly favorable to the creditors of the partnership.

SECTION 6. WHEN TRANSFER IS MADE OR OBLIGATION IS INCURRED. For the purposes of this [Act]:

(1) a transfer is made:

(i) with respect to an asset that is real property other than a fixture, but including the interest of a seller or purchaser under a contract for the sale of the asset, when the transfer is so far perfected that a good-faith purchaser of the asset from the debtor against whom applicable law permits the transfer to be perfected cannot acquire an interest in the asset that is superior to the interest of the transferee; and

(ii) with respect to an asset that is not real property or that is a fixture, when the transfer is so far perfected that a creditor on a simple contract cannot acquire a judicial lien otherwise than under this [Act] that is superior to the interest of the transferee;

(2) if applicable law permits the transfer to be perfected as provided in paragraph (1) and the transfer is not so perfected before the commencement of an action for relief under this [Act], the transfer is deemed made immediately before the commencement of the action;

(3) if applicable law does not permit the transfer to be perfected as provided in paragraph (1), the transfer is made when it becomes effective between the debtor and the transferee;

4: UNIFORM FRAUDULENT TRANSFERS ACT

(4) a transfer is not made until the debtor has acquired rights in the asset transferred;

(5) an obligation is incurred:

(i) if oral, when it becomes effective between the parties; or

(ii) if evidenced by a writing, when the writing executed by the obligor is delivered to or for the benefit of the obligee.

Comment

(1) One of the uncertainties in the law governing the avoidance of fraudulent transfers and obligations is the difficulty of determining when the cause of action arises. Subsection (b) clarifies this point in time. For transfers of real estate Section 6(1) fixes the time as the date of perfection against a good faith purchaser from the transferor and for transfers of fixtures and assets constituting personalty, the time is fixed as the date of perfection against a judicial lien creditor not asserting rights under this Act. Perfection typically is effected by notice-filing, recordation, or delivery of unequivocal possession. See U.C.C. §§ 9-302, 9-304, and 9-305 (security interest in personal property perfected by notice-filing or delivery of possession to transferee); 4 American Law of Property § 17.10-17.12 (1952) (recordation of transfer or delivery of possession to grantee required for perfection against bona fide purchaser from grantor). The provision for postponing the time a transfer is made until its perfection is an adaptation of § 548(d)(1) of the Bankruptcy Code. When no steps are taken to perfect a transfer that applicable law permits to be perfected, the transfer is deemed by paragraph (2) to be perfected immediately before the filing of an action to avoid it; without such a provision to cover that eventuality, an unperfected transfer would arguably be immune to attack. Some transfers – e.g., an assignment of a bank account, creation of a security interest in money, or execution of a marital or premarital agreement for the disposition of property owned by the parties to the agreement – may not be amenable to perfection as against a bona fide purchaser or judicial lien creditor. When a transfer is not perfectible as provided in paragraph (11), the transfer occurs for the purpose of this Act when the transferor effectively parts with an interest in the asset as provided in § 1(12) supra.

(2) Paragraph (4) requires the transferor to have rights in the asset transferred before the transfer is made for the purpose of this section. This provision makes clear that its purpose may not be circumvented by notice-filing or recordation of a document evidencing an interest in an asset to be acquired in the future. Cf. Bankruptcy Code § 547(e); U.C.C. § 9-203(1)(c).

4: UNIFORM FRAUDULENT TRANSFERS ACT

(3) Paragraph (5) is new. It is intended to resolve uncertainty arising from Rubin v. Manufacturers Hanover Trust Co., 661 F.2d 979, 989-91, 997 (2d Cir. 1981), insofar as that case holds that an obligation of guaranty may be deemed to be incurred when advances covered by the guaranty are made rather than when the guaranty first became effective between the parties. Compare Rosenberg, Intercorporate Guaranties and the Law of Fraudulent Conveyances: Lender Beware, 125 U.Pa.L.Rev. 235, 256-57 (1976).

An obligation may be avoided as fraudulent under this Act if it is incurred under the circumstances specified in § 4(a) or § 5(a). The debtor may receive reasonably equivalent value in exchange for an obligation incurred even though the benefit to the debtor is indirect. See Rubin v. Manufacturers Hanover Trust Co., 661 F.2d at 991-92; Williams v. Twin City Co., 251 F.2d 678, 681 (9th Cir. 1958); Rosenberg, supra at 243-46.

SECTION 7. REMEDIES OF CREDITORS.

(a) In an action for relief against a transfer or obligation under this [Act], a creditor, subject to the limitations in Section 8, may obtain:

(1) avoidance of the transfer or obligation to the extent necessary to satisfy the creditor's claim;

[(2) an attachment or other provisional remedy against the asset transferred or other property of the transferee in accordance with the procedure prescribed by [ ];]

(3) subject to applicable principles of equity and in accordance with applicable rules of civil procedure,

(i) an injunction against further disposition by the debtor or a transferee, or both, of the asset transferred or of other property;

(ii) appointment of a receiver to take charge of the asset transferred or of other property of the transferee; or (iii) any other relief the circumstances may require.

(b) If a creditor has obtained a judgment on a claim against the debtor, the creditor, if the court so orders, may levy execution on the asset transferred or its proceeds.

Comment

(1) This section is derived from §§ 9 and 10 of the Uniform Fraudulent Conveyance Act. Section 9 of that Act specified the remedies of creditors whose

4: UNIFORM FRAUDULENT TRANSFERS ACT

claims have matured, and § 10 enumerated the remedies available to creditors whose claims have not matured. A creditor holding an unmatured claim may be denied the right to receive payment for the proceeds of a sale on execution until his claim has matured, but the proceeds may be deposited in court or in an interestbearing account pending the maturity of the creditor's claim. The remedies specified in this section are not exclusive.

(2) The availability of an attachment or other provisional remedy has been restricted by amendments of statutes and rules of procedure to reflect views of the Supreme Court expressed in Sniadach v. Family Finance Corp. of Bay View, 395 U.S. 337 (1969), and its progeny. This judicial development and the procedural changes that followed in its wake do not preclude resort to attachment by a creditor in seeking avoidance of a fraudulent transfer or obligation. See, e.g., Britton v. Howard Sav. Bank, 727 F.2d 315, 317-20 (3d Cir. 1984); Computer Sciences Corp. v. Sci-Tek Inc., 367 A.2d 658, 661 (Del. Super. 1976); Great Lakes Carbon Corp. v. Fontana, 54 A.D.2d 548, 387 N.Y.S. 2d 115 (1st Dep't 1976). Section 7(a)(2) continues the authorization for the use of attachment contained in § 9(b) of the Uniform Fraudulent Conveyance Act, or of a similar provisional remedy, when the state's procedure provides therefor, subject to the constraints imposed by the due process clauses of the United States and state constitutions.

(3) Subsections (a) and (b) of § 10 of the Uniform Fraudulent Conveyance Act authorized the court, in an action on a fraudulent transfer or obligation, to restrain the defendant from disposing of his property, to appoint a receiver to take charge of his property, or to make any order the circumstances may require. Section 10, however, applied only to a creditor whose claim was unmatured. There is no reason to restrict the availability of these remedies to such a creditor, and the courts have not so restricted them. See, e.g., Lipskey v. Voloshen, 155 Md. 139, 143-45, 141 Atl. 402, 404-05 (1928) (judgment creditor granted injunction against disposition of property by transferee, but appointment of receiver denied for lack of sufficient showing of need for such relief); Matthews v. Schusheim, 36 Misc. 2d 918, 922-23, 235 N.Y.S.2d 973, 976-77, 991-92 (Sup.Ct. 1962) (injunction and appointment of receiver granted to holder of claims for fraud, breach of contract, and alimony arrearages; whether creditor's claim was mature said to be immaterial); Oliphant v. Moore, 155 Tenn. 359, 362-63, 293 S.W. 541, 542 (1927) (tort creditor granted injunction restraining alleged tortfeasor's disposition of property).

(4) As under the Uniform Fraudulent Conveyance Act, a creditor is not required to obtain a judgment against the debtor-transferor or to have a matured claim in order to proceed under subsection (a). See § 1(3) and (4) supra; American Surety

4: UNIFORM FRAUDULENT TRANSFERS ACT

Co. v. Conner, 251 N.Y. 1, 166 N.E. 783, 65 A.L.R. 244 (1929); 1 G. Glenn, Fraudulent Conveyances and Preferences 129 (Rev.ed. 1940).

(5) The provision in subsection (b) for a creditor to levy execution on a fraudulently transferred asset continues the availability of a remedy provided in § 9(b) of the Uniform Fraudulent Conveyance Act. See, e.g., Doland v. Burns Lbr. Co., 156 Minn. 238, 194 N.W. 636 (1923); Montana Ass'n of Credit Management v. Hergert, 181 Mont. 442, 449, 453, 593 P.2d 1059, 1063, 1065 (1979); Corbett v. Hunter, 292 Pa.Super. 123, 128, 436 A.2d 1036, 1038 (1981); see also American Surety Co. v. Conner, 251 N.Y. 1, 6, 166 N.E. 783, 784, 65 A.L.R. 244, 247 (1929) ("In such circumstances he [the creditor] might find it necessary to indemnify the sheriff and, when the seizure was erroneous, assumed the risk of error"); McLaughlin, Application of the Uniform Fraudulent Conveyance Act, 46 Harv.L.Rev. 404, 441-42 (1933).

(6) The remedies specified in § 7, like those enumerated in §§ 9 and 10 of the Uniform Fraudulent Conveyance Act, are cumulative. Lind v. O. N. Johnson Co., 204 Minn. 30, 40, 282 N.W. 661, 667, 119 A.L.R. 940 (1939) (Uniform Fraudulent Conveyance Act held not to impair or limit availability of the "old practice" of obtaining judgment and execution returned unsatisfied before proceeding in equity to set aside a transfer); Conemaugh Iron Works Co. v. Delano Coal Co., Inc., 298 Pa. 182, 186, 148 A. 94, 95 (1929) (Uniform Fraudulent Conveyance Act held to give an "additional optional remedy" and not to "deprive a creditor of the right, as formerly, to work out his remedy at law"); 1 G. Glenn, Fraudulent Conveyances and Preferences 120, 130, 150 (Rev.ed. 1940).

SECTION 8. DEFENSES, LIABILITY, AND PROTECTION OF TRANSFEREE.

(a) A transfer or obligation is not voidable under Section 4(a)(1) against a person who took in good faith and for a reasonably equivalent value or against any subsequent transferee or obligee.

(b) Except as otherwise provided in this section, to the extent a transfer is voidable in an action by a creditor under Section 7(a)(1), the creditor may recover judgment for the value of the asset transferred, as adjusted under subsection (c), or the amount necessary to satisfy the creditor's claim, whichever is less. The judgment may be entered against:

(1) the first transferee of the asset or the person for whose benefit the transfer was made; or

(2) any subsequent transferee other than a good-faith transferee or obligee who

4: UNIFORM FRAUDULENT TRANSFERS ACT

took for value or from any subsequent transferee or obligee.

(c) If the judgment under subsection (b) is based upon the value of the asset transferred, the judgment must be for an amount equal to the value of the asset at the time of the transfer, subject to adjustment as the equities may require.

(d) Notwithstanding voidability of a transfer or an obligation under this [Act], a good-faith transferee or obligee is entitled, to the extent of the value given the debtor for the transfer or obligation, to

(1) a lien on or a right to retain any interest in the asset transferred;

(2) enforcement of any obligation incurred; or

(3) a reduction in the amount of the liability on the judgment.

(e) A transfer is not voidable under Section 4(a)(2) or Section 5 if the transfer results from:

(1) termination of a lease upon default by the debtor when the termination is pursuant to the lease and applicable law; or

(2) enforcement of a security interest in compliance with Article 9 of the Uniform Commercial Code.

(f) A transfer is not voidable under Section 5(b):

(1) to the extent the insider gave new value to or for the benefit of the debtor after the transfer was made unless the new value was secured by a valid lien;

(2) if made in the ordinary course of business or financial affairs of the debtor and the insider; or

(3) if made pursuant to a good-faith effort to rehabilitate the debtor and the transfer secured present value given for that purpose as well as an antecedent debt of the debtor.

Comment

(1) Subsection (a) states the rule that applies when the transferee establishes a complete defense to the action for avoidance based on Section 4(a)(1). The subsection is an adaptation of the exception stated in § 9 of the Uniform Fraudulent Conveyance Act. The person who invokes this defense carries the burden of establishing good faith and the reasonable equivalence of the consideration exchanged.

4: UNIFORM FRAUDULENT TRANSFERS ACT

Chorost v. Grand Rapids Factory Showrooms, Inc., 77 F. Supp. 276, 280 (D.N.J. 1948), aff'd, 172 F.2d 327, 329 (3d Cir. 1949).

(2) Subsection (b) is derived from § 550(a) of the Bankruptcy Code. The value of the asset transferred is limited to the value of the levyable interest on the transferor, exclusive of any interest encumbered by a valid lien. See § 1(2) supra.

(3) Subsection (c) is new. The measure of the recovery of a defrauded creditor against a fraudulent transferee is usually limited to the value of the asset transferred at the time of the transfer. See, e.g., United States v. Fernon, 640 F.2d 609, 611 (5th Cir. 1981); Hamilton Nat'l Bank of Boston v. Halstead, 134 N.Y. 520, 31 N.E. 900 (1892); cf. Buffum v. Peter Barceloux Co., 289 U.S. 227 (1932) (transferee's objection to trial court's award of highest value of asset between the date of the transfer and the date of the decree of avoidance rejected because an award measured by value as of time of the transfer plus interest from that date would have been larger). The premise of § 8(c) is that changes in value of the asset transferred that occur after the transfer should ordinarily not affect the amount of the creditor's recovery. Circumstances may require a departure from that measure of the recovery, however, as the cases decided under the Uniform Fraudulent Conveyance Act and other laws derived from the Statute of 13 Elizabeth illustrate. Thus, if the value of the asset at the time of levy and sale to enforce the judgment of the creditor has been enhanced by improvements of the asset transferred or discharge of liens on the property, a good faith transferee should be reimbursed for the outlay for such a purpose to the extent the sale proceeds were increased thereby. See Bankruptcy Code § 550(d); Janson v. Schier, 375 A.2d 1159, 1160 (N.H. 1977); Anno., 8 A.L.R. 527 (1920). If the value of the asset has been diminished by severance and disposition of timber or minerals or fixtures, the transferee should be liable for the amount of the resulting reduction. See Damazo v. Wahby, 269 Md. 252, 257, 305 A.2d 138, 142 (1973). If the transferee has collected rents, harvested crops, or derived other income from the use or occupancy of the asset after the transfer, the liability of the transferee should be limited in any event to the net income after deduction of the expense incurred in earning the income. Anno., 60 A.L.R.2d 593 (1958). On the other hand, adjustment for the equities does not warrant an award to the creditor of consequential damages alleged to accrue from mismanagement of the asset after the transfer.

(4) Subsection (d) is an adaptation of § 548(c) of the Bankruptcy Code. An insider who receives property or an obligation from an insolvent debtor as security for or in satisfaction of an antecedent debt of the transferor or obligor is not a good faith transferee or obligee if the insider has reasonable cause to believe that the

4: UNIFORM FRAUDULENT TRANSFERS ACT

debtor was insolvent at the time the transfer was made or the obligation was incurred.

(5) Subsection (e)(1) rejects the rule adopted in Darby v. Atkinson (In re Farris), 415 F.Supp. 33, 39-41 (W.D.Okla. 1976), that termination of a lease on default in accordance with its terms and applicable law may constitute a fraudulent transfer. Subsection (e)(2) protects a transferee who acquires a debtor's interest in an asset as a result of the enforcement of a secured creditor's rights pursuant to and in compliance with the provisions of Part 5 of Article 9 of the Uniform Commercial Code. Cf. Calaiaro v. Pittsburgh Nat'l Bank (In re Ewing), 33 B.R. 288, 9 C.B.C.2d 526, CCH B.L.R. ¶ 69,460 (Bk.W.D.Pa. 1983) (sale of pledged stock held subject to avoidance as fraudulent transfer in § 548 of the Bankruptcy Code), rev'd, 36 B.R. 476 (W.D.Pa. 1984) (transfer held not voidable because deemed to have occurred more than one year before bankruptcy petition filed). Although a secured creditor may enforce rights in collateral without a sale under § 9-502 or § 9-505 of the Code, the creditor must proceed in good faith (U.C.C. § 9-103) and in a "commercially reasonable" manner. The "commercially reasonable" constraint is explicit in U.C.C. § 9-502(2) and is implicit in § 9-505. See 2 G. Gilmore, Security Interests in Personal Property 1224-27 (1965).

(6) Subsection (f) provides additional defenses against the avoidance of a preferential transfer to an insider under § 5(b). Paragraph (1) is adapted from § 547(c)(4) of the Bankruptcy Code, which permits a preferred creditor to set off the amount of new value subsequently advanced against the recovery of a voidable preference by a trustee in bankruptcy to the debtor without security. The new value may consist not only of money, goods, or services delivered on unsecured credit but also of the release of a valid lien. See, e.g., In re Ira Haupt & Co., 424 F.2d 722, 724 (2d Cir. 1970); Baranow v. Gibraltor Factors Corp. (In re Hygrade Envelope Co.), 393 F.2d 60, 65-67 (2d Cir.), cert. denied, 393 U.S. 837 (1968); In re John Morrow & Co., 134 F.686, 688 (S.D.Ohio 1901). It does not include an obligation substituted for a prior obligation. If the insider receiving the preference thereafter extends new credit to the debtor but also takes security from the debtor, the injury to the other creditors resulting from the preference remains undiminished by the new credit. On the other hand, if a lien taken to secure the new credit is itself voidable by a judicial lien creditor of the debtor, the new value received by the debtor may appropriately be treated as unsecured and applied to reduce the liability of the insider for the preferential transfer.

Paragraph (2) is derived from § 546(c)(2) of the Bankruptcy Code, which excepts certain payments made in the ordinary course of business or financial affairs from avoidance by the trustee in bankruptcy as preferential transfers. Whether a trans-

4: UNIFORM FRAUDULENT TRANSFERS ACT

fer was in the "ordinary course" requires a consideration of the pattern of payments or secured transactions engaged in by the debtor and the insider prior to the transfer challenged under § 5(b). See Tait & Williams, Bankruptcy Preference Laws: The Scope of Section 547(c)(2), 99 Banking L.J. 55, 63-66 (1982). The defense provided by paragraph (2) is available, irrespective of whether the debtor or the insider or both are engaged in business, but the prior conduct or practice of both the debtor and the insider-transferee is relevant.

Paragraph (3) is new and reflects a policy judgment that an insider who has previously extended credit to a debtor should not be deterred from extending further credit to the debtor in a good faith effort to save the debtor from a forced liquidation in bankruptcy or otherwise. A similar rationale has sustained the taking of security from an insolvent debtor for an advance to enable the debtor to stave off bankruptcy and extricate itself from financial stringency. Blackman v. Bechtel, 80 F.2d 505, 508-09 (8th Cir. 1935); Olive v. Tyler (In re Chelan Land Co.), 257 F.497, 5 A.L.R. 561 (9th Cir. 1919); In re Robin Bros. Bakeries, Inc., 22 F.S. 662, 663-64 (N.D.Ill. 1937); see Dean v. Davis, 242 U.S. 438, 444 (1917). The amount of the present value given, the size of the antecedent debt secured, and the likelihood of success for the rehabilitative effort are relevant considerations in determining whether the transfer was in good faith.

SECTION 9. EXTINGUISHMENT OF [CLAIM FOR RELIEF] [CAUSE OF ACTION]. A [claim for relief] [cause of action] with respect to a fraudulent transfer or obligation under this [Act] is extinguished unless action is brought:

(a) under Section 4(a)(1), within 4 years after the transfer was made or the obligation was incurred or, if later, within one year after the transfer or obligation was or could reasonably have been discovered by the claimant;

(b) under Section 4(a)(2) or 5(a), within 4 years after the transfer was made or the obligation was incurred; or

(c) under Section 5(b), within one year after the transfer was made or the obligation was incurred.

Comment

(1) This section is new. Its purpose is to make clear that lapse of the statutory periods prescribed by the section bars the right and not merely the remedy. See Restatement of Conflict of Laws 2d § 143 Comments (b) and (c) (1971). The section rejects the rule applied in United States v. Gleneagles Inv. Co., 565 F.S. 556, 583 (M.D.Pa. 1983) (state statute of limitations held not to apply to action by

4: UNIFORM FRAUDULENT TRANSFERS ACT

United States based on Uniform Fraudulent Conveyance Act).

(2) Statutes of limitations applicable to the avoidance of fraudulent transfers and obligations vary widely from state to state and are frequently subject to uncertainties in their application. See Hesson, The Statute of Limitations in Actions to Set Aside Fraudulent Conveyances and in Actions Against Directors by Creditors of Corporations, 32 Cornell L.Q. 222 (1946); Annos., 76 A.L.R. 864 (1932), 128 A.L.R. 1289 (1940), 133 A.L.R. 1311 (1941), 14 A.L.R.2d 598 (1950), and 100 A.L.R.2d 1094 (1965). Together with § 6, this section should mitigate the uncertainty and diversity that have characterized the decisions applying statutes of limitations to actions to fraudulent transfers and obligations. The periods prescribed apply, whether the action under this Act is brought by the creditor defrauded or by a purchaser at a sale on execution levied pursuant to § 7(b) and whether the action is brought against the original transferee or subsequent transferee. The prescription of statutory periods of limitation does not preclude the barring of an avoidance action for laches. See § 10 and the accompanying Comment infra.

SECTION 10. SUPPLEMENTARY PROVISIONS. Unless displaced by the provisions of this [Act], the principles of law and equity, including the law merchant and the law relating to principal and agent, estoppel, laches, fraud, misrepresentation, duress, coercion, mistake, insolvency, or other validating or invalidating cause, supplement its provisions.

Comment

This section is derived from § 11 of the Uniform Fraudulent Conveyance Act and § 1-103 of the Uniform Commercial Code. The section adds a reference to "laches" in recognition of the particular appropriateness of the application of this equitable doctrine to an untimely action to avoid a fraudulent transfer. See Louis Dreyfus Corp. v. Butler, 496 F.2d 806, 808 (6th Cir. 1974) (action to avoid transfers to debtor's wife when debtor was engaged in speculative business held to be barred by laches or applicable statutes of limitations); Cooch v. Grier, 30 Del.Ch. 255, 265-66, 59 A.2d 282, 287-88 (1948) (action under the Uniform Fraudulent Conveyance Act held barred by laches when the creditor was chargeable with inexcusable delay and the defendant was prejudiced by the delay).

SECTION 11. UNIFORMITY OF APPLICATION AND CONSTRUCTION.
This [Act] shall be applied and construed to effectuate its general purpose to make uniform the law with respect to the subject of this [Act] among states enacting it.

SECTION 12. SHORT TITLE. This [Act] may be cited as the Uniform

4: UNIFORM FRAUDULENT TRANSFERS ACT

Fraudulent Transfer Act.

SECTION 13. REPEAL. The following acts and all other acts and parts of acts inconsistent herewith are hereby repealed:

Comment

If enacted by this State, the Uniform Fraudulent Conveyance Act should be listed among the statutes repealed.

5: MEJIA V REED

RHINA MEJIA, Plaintiff and Appellant, v. DANILO REED et al., Defendants and Respondents.

(Superior Court of Santa Clara County, No. CV769375, Frank Cliff and Robert A. Baines, Judges.)

(The Court of Appeal, Sixth Dist., No. H020771, 97 Cal.App.4th 277.)

(Opinion by Kennard, J., expressing the unanimous view of the court.)

COUNSEL

Anderson & Blake, Hannig Law Firm and John H. Blake for Plaintiff and Appellant.

Douglas B. Schwab for Jeffrey W. Little as Amicus Curiae on behalf of Plaintiff and Appellant.

Olimpia, Whelan & Lively, Olimpia, Whelan, Lively & Ryan, Gary L. Olimpia, Adam R. Bernstein; Robinson & Wood and Helen E. Williams for Defendant and Respondent Danilo Reed.

Law Offices of Vanessa A. Zecher and Vanessa A. Zecher for Defendant and Respondent Violeta Reed. {Page 31 Cal.4th 661}

OPINION

KENNARD, J.- Danilo Reed (Husband) had an extramarital relationship with plaintiff Rhina Mejia that led to the birth of a child. In a later divorce proceeding, Husband and Violeta Reed (Wife) entered into a marital settlement agreement (MSA) under which Husband transferred all his interest in jointly held real property to Wife. Plaintiff claimed that the purpose of this transfer was to prevent her from collecting child support, and she asked the court to impose a lien on the real property. The trial court rejected her contentions and entered summary judgment for Husband.

The Court of Appeal reversed the trial court, holding that a transfer of real property under an MSA could be found invalid under the Uniform Fraudulent Transfer Act (UFTA) (Civ. Code, §§ 3439-3439.12). Because that holding conflicted with another Court of Appeal decision, Gagan v. Gouyd (1999) 73 Cal.App.4th 835, we granted review. We conclude that the Court of Appeal in this case correctly held that the provisions of the UFTA apply to marital settlement agreements.

5: MEJIA V REED

That conclusion requires us to address an additional issue. Under the UFTA, a transfer can be invalid either because of actual fraud (Civ. Code, § 3439.04, subd. (a)) or constructive fraud (id., §§ 3439.04, subd. (b), 3439.05); one form of constructive fraud is a transfer by a debtor, without receiving equivalent value in return, if the debtor is insolvent at the time of transfer or rendered insolvent by the transfer (§ 3439.05). The Court of Appeal held that there were triable issues of fact relating to both actual fraud and constructive fraud. Husband sought review only of the holding relating to constructive fraud. fn. 1 That holding rested on the proposition that a person is insolvent under section 3439.05 if the person's assets are less than the discounted cumulative value of future child support obligations. [1] We disagree, and hold that the discounted value of future child support, because it is generally paid from future income rather than current assets, should not be considered in determining solvency under section 3439.05. We therefore reverse the judgment of the Court of Appeal and remand the case for further proceedings. {Page 31 Cal.4th 662}

I. FACTS AND PROCEDURAL HISTORY

The facts are taken from the Court of Appeal opinion. Husband and Wife were married in 1970. In 1994, Husband had an extramarital relationship with plaintiff. Their daughter was born in February 1995. In May 1995, Wife petitioned for dissolution of her marriage to Husband. They entered into an MSA under which Husband conveyed all his interest in the couple's real estate to Wife, and she conveyed her interest in Husband's medical practice to him. The MSA provided that Husband would be solely responsible for his extramarital child support obligation. The MSA was merged into a judgment of dissolution entered in August 1995.

By June 1997, Husband had abandoned his medical practice. He now lives with his mother. He has no assets and little income.

Plaintiff, who had a pending paternity suit against Husband, filed a lis pendens against the real property awarded Wife under the MSA. The trial court in the paternity action awarded plaintiff child support of $750 per month, but it ruled that plaintiff had no standing to challenge the transfer of property under the MSA. The court later increased child support to $953 per month plus $200 per month for day care, or a monthly total of $1153.

Plaintiff then filed this action, asserting that the MSA was a fraudulent transfer by Husband to Wife, intended to hinder plaintiff in her collection of future child support. The complaint sought to establish a lien upon the real property trans-

5: MEJIA V REED

ferred under the MSA. (See Civ. Code, § 3439.07 [remedies of defrauded creditor].) Husband moved for summary judgment. His supporting papers did not expressly deny fraudulent intent, instead relying on plaintiff's failure to provide direct evidence of intent to defraud. Husband further declared that the value of his practice at the date of separation was $600,000, and consequently that the community property had been divided equally.

In response, plaintiff asserted that the transfer was accompanied by certain "badges of fraud" from which the trier of fact could infer intent to defraud. She presented an expert evaluation appraising the fair market value of Husband's medical practice at $100,000. Another expert calculated the discounted value of future child support at $164,829 to $205,975 on the assumption that child support, based on Husband's earning potential, would be set at $1146 to $1482 monthly (plus $200 per month for child care expenses). Under the lowest of these figures, the discounted value of future child support would still exceed the appraised value of Husband's practice.

The trial court assumed that the UFTA applied to the MSA, but it granted Husband's summary judgment motion on the grounds that no evidence was {Page 31 Cal.4th 663} presented of actual intent to defraud, and the transfer did not render Husband insolvent. The Court of Appeal reversed, holding that although the UFTA applies to marital settlement agreements, triable issues of fact precluded summary judgment.

II. THE UNIFORM FRAUDULENT TRANSFER ACT APPLIES TO TRANSFERS UNDER MARITAL SETTLEMENT AGREEMENTS

The UFTA permits defrauded creditors to reach property in the hands of a transferee. The Family Code, in section 916, protects property transferred to a spouse incident to divorce from the debts of the other spouse. Neither statute expressly refers to the other. Our task is to harmonize the two statutes. (DeVita v. County of Napa (1995) 9 Cal.4th 763, 778-779.)

"Under well-established rules of statutory construction, we must ascertain the intent of the drafters so as to effectuate the purpose of the law. [Citation.] Because the statutory language is generally the most reliable indicator of legislative intent, we first examine the words themselves, giving them their usual and ordinary meaning and construing them in context." (Esberg v. Union Oil Co. (2002) 28 Cal.4th 262, 268.) "[E]very statute should be construed with reference to the whole system of law of which it is a part, so that all may be harmonized and have effect." (Moore v. Panish (1982) 32 Cal.3d 535, 541.) "Where as here

5: MEJIA V REED

two codes are to be construed, they 'must be regarded as blending into each other and forming a single statute.' [Citation.] Accordingly, they 'must be read together and so construed as to give effect, when possible, to all the provisions thereof.' [Citation.]" (Tripp v. Swoap (1976) 17 Cal.3d 671, 679.)

[2] When the plain meaning of the statutory text is insufficient to resolve the question of its interpretation, the courts may turn to rules or maxims of construction "which serve as aids in the sense that they express familiar insights about conventional language usage." (2A Singer, Statutes and Statutory Construction (6th ed. 2000) p. 107.) Courts also look to the legislative history of the enactment. "Both the legislative history of the statute and the wider historical circumstances of its enactment may be considered in ascertaining the legislative intent." (Dyna-Med, Inc. v. Fair Employment & Housing Com. (1987) 43 Cal.3d 1379, 1387.) Finally, the court may consider the impact of an interpretation on public policy, for "[w]here uncertainty exists consideration should be given to the consequences that will flow from a particular interpretation." (Ibid.)

Following these principles of statutory construction, we turn first to the text of the UFTA and the Family Code. {Page 31 Cal.4th 664}

A. The Statutory Texts

1. The Uniform Fraudulent Transfer Act

The UFTA was enacted in 1986; it is the most recent in a line of statutes dating to the reign of Queen Elizabeth I. "This Act, like its predecessor and the Statute of 13 Elizabeth, declares rights and provides remedies for unsecured creditors against transfers that impede them in the collection of their claims." (Legis. Com. com., 12A West's Ann. Civ. Code (1997 ed.) foll. § 3439.01, p. 272.) Under the UFTA, a transfer is fraudulent, both as to present and future creditors, if it is made "[w]ith actual intent to hinder, delay, or defraud any creditor of the debtor." (Civ. Code, § 3439.04, subd. (a).) Even without actual fraudulent intent, a transfer may be fraudulent as to present creditors if the debtor did not receive "a reasonably equivalent value in exchange for the transfer" and "the debtor was insolvent at that time or the debtor became insolvent as a result of the transfer or obligation." (Civ. Code, § 3439.05.)

On its face, the UFTA applies to all transfers. Civil Code, section § 3439.01, subdivision (i) defines "[t]ransfer" as "every mode, direct or indirect, absolute or conditional, voluntary or involuntary, of disposing of or parting with an asset or an interest in an asset . . . ." The UFTA excepts only certain transfers resulting from lease terminations or lien enforcement. (Civ. Code, § 3439.08, subd. (e).)

5: MEJIA V REED

Thus, the UFTA on its face encompasses transfers made under an MSA. Consequently, most decisions of other states construing parallel provisions of the UFTA hold that it does apply to marital property transfers, including those in connection with divorce. (See, e.g., Scholes v. Lehmann (7th Cir. 1995) 56 F.3d 750, 758-759 [applying Ill. law]; Kardynalski v. Fisher (Ill.App.Ct. 1985) 482 N.E.2d 117, 121-122; Dowell v. Dennis (Okla.Ct.App. 2000) 998 P.2d 206, 209, 212-213; Greeninger v. Cromwell (Or.Ct.App. 1996) 915 P.2d 479, 482; see also Federal Deposit Ins. Co. v. Malin (2d Cir. 1986) 802 F.2d 12, 18 [under New York law, UFTA applies but ex-wife was good faith purchaser for value]; but see Britt v. Damson (9th Cir. 1964) 334 F.2d 896, 901 [Wash. law]; Witbart v. Witbart (Mont. 1983) 666 P.2d 1217, 1219.) Civil Code section 3439.11 provides expressly that the UFTA "shall be applied and construed to effectuate its general purpose to make uniform the law . . . among states enacting it."

Husband here points to section 10 of the UFTA (Civ. Code, § 3439.10), which provides: "Unless displaced by the provisions of this chapter, the principles of law and equity, including the law merchant and the law relating to principal and agent, estoppel, laches, fraud, misrepresentation, duress, coercion, mistake, insolvency, or other validating or invalidating cause, {Page 31 Cal.4th 665} supplement its provisions." He argues that Family Code section 916 is a law that "supplement[s]" the provisions of the UFTA by, in effect, establishing an exception to its provisions. But to "supplement" the UFTA means to provide something additional to the law, not to narrow or nullify the law. This point is illustrated in Monastra v. Konica Business Machines, U.S.A., Inc. (1996) 43 Cal.App.4th 1628. The defendants there argued that compliance with the Bulk Sales Act (Cal. U. Com. Code, § 6101 et seq.) immunized a transfer from attack under the UFTA. The Court of Appeal disagreed, concluding that the protections given creditors under the Bulk Sales Law supplemented, that is, added to, the protections of the UFTA. (Monastra v. Konica Business Machines, U.S.A., Inc., supra, at pp. 1639-1640.)

2. The Family Code

Before 1984, a spouse who received community property after a dissolution of marriage was liable for the community debts incurred by the other spouse during the marriage. (Dawes v. Rich (1997) 60 Cal.App.4th 24, 28; see Packard v. Arellanes (1861) 17 Cal. 525; Frankel v. Boyd (1895) 106 Cal. 608, 612-615.) Thus, a creditor of one spouse could often reach any property transferred to the other without resorting to an action to set aside a fraudulent transfer. Nevertheless, that remedy was available when needed to invalidate a fraudulent transfer made under an MSA. (See, e.g., McKnight v. Superior Court (1985) 170

5: MEJIA V REED

Cal.App.3d 291, 295-296, 299.)

In 1984, however, the Legislature substantially changed the postmarital liability of spouses. "The Legislature determined that, under most circumstances, after a marriage has ended, it is unwise to continue the liability of spouses for community debts incurred by former spouses." (Dawes v. Rich, supra, 60 Cal.App.4th at p. 30.) It enacted former Civil Code section 5120.160, which provided in pertinent part that, upon the dissolution of the marriage, "the property received by [a married] person in the division is not liable for a debt incurred by the person's spouse before or during marriage, and the person is not personally liable for the debt, unless the debt was assigned for payment by the person in the division of the property." (Stats. 1984, ch. 1671, § 9, p. 6021.) When the Family Code was enacted in 1992, Civil Code section 5120.160 became Family Code section 916.

When the Legislature enacted former Civil Code section 5120.160, it contemplated that " '[i]n allocating the debts to the parties, the court in the dissolution proceeding should take into account the rights of creditors so there will be available sufficient property to satisfy the debt by the person to whom the debt is assigned, provided the net division is equal.' " (Lezine v. {Page 31 Cal.4th 666} Security Pacific Fin. Services, Inc. (1996) 14 Cal.4th 56, 75, quoting Recommendation Relating to Liability of Marital Property for Debts (Jan. 1983) 17 Cal. Law Revision Com. Rep. (1984) pp. 23-24, fn. omitted.) Family Code section 2550, however, provides: "Except upon the written agreement of the parties, or on oral stipulation of the parties in open court, or as otherwise provided in this division, in a proceeding for dissolution of marriage or for legal separation of the parties, the court shall . . . divide the community estate of the parties equally." (Italics added.) [3] Whenever, as in this case, the parties agree upon the property division, no law requires them to divide the property equally, and the court does not scrutinize the MSA to ensure that it sets out an equal division. (In re Marriage of Cream (1993) 13 Cal.App.4th 81, 91.)

The only statutory exception to Family Code section 916's grant of immunity from liability is a provision that preserves the liability of property subject to a preexisting lien (Fam. Code, § 916, subd. (a)(2)); the statute does not mention fraudulent transfers. Thus, on its face, Family Code section 916 would appear to protect transfers of marital property incident to divorce from being set aside under the UFTA. We note, however, that section 916 states that it applies "[n]otwithstanding any other provision of this chapter." (Similar language appeared in former Civil Code section 5120.160.) This language indicates that section 916 may be subordinate to other statutes, such as the UFTA, not included in the same chapter of the Family Code as section 916.

5: MEJIA V REED

B. Canons of Statutory Construction

The parties call our attention to familiar canons of statutory interpretation, but these offer no assistance in resolving the apparent conflict between the statutes at issue here. Husband argues that the principle that specific provisions take precedence over general provisions (see Code Civ. Proc., § 1859; Collection Bureau of San Jose v. Rumsey (2000) 24 Cal.4th 301, 310) is controlling. He asserts that Family Code section 916, because it discusses only transfers in an MSA, is more specific than the UFTA, which regulates all transactions, and should therefore prevail over the UFTA. But one could as easily describe the UFTA as pertaining to only fraudulent transactions, and thus at least as specific as section 916, which concerns all marital settlement transactions. Neither statute appears to be significantly more specific than the other.

Plaintiff bases her argument on the adage of expressio unis est exclusio alterius -- the expression of some things implies the exclusion of things not expressed. She argues that the Legislature, when it enacted the UFTA, knew how to make a specific exemption for transfers under an MSA -- since it made exceptions for some other transfers -- and she asks us to infer from the {Page 31 Cal.4th 667} absence of an exception for marital settlements that the Legislature must have intended the UFTA to apply to marital settlement transactions. But one can equally argue that the Legislature, when it enacted former Civil Code section 5120.160 and later recodified that provision as Family Code section 916, knew how to make an exception for fraudulent transfers, but chose not to do so. Both the UFTA and the Family Code govern discrete subject areas, and the Legislature's failure to legislate expressly with respect to the rare instance in which they overlap does not suggest any legislative intent as to which should prevail.

C. Legislative History

Husband argues that the history of former Civil Code section 5120.160 (the predecessor to Family Code section 916) shows that the Legislature did not intend to allow creditors to challenge an MSA. In 1984, when the Legislature was considering former section 5120.160, Carol Bruch, a law professor at the University of California at Davis, proposed that the new law provide for notice to creditors and grant them a right to intervene in the dissolution proceedings. In connection with this proposal, she suggested amending the measure to provide that the section would not bar recovery by a creditor who was not notified, or did not approve the proposed marital settlement, and "successfully challenges the property division as a fraudulent conveyance in a motion to set aside the property division filed within 3 years after entry of the judgment dividing the property." (Carol

5: MEJIA V REED

Bruch, U.C. Davis Law School, Suggested Amendments to Assem. Bill 1460 (1983-1984 Reg. Sess.) Mar. 14, 1984.) The Law Revision Commission rejected Professor Bruch's suggested amendments, saying: "Carol proposes adoption of a 'bankruptcy' or 'probate' type scheme for imposing liability after dissolution of marriage, involving notice and an opportunity to appear for creditors, and fraudulent conveyance standards. While this scheme is theoretically interesting, the Commission rejected it because of the extensive procedures involved. It would transform simple divorce cases into elaborate proceedings involving many parties. We are unwilling to burden our bill with this; Carol can prepare and sponsor her own bill next session to adopt this sort of scheme if she is able to perfect it." (Nathaniel Sterling, Cal. Law Revision Com., letter to Assemblyman Alistair McAllister, Mar. 30, 1984, p. 2.) This historical account could support an inference that the Legislature did not intend to permit creditors to attack an MSA, as Husband contends, but it could also be viewed more narrowly as suggesting only a determination that creditors should not have standing to raise their claims in the dissolution proceeding itself.

The legislative history of the UFTA equally offers a weak inference in support of plaintiff's position. In 1986, when the Legislature considered the {Page 31 Cal.4th 668} UFTA, the Business Law Section of the California State Bar reported to the Legislature: "Serious consideration needs to be given to the effect of this statute in areas such as leveraged buyouts of businesses, marital property agreements, foreclosures sales of real property, to name a few examples." (Margaret Sheneman, State Bar of Cal. (Business Law Section), mem. to Judith Harper, Legis. Rep. on Sen. Bill No. 2150 (1985-1986 Reg. Sess.) Apr. 30, 1986, p. 2, italics added.) The Legislature, however, added no provisions relating to marital property transfers.

In sum, both when it enacted former Civil Code section 5120.160 and when it enacted the UFTA, the Legislature was advised that difficulties could arise from the intersection of family law and laws prohibiting fraudulent transfers. In both cases, it chose not to address the subject with specific legislation. In these circumstances, we cannot draw any conclusions as to what the Legislature intended based on the absence of legislative action.

D. Policy Considerations

The Court of Appeal here concluded that neither the language of the statutes nor their legislative history was dispositive, and that it would have to turn to an analysis of the relevant policy considerations as they bear on the question of legislative intent. The court that decided Gagan v. Gouyd, supra, 73 Cal.App.4th 835, also found that neither the statutory text nor legislative history was suffi-

5: MEJIA V REED

cient to resolve the conflict, requiring it to base its decision on policy considerations. We arrive at the same juncture.

The California Legislature has a general policy of protecting creditors from fraudulent transfers, including transfers between spouses. [4] A transfer before dissolution can be set aside as a fraudulent conveyance. (See Fam. Code, § 851 [transmutation of marital property subject to UFTA]; Reddy v. Gonzalez (1992) 8 Cal.App.4th 118, 122-123.) A transfer after dissolution can be set aside under the clear terms of the UFTA. When the court divides the marital property in the absence of an agreement by the parties, it must divide the property equally (Fam. Code, § 2550), which provides some protection for a creditor of one spouse only. In view of this overall policy of protecting creditors, it is unlikely that the Legislature intended to grant married couples a one-time-only opportunity to defraud creditors by including the fraudulent transfer in an MSA.

Husband puts forward two countervailing policy considerations. First, he argues that allowing MSA transfers to be considered fraudulent to creditors will complicate marital settlement negotiations. This contention is supported by Gagan v. Gouyd, supra, 73 Cal.App.4th at pages 842-843, which states: {Page 31 Cal.4th 669} "[A]s a matter of policy, we believe that to engraft the fraudulent transfer remedies onto a valid and approved marital settlement agreement would result in needlessly complicating the already emotionally laden dissolution process. It might result in the unraveling of a dissolution agreement painstakingly negotiated between the parties and their attorneys." We acknowledge Husband's contention, but we do not give it substantial weight. In our view, the parties' debts, and how to pay them, are matters that should be considered in marital settlement negotiations even if, like pension plans and income tax consequences, they make the process of reaching an agreement more complex.

Second, Husband argues that the state and the parties need to rely on the finality of dissolution judgments. [5] But California and federal law already permit such judgments to be set aside for fraud. Under state law, either spouse can attack the property division under a dissolution judgment on the ground that it was procured by extrinsic fraud. (Fam. Code, § 2122, subd. (a).) Under federal bankruptcy law, a bankruptcy trustee, acting in the interest of creditors, can set aside the property division of a dissolution judgment on the ground of fraud. (See Britt v. Damson (9th Cir. 1964) 334 F.2d 896, 902; In re Hope (Bankr. D.Colo. 1999) 231 B.R. 403, 415 & fn. 19, and cases cited.) Thus, while the law respects the finality of a property settlement agreement "that is not tainted by fraud or compulsion or is not in violation of the confidential relationship of the parties" (Adams v. Adams (1947) 29 Cal.2d 621, 624), we find no legislative policy to

5: MEJIA V REED

protect such agreements from attack as instruments of fraud. [6]

We therefore conclude, based on the policy considerations underlying the UFTA and the Family Code provisions governing dissolution judgments and settlements, that the UFTA applies to property transfers under MSA's. fn. 2

III. THERE IS NO TRIABLE ISSUE OF FACT AS TO CONSTRUCTIVE FRAUD

The Court of Appeal found triable issues of fact as to both actual fraud and constructive fraud. On review here, Husband challenges only the issue of constructive fraud.

There are two forms of constructive fraud under the UFTA. Civil Code section 3439.04, subdivision (b), provides that a transfer is fraudulent if the debtor did not receive reasonably equivalent consideration and either "(1) Was engaged or about to engage in a business or a transaction for which the {Page 31 Cal.4th 670} remaining assets of the debtor were unreasonably small in relation to the business or transaction; or [¶] (2) Intended to incur, or believed or reasonably should have believed that he or she would incur, debts beyond his or her ability to pay as they became due." Civil Code section 3439.05 provides that a transfer is fraudulent as to an existing creditor if the debtor does not receive reasonably equivalent value and "was insolvent at that time or . . . became insolvent as a result of the transfer . . . ." Only the form of constructive fraud defined in Civil Code section 3430.05 is at issue here.

Whether Husband here received equivalent value in the property division is a material disputed fact, as the trial court recognized. But constructive fraud under Civil Code section 3430.05 also requires that the transferor was insolvent at the time of the transfer, or rendered insolvent by the transfer. We find no triable issue of fact on the question of insolvency.

Under the UFTA's definition, a "debtor is insolvent if, at fair valuations, the sum of the debtor's debts is greater than all of the debtor's assets." (Civ. Code, § 3439.02, subd. (a).) [7] To determine solvency, the value of a debtor's assets and debts are compared. By statutory definition, a debtor's assets exclude property that is exempt from judgment enforcement. (Civ. Code, § 3439.01, subd. (a)(2).) Retirement accounts are generally exempt. (Code Civ. Proc., § 704.115; see Yaesu Electronics Corp. v. Tamura (1994) 28 Cal.App.4th 8, 13-15.) Here, when Husband's exempt retirement account is excluded, his sole postdissolution asset is his medical practice. That practice had a value as low as $72,000 at the time of the dissolution, according to plaintiff's appraisal evidence.

5: MEJIA V REED

Plaintiff argued that the trial court should compare the value of Husband's medical practice (his sole nonexempt asset) to the present value of the entire child support obligation (his sole debt), which plaintiff's expert estimated at between $164,829 and $205,975, and determine that Husband was insolvent after he executed the MSA. The trial court rejected plaintiff's argument on the ground that the unmatured portion of plaintiff's child support claim could not be fairly valued. The Court of Appeal disagreed. It held that Husband's child support debt should be taken into account at its present discounted value, and therefore it concluded that solvency, like consideration, was a triable issue of fact.

We disagree with the Court of Appeal's analysis. [8] Although the UFTA recognizes an unmatured contingent claim as a debt (Civ. Code, § 3439.01, subds. (b), (d)), child support claims present a special case. Support payments usually are paid from present earnings, not liquidation of preexisting assets. The amount of payments owed is computed on the basis of monthly disposable income. (Fam. Code, § 4055, subd. (a).) This figure is {Page 31 Cal.4th 671} generally based on actual earnings, although the trial court has discretion to consider earning capacity instead of actual income (Fam. Code, § 4058, subd. (b)), and child support payments may be changed, in some cases retroactively, if there is a change in actual earnings or earning capacity. (Fam. Code, § 3651, subd. (a); In re Marriage of Laudeman (2001) 92 Cal.App.4th 1009, 1015.) fn. 3

[9] Assets at the time of dissolution play little part in the computation of child support. They may enter indirectly into the calculation in two ways: (1) In assessing earning capacity, a trial court may take into account the earnings from invested assets (see, e.g., In re Marriage of Cheriton (2001) 92 Cal.App.4th 269, 292); and (2) a court may deem assets a "special circumstance" (Fam. Code, § 4057, subd. (b)(5)) that may justify a departure from the guideline figure for support payments (In re Marriage of Loh (2001) 93 Cal.App.4th 325, 332). But these are exceptional situations; the child support obligation is based primarily on actual earnings and earning capacity.

[10] Income not yet earned, however, is not an asset under the UFTA unless it is subject to levy by a creditor, as would be the case if, for example, the transferor possessed a promissory note payable at a future date. (See Civ. Code, § 3439.01, subd. (a)(2); Carter v. Carter (1942) 55 Cal.App.2d 13, 15-16.) Thus, Husband's future earnings, or his future earning capacity, would not appear on the balance sheet to offset his child support obligation.

We have found no cases that consider whether future child support obligations constitute a debt under the UFTA. In their briefs, the parties discuss In re Labrum

5: MEJIA V REED

& Doak, LLP (Bankr. E.D.Pa. 1998) 227 B.R. 383, a bankruptcy case involving whether future lease payments could be considered a debt, apparently the closest analogy they could find to the present case. The court there said: "[I]t is logical not to include all of the future rents as liabilities because this calculation miscategorizes the future rent liability as an obligation presently due in full . . . . [T]his would render any business with substantial projectable future expenses artificially deemed insolvent." (227 B.R. at p. 389.) But the parties dispute the meaning of this language. According to Husband, the court held that rents not yet due were not liabilities, while plaintiff claims that the court was concerned about only the failure to reduce future rent payments to present value.

[11] We conclude, however, that future child support payments should not be viewed as a debt under the UFTA. [12] In construing statutes, we {Page 31 Cal.4th 672} avoid any interpretation that will lead to absurd consequences. (People v. Coronado (1995) 12 Cal.4th 145, 151.) To treat future child support payments as a debt, while not viewing the earning capacity from which they will probably be paid as an asset, would yield an absurd result. Relatively few parents of young children have current assets sufficient to pay the present discounted value of years and years of future support obligations. Thus, treating future child support as a current debt would label many persons with child support obligations as insolvent under the UFTA even though they were current on their child support obligations and will be able to pay future obligations as they became due. This insolvency, moreover, is of a wholly artificial character, for the debtor cannot be compelled to convert future child support obligations into a present cash payment, and in fact generally cannot even voluntarily terminate liability for future support by paying the custodial parent the present value of such future payments. (See In re Marriage of Cheriton, supra, 92 Cal.App.4th 269.) No legislative purpose is served by treating a parent as insolvent because of child support obligations when that parent has paid all payments currently due and can pay future payments from future earnings or earning capacity.

In light of our conclusion that future child support payments should not be considered a debt under the UFTA, fn. 4 Husband here was not insolvent at the time of the transfer nor was he rendered insolvent by the transfer. There is thus no triable issue of fact as to constructive fraud. Actual fraud, however, remains a triable issue for decision by the trial court.

DISPOSITION

The judgment of the Court of Appeal is reversed, and the cause is remanded for further proceedings.

5: MEJIA V REED

George, C. J., Baxter, J., Werdegar, J., Chin, J., Brown, J., and Moreno, J., concurred.

↑FN 1. Wife joined in Husband's petition for review and brief on the merits. She did not raise any separate arguments.

↑FN 2. Gagan v. Gouyd, supra, 73 Cal.App.4th 835, is disapproved to the extent it is inconsistent with this opinion.

↑FN 3. The statements in this paragraph and the following two paragraphs are generalizations. There are many specific provisions that affect the calculation of child support, and our generalizations are not intended to override or modify such specific provisions.

↑FN 4. This reasoning would apply equally to future spousal support payments. We take no position, however, on the classification of other contingent or installment payments.

6: REDDY V GONZALEZ

SESHA REDDY, Plaintiff and Respondent,
v.
MELLINA GONZALEZ, Defendant and Appellant.

Docket No. H008719.

Court of Appeals of California, Sixth District.

July 17, 1992.

120*120 COUNSEL

Jesse W. Jack and Thomas P. Keegan for Defendant and Appellant.

Dennis Kollenborn for Plaintiff and Respondent.

OPINION

CAPACCIOLI, Acting P.J.

A transfer from Gilbert Gonzalez to his then-wife, defendant Mellina Gonzalez, of Gilbert's interest in the family home was set aside as a fraudulent conveyance. On appeal, defendant claims that the conveyance could not have been fraudulent since the property was subject to a homestead exemption. In addition, she asserts that there was insufficient evidence to support a finding of actual fraud. For the reasons expressed below, we affirm.

FACTS

In 1985 Gilbert was involved in an unsuccessful real estate transaction with plaintiff Sesha Reddy. Plaintiff subsequently sued Gilbert for losses incurred as a result of the transaction and obtained a judgment against him. Other than $1,300 attached from Gilbert's paychecks, plaintiff's judgment has not been satisfied. Gilbert currently has no other assets from which that judgment can be satisfied.

Defendant and Gilbert held title in joint tenancy to the family residence in Milpitas. The residence was purchased with community property funds. On March 23, 1987, Gilbert executed a deed which purportedly conveyed his interest in the residence to defendant. Defendant asked Gilbert to execute the deed "to protect the property from other parties [who] may wish to go after it because of some of [his] dealings ..." "[T]he main concern was to protect the home from being sought after by third parties." No consideration was given for the transfer. Gilbert believed that defendant would continue to protect his interest in the prop-

6: REDDY V GONZALEZ

erty, so he continued thereafter to contribute to the mortgage payments on the house. On March 9, 1988, Gilbert executed another deed purporting to convey his interest in the residence to defendant. Gilbert understood this document to convey merely "title" but not his interest in the property. He believed that he retained an interest in the property. Gilbert continues to maintain that he has an interest in the property.

Plaintiff brought an action to set aside as a fraudulent conveyance Gilbert's transfer to defendant of his interest in the Milpitas property. The trial court set aside the two conveyances as executed in fraud of creditors.

121*121 DISCUSSION

A. Potential Homestead Exemption Irrelevant

(1) Defendant asserts that the potential application of a homestead exemption to the Milpitas property negates any intent to defraud creditors. She argues that plaintiff would have been unable to obtain satisfaction of his judgment from the sale of the residence due to application of the homestead exemption and hence the conveyance did not shield any asset from creditors. We disagree.

Until 1975, universal homestead "exemptions" did not exist. (San Diego White Truck Co. v. Swift (1979) 96 Cal. App.3d 88, 91-92 [157 Cal. Rptr. 745].) Instead, protection of a dwelling could be accomplished only by execution and recordation of a "declaration of homestead." (Civ. Code, former §§ 1237, 1240, 1262, 1263, 1267, and 1268.) A judgment lien could not attach to real property upon which a homestead had been declared and homesteaded property was exempt from execution or forced sale. (Civ. Code, former § 1240; Code Civ. Proc., former § 674, subd. (a); Jacobson v. Pope & Talbot (1932) 214 Cal. 758, 760-761 [7 P.2d 1017].) Under this former statutory scheme, courts had held that the transfer of property upon which homestead had been declared was not a fraudulent conveyance because the property could not be reached to satisfy a judgment creditor. (Montgomery v. Bullock (1938) 11 Cal.2d 58, 62-63 [77 P.2d 846].) A fraudulent conveyance would occur, however, when the transferred property could have but had not yet been declared a homestead. (La Point v. Blanchard (1894) 101 Cal. 549, 552-553 [36 P. 98].)

In the mid-1970's the Legislature discarded much of "declared homestead" law and in its place enacted the current system of homestead exemptions. (1 Ogden's Revised Cal. Real Property Law (Supp.) pp. 66-69.) "Declared homesteads" were retained, as an alternative to automatic homestead exemptions, primarily "to continue the rule under former law that a judgment lien does not attach to a declared

6: REDDY V GONZALEZ

homestead." (Legis. committee com. to Code Civ. Proc., § 704.910, West's Ann. Codes, p. 363.) Under current law, a judgment lien can attach to real property used as a dwelling, even though the property may later be found to be subject to a homestead exemption.[1] (Code Civ. Proc., § 667.340; legis. committee com. to Code Civ. Proc., § 697.340, West's Ann. Codes, p. 160.) In addition, a 122*122 dwelling subject to a homestead exemption can be sold to satisfy a money judgment so long as prescribed statutory procedures are followed. (Code Civ. Proc., § 704.740.) Because, under the current statutory scheme, judgment liens do attach to dwellings potentially subject to a homestead exemption and judgment creditors can obtain court-ordered sale of such dwellings to satisfy judgments, such property is not outside the reach of creditors. Consequently, a conveyance by a debtor of an interest in such property with the intent to defraud creditors is a fraudulent conveyance under Civil Code section 3439.04.

The cases relied upon by defendant dealt only with property that had been declared a homestead under the prior laws. Property upon which a homestead had been declared under the former statutory scheme was insulated from the attachment of judgment liens and could not be sold to satisfy a money judgment. Hence, a conveyance of such property did not defraud creditors. The same cannot be said for property potentially subject to a homestead exemption. A judgment lien can attach to this property and it can be sold to satisfy a money judgment. Hence, a transfer of such property with the intent to shield it from creditors is a fraudulent conveyance.

B. Actual Fraud Alone Establishes That a Conveyance Is Fraudulent

"A transfer made or obligation incurred by a debtor is fraudulent as to a creditor, whether the creditor's claim arose before or after the transfer was made or the obligation was incurred, if the debtor made the transfer or incurred the obligation as follows: [¶] (a) With actual intent to hinder, delay, or defraud any creditor of the debtor. [¶] (b) Without receiving a reasonably equivalent value in exchange for the transfer or obligation, and the debtor: [¶] (1) Was engaged or was about to engage in a business or a transaction for which the remaining assets of the debtor were unreasonably small in relation to the business or transaction; or [¶] (2) Intended to incur, or believed or reasonably should have believed that he or she would incur, debts beyond his or her ability to pay as they became due." (Civ. Code, § 3439.04.)

(2) Defendant contends that Civil Code section 3439.04 requires proof of both actual fraud, as described in subdivision (a), and constructive fraud, as described in subdivision (b). She claims that proof of actual intent to defraud is insufficient

6: REDDY V GONZALEZ

to support the trial court's order setting aside the conveyance as fraudulent. This interpretation of the statute is unreasonable. The fact that subdivision (a) terminates with a period rather than a conjunction strongly indicates that the two subdivisions are alternative rather than conjunctive requirements. Furthermore, the statute from which section 3439.04, subdivision (a) was derived, former section 3439.07, required no 123*123 more than a showing that the debtor had the actual intent to defraud at the time of the conveyance. Section 3439.04 was enacted in 1986 as part of a statutory overhaul of the fraudulent conveyance statutes. Prior to 1986, former sections 3439.04, 3439.05, 3439.06 and 3439.07 each described a type of fraudulent conveyance. (Civ. Code, former §§ 3439.04- 3439.07.) Former section 3439.04 was reenacted in substantially similar form as section 3439.05. (Civ. Code, § 3439.05.) Former sections 3439.05, 3439.06 and 3439.07 were combined to form section 3439.04. Former section 3439.05 became section 3439.04, subdivision (b)(1); former section 3439.06 became section 3439.04, subdivision (b)(2); former section 3439.07 became section 3439.04, subdivision (a). Because these three sections set forth, under former law, three independent types of fraudulent conveyances, the mere combination of the three in section 3439.04 did not destroy their independence. Section 3439.04 instead comprehensively sets forth three types of fraudulent conveyances which do not require proof of insolvency. Hence, section 3439.04, subdivision (a) is independent of section 3439.04, subdivision (b) and does not require proof of anything more than an actual intent to defraud.

C. Sufficient Evidence of Fraudulent Intent

(3a) Defendant challenges the sufficiency of the evidence to establish actual fraudulent intent. (4) "`[O]ur power begins and ends with a determination as to whether there is any substantial evidence to support [the trial court's findings] ... we have no power to judge of the effect or value of the evidence, to weigh the evidence, to consider the credibility of the witnesses, or to resolve conflicts in the evidence....'" (In re Stephen W. (1990) 221 Cal. App.3d 629, 642 [271 Cal. Rptr. 319] quoting Overton v. Vita-Food Corp. (1949) 94 Cal. App.2d 367 [210 P.2d 757].) Our role is limited to determining whether there was evidence before the trial court to support its determination.

(3b) "If there is actual fraud a creditor can maintain an action to set aside the transfer without a showing that the defendant has no other assets to satisfy his judgment." (Freeman v. LaMorte (1957) 148 Cal. App.2d 670, 675 [307 P.2d 734]; accord Fross v. Wotton (1935) 3 Cal.2d 384, 388 [44 P.2d 350]; Civ. Code, § 3439.07, subd. (a)(1).) Actual intent to defraud must be shown by clear and convincing evidence. (Hansford v. Lassar (1975) 53 Cal. App.3d 364, 377 [125

6: REDDY V GONZALEZ

Cal. Rptr. 804].)

The evidence before the trial court amply supported its implicit finding of actual fraud. Gilbert testified that he conveyed his interest in the Milpitas property to defendant to protect the property from his creditors. This testimony clearly and convincingly evidenced Gilbert's intent to prevent his 124*124 creditors from obtaining satisfaction of their claims from Gilbert's interest in the Milpitas property. This is actual fraud. Thus, the evidence was sufficient to support the finding of actual fraud underlying the trial court's judgment setting aside the conveyances.

CONCLUSION

The judgment is affirmed.

Premo, J., and Elia, J., concurred.

[1] The amount of a homestead exemption is determined by the circumstances existing at the time the property is sold to satisfy the judgment. (Code Civ. Proc., § 704.730.)

7: U.S. V TOWNLEY

UNITED STATES DISTRICT COURT FOR THE EASTERN DISTRICT OF WASHINGTON AT SPOKANE

United States of America, Plaintiff,

v.

Bryce W. Townley, et al., Defendants.

Civil No. CS-02-0384-RHW

Date of Judgment: August 18, 2004

COUNSEL: James A. McDevitt, United States Attorney

W. Carl Hankla, Trial Attorney, Tax Division, U.S. Department of Justice

JUDGMENT AND ORDER OF FORECLOSURE SALE

Pursuant to the July 29, 2004 Order Granting the Government's Motion for Summary Judgment; Denying Defendants' Motion for Summary Judgment and pursuant to 26 U.S.C. § 7402(a) and 7403(c) and 28 U.S.C. § 2001 and 2002,

It is ordered, adjudged and decreed that:

1. Judgment is entered in favor of the United States and against Bryce W. Townley for the unpaid assessed balance of federal income tax liabilities and related interest, penalties, fees and costs shown below: [*2]

Tax Year	Assessment Date	Amount Assessed	Nature of Assessment
1994	04/15/95	($394.00)	Withholding Credit
	08/10/98	$ 3,319.00	Income Tax
	08/10/98	$ 149.51	Estimated Tax Penalty
	08/10/98	$ 731.25	Late Filing Penalty
	08/10/98	$ 1,253.54	Interest to Assessment Date
	11/24/98	$ (808.39)	Subsequent Payment
	11/30/98	$ 16.00	Fees and Collection Costs
	08/23/99	$ 16.00	Fees and Collection Costs
	04/16/01	$ 16.00	Fees and Collection Costs
1995	04/15/96	$ (346.00)	Withholding Credi)
	08/10/98	$ 1,811.00	Income Tax
	08/10/98	$ 77.37	Estimated Tax Penalty
	08/10/98	$ 366.25	Late Filing Penalty

7: U.S. V TOWNLEY

Tax Year	Assessment Date	Amount Assessed	Nature of Assessment
	08/10/98	$ 412.07	Interest to Assessment Date
1996	08/10/98	$ 48,188.00	Income Tax
	08/10/98	$ 2,564.82	Estimated Tax Penalty
	08/10/98	$ 3,855.04	Failure to Pay Tax Penalty
	11/16/98	$ 722.82	Failure to Pay Tax Penalty
	05/22/00	$ 7,469.14	Failure to Pay Tax Penalty
	08/10/98	$ 10,842.30	Late Filing Penalty
	08/10/98	$ 7.208.73	Interest to Assessment Date
Total Assessments:		**$ 87.470.45**	

plus all penalties accruing under law after the dates of assessment, plus interest accruing after the dates of assessment pursuant to 26 U.S.C. § 6601, 6621, and 6622, and 28 U.S.C. § 1961 (c) until paid.

2. Judgment is entered in favor of the United States and against Charlene R. Townley for the unpaid assessed balance of federal income tax liabilities and related interest, penalties, fees and costs shown below: [*3]

Tax Year	Assessment Date	Amount Assessed	Nature of Assessment
1994	04/15/95	$ (394.00)	Withholding Credit)
	08/10/98	$ 3,319.00	Income Tax
	08/10/98	$ 149.51	Estimated Tax Penalty
	08/10/98	$ 731.25	Late Filing Penalty
	08/10/98	$ 1,253.54	Interest to Assessment Date
	11/30/98	$ 16.00	Fees and Collection Costs
	08/23/99	$ 16.00	Fees and Collection Costs
	04/16/01	$ 16.00	Fees and Collection Costs
1995	04/15/96	$ (346.00)	Withholding Credit
	08/10/98	$ 1,811.00	Income Tax
	08/10/98	$ 77.37	Estimated Tax Penalty
	08/10/98	$ 366.25	Late Filing Penalty
	08/10/98	$ 412.07	Interest to Assessment Date
1996	08/10/98	$ 48,188.00	Income Tax
	08/10/98	$ 2,564.82	Estimated Tax Penalty
	08/10/98	$ 3,855.04	Failure to Pay Tax Penalty
	11/16/98	$ 10,872.30	Late Filing Penalty
	08/10/98	$ 7.208.73	Interest to Assessment Date
	11/16/98	$ 5,059.74	Failure to Pay Tax Penalty
Total Assessments:		**$ 85,146.62**	

7: U.S. V TOWNLEY

plus all penalties accruing under law after the dates of assessment, plus interest according after the dates of assessment pursuant to 26 U.S.C. § 6601, 6621, and 6622, and 28 U.S.C. § 1961 (c) until paid.

3. The federal tax liens arising under 26 U.S.C. § 6321 from the unpaid income tax assessments described in paragraphs 1 and 2 above against Bryce W. Townley and Charlene R. Townley, for tax years 1994, 1995 and 1996, are hereby enforced against the real property described below as the Residence Property and the Investment Property.

4. The Residence Property, tax parcel number 2661712469090, is located at 18832 Pine Loop Road, Leavenworth, Washington 98826 and is legally described as Lot 19, Block 1, Alpine Acres according to the plat thereof recorded in Volume 7 of plats, page 33 and 34, records of Chelan County.

5. The Investment Property, tax parcel number 241701680365, is located at 226 Evans Street and 201 Orchard Street, Leavenworth, Washington 98826, and is [*4] legally described as the east 100 feet of Lot 6, Block 5, Leavenworth Gardens, according to the plat thereof recorded in Volume I of Plats, page 85, records of Chelan County, Washington.

6. An Internal Revenue Service Property Appraisal and Liquidation Specialist, or such representative as he may appoint or employ, is authorized and directed under 28 U.S.C. § 2001 and 2002 to offer for public sale and to sell the Residence Property and the Investment Property, along with any improvements, buildings, and appurtenances thereon or thereto, and this Judgment and Order of Foreclosure Sale shall serve as a special writ of execution and no further orders or process from the Court shall be required;

7. The Internal Revenue Service Property Appraisal and Liquidation Specialist or his representative is authorized to have free access to the Residence Property and Investment Property and to take all actions necessary to preserve the Residence Property and Investment Property, including, but not limited to, retaining a lock-smith or other person to change or install locks or other security devices on any part of the property, until the deeds to the Residence Property and Investment Property are delivered to the ultimate purchaser.

8. Bryce W. Townley, Charlene R. Townley, Bruce Alden Banister as Trustee of Beaver Valley Trust, their agents, successors and assigns, tenants, occupants, or other persons in possession or control of the Residence Property and Investment Property shall take all reasonable steps necessary to preserve the Residence Property and Investment Property (including all buildings, improvements, fixtures

7: U.S. V TOWNLEY

and appurtenances on the property) in their current condition. They shall not commit waste against the Residence Property and Investment Property, nor shall they cause or permit anyone else to do so. They shall not do anything that tends to reduce the value or marketability of the Residence Property arid Investment Property, nor shall they cause or permit anyone else to do so. They shall not record any instruments, publish [*5] any notice, or take any other action (such as running newspaper advertisements or posting signs) that may directly or indirectly tend to adversely affect the value of the Residence Property and Investment Property or that may tend to deter or discourage potential bidders from participating in the public auction, nor shall they cause or permit anyone else to do so. Violation of this paragraph shall be deemed a contempt of court and punishable as such.

9. All persons occupying the Residence Property and Investment Property shall leave and vacate the Residence Property and Investment Property permanently within twenty (20) days of the date of this Order, taking with them their personal property (but leaving all improvements, buildings, and appurtenances to the property). If any person fails or refuses to leave and vacate the property by the time specified in this Order, the Internal Revenue Service Property Appraisal and Liquidation Specialist or his representative is authorized (but not required) to take all actions that are reasonably necessary to bring about the ejectment, of those persons. A writ of assistance may, without further notice, be issued by the Clerk of Court pursuant to Rule 70 of the Federal Rules of Civil Procedure to compel delivery of possession of the Residence Property and Investment Property. If any person fails or refuses to remove his or her personal property from the premises by the time specified herein, the personal property remaining on the property thereafter is deemed forfeited and abandoned, and the Internal Revenue Service Property Appraisal and Liquidation Specialist or his representative is authorized to remove it and dispose of it in any manner he sees fit, including sale, in which case the proceeds of the sale are to be applied first to the expenses of sale and the balance to be applied toward the subject tax liabilities of Bryce W. Townley and Charlene R. Townley.

10. The terms and conditions of the sale of the Residence Property and Investment Property are as follows:

a. The sale of the Residence Property and Investment Property shall be free [*6] and clear of all liens or interests, specifically including those of the United States; Bryce W. Townley and Charlene R. Townley; Bruce Alden Banister, Trustee of Beaver Valley Trust; Jennifer and Daniel Sidebottom; and the current tenants or occupants.

7: U.S. V TOWNLEY

b. The sale shall be subject to building lines, if established, all laws, ordinances, and governmental regulations (including building and zoning ordinances) affecting the Residence Property and Investment Property, and easements and restrictions of record, if any;

c. The sale shall be held on the premises of the Residence Property and/or Investment Property or any other place permitted by the provisions of 28 U.S.C. § 2001;

d. The date and time for sale are to be announced by the Internal Revenue Service Property Appraisal and Liquidation Specialist or his representative;

e. Notice of the sale shall be published once a week for at least four consecutive weeks before the sale of the Residence Property and Investment Property in at least one newspaper regularly issued and of general circulation in the county wherein the Residence Property and Investment Property are situated, and, at the discretion of the Internal Revenue Service Property Appraisal and Liquidation Specialist or his representative, by any other notice that he or his representative deems appropriate. The notice shall contain a description of the Residence Property and Investment Property and shall contain the terms and conditions of sale in this Judgment and Order of Foreclosure Sale;

f. The sale of the Residence Property and Investment Property shall be subject to a minimum bid, the amount of which shall be determined by the Internal Revenue Service Property Appraisal and Liquidation Specialist or his representative at his sole discretion. If the minimum bid is not met or exceeded, the Internal Revenue Service Property Appraisal and Liquidation Specialist or his representative may, without further permission of this Court, and under the terms and conditions in this [*7] judgment and Order of Foreclosure Sale, reduce the minimum bid, and, if necessary, hold a new public sale;

g. At the time of the sale of the Residence Property and Investment Property, the successful bidder shall be required to deposit with the Internal Revenue Service Property Appraisal and Liquidation Specialist or his representative a minimum of ten (10) percent of the bid, with the deposit to be made by cash, certified check or cashier's check payable to the United States Treasury. Before being permitted to bid at the sale, bidders shall display to the Internal Revenue Service Property Appraisal and Liquidation Specialist, or his representative, proof that they can make the deposit required by this Judgment and Order of Foreclosure Sale (the United States may bid as a credit against the outstanding amount of the above-described judgment, without tender of cash);

7: U.S. V TOWNLEY

h. The balance of the purchase price for the Residence Property and Investment Property is to be paid to the Internal Revenue Service Property Appraisal arid Liquidation Specialist or his representative by the successful bidder within twenty (20) days following the date of the acceptance of the bid. The payment shall be made by certified check, cashier's check or money order payable to the United States Treasury. In the event that the bidder fails to fulfill this requirement, the deposit shall be forfeited and applied to cover the expenses of the sale, with any amount remaining to be applied to the outstanding federal tax liabilities of Bryce W. Townley and Charlene R. Townley as stated above, and the Residence Property and Investment Property shall be again offered for sale in accordance with the provisions of this Judgment and Order of Foreclosure Sale;

i. The sale of the Residence Property and Investment Property shall be subject to confirmation by this Court. Upon confirmation of the sale, the Internal Revenue Service Property Appraisal and Liquidation Specialist or his representative shall execute and deliver quit claim deeds conveying the Residence Property and [*8] Investment Property to the purchaser. Upon confirmation of the sale, all interests in, liens against, or claims to the Residence Property and Investment Property that are held or asserted by all parties to this action are discharged and extinguished, and redemption rights under state law shall not apply to this sale under federal law;

j. The purchaser is responsible to take the necessary action for the ejection of anyone who may be occupying the Residence Property and Investment Property on the date of the sale; and

k. The sale is ordered pursuant to 28 U.S.C. § 2001 and is made without right of redemption.

l. When the sale of the Residence Property and Investment Property is confirmed by this court, the Chelan County Auditor shall permit the transfer of the Residence Property and Investment Property to be reflected upon that county's register of title.

12. After the confirmation of the sale of the Residence Property and Investment Property, the Internal Revenue Service Property Appraisal and Liquidation Specialist or his representative shall distribute the amount paid by the purchaser in the following order of preference, until that amount is exhausted. First, the Internal Revenue Service Property Appraisal and Liquidation Specialist or his representative shall retain an amount sufficient to cover the expenses of sale, including any costs incurred to secure or maintain the Residence Property and

7: U.S. V TOWNLEY

Investment Property. Second, the Internal Revenue Service Property Appraisal and Liquidation Specialist or his representative shall satisfy any delinquent Chelan County property taxes that may constitute a lien against the Residence Property and/or Investment Property under 26 U.S.C. § 6323(b)(6). Third, the Internal Revenue Service Property Appraisal and Liquidation Specialist or his representative shall pay to the United States by check made payable to the United States Treasury arid delivered by certified or overnight express mail addressed to Carl Hankla, United States Department of Justice, Tax [*9] Division, 555 Fourth Street N.W. Room 7225, Washington. D.C., 20001, an amount to cover the federal tax liabilities of Bryce W. Townley and Charlene R. Townley for tax years 1994, 1994 and 1996, which liabilities have been reduced to judgment by this Court as set forth in paragraphs 1 and 2 above, plus all penalties accruing under law after the dates of assessment, plus interest accruing after the dates of assessment pursuant to26 U.S.C. § 6601, 6621, and 6622, and 28U.S.C. § 1961(c) until paid. In the event that the federal tax liabilities are satisfied, the Internal Revenue Service Property Appraisal and Liquidation Specialist or his representative shall interplead the surplus sale proceeds into the registry of the Court.

8: U.S. V TOWNLEY

UNITED STATES OF AMERICA, Plaintiff - Appellee, v. BRYCE W TOWNLEY, individually and as Trustee for Bryce and Charlene Townley Living Trust; CHARLENE R TOWNLEY, individually and as Trustee for Bryce and Charlene Townley Living Trust, Defendants - Appellants, and BRUCE ALDEN BANISTER, Trustee for Beaver Valley Trust; DANIEL SIDEBOTTOM; JOHN DOE; GEORGE BARTH; BEAVER VALLEY TRUST, Defendants.

No. 04-35767

UNITED STATES COURT OF APPEALS FOR THE NINTH CIRCUIT

181 Fed. Appx. 630; 2006 U.S. App. LEXIS 12372; 97 A.F.T.R.2d (RIA) 2484

May 4, 2006, Argued and Submitted, Seattle, Washington

May 17, 2006, Filed

NOTICE:

[*1] RULES OF THE NINTH CIRCUIT COURT OF APPEALS MAY LIMIT CITATION TO UNPUBLISHED OPINIONS. PLEASE REFER TO THE RULES OF THE UNITED STATES COURT OF APPEALS FOR THIS CIRCUIT.

PRIOR HISTORY:

Appeal from the United States District Court for the Eastern District of Washington. D.C. No. CV-02-00384-RHW. Robert H. Whaley, Chief District Judge, Presiding.

COUNSEL: For UNITED STATES OF AMERICA, Plaintiff - Appellee: James A. McDevitt, Esq., USSP - OFFICE OF THE U.S. ATTORNEY, Spokane, WA; W. Carl Hankla, Esq., U.S. DEPARTMENT OF JUSTICE, Tax Division, Washingon, DC; Charles Bricken, Esq., Frank P. Cihlar, Attorney, Richard Farber, Esq., Francesca U. Tamami, Esq., DOJ - U.S. DEPARTMENT OF JUSTICE, Tax Division, Washington, DC.

For BRYCE W TOWNLEY, individually and as Trustee for Bryce and Charlene Townley Living Trust, CHARLENE R TOWNLEY, individually and as Trustee for Bryce and Charlene Townley Living Trust, Defendant - Appellant: Alan Stuart Richey, Esq., Port Hadlock, WA.

For DANIEL SIDEBOTTOM, Defendant: Daniel Sidebottom, S. Africa.

For John Doe, No appearance, No Appearance.

8: U.S. V TOWNLEY

For GEORGE BARTH, Defendant: No appearance, No appearance.

JUDGES: Before: REINHARDT, McKEOWN, and CLIFTON, Circuit [*2] Judges.

OPINION

MEMORANDUM *

- - - - - - - - - - - - - Footnotes - - - - - - - - - - - - - -*
This disposition is not appropriate for publication and may not be cited to or by the courts of this circuit except as provided by 9th Cir. R. 36-3.

- - - - - - - - - - - End Footnotes- - - - - - - - - - - - - -
Before: REINHARDT, McKEOWN, and CLIFTON, Circuit Judges.

Defendants Bryce and Charlene Townley appeal the district court's grant of summary judgment in favor of the government. We affirm.

The district court did not err in holding that the Townleys transferred their real property into the Beaver Valley Trust in violation of the Washington Uniform Fraudulent Transfers Act. The Townleys' repeated admissions that they transferred property to the Trust in order to avoid potential future creditors provide direct evidence of fraud. Further, by demonstrating that the property transfer was. characterized by multiple badges of fraud, the government also showed compelling circumstantial evidence of fraud. Therefore, the government provided the requisite "clear and satisfactory proof that the Townleys possessed an "actual intent to hinder, [*3] delay or defraud a[] creditor" under the UFTA. R.C.W.A § 19.40.041(a)(1); see also Sedwick v. Gwinn, 73 Wn. App. 879, 873 P.2d 528, 531 (Wash. App. 1994); Clearwater v. Skyline Construction Co., Inc., 67 Wn. App. 305, 835 P.2d 257, 264-67 (Wash. App. 1992).

The Townleys also argue that collateral estoppel or, alternatively, res judicata precludes the government from bringing the foreclosure action altogether. This argument is without merit. Neither the claims nor the issues litigated and decided in the bankruptcy proceedings were identical to those raised before the district court. While the court determined that the residential property was not part of the estate, it did not discuss whether the real property parcels had been fraudulently transferred from the estate or whether the Trust should be considered a distinct legal entity. See Kourtis v. Cameron, 419 F.3d 989, 994 (9th Cir. 2005); Mpoyo v. Litton Electro- Optical Systems, 430 F.3d 985, 987 (9th Cir. 2005). Further, the record suggests that the IRS was precluded from meaningfully partici-

8: U.S. V TOWNLEY

pating in the bankruptcy proceeding such that it was unable to assert its unique interests before the [*4] court, even had it desired to do so.

Finally, the Townleys argue that the action is barred because the government failed to obey administrative procedures and exhaust applicable administrative remedies. As noted by the district court, this claim is frivolous. The IRS is permitted to prepare substitute Form 1040 tax returns. See 26 U.S.C. § 6020(b)(1) ("If any person fails to make any return required by any internal revenue law or regulation . . . the [IRS] shall make such return from his own knowledge and from such information as he can obtain through testimony or otherwise."); see also Rapp v. Commissioner, 774 F.2d 932, 935 (9th Cir. 1985). Similarly, the IRS did not err in failing to produce a 23C Assessment Certificate. We have repeatedly held that a Form 4340 Certificate of Assessment and Payment, complete with an assessment date, is alone sufficient to establish that a tax assessment was properly made. See Koff v. United States, 3 F.3d 1297, 1298 (9th Cir. 1993)("[When provided with Forms 4340,] which set forth all the information th[e] regulation requires, [taxpayers] have already been given all the document [*5] to which they are entitled by section 6203.").

AFFIRMED

United States Bankruptcy Court, E.D. Virginia.

In re DEP, INC. Debtor.

C.F. Trust, Inc., Plaintiff,

v.

DEP, Inc., et al., Defendants.

Nos. 95-14438-SSM, 97-1017
Oct. 31, 1997

Harvey A. Levin, Birch, Horton, Bittner and Cherot, Washington, DC, for plaintiff. Robert Rae Gordon, Gordon & Pesner, L.C., McLean, VA, for defendant J.P. Development, Inc. Thomas P. Gorman, Tyler, Bartl, Burke & Albert, P.L.C., Alexandria, VA, for Gordon Peyton, Chapter 7 Trustee: James R. Schroll, Bean, Kinney & Korman, P.C., Arlington, VA, for Atlantic Funding Corporation. Paul D. Pearlstein, Pearlstein & Jacques, Washington, DC, for defendant Brent Jacques, Substitute Trustee

MEMORANDUM OPINION

8: U.S. V TOWNLEY

STEPHEN S. MITCHELL, Bankruptcy Judge. *1 A hearing was held in open court on September 10, 1997, on the plaintiff's motion for summary judgment in this action to determine the priority and extent of liens against certain real property owned by the debtor. At the conclusion of the hearing the court took the motion under advisement in order to review the evidence and the applicable law. [FN1] Having done so, the court concludes that a challenged first-lien deed of trust has not been extinguished but that a challenged judgment lien has.

FN1. Subsequent to the hearing, J.P. Development filed on September 24, 1997, in opposition to the summary judgment motion, an affidavit of Barrie M. Peterson. On October 8, 1997, C.F. Trust filed a motion to strike the affidavit. At a hearing held on October 28, 1997, the court granted the motion to strike the affidavit.

Background This is an action to determine the priority and extent of a judgment lien, purchased by J.P. Development, Inc. ("J.P.Development") vis-a-vis a deed of trust purchased by C.F. Trust, Inc. ("C.F.Trust"). Both liens are claimed to encumber twenty-two office condominium units, owned by the debtor, known as the Dominion Professional Center. The debtor, DEP, Inc. ("DEP" or "the debtor"), is a Virginia corporation, the stock of which is now entirely owned by Barrie M. Peterson. At all times during the events giving rise to the present controversy, however, the president of DEP was Scott Peterson, his son, who is also the president and sole shareholder of J.P. Development. DEP, Inc. filed a voluntary petition under chapter 11 of the Bankruptcy Code in this court on October 10, 1995, and operated for some 17 months as a debtor in possession. On its original schedules, DEP did not list the judgment lien now at issue, nor did it recognize or provide for the judgment lien in the first proposed chapter 11 plan it filed. Pltf. Exh. 26 and 27. On March 11, 1997, the debtor's case was converted to a case under chapter 7, and Gordon P. Peyton has qualified as trustee. At the time the debtor filed its petition, it owned three pieces of real estate. One consists of an undeveloped 61.25 acre parcel known as the "Pick-A-Pair" tract. The second consists of a mobile home park and three adjacent parcels known collectively as the Elm Farm mobile home park. The third, which is the subject of the present adversary proceeding, consists of 22 office condominium units in a complex known as the Dominion Professional Center. [FN2]

FN2. The Dominion Professional Center actually consists of a total of 23 units. One was sold to an unrelated party before the market for office condominiums dried up, and the remaining 22 are currently being rented. At a hearing held on July 2, 3, and 10, 1996, on a motion for relief from the automatic stay brought by C.F. Trust and Atlantic Funding Corporation, this court determined that the

8: U.S. V TOWNLEY

fair market value of the Dominion Professional Center was $2,100,000.00.

The property upon which the Dominion Professional Center stands was purchased by Barrie M. Peterson, Trustee on July 13, 1983. Pltf. Exh. 6. The construction of the Dominion Professional Center was financed by a $1.6 million loan made on or about December 21, 1984, by Dominion Federal Savings and Loan Association and was backed by an industrial development revenue bond issued by the Industrial Development Authority of Prince William County, Virginia. Pltf. Exh. 7. A deed of trust against the property to secure the note and the bond was recorded on December 23, 1984. Pltf. Exh. 8. Subsequently, a second-lien deed of trust in the amount of $1 million was recorded against the property in November 1986 to secure a loan made by Dominion Federal Savings and Loan Association. [FN3]

FN3. The note secured by the second deed of trust was subsequently transferred to Trustbank Savings Bank, FSB. Trustbank was later taken over by the Resolution Trust Corporation, which sold the note as part of a portfolio of non-performing loans to Superior Financial Services, Inc., which in turn sold it to Atlantic Funding Corporation, the current noteholder. At the relief from stay hearing, the court determined that the amount then due on Atlantic's note was $1,719,923.00.

In November 1991, Barrie M. Peterson, Trustee, conveyed the property to an entity known as Dominion Professional Center, L.P. For reasons that are unexplained, the conveyance was done in two stages. [FN4] A quitclaim deed was executed first conveying the property from Barrie M. Peterson, Trustee, to Barrie M. Peterson and Nancy A. Peterson, his wife, as tenants in common (he as to an undivided 99% interest and she as to an undivided 1% interest). Pltf. Exh. 12. A second quitclaim deed was then executed from Barrie M. Peterson and Nancy A. Peterson to Dominion Professional Center, L.P. [FN5] Pltf. Exh. 13. Both deeds are dated, and appear to have been signed, on November 13, 1991. Both deeds were recorded the next day, November 14, 1991, at 1:52 p.m.; were given successive instrument numbers by the clerk; and appear in the deed books one immediately after the other .

FN4. C.F. Trust asserts in its memorandum that the purpose of the two-step transfer was to save recording taxes. See Va.Code Ann. Â§ 58.1- 811(A) (exempting certain deeds from recording taxes). This conclusion is consistent with the notations placed on both deeds claiming exemption from recording taxes. Subsequent to the summary judgment hearing, however, J.P. Development filed an affidavit of Barrie M. Peterson asserting that the purpose of passing title through

8: U.S. V TOWNLEY

him and his wife, "was not to save recordation taxes but, according to Wendy Fields [the attorney handling the transaction], was the way the title company wanted it done." By separate order, this court has struck the affidavit from the record. But even if the affidavit were part of the record, this court, based on its assessment of Mr. Peterson's credibility in prior litigation in this case, would not be inclined to give the affidavit any credence--particularly as Mr. Peterson invoked the attorneyclient privilege during his deposition to block further inquiry into the reasons for the two deeds. For the purpose of this opinion, however, the actual reason the conveyance was structured the way it was is immaterial.

FN5. Barrie Peterson was the general partner, and he and his wife the sole limited partners, of Dominion Professional Center, L.P.

*2 The controversy before the court arises from the fact that some eight months prior to this transaction, a judgment against Barrie M. Peterson, individually, had been docketed among the land records of Prince William County, Virginia, where the Dominion Professional Center is located. The judgment, in the amount of $1,003,850.00, had been obtained in the United States District Court for the Central District of California on January 30, 1990 by Grant K. MacCoon and others ("the MacCoon judgment"). It was domesticated in Virginia by a judgment of the Circuit Court of Fairfax County dated December 12, 1990 and was docketed in Prince William County on March 4, 1991. The judgment was purchased for $200,000 on December 28, 1994, by J.P. Development, Inc., a corporation wholly owned by Scott Peterson, in a transaction orchestrated by Barrie M. Peterson using funds that came from the sale of two properties titled in his name as trustee. Pltf. Exh. 30-42, 45-46, and 49. At some point in 1992, the $1.6 million first-trust note, then held by Signet Bank ("Signet"), went into default, and in August, Signet began foreclosure proceedings. Pltf. Exh. 19. Barrie Peterson sought to borrow money from Central Fidelity Bank ("Central Fidelity"), which at that point held deeds of trust against the Pick-A-Pair tract and the Elm Farm mobile home park, to purchase the Signet note, which Signet was apparently willing to sell for $900,000. Central Fidelity, apparently concerned because of the existence of the $1 million second deed of trust against the property and an inability to otherwise acquire a first-lien position, decided to purchase the Signet note directly rather than loan Barrie Peterson the money to acquire it. Pltf. Exh. 25. Central Fidelity purchased the Signet note for $900,000 on or about September 23, 1992.

[FN6] Pltf. Exh. 10. At that time, the principal balance due on the note was $1,170,355.88, and accrued unpaid interest was due in the amount of $1,404.36. [FN7] Contemporaneously with the assignment of Signet's deed of trust, the

8: U.S. V TOWNLEY

Dominion Professional Center was conveyed to DEP, Inc., by a deed of assumption dated September 18, 1992, under which the debtor expressly assumed and agreed to pay the Signet note. Pltf. Exh. 20. By a separate amended and restated note of that same date, signed by DEP as the maker and by Barrie M. Peterson, Trustee, Barrie M. Peterson, individually, and Nancy A. Peterson as guarantors, the principal amount of the note was reduced to $1 million. Pltf. Exh. 21. Also dated September 18, 1992, is a second promissory note in the amount of $6,167,999.82 signed by the same parties and an "amended and restated" deed of trust against the Dominion Professional Center in the amount of $6,167,999.82. Pltf. Exh. 3 and 22. That amount represents the aggregate of all the indebtedness then due on the Pick-A-Pair, Elm Farm, and Dominion Professional Center loans, including the sums represented by the $1 million note. The deed of trust recites that "the liens and security interests represented by [the existing deed of trust against the Pick-a-Pair and Elm Farm parcels] are each hereby merged and consolidated into this deed of trust." It further recites that the modified Signet note and the Pick-a-Pair and Elm Farm note "and all debts and obligations represented by each are hereby merged and consolidated into a single promissory note." On November 1, 1993, as part of a workout attempt, the total debt then owed Central Fidelity was split into two promissory notes (each with a different interest rate), one in the amount of $4,414,903.57 and the other in the amount of $1,650,000, both of which continued to be secured by the 1992 "amended and restated" deed of trust. Pltf. Exh. 1 and 2. On August 29, 1995, Central Fidelity sold the notes--which were in default--and the deed of trust to C.F. Trust, an entity that had been formed for the express purpose of acquiring them. [FN8] FN6. With the exception of the assignment from Signet, which is both dated and acknowledged on September 23, 1992, all the remaining documents are dated September 18, 1992, but were acknowledged on September 21, 1992. All the documents, including the assignment, were recorded September 24, 1992 .

FN7. These are the figures recited in an estoppel certificate prepared by Central Fidelity at the time of the loan purchase and signed by Scott Peterson and Barrie M. Peterson, as the debtor's president and vice- president, respectively, on September 18, 1997. See Pltf. Exh. 11. Other (higher) interest figures are shown on various other exhibits, but the record is far from clear as to how those figures were calculated. For that reason, the court adopts the figures shown on the estoppel certificate.

FN8. Briefly, Atlantic Funding had already purchased the second trust note and was afraid that Central Fidelity would foreclose under its deed of trust, thereby wiping out Atlantic's position. Atlantic's president president and sole shareholder, William Cooley, then recruited additional investors and formed C.F. Trust to pur-

8: U.S. V TOWNLEY

chase the Central Fidelity deed of trust. The purchase was made with borrowed funds, and the Central Fidelity note and deed of trust have been assigned to the lender as security.

Discussion *3 Under Fed.R.Civ.P. 56(c), made applicable to bankruptcy proceedings by Fed.R.Bankr.P. 7056, summary judgment may be entered in favor of a party on that party's motion "if the pleadings, depositions, answers to interrogatories, and admissions on file, together with the affidavits, if any, show that there is no genuine issue as to any material fact and that the moving party is entitled to a judgment as a matter of law." When a motion for summary judgment is made and supported as provided in Rule 56, an adverse party may not rest upon the mere allegations or denials of the adverse party's pleading, but the adverse party's response, by affidavits or otherwise as permitted by Rule 56, must set forth specific facts showing that there is a genuine issue for trial. Fed.R.Civ.P. 56(e). Four issues are raised by the motion for summary judgment and the opposition filed by J.P. Development. The first is whether the lien securing the $1.6 million note formerly held by Signet was extinguished when Central Fidelity purchased and refinanced it. The second is whether the MacCoon judgment lien attached to the property during the short instant that title was vested in Barrie M. Peterson individually. The third is whether the judgment lien was extinguished when it was purchased by J.P. Development with money that is said to have been Mr. Peterson's own. And the fourth, finally, is whether--assuming J.P. Development has a lien--that lien ought to be equitably subordinated to the claims of other creditors secured by the property. These issues will each be discussed in turn. A. Has Central Fidelity's First Trust Position Been Extinguished? J.P. Development argues that, notwithstanding the express intention of Central Fidelity and DEP to preserve the first-lien position of the $1.6 million Signet note, that position was nevertheless lost when the note was "restated" in September 1992 and then "merged" into the $6,167,999.82 note and deed of trust. [FN9] The only authority cited for this proposition is a passing reference to Virginia's doctrine of merger in Fox v. Templeton, 229 Va. 380, 386, 329 S.E.2d 6, 9 (1985) ("The acceptance of title in satisfaction of a preexisting security interest is presumed, in the absence of a contrary intention, to constitute a merger of the original secured interest into the legal title acquired....[S]uch a merger carries with it all liens, securities, and remedies which were incidental to the original secured interest"). The facts in Fox v. Templeton, however, are wholly unlike those in the present case. In Fox, an existing noteholder secured by an equitable mortgage against real estate accepted a conveyance of the property in satisfaction of the debt. At the time the mortgage had been recorded, there was an existing judgment lien against the property. That judgment lien was erroneously released the following day. Some time after the

8: U.S. V TOWNLEY

judgment was released, the noteholder accepted a deed to the property in satisfaction of the note. The noteholder had not done a title search either at the time the original mortgage was recorded or when she subsequently accepted the deed in satisfaction of the indebtedness. The judgment lien was then reinstated, and the issue was whether the property, now titled in the name of the former noteholder, was subject to the judgment lien

FN9. It is important to emphasize that C.F. Trust is not arguing that the recording of the amended and restated deed of trust gave Central Fidelity any greater lien than it already enjoyed. That is, C.F. Trust expressly recognizes in its motion that its first-lien position is limited to the amount due on the Signet note at the time the note was purchased by Central Fidelity, and that the roughly $5 million in additional indebtedness for which the property was made subject as a result of the amended and restated deed of trust is subordinate to any then-existing legitimate liens of record against the property. Pltf's Mot. for Summary Judgment 23-24. See, Pltf. Exh. 28 (opinion letter of counsel to Central Fidelity that consolidated deed of trust had first priority only to the extent of principal balance plus accrued and unpaid interest on the industrial revenue bond.

The Court in Fox held that the noteholder was charged with constructive knowledge of the judgment lien at the time the original mortgage was recorded and that, as a necessary corollary of the doctrine of merger, there was a rebuttable presumption that such knowledge still existed when she accepted the deed in satisfaction of the debt. Because she could not show any detrimental reliance on the mistaken release--not having examined the land records before accepting the conveyance of the property--she was in no position to complain when the judgment was restored. Accordingly, her ownership interest in the property was subject to the judgment lien. *4 In the present case, unlike Fox, there is no issue of Central Fidelity, as mortgagee, accepting title to the property in satisfaction of the debt. Even in such a circumstance, it by no means follows that the mortgage lien will necessarily merge into the fee simple title. As noted in Fox, merger is "presumed" only "in the absence of evidence of a contrary intent." See Rorer v. Ferguson, 96 Va. 411, 31 S.E. 817 (1898). In Rorer, the holder of a second deed of trust accepted a deed to real estate that was subject to both a senior deed of trust and a junior judgment lien. In a suit to sell the land to satisfy the judgment, the junior judgment lien holder argued that the second deed of trust had been extinguished when the noteholder acquired the property. Addressing this argument, the then-Supreme Court of Appeals of Virginia reasoned: Equity will, in the absence of any declaration of intention, destroy [the lien]; but if there is any reason for keeping it alive--such as the existence of another incumbrance,--equity will not destroy [the lien]. 31 S.E. at 818 (emphasis added). The court held that since a junior lien was

8: U.S. V TOWNLEY

in place, it was in the best interest of the deed of trust holder (now the owner) to have his lien kept intact. Id. at 819. In the present case, there has been no joinder of legal title with a beneficial interest, as in Fox and Rorer. Rather, the court understands the "merger" argument to be that the original deed of trust securing the $1.6 million Signet note, although never formally released of record, was merged into, and extinguished by, the "amended and restated" $6,167,999.82 deed of trust executed by DEP after Central Fidelity purchased the Signet note. However, the decision of the Virginia Supreme Court in Sackadorf v. JLM Group L.P., 250 Va. 321, 462 S.E.2d 64 (1995) makes it clear that a note can be purchased and modified without losing the lien position securing the note. In Sackadorf, American Security Bank, as part of a loan transaction intended to "refinance" or "retire" an existing secured loan, received from the existing lender an "assignment" of two notes and the deeds of trust securing them. At the time the transaction occurred, there were two junior deeds of trust against the property. Following the assignment of the original note, the borrower executed a "replacement" promissory note in the same amount as the aggregate of the two original notes, but at a lower rate of interest, a longer amortization, and a lower payment amount. The borrower also executed an instrument entitled "Amendment, Restatement and Consolidation of Deeds of Trust" reciting "the existence and validity" of the original notes and providing for the amended deed of trust to have "the same lien and priority" as the original deed of trust. As in the present case, the junior lien holders in Sackadorf argued that the first lien was extinguished when the original notes were assigned to the new lender, and that the funds advanced by the new lender for the purchase constituted a "new loan" that was subordinate to all existing encumbrances against the property. The Court observed, as a general principle, that if the "sole obligor" on a note was the "payor" of funds received by the original secured noteholder for the surrender of the note, the sole obligor's liability on the note was discharged, and the lien securing the note was discharged. Sackadorf, 250 Va. at 330, 462 S.E.2d at 69; see also Bank of Russell Co. v. Griffith, 176 Va. 1, 10 S.E.2d 481 (1940) (where attorney gave fees earned in his practice to his daughter to purchase a deed of trust securing the attorney's own property, the lien of the deed of trust was extinguished). The Court held, however, that "if the person or entity supplying the funds is not a party to the instrument alleged to have been paid, and is not obligated in any way for its payment, then the question whether the transaction 'is a payment or a purchase is a question of intention....' " Sackadorf, 250 Va. at 330, 462 S.E.2d at 69. In Sackadorf, the trial court had found that the funds paid to the first noteholder came from the successor lender and were not under the control of the borrower. The Virginia Supreme Court held: *5 [T]he evidence presented was not only consistent with an assignment: it was inconsistent with payment.

8: U.S. V TOWNLEY

There was no evidence that [the former lender] recorded a certificate of satisfaction to release its deeds of trust, or that [the borrower] demanded that it do so. Similarly, the evidence showed that [the former lender] neither canceled the notes nor returned them to [the borrower], but instead endorsed and delivered the notes to [the new lender]. Thus, we conclude that the trial court did not err in holding that [the original lender's] lien was not extinguished by its receipt of funds [from the loan proceeds escrow account], and that [the new lender] acquired a valid first lien on the property. 250 Va. at 331, 462 S.E.2d at 70. J.P. Development argues that Sackadorf is distinguishable on its facts, because in Sackadorf the party that signed the "replacement" note and the amended deed of trust was the same party that signed the original note and deed of trust. This contrasts with the present case, where, it is argued, the amended and restated note and deed of trust were signed by an entirely different entity (DEP, Inc.) from the party (Barrie Peterson, Trustee) who signed the original note and deed of trust. However, while Barrie Peterson, Trustee, was not the maker of the amended and restated note, he did sign as guarantor. Nothing in Sackadorf, moreover, even remotely suggests that the Virginia Supreme Court was hanging its analytical hat on the obligor's continuity of interest: the issue was simply whether the funds paid to the first noteholder came from some party other than the "sole obligor" on the note and whether the intention of the party who supplied the funds was to pay the note or to purchase it. In the present case, there is no factual dispute that the funds paid to Signet Bank on account of the note came from Central Fidelity Bank, and that Central Fidelity Bank was not otherwise obligated on the note. Nor is there any dispute that Central Fidelity's intention was to purchase the note, not to pay it. There is no evidence that the original note was ever marked "paid" or that a certificate of satisfaction was ever recorded with respect to the original deed of trust. Additionally, the language used in all the instruments executed at the time of the transaction clearly expresses an intent to purchase, not to pay, the note. Thus, under Sackadorf, the lien of the Signet deed of trust was not extinguished unless, as argued by J.P. Development, the subsequent "restatement" of the note and deed of trust somehow created a "new" obligation. [FN10]

FN10. Although it has not used the term in its memorandum, J.P. Development is essentially arguing that the "restated" note constituted a novation, that is, "a mutual agreement among all parties concerned for discharge of a valid existing obligation by the substitution of a new valid obligation on the part of the debtor or another." Honeywell, Inc. v. Elliott, 213 Va. 86, 189 S.E.2d 331 (1972). Three types of novation are recognized: "(1) Where the debtor and the creditor remain the same, but a new debt takes the place of the old one; (2) where the debt remains the same, but a new debtor is substituted; [and] (3), where the debt and

8: U.S. V TOWNLEY

debtor remain, but a new creditor is substituted." Wheeler v. Wardwell, 173 Va. 168, 3 S.E.2d 377 (1939) (series of renewal notes endorsed by the defendant were "a continuance of the transaction between the parties" and not a novation.) However, a novation is never presumed; rather, in the absence of satisfactory proof to the contrary, the presumption is that the debt has not been extinguished by taking the evidence of indebtedness. Gullette v. F.D.I.C., 231 Va. 486, 344 S.E.2d 920 (1986).

*6 The evidence overwhelmingly supports an intent to modify the terms of an existing indebtedness and not to create a new one. Having acquired for $900,000 a note with a outstanding principal balance of $1,170,355.88, Central Fidelity agreed with the debtor and Mr. and Mrs. Peterson to reduce the principal balance to $1,000,000. It is true that the modified obligation was evidenced by a newly-drawn form of promissory note, but the mere drawing-up of a new instrument does not necessarily constitute a novation. [FN11] See, F.D.I.C v. Wald, 630 F.2d 239 (4th Cir.1980) (liability of guarantors under written guarantee of first note not discharged when note was paid by renewal note guaranteed by only one of the original guarantors).

FN11. There is no evidence that the original $1.6 million note was ever surrendered by Central Fidelity. But even if it had been, such surrender would not necessarily have discharged the indebtedness evidenced by that note. Hubbard Realty Co., Inc. v. First Nat'l Bank of Pikeville, 704 F.2d 733 (4th Cir.1983) (deed of trust securing earlier note that was paid by renewal and had been surrendered could be enforced even though the renewal note was invalid because it was executed after the bank received actual notice that the former president who signed it had been removed from office).

A more difficult issue, factually, is presented by the language in the 1992 amended and restated deed of trust that the Signet note (now written down to $1 million) was being "merged and consolidated" with the other outstanding obligations of DEP "into a single promissory note." The $1 million "amended and restated" note, successor to the $1.6 million note purchased from Signet, appears to have been treated as a mere formality by Central Fidelity, since it was immediately subsumed, before the ink on it had even dried, into the $6,167,999.82 note. Certainly, it appears that the parties thereafter treated the debt on all three parcels as a unitary obligation. Nevertheless, nothing in the documents executed or recorded in connection with the purchase of the Signet note in 1992 evidences any intent to relinquish or extinguish the lien securing the indebtedness represented by that note. There is no language in the 1992 amended and restated deed of trust releasing the 1984 deed of trust, or even "merging" it into the deed of trust

8: U.S. V TOWNLEY

against the Pick-A-Pair and Elm Farm tracts. Rather, the merger language runs the other way: the Pick-A-Pair and Elm Farm deed of trust is merged into the Dominion Professional Center deed of trust. Thus, while the sum secured by the Dominion Professional Center deed of trust is increased, the continuity of the original lien is clearly and expressly maintained. Given the clear language in the 1992 instruments preserving the lien of the 1984 deed of trust, and since Central Fidelity, as the party purchasing the note secured by the 1984 deed of trust, was not "the sole obligor"--or, indeed, an obligor at all--on the note, the court concludes that the lien created by the 1984 deed of trust remains intact without alteration of priority as to the amount due on the Signet note at the time it was purchased by Central Fidelity and any accrued interest on that sum. [FN12] Accordingly, summary judgment will be entered in favor of C.F. Trust determining that it has a first-lien position as to that amount, subject only to any valid real estate tax liens and mechanic's liens.

FN12. The calculation of the accrued interest is not without its difficulties, in light of the subsequent splitting of the $6,167,999.82 note into two separate notes, each of which has a separate rate of interest.

B. Did the MacCoon judgment attach to the property? *7 There is no dispute that the lien securing the Atlantic Funding note is superior to any amount owed C.F. Trust over and above the amount that was due on the Signet note at the time it was acquired by Central Fidelity. That leaves the question of the priority to be accorded the remaining amount due C.F. Trust under its notes. As discussed above, the amended and restated deed of trust was recorded on September 24, 1992, some 18 months after the MacCoon judgment against Barrie M. Peterson was docketed and some ten months after title to an undivided 99% interest in the Dominion Professional Center vested in Barrie M. Peterson individually. If the MacCoon judgment became a lien against the property on November 14, 1991, when the deed to Barrie Peterson was recorded, it is clearly in third order of priority, and the balance owed C.F. Trust under the 1992 deed of trust is in fourth position. On the other hand, if the MacCoon judgment did not attach to the property, C.F. Trust is in third position. [FN13]

FN13. To be sure, this wrangling over who is in third position is largely academic. As noted above, this court has previously determined that the fair market value of the Dominion Professional Center is $2.1 million. Since the court has determined that C.F. Trust is in first position to the extent of $1,170,355.88 and accrued interest, and since the court has also determined that $1,719,923.00 was due on the second-trust note held by Atlantic Funding, it seems clear that in any foreclosure or judicial sale, nothing is likely to be paid on account of whatever

8: U.S. V TOWNLEY

lien is in third position. Nevertheless, since the court's holding as to the priority of C.F. Trust's lien may be appealed, the court finds it appropriate to reach the question of whether J.P. Development has any lien at all against the Dominion Professional Center.

Under Virginia law, a judgment, once docketed in the clerk's office of the circuit court for a city or county, becomes a lien against all real estate owned by or thereafter acquired by the judgment debtor in that jurisdiction. Va.Code Ann. § 8.01-458. [FN14] Thus, there can be no question that the MacCoon judgment, which was docketed in Prince William County on March 4, 1991, became a lien against the Dominion Professional Center when title to the real estate became vested in Barrie M. Peterson individually on November 14, 1991, unless, as argued by C.F. Trust, the doctrine of "transitory seisin" applies to prevent the judgment from attaching. That doctrine, simply stated, is that, as a general rule, transitory seisin is not such an interest as becomes subject to a lien of a judgment, and that where land is conveyed to a judgment debtor, and eo instanti reconveyed by him to a trustee to secure the purchase money, the judgment debtor has no interest that is subject to a judgment lien or a wife's dower as against the deed of trust. Straus v. Bodeker's Ex'x, 86 Va. 543, 10 S.E. 570 (1889) (judgment lien); Hurst v. Dulaney, 87 Va. 444, 12 S.E. 800 (1891) (dower); see also Charlottesville Hardware Co. v. Perkins, 118 Va. 34, 86 S.E. 869 (1915) (judgment lien was subordinate to the deed of trust securing the purchase price even though the deed of trust was not recorded until almost a year after the sale, where recitals in the deed stated that a deed of trust had been executed.) As explained in an early case, the doctrine of transitory seisin is grounded in the principal that a judgment creditor takes the property or applies it to the satisfaction of his lien "in subordination to all the equities which exist at the time in favor of third persons." Summers v. Darne, 72 Va. (31 Gratt. 791) 567 (1879). The Court explained:

FN14. Va.Code Ann. § 8.01-458 provides in relevant part as follows:

Every judgment for money rendered in this Commonwealth by any state or federal court or by confession of judgment, as provided by law, shall be a lien on all the real estate of or to which the defendant in the judgment is or becomes possessed or entitled, from the time such judgment is recorded on the judgment lien docket of the clerk's office of the county or city where such land is situated[.]

When, therefore, land is conveyed and the purchaser at the same time gives back a mortgage or other incumbrance to secure the purchase-money, he does not thereby acquire any such seisin or interest as will entitle his wife to dower, or his creditor to subject the land to his debts discharged of the mortgage. In such cases

8: U.S. V TOWNLEY

the deed and mortgage are regarded as parts of the same contract, and constitute but a single transaction, investing the purchaser with seisin for a transitory instant only. *8 Id. at 570 (72 Va. 791, 31 Gratt. at 801). There can hardly be a stronger case, factually, for arguing that the vesting of title in Barrie Peterson individually was a purely instantaneous or transitory event. The deed from himself as trustee to himself and his wife individually was apparently executed at the same time as the deed from him and his wife to Dominion Professional Center, L.P. Both deeds were recorded at the same time, down to the very minute; they were given successive instrument numbers by the clerk; and they appear, one immediately following the other, in the same deed book. Whatever the motivation for the two-stage conveyance-- whether to avoid recording taxes or to solve some title problem or perhaps to confer some income tax benefit--the two deeds were clearly intended to be part of a single transaction by which the property, titled up to that point in the name of Barrie M. Peterson, Trustee, would be transferred to Dominion Professional Center, L.P. J.P. Development, however, urges that the Virginia courts have never applied the rule of transitory seisin except to protect deeds of trust taken back to secure the purchase price of the property and that, as a legal fiction, the doctrine ought to be limited to that type of factual situation. Upon a review of the cases, the court is constrained to agree. [FN15] The underpinning of the cases articulating the transitory seisin analysis is that, as the deed and the mortgage taken back are parts of the same contract, "justice and policy equally require that no prior judgment against the mortgagor should intervene and attach upon the land during the transitory seisin, to the prejudice of the mortgagee." Straus, 86 Va. at 548, 10 S.E. 570. As an alternative approach to achieving the same result, the Virginia courts have also analyzed the vendee's interest as being held in a resulting or implied trust for the unpaid vendor. Borst v. Nalle, 69 Va. (28 Gratt. 423) 139 (1877). In short, it appears that in Virginia, the application of the doctrine of transitory seisin requires not only that the period of vesting be brief, but that it be subject to superior equities arising as part of an integrated transaction.

FN15. It is not quite true, however, that the doctrine of transitory seisin has been applied only in the context of protecting a purchase-money lien. In Devers v. Chateau Corp., 792 F.2d 1278 (4th Cir.1986), the Fourth Circuit, applying Virginia law, held that a lessee's cancellation of a 99-year lease, followed immediately by the lessor's absolute conveyance of the property to the former lessee, did not result in a wife's dower interest attaching to the freehold during the fleeting period between the cancellation of the lease and the recording of the deed.

There is nothing in the summary judgment record to suggest that, when the undivided 99 percent interest in the property vested, however briefly, in Barrie M.

8: U.S. V TOWNLEY

Peterson, there were superior equities in favor of Dominion Professional Center, L.P., or that Barrie Peterson and his wife held title to the property merely as the partnership's agent. Nor does the record disclose that the partnership advanced any funds for the purchase. In short, notwithstanding the extreme brevity of Mr. and Mrs. Peterson's ownership, it does not appear that they were under any legal duty or compulsion at the time they acquired title to further convey the property, or that the second conveyance was other than for their own personal benefit or convenience, they being the sole partners of the limited partnership. The court concludes, therefore, that there is no equitable basis upon which to hold that the lien of the MacCoon judgment did not attach to the property on November 14, 1991. Accordingly, unless the judgment lien has been otherwise extinguished or is subject to equitable subordination, it stands in third position, behind the Atlantic Funding deed of trust and ahead of the amounts owed to C.F. Trust over and above the $1,170,355.88 principal plus accrued interest thereon that the court has determined are entitled to first priority. C. Has the MacCoon judgment lien been extinguished? *9 C.F. Trust asserts that, even if the MacCoon judgment attached to the property, the judgment lien was extinguished when Barrie M. Peterson arranged for the judgment to be purchased by J.P. Development and supplied the funds for its purchase. It is on this issue that J.P. Development most strenuously argues that summary judgment is not appropriate because, it is urged, there is a genuine factual dispute as to whether Barrie M. Peterson supplied the funds to purchase the judgment. There can be little doubt that under Virginia law, "[t]he payment of a judgment by any one of the judgment debtors extinguishes the judgment at law." Grizzle v. Fletcher, 127 Va. 663, 105 S.E. 457 (1920) (surety who paid judgment that had been entered against him and his principal and took an assignment of the judgment could not have execution issued on the judgment against his principal but had to proceed separately against his principal on the implied contract of indemnity). As explained by the Court in Grizzle, the payment of the judgment by one of the judgment debtors is a union of debtor and creditor in the same person and this operates to discharge the debt. A person cannot buy his own debt without extinguishing it. Of course, the creditor may sell the judgment to a third person, but not to one of the judgment debtors, so as to keep it alive at law. Id. The Grizzle court did recognize that an exception existed when payment was made by a surety: "[A] judgment paid by a surety thereon will be kept alive by a court of equity for the benefit of the surety, but this arises out of the doctrine of subrogation[.]" Id; see also Lillie v. Dennert, 232 F. 104 (6th Cir.1916) (where one of two joint tort-feasors satisfied a judgment against both, the judgment was discharged, even though the judgment debtor had induced a third person to pay the judgment for him and to take an assignment of it); Parker v. Mauldin, 353 So.2d 1375 (Ala.1977) (judgment not extinguished where evi-

8: U.S. V TOWNLEY

dence supported finding that bank that purchased judgment against one of its customers was acting independently and in a regular businesslike manner); Hart v. Harrell, 17 S.W.2d 1093 (Tex.Civ.App.1929) (purchase of judgment by judgment debtor's agent constituted payment thereof, precluding further execution). In the present case, there can be no serious dispute that Barrie M. Peterson orchestrated the purchase by J.P. Development of the MacCoon judgment. On February 1, 1994, Barrie Peterson wrote to counsel for Grant MacCoon confirming the agreement that had been reached for "settlement of all outstanding matters." Pltf. Exh. 30. The terms relevant to the present issue were as follows: 1. I will pay $100,000 to Mr. MacCoon, by certified or cashier's check, within 60 days....

* * * *10 3. I, or at my option a purchaser reasonably acceptable to both Mr. MacCoon and me (the "Purchaser"), will pay another $100,000 to Mr. MacCoon, by certified or cashier's check, within 6 months after the date of the first payment. 4. At the time of the second payment, Mr MacCoon will cause all parties having interests in the Judgment to execute one of the following types of documents, in accordance with my request ...: a. Appropriate documents, as indicated by the Purchaser's attorneys, to assign all interests in the Judgment to the Purchaser; or b. Appropriate documents, as indicated by my attorneys to be filed in California and every other jurisdiction where the Judgment has been filed, indicating that the Judgment has been fully paid and satisfied. Id. (emphasis added). The letter bears Mr. MacCoon's signature dated February 4, 1994, agreeing to the terms. Id. On April 8, 1994, Barrie Peterson sent Mr. MacCoon's attorney a proposed modification of the settlement agreement extending the time for the first payment upon delivering to an escrow agent a deed to a condominium unit Barrie Peterson owned as trustee in Keystone, Colorado. Pltf. Exh. 31. Throughout the extension agreement, Barrie Peterson consistently refers to himself ("I") as the party who would make the first $100,000.00 payment. Mr. MacCoon agreed to the proposed terms on April 12, 1994. Id. On April 26, 1994, Barrie Peterson transmitted to Mr. MacCoon's attorney a $100,000.00 cashier's check with a cover letter over his own signature stating, "In accordance with our settlement agreement in the above-referenced case, enclosed herewith is a cashier's check in the amount of $100,000.00 as timely first payment." Pltf. Exh. 32. The check, drawn on Central Fidelity Bank, contained the notation, "PURCHASER: JUBAL CORPORATION." Id. Scott Peterson is the president of "Jubal Corporation" (or more properly, it appears, Jubal, Inc.), which shares offices with a number of other corporations and entities owned by Scott Peterson and Barrie Peterson. The funds used to purchase the cashier's check appear to have come from a $230,000.00 loan made to Jubal, Inc. on April 15, 1994, by Dr. James G. McClure. Pltf. Exh. 34. That same date, Barrie Peterson, as trustee, had entered

8: U.S. V TOWNLEY

into a written contract to sell a 44.3960 acre tract known as the "Fortuna property" to Dr. McClure and Scott Peterson for $1,750,000.00, with Dr. McClure to pay $875,000.00 in cash at settlement, and Scott Peterson to pay $875,000 to Jubal, Inc., described in the contract as the holder of the first deed of trust against the parcel. Pltf. Exh. 35. That transaction closed on May 3, 1994, at which time Dr. McClure paid the $875,000.00 in cash, and Jubal, Inc. repaid the $230,000.00 loan to Dr. McClure. Pltf. Exh. 39. Scott Peterson's share of the purchase price is shown on the settlement statement as having been made by an unsecured promissory note, which was then assigned to Jubal, Inc. The settlement statement also shows a payment to Jubal, Inc., purportedly on account of its deed of trust, directly out of the sales proceeds in the precise amount ($230,680.58) necessary to pay off Jubal's note to Dr. McClure.

The $875,000 note given by Scott Peterson at settlement, and assigned to Jubal, Inc., is not only unsecured, it is by its express terms non-recourse:
Notwithstanding anything contained in this Note to the contrary, the Borrower shall have no personal liability to pay any amounts required to be paid hereunder and the noteholder shall not take any action against the Borrower to collect or enforce this Note. The loan evidenced hereby is a non-recourse loan to the Borrower.... This Note is an unsecured note representing the deferred purchase price owned by the Borrower to Barrie M. Peterson, Trustee.... *11 (emphasis added). Pltf. Exh. 43. Of course, there is only one way to describe a note that is simultaneously unsecured and non-recourse: a sham. The second $100,000.00 payment required under the settlement agreement was made to Mr. MacCoon on September 23, 1994, directly out of the proceeds of sale of a condominium unit in Dillon, Colorado, owned by Barrie M. Peterson, Trustee. [FN16] Pltf. Exh. 46. On December 28, 1994, a written assignment of judgment was executed by Mr. MacCoon in favor of J.P. Development. Pltf. Exh. 49. J.P. Development, as noted above, is wholly owned by Scott Peterson, Barrie Peterson's son, and shares office space with various entities owned and controlled by Barrie Peterson. On April 15, 1996, J.P. Development obtained from the Circuit Court of Prince William County, Virginia, a charging order against the interests of Barrie M. Peterson and Barrie M. Peterson, Trustee, in four limited partnerships. Pltf. Exh. 50. That charging order, which was drafted by counsel for J.P. Development, recited, as a credit against the judgment, "The Two Hundred Thousand and NO/100 ($200,000.00) payment made on December 28, 1994, by Barrie M. Peterson ... in partial satisfaction of the Judgment[.]" (emphasis added).

FN16. Barrie Peterson purported to hold title to the condominium unit as trustee for the benefit of his two minor children under a 1985 trust agreement. Pltf. Exh. 47.

8: U.S. V TOWNLEY

Against this mass of evidence, direct and circumstantial, the only evidence offered by J.P. Development to refute the contention that the funds to purchase the judgment came from Barrie M. Peterson is an affidavit of Barrie Peterson, which the court has ordered stricken from the record, containing a bare denial that he supplied the funds. Even if the affidavit had not been struck, it would not have been sufficient to raise a genuine issue of material fact. The affidavit does not address any of the details of the transaction. It only says, in effect, "I didn't do it." Such a general denial is insufficient to create a genuine issue of material fact. [FN17] The objective evidence, on the other hand, is overwhelming that Barrie Peterson arranged all the terms of the sale, orchestrated the financing, and directed to whom the judgment would be assigned. The first $100,000.00 to purchase the judgment came indirectly, and the second $100,000 directly, from the sale of property Barrie Peterson owned as trustee. The conclusion is inescapable that J.P. Development was nothing but Barrie Peterson's straw in the transaction and holds the assignment of judgment for his benefit. [FN18] Accordingly, since the payment of a judgment by any one of the judgment debtors extinguishes the judgment at law, Grizzle v. Fletcher, supra, and since there are no circumstances that would justify keeping the judgment alive in equity by application of the doctrine of equitable subrogation, the court concludes that the judgment lien against the Dominion Professional Center has been extinguished FN17. In addition, the court has already had an opportunity to assess the credibility of Barrie Peterson during the three-day hearing on relief from the automatic stay. To put the matter charitably, truth is not the brightest star in Mr. Peterson's constellation, and the court would not be inclined to give any credence to Mr. Peterson's denials that he supplied the funds to purchase the judgment. Nor, it might be added, does the deposition testimony of Scott Peterson assist J.P. Development's position. The younger Mr. Peterson's testimony as to the source of the funds used to purchase the judgment is an astonishing mass of evasion. It is not often that a trier of fact can make a credibility determination based on a cold transcript, but in this particular case there can be no doubt, based on the deposition transcript, that the younger Mr. Peterson had no intention of giving straight answers to straight questions or of supplying relevant information concerning the transaction.

FN18. In particular, it would appear that a primary purpose of having J.P. Development hold the judgment was in order to obtain friendly liens against Barrie Peterson's assets that could be used to shield those assets from his creditors. See Pltf. Exh. 51, Memorandum Opinion in C.F. Trust, Inc. v. Peterson, No. 96-1128-A (E.D.Va., Dec. 9, 1996) (Cacheris, C.J.) (determining that alleged $450,000 second deed of trust against Barrie and Nancy Peterson's home in favor of Jubal, Inc. was a fraudulent conveyance).

8: U.S. V TOWNLEY

D. Should the judgment lien be equitably subordinated? *12 The final issue is whether, assuming the court is wrong and there is a valid judgment lien against the Dominion Professional Center, it should be subordinated under Â§ 510, Bankruptcy Code, to the claims of C.F. Trust. Under Â§ 510(c), Bankruptcy Code, [A]fter notice and a hearing the court may-- (1) under principles of equitable subordination, subordinate for purposes of distribution all or part of an allowed claim to all or part of another allowed claim or all or part of an allowed interest to all or part of another allowed interest; or (2) order that any lien securing such a subordinated claim be transferred to the estate. In United States v. Noland,--U.S.-- ,517 U.S. 535, 116 S.Ct. 1524, 134 L.Ed.2d 748 (1996), the Supreme Court explained that, although Congress, in enacting Â§ 510(c), "included no explicit criteria for equitable subordination," the language of the statute "clearly indicates congressional intent at least to start with existing doctrine." That existing doctrine, as the Court observed, was judge-made and was generally triggered by a showing that the creditor had engaged in "some type of inequitable conduct" that "resulted in injury to the creditors of the bankrupt or conferred an unfair advantage on the claimant." In an often-cited opinion decided under the former Bankruptcy Act of 1898, the Fifth Circuit in Benjamin v. Diamond (In re Mobile Steel Corp.), 563 F.2d 692 (5th Cir.1977) set forth a number of principles to be considered in determining whether or not a particular claim should be equitably subordinated, among them that claims arising from the dealings between the debtor and its fiduciaries must be subjected to rigorous scrutiny. Id. at 701. See also Pepper v. Litton, 308 U.S. 295, 60 S.Ct. 238, 84 L.Ed. 281 (1939). However, simply because a creditor is an insider does not warrant subordination of an otherwise valid secured claim. EEE Comm'l Corp. v. Holmes (In re ASI Reactivation, Inc.), 934 F.2d 1315, 1320-1321 (4th Cir.1991) (purchase by president with his own funds of note secured by assets of corporation). C.F. Trust's equitable subordination argument focuses, not on the original character of the claim, but on the inequitable use to which J.P. Development has attempted to put the judgment. As noted above, J.P. Development is wholly owned by Scott Peterson, who, until very shortly prior to the chapter 11 filing, was the president of DEP. Notwithstanding that J.P. Development had purchased the MacCoon judgment over 9 months earlier, neither J.P. Development's alleged claim nor its alleged lien was shown on the schedule of liabilities filed by the debtor, nor was such claim acknowledged or treated in the original plan of reorganization filed by the debtor. It was only after the "drop dead" date approached at which C.F. Trust would have relief from the automatic stay [FN19] that the debtor, for the first time, asserted the existence of the MacCoon judgment lien and sought to treat J.P. Development as a creditor. The debtor has provided no explanation as to why the lien was not previously disclosed. As discussed above,

8: U.S. V TOWNLEY

it appears that Barrie Peterson arranged for the MacCoon judgment to be acquired by J.P. Development, rather than paid off, so that he could have the benefit of a friendly lien to shield his assets from collection efforts by C.F. Trust and other creditors.

FN19. On July 10, 1996, the court entered an order that, among other conditions for continuing the automatic stay, required the debtor to obtain confirmation of a plan not later than October 25, 1996. The amended plan that, for the first time, listed J.P. Development as a creditor was filed on October 18, 1996. It would have treated Atlantic Funding's claim as being in first position, but limited to the $250,000.00 that Atlantic Funding paid for it. Then it would have treated the J.P. Development claim as being in second position to be paid in full at its face amount (notwithstanding that it, like the Atlantic Funding claim, had been purchased at a substantial discount). Then the plan would have treated C.F. Trust as being in third position. The plan, in short, would simply have siphoned out to the Petersons essentially all the value of the Dominion Professional Center. .

In short, C.F. Trust has made out at least a prima facie case for equitable subordination of the judgment lien, and J.P. Development has offered no evidence sufficient to rebut that showing. The concern the court has, however, is that §510(c) by its very terms allows a court to subordinate claims "for the purposes of distribution." In the present case, C.F. Trust has already been granted relief from the automatic stay and is apparently prepared to foreclose. [FN20] While the Dominion Professional Center has not been abandoned by the trustee and remains technically property of the bankruptcy estate, in light of the court's previous determination as to fair market value, there is no realistic possibility that the foreclosure sale will result in a surplus that would be subject to "distribution" by the trustee. [FN21] Consequently, any order subordinating the MacCoon judgment lien for the purposes of distribution would be essentially meaningless. Were the Dominion Professional Center to be sold by the chapter 7 trustee free and clear of liens under §363(f), Bankruptcy Code, the court's duty to decide the equitable subordination issue would be clear, but where a foreclosure sale is being conducted in accordance with state law, and where there is no realistic likelihood of excess proceeds for distribution by the trustee, this court does not believe that §510(c), Bankruptcy Code, may be employed to alter the distribution priorities under state law. Accordingly the court will deny summary judgment on the equitable subordination issue at this time, without prejudice to the plaintiff's right to renew the motion for summary judgment on that issue if the chapter 7 trustee moves to sell the property under §363(f), Bankruptcy Code.

FN20. The court has been advised that foreclosure sales of the Pick-A-Pair tract

8: U.S. V TOWNLEY

and the Elm Farm mobile home park have already been held.

FN21. Va.Code Ann. §§ 55-59.4(A)(3) directs distribution of the proceeds of a foreclosure sale to be made as follows:

The trustee shall receive and receipt for the proceeds of sale, no purchaser being required to see to the application of the proceeds, and apply the same, first, to discharge the expenses of executing the trust, including a commission to the trustee of five per centum of the gross proceeds of sale; secondly, to discharge all taxes, levies, and assessment, with costs and interest if they have priority over the lien of the deed of trust, including the due pro rata thereof for the current year; thirdly, to discharge in the order of their priority, if any, the remaining debts and obligations secured by the deed, and any liens of record inferior to the deed of trust under which sale is made, with lawful interest; and, fourthly, the residue of the proceeds shall be paid to the grantor or his assigns; provided, however, that the trustee as to such residue shall not be bound by any inheritance, devise, conveyance, assignment or lien of or upon the grantor's equity, without actual notice thereof prior to distribution; provided further that such order of priorities shall not be changed or varied by the deed of trust.

*13 A separate order will be entered consistent with this opinion.

9: WU V TSENG

Hung-Lin WU and Wu Trust, Plaintiffs,

v.

Stanley TSENG, Richard L. Kreger, Individually and as Custodian for Richard H. Kreger, Robert C. Jackson, Ryan S. Kreger, Toni M. Kreger, and Patricia House, Richard H. Kreger, Robert C. Jackson, Ryan S. Kreger, Toni M. Kreger, Patricia House, Peter McBride, Trustee, and Davis Wetlands Bank, L.L.C., Defendants.

Civil Action No.: 2:05cv699.

United States District Court, E.D. Virginia, Norfolk Division.

October 24, 2006.

469*469 Brett Alexander Spain, John Dinshaw McIntyre, Willcox & Savage PC, Norfolk, VA, for Plaintiffs.

Gregory Slack Larsen, Roy Larsen Romm & Lascara PLC, Chesapeake, VA, for Defendants.

Peter McBride, Kreger & McBride, Chesapeake, VA, pro se.

470*470 Douglas Eugene Kahle, Mark Randolf Baumgartner, Pender & Coward PC, Virginia Beach, VA, for Defendant Davis Wetlands Bank, L.L.C.

AMENDED OPINION & ORDER

HENRY COKE MORGAN, JR., Senior District Judge.

Plaintiffs Hung-Lin Wu and Wu Trust ("Plaintiffs") and Defendants Richard L. Kreger individually and as custodian for the other individually-named defendants, Richard H. Kreger, Robert C. Jackson, Ryan S. Kreger, Toni M. Kreger, and Patricia House ("the Kreger Defendants"), have moved for Partial Summary Judgment against Defendant Davis Wetlands Bank, LLC ("Defendant Davis"). Defendant Davis asserts its claim to the disputed real property under theories of equitable lien and resulting trust. Plaintiffs and the Kreger Defendants contend that Defendant Davis' claim is without merit because there is no written agreement conveying the real property to Defendant Davis, and because any interest Defendant Davis had in the property was not recorded until after the interests of Plaintiffs and the Kreger

Defendants had been registered. The Court agrees. Plaintiffs' and the Kreger Defendants'

9: WU V TSENG

Motions for Partial Summary Judgment are thus GRANTED.

I. PROCEDURAL HISTORY

This action was filed on December 2, 2005, by Plaintiffs against Stanley Tseng ("Mr. Tseng"), the Kreger Defendants, and Peter McBride ("Mr. McBride"). Doc. 1. On March 31, 2006, Defendant Davis filed a Motion to Intervene and a Memorandum in Support of the Motion, seeking to intervene as of right. Does. 9, 10. On April 14, 2006, Plaintiffs submitted a Brief in Opposition to the Motion to Intervene, and the Kreger Defendants submitted their Brief in Opposition, incorporating Plaintiffs' arguments in opposition to the Motion. Does. 11, 12. On April 19, 2006, Defendant Davis filed its reply brief. Doc. 13. The Court granted Defendant Davis' Motion to Intervene on June 6, 2006. Doc. 17.

Defendant Davis filed its Answer to Plaintiffs' Complaint on June 6, 2006. Doc. 18. Plaintiffs filed an Amended Complaint against Mr. Tseng, Mr. McBride, the Kreger Defendants and Defendant Davis on June 26, 2006. Doc. 19. Mr. McBride answered the Amended Complaint on June 28, 2005 (Doc. 20), the Kreger Defendants answered on July 11, 2006 (Doc. 21), and Defendant Davis answered on July 17, 2006 (Doc. 22).

On August 30, 2006, the Kreger Defendants and Plaintiffs each filed a Motion for Partial Summary Judgment against Defendant Davis.[1] Does. 23 and 24, respectively. Only Plaintiffs filed a Memorandum of Support for the Motion. Doc. 25. Defendant Davis filed its Brief in. Opposition to Motions for Partial Summary Judgment on September 11, 2006. Doc. 26. On September 18, 2006, the Kreger Defendants and Plaintiffs filed Reply Briefs in Support of their Motion for Partial Summary Judgment. Does. 27 and 28, respectively. A hearing on the two Motions for Partial Summary Judgment was held on October 12, 2006. Doc. 32.

II. FACTUAL BACKGROUND

The subject of the pending litigation and the instant Motion is approximately 880 acres of real property located in Chesapeake, Virginia ("the Property"). Mr. Tseng purchased the Property in or about 471*471 April of 1984 and has held record title until or about[2] the date that default judgment was recorded in favor of Plaintiffs on August 17, 2005. Doc. 11, Ex. A ¶ 7; Doc. 1 at ¶ 14, 16.

A. Claims on the Property

In this action, Plaintiffs are seeking to set aside as fraudulent a deed of trust executed by Mr. Tseng in favor of the Kreger Defendants and Mr. McBride. See Doc.

9: WU V TSENG

1 ¶¶ 20-23. The deed of trust, purportedly securing six (6) individual promissory notes, was allegedly negotiated on April 29, 2005, just prior to Plaintiffs obtaining a $11,279,836.00 judgment against Mr. Tseng on May 12, 2005. Id at ¶¶ 14, 16. Plaintiffs desire to sell the Property in order to satisfy their judgment against Mr. Tseng. Id. at ¶¶ 20-23. Plaintiffs' judgment lien on the Property was properly docketed on August 17, 2005. See id. at ¶ 14, 16.

On January 3, 2006, one month after the instant action was filed, Douglas S. Davis ("Mr. Davis"), an environmental consultant, and Davis Environmental Consultants, Inc. ("Consultants"), an entity wholly owned and operated by Mr. Davis, filed a "Bill of Complaint for Specific Performance" against Mr. Tseng in the Virginia Beach Circuit Court, seeking specific performance of a contract entered into between Mr. Tseng, Mr. Davis, and Consultants in 1998 ("the 1998 Contract") to convey the Property to Davis Wetlands Bank, LLC ("Defendant Davis").[3] See Doc. 10, Ex 1. In the Bill of Complaint, Mr. Davis and Consultants represented the following to the Virginia Beach Circuit Court, in relevant part:

The [1998 Contract] provides that Davis or Tseng may demand that the Property and the Project be "converted to entity ownership," with each party to have an ownership interest in the entity equivalent to their interest in the net income of the Project. . . . Despite demand by Davis, Tseng refuses to convey the Property into [Davis] as set forth in the [1998 Contract]. . . . Now therefore, Plaintiffs respectfully request this Court to enter an order directing Tseng to convey the Property into the [Intervenor].

Id. at ¶¶ 14, 17. Neither Plaintiffs, the Kreger Defendants, nor Mr. McBride were named as parties to the action in Virginia Beach, nor were they given notice of such. Doc. 25 at 2.

Mr. Tseng made no appearance in the action and Defendant Davis sought a default judgment. Doc. 10, Ex. 1 at 2. On February 10, 2006, the Virginia Beach Circuit Court granted default judgment as follows: "judgment by default be, and it hereby is, entered for Plaintiffs, Douglas D. Davis and Davis Environmental Consultant, Inc. . . . The Property . . . is hereby conveyed to Davis Wetlands Bank, LLC as required by the parties' 1998 agreement." Id.

472*472 Defendant Davis moved to intervene in this action on March 31, 2006, claiming that it is the owner of the Property by virtue of the Virginia Beach Circuit Court's Order of Judgment and by having established an equitable lien pursuant to the 1998 Contract. See generally Doc. 10. Defendant Davis also

9: WU V TSENG

claims that it has a priority interest in the Property by virtue of having established, inter alia, a resulting trust through the 1998 Contract, as well as ancillary oral agreements and understandings. Doc. 13 at 3-4.

In granting Defendant Davis' Motion to Intervene, this Court did not pass on the validity of the theories set forth by Defendant Davis, by which it claims priority interest over the Plaintiffs' and the other Defendants interests in the subject Property. Doc. 17 at 5. The Court found only that Defendant Davis had a "direct and substantial interest in the Property" by virtue of the default judgment of the Virginia Beach Circuit Court; thus, as a threshold matter, Defendant Davis met the requirements to intervene in this action pursuant to Rule 24(a)(2) of the Federal Rules of Civil Procedure. Id.

B. The 1998 Contract

The stated purpose of the 1998 Contract, entered into on January 15, 1998, was to form a joint venture for the purpose of developing the Property to make it available for "compensatory wetlands mitigation." See Doc. 11, Ex. A preamble and ¶ 1. The contract apportions rights and responsibilities as between the parties for purposes of developing the Property; notably, that Mr. Tseng, as owner of the Property, shall make it available for wetlands migration and will advance the first $100,000 of all fees and costs for the project, and that Mr. Davis would be responsible for overseeing construction and conversion of the Property. Id. at ¶¶ 1, 2.

Defendant Davis' legal claim to the Property relies upon paragraph five (5) of the 1998 Contract, which provides that the Property and the wetlands project "may be converted to entity ownership, in which case, if there has been no breach or default by Davis at the time of conversion, the parties shall have ownership interests in said entity(ies) as set forth in paragraph 3 above." Id. at ¶ 5. Paragraph three (3) specifies that profits in the wetlands mitigation project were to be apportioned 82% to Mr. Tseng and 18% to Mr. Davis and Consultants. Id. at ¶ 3.

After entering into the 1998 Contract, the parties to that agreement executed an addendum extending the original term. Doc. 11, Ex. C. In addition, Mr. Davis and Mr. Tseng executed a Sales Commission Agreement dated June 15, 2004, which provides in relevant part that the "commission fee to be paid to [Davis Environmental] will not exceed 50% of the sale price" of each wetlands mitigation credit sold from the mitigation bank. Id., Ex. B. The Sales Commission Agreement further states that "[t]his commission is not based on any hourly rate but is based on the difficulty and complexity of the sale of wetland bank credits."

9: WU V TSENG

Id. Neither the 1998 Contract, the addendum, nor the Sales Commission Agreement contain any other substantive provisions relevant to a transfer of the Property to Defendant Davis. Id., Exs. A, B, & C.

III. SUMMARY JUDGMENT STANDARD OF REVIEW

Summary judgment is proper only "if the pleadings, depositions, answers to interrogatories, and admissions on file, together with the affidavits, if any, show that there is no genuine issue as to any material fact and that the moving party is entitled to a judgment as a matter of law." FED.R.Civ.P. 56(c); see also Miller v. Leathers, 913 F.2d 1085, 1087 (4th Cir. 473*473 1990). Summary judgment is appropriate when the record, taken as a whole, could not lead a rational trier of fact to find for the nonmoving party. Anderson v. Liberty Lobby, Inc., 477 U.S. 242, 247- 49, 106 S.Ct. 2505, 91 L.Ed.2d 202 (1986). The facts and inferences drawn from the pleadings must be viewed in the light most favorable to the nonmoving party. Nguyen v. CNA Corp., 44 F.3d 234, 237 (4th Cir.1995). If the Plaintiff and Defendants dispute the facts of the case, "plaintiff s version of the facts must be presented where the parties' versions conflict, at least to the degree that [her] allegations have support in affidavits, depositions or other documentary evidence." Magnuson v. Peak Technical Servs., 808 F.Supp. 500, 504 (E.D.Va.1992) (citations omitted).

In order to successfully defeat a motion for summary judgment, a nonmoving party cannot rely on "mere belief or conjecture, or the allegations and denials contained in the pleadings." Doyle v. Sentry Ins., 877 F.Supp. 1002, 1005 (E.D.Va.1995) (citing Celotex Corp. v. Catrett, 477 U.S. 317, 324, 106 S.Ct. 2548, 91 L.Ed.2d 265 (1986)). Rather, the nonmoving party must set forth specific facts through affidavits, depositions, interrogatories, or other evidence to show genuine issues for trial. Celotex, 477 U.S. at 324, 106 S.Ct. 2548. When the nonmoving party fails to make a sufficient showing establishing an essential element of his case and he bears the burden of proof on that issue, "there is `no genuine issue of material fact,' since a complete failure of proof concerning an essential element of the nonmoving party's case necessarily renders all other facts immaterial." Id at 322, 106 S.Ct. 2548; Anderson, 477 U.S. at 254, 106 S.Ct. 2505.

IV. ANALYSIS

Defendant Davis, in its Motion to Intervene (Does. 9, 10) and Reply in Support of its Motion to Intervene (Doc. 13), asserts that the 1998 Contract and its possession of the Property since that time, created an equitable lien on the Property. Doc. 10 at 3; see Doc. 26 at 3. In the alternative, Defendant Davis contends that,

9: WU V TSENG

as evidenced by the 1998 Contract and oral communications between Mr. Tseng and Mr. Davis, Defendant Davis is entitled to the Property as a resulting trust.[4] Doc. 13 at 3-4. In their Motions for Partial Summary Judgment, Plaintiffs and the Kreger Defendants allege that Defendant Davis' claim to the Property is meritless. Plaintiffs and the Kreger Defendants assert that Defendant Davis has no claim to the Property for purposes of this matter, because (1) under Virginia law, an agreement creating an equitable lien must be in writing; (2) the only writing that could create an equitable lien is the 1998 Contract, which fails to sufficiently evidence Mr. Tseng's intent to create an equitable lien on the Property, and thus Defendant Davis has no legal claim to the land; and, (3) even if an equitable lien was created, Defendant Davis failed to comply with Virginia's recording statute, and therefore its claim is junior to Plaintiffs' and the Kreger Defendants' prior recorded interests. Does. 25, 28 at 4.

In its Motion in Opposition to Partial Summary Judgment, Defendant Davis asserts that an oral agreement and equitable lien cannot be recorded; therefore, it did not have to comply with the Commonwealth 474*474 of Virginia's recording statute.[5] Doc. 26 at 4-6; see Doc. 13 at 3-5. Defendant Davis thus concludes that because it was not bound by the recording statute, it was entitled an interest in the Property as of the date of the 1998 Contract, giving it superior claim to the Property. Doc. 26 at 7.

A. Equitable Lien

Defendant Davis asserts that in the 1998 Contract, Mr. Tseng expressed an intention to convey the Property to Defendant Davis; that ¶ 5 of the agreement represents Mr. Tseng's desire that the Property be "converted to entity ownership." Doc. 11 at 3. Defendant Davis further asserts that by "entity" the agreement meant Davis Wetlands Bank, LLC. Id. Thus, Defendant Davis claims an equitable lien was created. Id.

It is settled law in the Commonwealth of Virginia that an equitable lien must be in writing. As explained by the Supreme Court of Virginia:

The doctrine may be stated in its most general form that every express executory agreement in writing, whereby the contracting party sufficiently indicates an intention to make some particular property, real or personal, or fund, therein described and identified, security for a debt or other obligation . . . created an equitable lien upon the property so indicated which is enforceable against the property. . . . Under like circumstances a mere verbal agreement may create a similar lien upon personal property.

9: WU V TSENG

Harnsberger v. Wright, 185 Va. 586, 589, 39 S.E.2d 737 (1946) (emphasis added). This distinction has been recognized repeatedly in both state and federal cases applying Virginia law. See, e.g., Harper v. Harper, 159 Va. 210, 218, 165 S.E. 490 (1932) (same); Brown v. Ford, 120 Va. 233, 245, 91 S.E. 145 (1917) (same); In re James B. Corbitt Co., 20 B.R. 460, 461 (Bankr.E.D.Va.1982)("To establish an equitable lien, Virginia law requires a written contract that shows intent to charge a particular piece of property.")(citing Hoffman v. First Nat'l Bank of Boston, 205 Va. 232, 135 S.E.2d 818 (1964)); 51 Am. Jur.2d Liens § 42 (2000) ("Unless otherwise provided by statute, a lien on personal property that is valid as between the parties and their privies may be created by an oral agreement. However, a written agreement is generally necessary to create an equitable lien on real property by contract."). The only written agreement offered by Defendant Davis to date is the 1998 Contract. The 1998 Contract does not in any manner contain the necessary elements of an equitable lien. In order to 475*475 create such a lien, there must be a clear intent to make a specific piece of property security for an identifiable debt and proof that the "property had actually been set aside and appropriated for this particular purpose. . . ." Hoffman v. First Nat'l Bank of Boston, 205 Va. 232, 237, 135 S.E.2d 818 (1964). The language of the written contract only states that the Property "may" be conveyed to entity ownership. Doc. 11, Ex. A ¶ 5. The 1998 Contract nowhere states when, why, specifically to whom, or upon happening of what event the Property would be transferred. See Doc. 11, Ex. A. Further, because the Property is real property, the existence of Defendant Davis' alleged equitable lien cannot be based on oral agreements beyond the scope of the 1998 Contract. Therefore, Defendant Davis cannot claim the benefit of an equitable lien as a matter of law.

At hearing, Defendant Davis' counsel argued that it had an equitable lien by virtue of its part performance of an oral contract for transfer of land, including that Defendant Davis was in possession of the land, that Defendant Davis provided services pursuant to this oral agreement, and that refusal to transfer interest to Defendant Davis as part performer would operate a fraud. Defendant Davis' thus alleges that his possession of the Property entitles him to the Property. This is not the case.

Defendant Davis relies on two cases, In re Wells, 296 B.R. 728 (Bankr.E.D.Va. 2003), and In re Smith, 348 F.Supp. 1290 (E.D.Va.1972), to support its position that an oral agreement to convey property is removed from the Statute of Frauds by part performance, and that a trustee in bankruptcy (as was the case in Wells) occupies the position of a lien creditor. See Smith, 348 F.Supp. at 1293 ("the trustee in bankruptcy occupies the position of a lien creditor"); Wells, 296 B.R. at 731. Therefore, Defendant Davis's counsel contends that an oral agreement for

9: WU V TSENG

transfer of land where there has been part performance is valid and effective as against lien creditors.

While counsel correctly states the law, he misconstrues its application to the present case. The two cases on which Defendant Davis' counsel so heavily relies are inapplicable to the present case because Smith, which modifies Wells as it applies in the district court context, only applies to those agreements between a debtor and creditor; it does not, and could not logically, apply to third party creditors, because there is no means to put third parties on notice of the oral agreement and the creditor's rights in the subject property. See Smith, 348 F.Supp. at 1293-94; Wells, 296 B.R. at 733 ("the trustee can take title only to the extent that debtors have title"). Further, Smith applies specifically to resulting trusts, Wells to constructive trusts, and neither exists here. See supra IV(C); See Smith, 348 F.Supp. at 1293-94 (noting that Virginia's recording statutes do not apply to resulting trusts); Wells, 296 B.R. at 731 (observing that § 11- 1, the statute that requires transfers of real property to be in writing, would invalidate the constructive trust at issue); Doc. 26 (arguing only for the existence of an equitable lien, and not of a resulting trust or constructive trust). While the Court understands how Defendant Davis' counsel found these cases appealing, a mere reading of the cases reveals them to be inapposite to the facts of the present matter.

B. Virginia's Recording Statute

Defendant Davis asserts that, whether its claim of interest in the land be based on a theory of equitable lien or resulting trust (infra, IV(C)), it was not bound to comply with Virginia's recording statutes, because these statutes do not apply (1) to equitable liens where the grantee is in possession of the property, or (2) to 476*476 resulting trusts or equitable liens grounded in oral agreements. Doc. 26 at 3-4. As discussed above, an equitable lien must be in writing, and no equitable lien was created by the 1998 Contract or any other writing in the Record. See infra, IV(A). Should the Court, however, find that an equitable lien existed or that Defendant Davis is otherwise entitled to the Property, it nevertheless failed to comply with Virginia's recording statutes. Failure to comply with the statutes renders Defendant Davis' claim junior to those of Plaintiffs[6] and the Kreger Defendants.

Record title in the Commonwealth of Virginia is governed by two sections of the Virginia Code: §§ 11-1 and 55-96. These two sections, read together, require that every contract for conveyance of real estate be in writing, and that every contract conveying real estate be recorded. See Va.Code Ann. §§ 11-1 and 55-96.

9: WU V TSENG

1. Section 11-1 of the Virginia Code

Section 11-1 addresses those contracts that are void unless in writing. Specifically, § 11-1 provides:

Every contract, not in writing, made in respect to real estate or goods and chattels in consideration of marriage, or made for the conveyance or sale of real estate, or a term therein of more than five years, and, except as otherwise provided in § 8.2-402 of the Uniform Commercial Code, every bill of sale or contract for the sale of goods and chattels when the possession is allowed to remain with the seller, shall be void, both at law and in equity, as to purchasers for value and without notice and creditors. . . .

Va.Code Ann. § 11-1 (2006). Relevant to the instant matter, this section states that every contract made in the conveyance or sale of real estate that is not in writing is void as to a purchaser for value without notice and creditors (bona fide purchasers/creditors).

Defendant Davis argues that an oral agreement is removed from the recording statutes, because of the mere impossibility of recording something not committed to writing. This neither bears logic, nor the law.[7]

Because the language of the statute specifically refers to "written" contracts, an early line of cases in Virginia — those cited substantially by Defendant Davis in support of its claim — held that the statute had no application to oral contracts for the conveyance of real property, and thus a party to an oral contract could not be affected by a subsequently recorded judgment lien. See Floyd v. Harding, 69 Va. (28 Gratt.) 401 (1877); Doc. 26 at 4 citing Young v. Devries, 72 Va. 304 (1879)(progeny of Floyd). This line of cases later 477*477 came under criticism. As noted by the Supreme Court of Virginia:

The course of [these] decision[s] in Virginia had led to this remarkable result: that on an oral contract for the sale of land under which the purchaser took possession and paid all the purchase money before a creditor of the vendor obtain judgment, the purchaser acquired a good title in equity as against such creditor, while under a written contract and a deed of conveyance, neither of which was recorded, the creditor's right was paramount to that of the purchaser. The purchaser by parol got a good title in spite of the statute of frauds and perjuries, and his title was not effected by the registry law, because he could not have that recorded which was not written, while the purchaser by writing, who complied with the statute of frauds, lost his rights as against a creditor, by failing to comply with a registry law when it was in his power to do so.

9: WU V TSENG

Straley v. Esser, 117 Va. 135, 143, 83 S.E. 1075 (1915)(discussing Floyd v. Harding, supra and its progeny). Notably, this "remarkable result" is the same irrational conclusion that Defendant Davis wishes this Court to reach. See Doc. 26 at 4 (citing Young's holding that "oral agreements were `not held under titles which come under the influence of the registration acts, but under equitable titles which could not be affected by the provisions of those acts.'").

In order to resolve the inequity which resulted from the Floyd and Young line of cases, the Virginia legislature enacted what is now § 11-1 of the Virginia Code. Section 11-1 was intended to remedy the anomaly caused by Floyd and its progeny. See Stein v. Pulaski Furniture Corp., 217 F.Supp. 587, 589-90 (W.D.Va.1963); Page v. Old Dominion Trust Co., 257 F. 402, 403-04 (4th Cir.1919).

Accordingly, § 11-1 expressly addresses, and nullifies, Defendant Davis' contention that conveyances of land could be achieved by oral agreement without need for recording. Because this argument is illogical and, unsubstantiated by the law, the Court rejects it and finds the terms of § 11-1 controlling.

2. Section 55-96 of the Virginia Code

Section 55-96 provides for the contracts that are void as to creditors and purchasers until recorded. This section states:

A. 1. Every (i) such contract in writing, (ii) deed conveying any such estate or term, (iii) deed of gift, or deed of trust, or mortgage conveying real estate or goods and chattels and (iv) such bill of sale, or contract for the sale of goods and chattels, when the possession is allowed to remain with the grantor, shall be void as to all purchasers for valuable consideration without notice not parties thereto and lien creditors, until and except from the time it is duly admitted to record in the county or city wherein the property embraced in such contract, deed or bill of sale may be. . . . The mere possession of real estate shall not, of itself, be notice to purchasers thereof for value of any interest or estate therein of the person in possession.

Va.Code Ann. § 55-96 (1950, as amended)(emphasis added). Essentially, under this section, every contract conveying property shall be void as to all bona fide purchasers or creditors without notice until the deed or written contract conveying the property is duly recorded.

Defendant Davis argues that § 55-96 exempts it from the recording requirement (a similar argument can be made, but is not asserted, for § 11-1), because Davis reads the section to apply only to those grantees of land who are not in posses-

9: WU V TSENG

sion. Doc. 26 at 5-6 (citing "such bill of sale, or 478*478 contract for the sale of goods and chattels, when the possession is allowed to remain with the grantor"); see Va.Code Ann. § 11-1 (2006)(a similar portion of § 11-1 reads "every bill of sale or contract for the sale of goods and chattels when the possession is allowed to remain with the seller"). Defendant Davis suggests that the phrase "when the possession is allowed to remain with the grantor" was meant to modify all four subsections listed before it. Doc. 26 at 5-6. However, this interpretation neither squares with the language of the statute nor its history.

As an initial matter, Defendant Davis' interpretation is expressly contradicted by the history of the statute; specifically, the last sentence of the section, which provides that possession of real estate alone is not sufficient notice of ownership to protect against claims of subsequent purchasers of creditors. That provision was added to change the common law rule that possession by a grantee put a prospective purchaser on notice of the grantee's rights. Norfolk & Portsmouth Traction Co. v. C.B. White & Bros., 113 Va. 102, 105-06, 73 S.E. 467 (1912). The change was intended to protect parties dealing with the grantor by allowing those parties to rely on the land records to determine interests in property rather than to subject them to hidden liens. Id. This change was explained by the Supreme Court of Virginia in Norfolk & Portsmouth Traction Co. v. C.B. White & Bros., 113 Va. 102, 73 S.E. 467 (1912). After highlighting the passage concerning possession in § 2465 (the predecessor to § 55-96), the Court stated:

As will be observed, section 2463 relates to contracts not in writing, while the provisions of sections 2464 and 2465 relate to written instruments. . . . Those sections are the same now as they were when the case of Chapman v. Chapman, 91 Va. 397, 21 S.E. 813, 50 Am.St.Rep. 846 (1895), was decided, except the language italicized in section 2465. . . . That section was amended by adding that language after the decision in the case of Chapman. . . . In that case it was held that a purchaser for value of real property in the possession of another was put upon his inquiry as to the rights of the one in possession, and is affected with knowledge of whatever rights such possessor has, and such knowledge was held to be the same in effect as the notice which is imputed by the registry laws. The object of that amendment of section 2465, as generally understood by the courts and the legal profession, was to abolish the common-law doctrine of Chapman v. Chapman, and to provide that the possession of such estate or term, without notice of other evidence of title in such occupant, should not be notice to such subsequent purchaser for valuable consideration.

Id. at 105-06, 73 S.E. 467 (emphasis added).

9: WU V TSENG

As explained by the Supreme Court of Virginia, the only time when the language concerning possession is relevant is when that possession has been transferred to the grantee. Under those circumstances, the law of Virginia is that mere possession by an alleged grantee, as Defendant Davis claims here, is not sufficient to put bona fide purchasers on notice. See Norfolk & Portsmouth, 113 Va. at 107, 73 S.E. 467 (holding that mere possession by a grantee under an oral agreement is not notice); Kiser v. Clinchfield Coal Corp., 200 Va. 517, 521-22, 106 S.E.2d 601 (1959)(noting the statutory change in the Chapman common-law rule and stating that possession by the grantee "shall not be notice to subsequent purchasers for valuable consideration").

Defendant Davis' interpretation also renders the final sentence of the statute meaningless, in contravention of fundamental canons of statutory analysis. As the Fourth Circuit has noted, it is a 479*479 classic canon of statutory construction that courts must give effect to every provision and word in a statute and avoid any interpretation that may render statutory terms meaningless or superfluous." Discover Bank v. Vaden, 396 F.3d 366, 369 (4th Cir.2005) (internal quotations omitted); Soliman v. Gonzales, 419 F.3d 276, 283 (4th Cir.2005) ("[W]e are `loath' to read one statutory provision so as to render another provision of the same statute superfluous").

Because Defendant Davis' characterization of § 55-96 neither comports with the plain language of the statute, nor with its history, it cannot avail itself of the argument that its possession of the Property did not require it to record its interest in it. The Court finds that the phrase upon which Defendant Davis relies was meant only to modify the terms directly before it — subsection (iv) — and not the list of scenarios that precede it (subsections (I), (ii), and (iii)). Thus, where Defendant Davis does not have a written agreement entitling him to the Property, and because its right to the property was not recorded until default judgment was entered in its favor by the Virginia Beach Circuit Court on February 10, 2006, the Court finds that Defendant Davis does not have an interest in the Property superior to that of Plaintiffs and the Kreger Defendants.

C. Resulting Trust

Defendant Davis alleges that, even if the Court does not find that an equitable lien was created by the 1998 Contract, a resulting trust was created by Mr. Tseng's intention to transfer the Property to Defendant Davis in the 1998 Contract and in oral communications[8] between Mr. Tseng and Mr. Davis. Doc. 13 at 3-4 ("Tseng's state of mind, his intention, to create an equitable lien also served to establish a resulting trust, when Tseng retained title."); see Salyer v.

9: WU V TSENG

Salyer, 216 Va. 521, 525, 219 S.E.2d 889 (1975)("A resulting trust . . . is enforceable in equity and may arise without a writing."). Defendant raised the resulting trust argument in his Reply Memorandum in support of his Motion to Intervene, but has not raised it again in his Motion in Opposition to Partial Summary Judgment. Accordingly, Plaintiffs and the Kreger Defendants assert that by virtue of the lack of argument in its latest motion, Defendant Davis has "abandoned" the resulting trust argument. While the Court cannot be certain that this is the case, there is little support for the accuracy of Defendant Davis' claim.

"A resulting trust is an indirect trust which arises from the intention of the parties, or the nature of the transaction." Tiller v. Owen, 243 Va. 176, 180, 413 S.E.2d 51 (1992). "In order for a resulting trust to arise, the would-be beneficiary must pay for the property, or assume payment of all or part of the purchase money prior to or at the time of purchase, and have legal title conveyed to another without any mention of a trust in the conveyance." Id. citing Leonard v. Counts, 221 Va. 582, 588, 272 S.E.2d 190 (1980). However, "[t]he trust must arise from the original transaction, and at the time it takes place, and at no other time." Morris v. Morris, 248 Va. 590, 594, 449 S.E.2d 816 (1994); see Salyer v. Salyer, 216 Va. 521, 526, 219 S.E.2d 889 (1975)("It is necessary that the beneficiary prior to or at the time of the purchase should pay or assume an obligation to pay the purchase price. It is not enough that subsequent to the purchase he pays or agrees to pay the purchase price.")(internal quotations omitted).

While Defendant Davis does not substantiate its argument with many facts, 480*480 applying Virginia law, Defendant Davis essentially suggests that Mr. Tseng, as "would-be beneficiary" of the trust, paid for the land in 1984 and then conveyed it in 1998 to Defendant Davis without mentioning the trust in the conveyance. See Doc. 13 at 3-4. These facts, however, fail to create a resulting trust. Mr. Tseng purchased the property in 1984 and was the title owner until he conveyed it by Deed of Trust to the Kreger Defendants in 2005; or in the alternative, until the Property became subject to the judgment lien in favor of Plaintiffs on August 17, 2005. Doc. 11, Ex. A ¶ 7; Doc. 1 at ¶ 14, 16 (the Record is unclear). Mr. Tseng did not contract with Mr. Davis until January 15, 1998, and Defendant Davis was not incorporated until August 25, 1998. See Does. 10 ¶ 15; 25, Ex. 7. To create a resulting trust, Defendant Davis would have had to have given Mr. Tseng the purchase money (or services in lieu of payment)[9] at the time the property was purchased; thus, making Mr. Tseng trustee for land paid for and owned by Defendant Davis. This, however, would be impossible under the given facts, because the alleged transfer of land and money as between would-be trustee and beneficiary, did not occur until fourteen (14) years after the Property had been purchased by Mr. Tseng.

9: WU V TSENG

Because a resulting trust must be created at the time of purchase — that is, when money is paid for the benefit of another — there can be no resulting trust here.

V. CONCLUSION

Defendant Davis has failed to meet its burden to withstand summary judgment. It has not alleged any specific facts that show it has a legally-grounded interest in the Property. Specifically, Defendant Davis has been unable to present facts that meet the requirements of the two theories upon which it relies: equitable lien and resulting trust. Further, its attack on the recording statutes is rooted in inapplicable and overruled law. It has made inconsistent arguments that are supported by meager facts. Accordingly, Plaintiffs and the Kreger Defendants have successfully shown, based on the evidence in the Record, that Defendant Davis does not have a cognizable claim before this Court. The Court GRANTS Plaintiff and the Kreger Defendants' Motions for Partial Summary Judgment. Defendant Davis's claims are DISMISSED. Defendant Davis remains a nominal party to this action, however, for purposes of prioritizing creditors' rights in selling the Property to satisfy Mr. Tseng's debts.

It is so ORDERED.

[1] Mr. McBride did not file a brief in either support or opposition to the pending Motion for Partial Summary Judgment.

[2] The only title search on the Record is dated April 8, 2005 and shows Stanley Tseng as the title holder. Doc. 11 at 3, Ex. D. This date is prior to the transfer of the deed of trust to the Kreger Defendants (April 29, 2005), and prior to the default judgment of the Virginia Beach Circuit Court, conveying the Property to Defendant Davis (February 10, 2006). Accordingly, based on the facts before the Court, it can be said only that the last record owner as of April 8, 2005 is Mr. Tseng, and the Plaintiffs recorded their judgment lien on the Property on August 17, 2005.

[3] Davis Wetlands Bank, LLC was allegedly formed on August 25, 1998 by agreement of Mr. Davis and Mr. Tseng. See Docs. 10 ¶ 15; 25, Ex. 7 (printout of State Corporation Commission). Davis Wetlands is a Virginia limited liability company with its principal place of business located in Virginia Beach. Doc 25, Ex. 7.

[4] It appears that Defendant Davis has abandoned this argument. It was raised only in its Rebuttal brief to the Motion to Intervene, and was not mentioned in the Motion in Opposition to Partial Summary Judgment. See Does. 11, 13, 26. At

9: WU V TSENG

hearing, this was not pursued by Defendant Davis' counsel. This matter will nevertheless be discussed by the Court for the sake of thoroughness and clarity.

[5] Defendant Davis' brief is not entirely clear when stating which arguments it is relying upon, and which facts allegedly support these arguments. Defendant Davis appears to state that both its 1998 Contract with Mr. Tseng and later oral communications between these parties created an equitable lien. Doc. 26 at 4 ("Virginia's recording statutes . . . are further inapplicable to void Davis Wetlands Bank's equitable lien because the agreement between Tseng and Douglas Davis, that gave rise to Davis Wetlands Bank's claim of equitable lien, arose, at least in part, from an oral contract."). The confusion may be attributed to Defendant Davis' attempts to bolster weaker arguments with viscerally persuasive, but ultimately spurious, facts. As will be discussed infra, only the written instrument may establish a claim for equitable lien; therefore, Defendant Davis' argument that oral agreements supplement a finding of equitable lien are irrelevant. See infra, IV(A). Oral agreements may support a resulting trust; however, the facts do not show that a resulting trust was created here. See infra, IV(C); Doc. 26 ¶ 4 (the only facts alleged in support of the existence of an oral agreement are contained in Defendant Davis' Motion in Opposition: "Pursuant to an oral contract, Tseng and Davis agreed that, upon Douglas Davis' request, the subject Property could be conveyed into Davis Wetlands Bank.").

[6] Right to title by way of judgment lien, docketed on August 17, 2005. Doc. 25 at 6.

[7] Defendant Davis cites a number of cases in support of this argument; unfortunately, all of them are either inapplicable or are no longer good law. See Doc. 26 4-7. Specifically, Defendant Davis cites: Borst v. Nalle, 69 Va. (28 Gratt.) 423 (1877) (overturned by enactment of § 11-1); Barnes v. American Fertilizer Co., 144 Va. 692, 130 S.E. 902 (1925) (expressly acknowledging that the rule in Floyd and Young is no longer the law of Virginia, but holding that consent decrees are not subject to the recording statutes); Dulany v. Willis, 95 Va. 606, 29 S.E. 324 (1898) (equitable mortgage based upon a clear and unambiguous written agreement may be defeated by a judgment lien); In re Wells, 296 B.R. 728, 731 (Bankr.E.D.Va.2003) (section 11-1 renders the parol agreement void); In re Smith, 348 F.Supp. 1290 (E.D.Va.1972)(resulting trusts are not circumscribed by Virginia's recording statutes). Because Defendant Davis is not asserting a right under a consent decree or equitable mortgage theory, and his argument for resulting trust fails, these cases fail to support its argument. See supra IV(C).

[8] Defendant Davis does not substantiate what these oral agreements entailed.

9: WU V TSENG

Rather, it only alleges that agreements were made in which Mr. Tseng stated his intention to transfer the Property to Defendant Davis. Doc. 24 ¶ 4.

[9] Defendant Davis alleges that a resulting trust was created at the time the 1998 Contract when Mr. Tseng intended to convey the Property to Defendant Davis in exchange for its efforts developing the Property into wetlands. Doc. 13 at 4.

10: FLEET CREDIT V TML BUS SALES

FLEET CREDIT CORPORATION, a Rhode Island Corporation, Plaintiff-Appellee,

v.

TML BUS SALES, INC., Applicant-Appellant.

No. 93-17218.

United States Court of Appeals, Ninth Circuit.

Argued and Submitted May 11, 1995.
Memorandum May 23, 1995.
Order and Opinion September 1, 1995.

Bruce Sherman, Law Office of Kendall M. Squires, San Diego, CA, for appellant.

Thomas E. Shuck, Ivanjack & Lambirth, Los Angeles, CA, for appellee.

Before GOODWIN, POOLE and KLEINFELD, Circuit Judges.

120*120 ORDER

The memorandum decision filed May 23, 1995, is redesignated as an authored opinion by Judge Kleinfeld with modification.

OPINION

KLEINFELD, Circuit Judge:

We decide a question of lien priorities arising out of a bankruptcy and a fraudulent conveyance.

I. Facts.

Berthold owned Taylor Bus Service, which filed chapter 11 bankruptcy. TML Bus Sales secured a judgment for more than $17 million against Berthold personally for embezzlement and conversion of TML's funds. Fleet Credit obtained a default judgment against Berthold personally in the amount of $153,275.89 plus interest.

After the bankruptcy filing, two longtime friends and employees of Berthold's incorporated Victory Enterprises as a Nevada Corporation. Taylor Bus Service emerged from the bankruptcy and received $1.9 million from the bankruptcy trustee. Taylor Bus loaned the $1.9 million to Victory, using falsified dates on documents to hide the true nature of the transaction. The district court found that the promissory note was a falsely dated instrument drafted to "disguise a fraudulent transfer."

10: FLEET CREDIT V TML BUS SALES

Victory deposited the $1.9 million into a Schwab brokerage account. Fleet believed that the money in the Schwab account really belonged to its judgment debtor, Berthold, and filed a lien against the Schwab account on March 30, 1992, in order to satisfy the judgment. Schwab refused to turn the money over to Fleet, because the account was Victory's corporate account.

Fleet then filed this diversity suit in federal court. The court determined that Taylor Bus Service was an alter ego of Berthold, and Taylor Bus's conveyance to Victory was a fraudulent conveyance, so Fleet could reach the money in Victory's Schwab account:

The $1.9 million transfer to Victory was made `[w]ith actual intent to hinder, delay, or defraud' Taylor's and Berthold's creditors. Cal.Civ.Code. § 3439.04(a) * * *

The avoidance of the transfer to Victory effectively `revests' in Taylor the property transferred. * * *

Berthold operated Taylor as an extension of himself. He personally directed the transfer of large sums of money, and did so for reasons that had nothing whatsoever to do with the operation of the corporate entity. Based on all the facts presented to the Court, it is clear beyond cavil that an inequitable result would follow were the Court to permit Berthold to shield himself with Taylor's corporate form.

Meanwhile, TML sued Victory in state court to establish its own rights to the money in the Schwab account. The state court likewise held that Berthold's creditor, TML, could reach the money in what was nominally Victory's Schwab account.

TML filed a notice of lien in Fleet's federal case, claiming a right under California Code of Civil Procedure § 708.410 to all amounts remaining after Fleet satisfied its state court judgment for $153,274.89 plus interest. Fleet moved for attorneys' fees as well, as a priority ahead of TML's lien. The district court held that TML could not secure a lien against Berthold at all, and Fleet was entitled to attorneys' fees.

II. Analysis.

TML appeals the determination that it had no right to a lien under the applicable statute and asks us to find that, if it did have a right to secure a lien, its lien was superior to Fleet's as to the amount of attorneys' fees. We reverse, and hold that

10: FLEET CREDIT V TML BUS SALES

TML did have a lien, behind Fleet's lien for the amount of its earlier judgment, but ahead of Fleet's lien for attorneys' fees.

TML obtained a $17 million, and Fleet a $153,000, judgment against Berthold in state court. Berthold hid $1.9 million in an account at Charles Schwab. His alter ego corporation loaned the money to another corporation in a fraudulent conveyance designed 121*121 to keep the money away from creditors, as established by findings of fact after trial. The Schwab account was in the name of the second corporation, so for Berthold's creditors to get it, they had to penetrate two layers of fraud, the alter ego corporation, and the fraudulent conveyance. Fleet did so, in federal court, and TML established substantially the same thing in state court. The attorneys' fees of Fleet at issue are those Fleet won in the federal court case establishing the fraudulent conveyance and alter ego, not the earlier case establishing Berthold's debt to Fleet of $153,000.

The district court concluded that because Berthold did not obtain a judgment in his favor in the fraudulent conveyance action in federal court in which TML sought to assert its lien, TML could not assert a lien on Berthold's interest. We read the California statute differently, and conclude that TML's motion for an order enforcing his lien should have been granted. We review this question of California law de novo, Ravell v. United States, 22 F.3d 960, 961 n. 1 (9th Cir.1994).

The statute at issue reads:

(a) A judgment creditor who has a money judgment against a judgment debtor who is a party to a pending action or special proceeding may obtain a lien under this article, to the extent required to satisfy the judgment creditor's money judgment, on both of the following: (1) Any cause of action of such judgment debtor for money or property that is the subject of the action or proceeding. (2) The rights of such judgment debtor to money or property under any judgment subsequently procured in the action or proceeding.

Cal.Code Civ.P. § 708.410.

Subsection (2) entitles TML to a lien for the amount of its judgment even though Berthold did not have a cause of action which was the subject of the lawsuit, because the action established that Berthold had an interest in the Schwab account for purposes of awarding his interest to creditors defrauded by his alter ego corporation and fraudulent conveyance. The first subsection lets a judgment creditor take a lien when the judgment debtor sues a third party for money. The second subsection broadens the judgment creditor's rights, so that it can take a

10: FLEET CREDIT V TML BUS SALES

lien where the proceeding establishes that the judgment debtor has an interest in money or property, even though the judgment debtor was not the plaintiff. If there were doubt about this reading, it would be resolved by the legislative history. In the Legislative Committee Comment, immediately following the statute, the section is interpreted as follows:

A lien under this article reaches the judgment debtor's right to money under the judgment in the pending action or proceeding as permitted by former law [referring to the superseded section 688.1]. See Abatti v. Eldridge, 103 Cal.App.3d 484, 163 Cal.Rptr. 82 (1980). The lien also reaches any right of the judgment debtor to property under the judgment.

Cal.Code Civ.P. § 708.410 Legislative Committee Comment — Assembly 1982 Addition (emphasis added).

Fleet urges that the fraudulent conveyance lawsuit did not establish a right in Berthold to anything, because the district court's conclusion of law number 14 in its July 9, 1993, order sets aside the fraudulent transfer to the second corporation only to the extent necessary to satisfy Fleet's claim. The findings of fact, however, establish that the conveyance was fraudulent, and the first corporation an alter ego, without regard to any special circumstances attributable only to Fleet and not to other similarly situated creditors. This is not to say that Berthold could take the money for himself under the judgment. Whether he would be entitled to any excess, or Victory could keep it, would be adjudicated only in the event (an impossibility in the facts of this case) that a surplus remained after satisfying the liens of the creditors defrauded. The findings of fact establish Berthold's right to the Schwab account insofar as his right is subject to claims of creditors defrauded by his alter ego corporation and fraudulent transfer.

Fleet sued under California Code of Civil Procedure § 708.210, which allows a judgment creditor to collect its money by suing a 122*122 third person who has possession or control "of property in which the judgment debtor has an interest...." The district judge correctly analyzed the case when he said "Fleet nevertheless may recover its judgment out of the Schwab One account by establishing that the money in that account belongs to Berthold." (CR 178 at 16) (emphasis added). Abatti, 163 Cal.Rptr. at 85, 163 Cal.Rptr. 82, establishes that a judgment debtor does not have to be a plaintiff in a subsequent suit for its judgment creditor to obtain a lien in that suit. Berthold got a right to funds and under these circumstances, the statute permitted TML to secure a lien under § 708.410.

Fleet argues that even if TML is entitled to a lien, its attorneys' fees obtained in

10: FLEET CREDIT V TML BUS SALES

the fraudulent conveyance suit have priority over TML's lien. TML argues that the court erred in awarding Fleet attorneys' fees at all in the fraudulent conveyance suit. We conclude that TML's lien has priority over Fleet's attorneys' fees, so we need not reach the question of whether the court erred in awarding Fleet attorneys' fees. TML's lien will exhaust the account.

Fleet was a judgment creditor based on its state court judgment for $153,000 with interest on the judgment until paid. The later federal court judgment in the fraudulent conveyance case, not the state court judgment which made Fleet a judgment creditor for $153,000, awarded Fleet the $79,000 in attorneys' fees at issue.

Fleet's lien based on its state court suit arose upon filing, and was for the amount of the judgment in that suit. In re Marriage of Kerr, 185 Cal.App.3d 130, 229 Cal.Rptr. 610, 611 (1986). TML won a money judgment against Berthold in state court in 1989, and filed a notice of lien in this action on July 15, 1993, before Fleet requested an amendment to the July 9 order so it could get fees, and three months before those fees were awarded.

In California, "[o]ther things being equal, different liens upon the same property have priority according to the time of their creation, except in cases of bottomry and respondentia." Cal.Civ.Code § 2897. This first in time, first in right rule controls. Fleet was first in time for $153,000, but TML was first in time for $17 million as against Fleet's subsequent $79,000 lien for its attorneys' fees judgment obtained in the federal fraudulent conveyance action. The lien established when a judgment creditor files a suit under § 708.410, is "a lien for the amount required to satisfy the money judgment...." Cal.Code Civ.P. § 697.010 (emphasis added),[1] unless otherwise stated by statute. There is no statute altering that equation, so Fleet's initial filing only entitled it to a lien for the amount of its money judgment, not its fees. "A lien created by statute is limited in operation and extent by the terms of the statute, and can arise and be enforced only in the event and under the facts provided for in the statute.... The lien cannot be extended by the courts to cases not provided for...." 51 Am.Jur.2d § 38 at 176-77.

No exception to the first in time, first in right rule entitles Fleet to augment its lien by subsequent awards, so the first lien created takes priority. Roseburg Loggers, Inc. v. U.S. Plywood- Champion Papers, Inc., 14 Cal.3d 742, 122 Cal.Rptr. 567, 572-73, 537 P.2d 399, 404-05 (1975). As between TML's lien and Fleet's lien, if any, for the $79,000 in subsequently awarded attorneys' fees, TML's lien is first in time.

10: FLEET CREDIT V TML BUS SALES

Because we find that under California law TML was entitled to a lien and that lien had priority over Fleet's right to obtain attorneys' fees, we do not reach TML's claim that no award of fees was permissible under California Code of Civil Procedure § 708.290.

Fleet has obtained the money from the Schwab account, pursuant to the district court judgment. Our decision entitles TML to all that is left after Fleet's $153,274.89 lien plus interest. TML has requested an award of interest on the money which Fleet obtained in excess of its state court judgment with interest, and which should have been paid to TML, from the time the money was 123*123 distributed to Fleet. Its entitlement is not governed by 28 U.S.C. § 1961, for the time between the distribution to Fleet and entry of the judgment in district court pursuant to this decision, because TML was entitled to a priority with respect to the Schwab account during that period, not a money judgment against Fleet. The district court shall determine whether interest is payable for some or all of the time between the distribution to Fleet and the judgment based on this decision, and in what amount, under the principle stated in the Restatement of Restitution § 156 or other applicable law.

REVERSED.

[1] See also Cal.Code of Civ.P. §§ 697.540(a), 708.410(a), which also allow liens, but only to satisfy the amount of a prior money judgment.

11: IN RE TURNER

In re Stephen Brian TURNER, etc., Debtor. John T. Kendall, Chapter 7 Trustee, Plaintiff,

v.

Susana C. Turner, et al., Defendants. Ah Beng Yeo and E.A. Martini, Plaintiffs,

v.

Stephen Brian Turner, M.D., etc., Defendant.

Bankruptcy No. 02-44874TK. Adversary Nos. 02-7273 AT, 02-7298 AT.

United States Bankruptcy Court, N.D. California.

December 5, 2005.

141*141 142*142 Timothy Carl Aires, Aires Law Group, Newport Beach, CA, for Plaintiffs Ah Beng Yeo and E.A. Martini.

Chris Kuhner, Kornfield, Paul & Nyberg, Oakland, CA, for Plaintiff John T. Kendall.

Drew Henwood, Law Offices of Drew Henwood, San Francisco, CA, Herman A.D. Franck, Law Offices of Herman Franck, Sacramento, CA, for Defendant Susana Turner.

143*143 MEMORANDUM OF DECISION AFTER TRIAL

LESLIE TCHAIKOVSKY, Bankruptcy Judge.

The two above-captioned adversary proceedings were consolidated for trial. The Court conducted a trial on most of the claims asserted on March 8, 9, and 10, 2005.[1] At the conclusion of the trial, the Court took the claims under submission. It deferred rendering a decision pending receipt of the above-captioned debtor's (the "Debtor") tax returns. Pursuant to the Court's direction, the parties filed closing briefs on or about November 7, 2005. Having considered the evidence and argument presented by the parties, the Court finds and concludes as set forth below.

SUMMARY OF FACTS

The Debtor graduated from medical school in or about 1980. The Debtor and Susana Turner ("Susana") were married on February 16, 1981. After five years of post-graduate work, the Debtor began practicing medicine. Some time during the 1980s, a complaint about the Debtor's professional conduct was lodged with the Medical Board of California, Department of Consumer Affairs. Thereafter, the

11: IN RE TURNER

Debtor was placed on probation and permitted to practice medicine only on certain conditions.

In November 1991, the Debtor and Susana acquired title to and began living in a residence located in Alameda County, California (the "Home"). The deed by which they acquired title was recorded shortly thereafter. In 1994, while the Debtor was still practicing medicine on probation, he was convicted of a misdemeanor based on an incident involving a patient. This second incident ultimately led to a license revocation proceeding and to the Debtor's surrender of his medical license. Thereafter, the Debtor supported himself and his family by performing paramedical examinations for insurance companies.

In 1994, the Debtor attended a seminar on "asset protection" given by Robert Matthews ("Matthews"). At the conclusion of the seminar, Matthews referred the Debtor to a tax attorney knowledgeable about "asset protection." The attorney provided the Debtor with a form of document entitled Declaration of Trust (the "GG Trust Declaration") which the Debtor and Susana signed but did not record. The GG Trust Declaration purported to establish a Bahamian Trust and declared that certain of the Debtor's and Susana's assets, including the Home, were held in trust for the Debtor's and Susana's three children.

Beginning in the Spring of 1995, the Debtor engaged in conduct with respect to the plaintiffs Ah Beng Yeo and E.A. Martini (the "Plaintiffs") that was ultimately found by a jury to be tortious. At about the same time, the Debtor met with Matthews in Ventura to discuss the subject of "asset protection." The Debtor showed Matthews a transmutation agreement, purporting to change the character of the Home to Susana's separate property (the "Transmutation Agreement") and the GG Trust Declaration as evidence of what efforts he had made previously to "protect" his assets. Matthews advised the Debtor about some of the disadvantages of holding real property in an offshore trust. They discussed the use of limited liability companies to "protect" assets.

In September 1997, the Plaintiffs filed a lawsuit (the "Tort Action") against the 144*144 Debtor and in August 1998 obtained a money judgment (the "Judgment"). At about the same time, at the Debtor's direction, Matthews created a Nevada limited liability company named Real Investment Capital Holdings LLC ("RICH LLC") and a Nevada corporation named Proset Enterprises, Inc. ("Proset").[2] In publicly filed documents, the GG Trust was identified as the 99 percent owner and Proset was identified as the 1 percent owner of RICH LLC. Alfred Cheung, Susana's brother, a resident of Hong Kong, was identified as Proset's President and Secretary.

11: IN RE TURNER

In March 1998, after the Civil Action was filed but before the Judgment was entered, Susana and the Debtor executed a grant deed (the "1998 Deed"), transferring title to the Home to RICH LLC. The 1998 Deed was recorded in April 1998. On March 16, 1999, approximately seven months after the Judgment was entered, the Debtor, acting on behalf of RICH LLP, executed a deed of trust in favor of Proset (the "Proset Deed of Trust"), encumbering the Home to secure a line of credit. The Proset Deed of Trust was recorded on March 18, 1999.[3] The Debtor is identified in the Proset Deed of Trust as the managing partner of RICH LLC.

In October 1999, the Plaintiffs filed a fraudulent transfer action against the Debtor and Susana.[4] On May 31, 2001, the Plaintiffs obtained a writ of execution and attempted to execute the writ against the Home. In June 2001, the Debtor prepared a dissolution petition for Susana in which she sought to dissolve her marriage to the Debtor. In the petition, the Debtor and Susana stipulated that the Home (which had previously been transferred to RICH LLC) should be "confirmed" as Susana's separate property. A dissolution judgment (the "Dissolution Judgment") was entered in September 2001. Notwithstanding their divorce, the Debtor and Susana both continue to live in the Home and file joint tax returns, identifying themselves as married.

On December 27, 2001, RICH LLC executed a deed, transferring title to the Home to Susana (the "2001 Deed").[5] The 2001 Deed was recorded the same day.[6] 145*145 On September 10, 2002, less than one year after the recordation of the 2001 Deed, the Debtor filed a petition seeking relief under chapter 7 of the Bankruptcy Code, thereby commencing this case.

DISCUSSION

As noted above, the trial addressed claims asserted in two adversary proceedings: (1) A.P. No. 02-7273 AT (the "Fraudulent Transfer Action") and (2) A.P. No. 02-7298 AT (the "Objection to Discharge Action"). The Fraudulent Transfer Action was filed by the Plaintiffs in state court in October 1999. It was removed to this court when the Debtor filed his chapter 7 bankruptcy petition in September 2002. Pursuant to Rule 6009 of the Federal Rules of Bankruptcy Procedure, the Trustee took over the prosecution of this action. The Plaintiffs filed the Objection to Discharge Action in the bankruptcy court after the Debtor filed his chapter 7 bankruptcy petition. They remain the plaintiffs in that action. The Court will address each action in turn.

A. FRAUDULENT TRANSFER ACTION

11: IN RE TURNER

The Fraudulent Transfer Action asserts four claims for relief. The first two claims seek to avoid the various pre-petition transfers of the Home by the Debtor as actually and constructively fraudulent pursuant to bankruptcy and state law. Section 548 of the Bankruptcy Code permits a trustee to avoid a transfer of an interest of the debtor in property that is actually or constructively fraudulent provided it was made within one year of the bankruptcy filing. See 11 U.S.C. § 548.

Section 544(b) of the Bankruptcy Code permits a trustee to avoid a transfer that would have been avoidable by an unsecured creditor under applicable state law provided that there is such a creditor with a claim against the bankruptcy estate. See 11 U.S.C. § 544(b). Section 3439 et seq. of the California Civil Code permits a creditor to avoid the transfer of an "asset" of the debtor that is actually or constructively fraudulent that is made within four years prior to the date the avoidance action is filed. See Cal. Civ.Code §§ 3439.07, 3439.09. "Asset" is defined to include only the unencumbered, nonexempt value of the property transferred. See Cal. Civ.Code § 3439.01(a).

Both bankruptcy law and California law define an actually fraudulent transfer as one made with "actual intent to hinder, delay, or defraud a creditor." See 11 U.S.C. § 548(a)(1)(A); Cal. Civ.Code § 3439.04(a)(1). Both bankruptcy law and California law define a transfer that is constructively fraudulent, in essence, as one for which the debtor does not received reasonably equivalent value and which is made when the debtor is insolvent or which renders the debtor insolvent. See 11 U.S.C. § 548(b); Cal. Civ.Code § 3439.05. In sum, despite their similarities, the right to avoid a fraudulent transfer under the Bankruptcy Code differs from the right to avoid a fraudulent transfer under California law in two significant respects. First, the "reach back" period under the Bankruptcy Code is only one year. The "reach back" period under California law is four years or, in the case of "actual fraud," if later, one year after the transfer could reasonably have been discovered. See Cal. Civ.Code § 3439.09(a). Second, under the Bankruptcy Code, the entire transfer is avoided. Under California law, only the transfer of the "asset" is avoided.

146*146 In the first claim for relief, the Trustee seeks to avoid all of the transfers referred to above as actually fraudulent under both 11 U.S.C. § 548 and Cal. Civ.Code § 3439 et seq. In the second claim for relief, the Trustee seeks to avoid all of the transfers referred to above as constructively fraudulent under both 11 U.S.C. § 548 and Cal. Civ.Code § 3439 et seq. In the third claim for relief, the Trustee seeks a determination that, despite the numerous transfers, the Debtor retained his equitable interest in the Home at the time he filed his bankruptcy petition. Thus, he seeks a determination that the Home is property of the

11: IN RE TURNER

Debtor's bankruptcy estate. In the fourth claim for relief, he seeks turnover of the Home.

The evidence presented at trial persuaded the Court that all of the transfers in question were made with actual intent to hinder, delay, or defraud creditors. Actual intent must generally be established by reference to external circumstances. California fraudulent transfer law has codified some of the types of circumstances commonly found to indicate actual intent to defraud. Several of these "badges of fraud" are present here.[7] The Court was also persuaded that the Debtor received no consideration for any of the transfers and that they rendered the Debtor insolvent.

The Court did not believe the Debtor's and Susana's testimony that the transfer reflected by the Transmutation Agreement was made to restore marital harmony and to give Susana a sense of financial security. It was obvious to the Court that the Debtor exerted complete control over the disposition of the Home both before and after the execution of the Transmutation Agreement. However, the transfer reflected by the Transmutation Agreement is irrelevant because, as noted above, in 1998, Susana transferred her separate property interest in the Home to RICH LLC pursuant to the 1998 Deed. The Debtor obviously considered the GG Trust Declaration as not having effected a transfer because he did not bother to have any document executed by the trustee of the GG Trust, transferring title back to the Debtor and Susana (or to Susana alone) before he and Susana executed the 1998 Deed.

During the pre-trial motion stage of the proceeding, the Court viewed the 1998 Deed as the critical transfer for fraudulent transfer purposes. Because this transfer occurred more than one year before the filing of the Debtor's bankruptcy petition, the Court assumed that the Trustee's remedies were limited to avoidance of the "asset" transferred pursuant to the 1998 Deed. As a result, at the Court's direction, Susana and the Trustee each called appraisers as expert witnesses to testify as to the unencumbered, nonexempt value of the Home at the time of the 1998 transfer.

Susana's appraiser testified that the Home had no "asset" value at that time. The Trustee's appraiser testified that the Home had approximately $7,700 in unencumbered, nonexempt value. Although both appraisers were competent and credible, the Court found the Trustee's appraiser methodology more reasonable. Thus, if the Trustee were forced to rely on California fraudulent transfer avoidance law, the Court would grant the Trustee a judgment avoiding the transfer of the Home to the extent of $7,700. However, based on the testimony at trial and further

11: IN RE TURNER

analysis of the series of transfers persuades the Court 147*147 that the critical transfer is reflected by the 2001 Deed.

The evidence presented persuaded the Court that RICH LLC and Proset were the Debtor's alter egos. The Debtor admitted that these entities were created and their relationship structured to maximize the protection of his assets: i.e., the Home. "Asset protection" is not illegal and is honored by the law if done for a legitimate purpose. For example, an individual may do business through a corporation or limited liability company and will not be held personally liable for the debts of the entity. The assets of the corporation or limited liability company will not be considered the assets of the individual interest holder. However, an entity or series of entities may not be created with no business purpose and personal assets transferred to them with no relationship to any business purpose, simply as a means of shielding them from creditors.

Under such circumstances, the law views the entity as the alter ego of the individual debtor and will disregard it to prevent injustice. Under similar facts, a trial court found that the corporation created by a judgment debtor to hold his assets was the judgment debtor's alter ego. This finding was noted with approval by the Ninth Circuit Court of Appeals. See Fleet Credit Corp. v. TML Bus Sales, Inc., 65 F.3d 119, 120 (9th Cir.1995). In Fleet, the trial court found that Berthold, the judgment debtor, had operated a corporation:

... as an extension of himself. He personally directed the transfer ... and did so for reasons that had nothing whatsoever to do with the operation of the corporate entity.... [I]t is beyond cavil that an inequitable result would follow were the Court to permit Berthold to shield himself with Taylor's corporate form.

Id. at 120.

Moreover, in Fleet, as here, Berthold caused his alter ego corporation to make a further fraudulent transfer. The Court of Appeals noted that: "for Berthold's creditors to get ... [Berthold's assets], they had to penetrate two layers of fraud, the alter ego corporation, and the fraudulent conveyance." Id. at 121. Thus, the fraudulent transfer by the alter ego corporation could be treated as a fraudulent transfer by Berthold. Id. at 121-22.

Thus, the only relevant transfer to be avoided is the transfer reflected by the 2001 Deed: i.e., by the Debtor (through his alter ego, RICH LLC) to Susana. The Court has received no evidence of the value of the "asset" transferred pursuant to the 2001 Deed. However, because this transfer occurred within one year of the bankruptcy filing, there is no need to reopen the evidence for this purpose. The Trustee

11: IN RE TURNER

is entitled to avoid the transfer in its entirety under 11 U.S.C. § 548(a).

The avoidance of this transfer causes the interest in the Home to revert to RICH LLC which, as discussed above, the Court views as the Debtor's alter ego. Because the Debtor and Susana were divorced before the bankruptcy was filed, the avoidance of the transfer reflected by the 2001 Deed causes the entire interest in the Home to reverts to the Debtor as his separate property. Thus, the Home is property of the Debtor's bankruptcy estate in its entirety. As a result, the Trustee is also entitled to a judgment on his fourth claim for relief: i.e., for turnover of the Home pursuant to 11 U.S.C. § 542.

B. DENIAL OF DISCHARGE CLAIM

The Denial of Discharge Action seeks denial of the Debtor's discharge under 148*148 11 U.S.C. § 727(a)(2), (4), and (5). Section 727(a)(2) of the Bankruptcy Code provides, in pertinent part, that an individual chapter 7 debtor may not obtain a discharge if "the debtor, with intent to hinder, delay, or defraud a creditor ... has transferred ... or concealed ... (A) property of the debtor, within one year before the date of the filing of the petition; or (B) property of the estate, after the date of the filing of the petition." The transfer of the Home by RICH LLC to Susana pursuant to the 2001 Deed occurred within one year of the bankruptcy filing. As discussed above, the Court finds and concludes that RICH LLC was the Debtor's alter ego and that the transfer reflected by the 2001 Deed was made with actual intent to hinder, delay, or defraud the Plaintiffs. Thus, the Debtor's discharge should be denied based on 11 U.S.C. § 727(a)(2).

The Debtor's discharge should also be denied under 11 U.S.C. § 727(a)(4). Section 727(a)(4) provides, in pertinent part, that an individual chapter 7 debtor may not obtain a discharge if "the debtor knowingly and fraudulently, in or in connection with the case(A) made a false oath or account...." The Court concludes that the Debtor knowingly and fraudulently made several false oaths on the Debtor's Schedules of Assets and Liabilities (the "Debtor's Schedules") and Statement of Financial Affairs (the "SOFA"). Both documents were signed by the Debtor under penalty of perjury.

First, the Court views as a knowing and false oath the Debtor's omission of any reference to his interest in the Home. Schedule A of the Debtor's Schedule of Assets and Liabilities (the "Debtor's Schedules") asked the Debtor to list any interest in real property and to describe the nature of the interest. The Court was persuaded that, notwithstanding the numerous paper transfers of his interest in the Home, at the time he filed his bankruptcy petition, the Debtor retained an

11: IN RE TURNER

equitable interest in the Home. He failed to list that interest on Schedule A.

In addition, item 10 on the Debtor's SOFA directed him to list any transfers of property other than in the ordinary course of business within one year prior to the bankruptcy filing. As discussed above, the Court views the 2001 Deed as a transfer by the Debtor. The Debtor failed to list this transfer and marked the box indicating that there were no such transfers. The Court views this omission and mark as a knowing and fraudulent false oath.

Second, Schedule B of the Debtor's Schedules, item 12, asked the Debtor to list any interests in incorporated or unincorporated businesses. As discussed above, the Court was persuaded that the Debtor was the equitable owner of RICH LLC and Proset at the time he filed his bankruptcy petition. The Debtor failed to list these interests and instead checked the space in the column indicating that he had no interest in any incorporated or unincorporated business. The Court also views this omission and mark as a knowing and fraudulent false oath.

Third, Schedule I and J required the debtor to list his income and expenses at the time the bankruptcy petition is filed. On Schedule I, the Debtor identified himself as divorced. He listed a monthly income of $5,000 and, on Schedule J, listed expenses of $5,106, the largest item being an alimony payment of $4,657. This was inconsistent with the Debtor's sworn statements in his tax returns for that year in two respects. As noted above, in their tax returns, filed jointly notwithstanding their prior divorce, the Debtor and Susana identified themselves as married. Not surprisingly, they also listed no alimony payment.

149*149 Although the Court believes that the Debtor's and Susana's divorce was effected for fraudulent purposes, they are nonetheless divorced. Thus, the Debtor's false statement under oath concerning his marital status is the one made on his tax returns, not the one made on Schedule I. However, based on the evidence presented, the Court finds and concludes that the Debtor's statement on Schedule J that his monthly expenses included an alimony payment of $4,675 was a knowing and fraudulent false statement. Susana testified credibly that the Debtor did not pay her alimony of $4,675 a month. Instead, he simply gave her money when she asked for it. The Court is persuaded that this false statement, standing alone, warrants denial of the Debtor's discharge.

Finally, 11 U.S.C. § 727(a)(5) of the Bankruptcy Code provides, in pertinent part, that an individual chapter 7 debtor may not obtain a discharge if "the debtor has failed to explain satisfactorily, before determination of denial of discharge ... any loss of assets or deficiency of assets to meet the debtor's liabilities...." The

11: IN RE TURNER

Plaintiffs failed to present sufficient evidence to meet their burden of establishing a claim for denial of the Debtor's discharge under this subsection.

CONCLUSION

With respect to the Fraudulent Transfer Action:

1. With respect to the First Claim for Relief, the Trustee is entitled to a judgment declaring that RICH LLC and Proset were alter egos of the Debtor and avoiding the transfer of the Home to Susana pursuant to the 1998 Deed as an actually fraudulent transfer under 11 U.S.C. § 548(a)(1)(A).

2. Alternatively, with respect to the Second Claim for Relief, the Trustee is entitled to a judgment avoiding the Home to Susana pursuant to the 1998 Deed as a constructively fraudulent transfer under 11 U.S.C. § 548(a)(1)(B).

3. With respect to the Third Claim for Relief, the Trustee is entitled to a judgment declaring that, at the time he filed his bankruptcy petition, the Debtor retained his equitable interest in the Home.

4. With respect to the Fourth Claim for Relief, the Trustee is entitled to a judgment ordering turnover of the Home to the Trustee. With respect to the Denial of Discharge Action:

1. The Plaintiffs are entitled to a judgment denying the Debtor's discharge pursuant to 11 U.S.C. § 727(a)(2) and (4). Their claim for denial of the Debtor's discharge pursuant to 11 U.S.C. § 727(a)(5) will be dismissed with prejudice.

2. The second claim for relief, seeking to except the Plaintiffs' Judgment from the Debtor's discharge, is dismissed as moot.

Counsel for the Trustee is directed to submit a proposed form of judgment in accordance with this decision.

[1] The Court severed the dischargeability claim asserted in A.P. No. 02-7298 AT for a later trial, if necessary.

[2] The Debtor and Matthews continue to maintain a business relationship. Matthews owns a company with an office in Las Vegas that serves as the resident agent for the RICH LLC and Proset, as well as for numerous other companies. In addition, for a small annual payment, the Debtor serves as the "nominee" president for at least six limited liability companies formed by Matthews for other clients who do not wish their names to be listed in a public filing. The public filing does not reveal that the Debtor is not a bona fide officer of the companies.

[3] The Debtor testified at trial that there was never any draw on the line of cred-

11: IN RE TURNER

it. As a result, the Proset Deed of Trust did not secure any debt. Moreover, there was no credible testimony at trial that Proset ever had the ability to answer a draw. No credible evidence was provided that either Proset or the GG Trust, Proset's interest holder, had any assets other than their interest the Home. The Debtor testified vaguely that the GG Trust had held investments which generated income. The Court did not believe him.

[4] After the Debtor filed his bankruptcy petition, this action was removed to the bankruptcy court and was designated A.P. No. 02-7273 AT. Thus, it is one of the two above-captioned adversary proceedings. As fraudulent transfer actions belong to the bankruptcy estate, the Trustee has assumed the prosecution of this proceeding in place of the Plaintiffs. See Fed. R. Bankr.Proc. 6009.

[5] The Court has not been provided with a copy of the 2001 Deed. However, the Court assumes that the Debtor signed the 2001 Deed on behalf of RICH LLC.

[6] The Dissolution Judgment had no legal effect on Susana's interest in the Home. Prior to the entry of the Dissolution Judgment, Susana had transferred her separate property interest in the Home, acquired pursuant to the Transmutation Agreement, to RICH LLC.

[7] For example, all of the transfers were to insiders; the Debtor retained possession and control of the Home after the all of the transfers; the Debtor had been sued before most of the transfers; no consideration was received for the transfers; and the Debtor was rendered insolvent by the transfers. See Cal. Civ.Code § 3439.04(b).

12: ASSOCIATED VENDORS V OAKLAND MEAT

ASSOCIATED VENDORS, INC., Plaintiff and Appellant,

v.

OAKLAND MEAT CO., INC. et al., Defendants and Respondents.

Civ. No. 20302.

California Court of Appeals. First Dist., Div. One.

Dec. 17, 1962.

Robert C. Burnstein and Sandra J. Shapiro for Plaintiff and Appellant.

Connella, Sherburne & Myers and E. Conrad Connella for Defendants and Respondents.

MOLINARI, J.

Appellant, Associated Vendors, Inc., brought this action against respondents Oakland Meat Co., Inc., (hereinafter referred to as Meat Co.) Oakland Meat & Packing Co., (hereinafter referred to as Packing Co.), and several individuals, to collect unpaid rental on property leased by appellant to respondent Packing Co., and to recover the difference between the rental provided in the lease with Packing Co. and the rental now being paid by a new tenant. Appellant alleged that, upon Packing Co.'s default in payment of rent and vacation of the premises, appellant relet the premises to one Frank H. Black, on Packing Co.'s behalf, at a monthly rental which was less than the rental Packing Co. was obligated to pay under the terms of the lease. Appellant sought to impose liability upon the Meat Co. and the individuals on the theory that Packing Co., the lessee under the lease, was the alter ego of the other respondents. Appellant also sought attorney's fees and an injunction against respondents restraining them from selling or otherwise transferring certain obligations incurred by Frank H. Black.

Following a trial on the merits, the court found in favor of appellant as against Packing Co., and in favor of the other defendants to the action. Appellant appeals from the judgment. 828*828

The sole issue on appeal is whether the trial court erred in holding that Packing Co. was not the alter ego of respondents.

Statement of Facts

The appellant, as lessor, leases market space in the Housewives Market in Oakland. In November 1956, one of the appellant's tenants, Clarence Klieman,

12: ASSOCIATED VENDORS V OAKLAND MEAT

went into bankruptcy. The appellant thereupon entered into the negotiations here-inafter set forth for a lease of the premises formerly occupied by Klieman. At the time of said negotiations Meat Co. was an established meat wholesaler. The directors and officers of Meat Co. were Zaharis, Lafayette, White and Frueh. Zaharis was its president and the owner of 26 per cent of its stock. He had been an officer, director and shareholder since it was formed. Lafayette owned 26 per cent of the stock, while White and Frueh owned 24 per cent each. The preliminary negotiations for said lease were held at a meeting in November of 1956.

Allan Schulman, president of the appellant corporation, testified concerning said meeting as follows: that he, in his then capacity as secretary-treasurer of appellant, and Phil Davidson, one of its directors, met with respondents, Zaharis and Lafayette, at the office of Meat Co. to discuss the possible lease to Meat Co. of the meat department premises formerly occupied by Klieman; that Zaharis and Lafayette stated to him that "they" wanted to lease said department in order to recoup certain losses which they had sustained in sales of meat to Klieman; that he (Schulman) stated the rent would be $3,000 for the first month, and $1,500 every month thereafter, for a term of eight years; that he further stated that $4,500 was to be paid in advance, $1,500 thereof being lease security; and that no mention was made of the name of the person who would appear as lessee on the lease. Davidson's testimony regarding this meeting was substantially the same as Schulman's. He testified that at said meeting there was no mention of a lease to anyone other than Meat Co., and that he was of the opinion, then, that Associated Vendors was dealing with Meat Co.

Zaharis testified as follows with reference to the said meeting: That it was held on November 20, 1956, in Davidson's office, and not at that of the Meat Co.; that present, besides himself, were Davidson, Klieman, and Arthur Weikert. (Weikert was General Manager of the market.) That there never was any meeting between Schulman, Davidson, Lafayette 829*829 and himself; that at said meeting he (Zaharis) stated that he was interested in purchasing the fixtures which were being foreclosed, running the retail business, and signing a lease, providing the officers of Meat Co., who were meeting the next day, were interested; that he "was not interested in personal liability" and that he asked Weikert and Davidson if he "could use the name Housewives Meat Company for the new business as a new corporation"; that they said "no, it was too similar to the Housewives Market," and that then he (Zaharis) stated: " 'If you are interested in me signing a lease it will have to be a separate corporation.' " Zaharis testified further as to the terms of the proposed lease. (These were the same as those specified above by Schulman.) Lafayette denied being present at any such meeting.

12: ASSOCIATED VENDORS V OAKLAND MEAT

Klieman testified that such a meeting was held, and that present were the same persons mentioned by Zaharis. Klieman testified further that at this meeting Zaharis stated that "he would have to have a new corporation because he wanted no personal liability on himself" or the Meat Co. Weikert denied being present at the meeting and stated that he did not meet Zaharis until 1959.

The evidence discloses that contemporaneously with these negotiations Zaharis had been in contact with a Mr. Stanley Whitney concerning the acquisition of a corporation known as Town & Country Farms, which was organized for the purpose of developing real estate, had not issued any stock and had never commenced doing any business. Whitney was the attorney for said corporation and pursuant to negotiations with Zaharis undertook to amend the articles and certificate of said corporation by changing its name to Oakland Meat & Packing Company (referred to herein as Packing Co.).

Zaharis testified, further, that the day after the aforesaid meeting, Weikert phoned him for "his answer"; that he told Weikert he "personally was interested in it" and that he "told them that if they wanted me to form a new corporation, sign the lease, that I wanted no personal liability, I would be glad to do it"; that Weikert said he would discuss it with the officials of appellant, and that if they agreed that they would make a lease and bring it to him; that a "day or two after the market was opened" he received another telephone call from Weikert wherein Weikert stated that "the officials of the corporation at the Housewives Market was interested in getting the lease signed because we were operating without 830*830 a lease"; that he replied that he "couldn't sign the lease until the corporation papers were back from Sacramento"; that a similar conversation was had one or two days later; and that the day following the last conversation the papers were obtained. Zaharis also testified that "we were operating for two or three days before there was a lease signed."

Copies of the lease in question had, in the meantime, been prepared by Robert C. Burnstein, attorney for appellant, who forwarded them to Whitney with a letter of transmittal specifically requesting that the lease be signed by an authorized officer of Packing Co. and that the seal of said corporation be impressed upon it. Whitney had continued to act as attorney for Packing Co., and upon the change of name becoming effective, proceeded to make application for a permit to issue stock under the new name. Both copies of the lease were subsequently signed in Whitney's office by Zaharis and White as president and secretary-treasurer, respectively, of Packing Co. and its seal was affixed thereto. Whitney then brought both copies of the lease, together with Packing Co.'s check for $4,500 representing the first month's rent and the security deposit, to the appellant's

12: ASSOCIATED VENDORS V OAKLAND MEAT

premises where they were signed by two officers of the appellant. The said lease designates the appellant as lessor and Packing Co. as lessee, and bears an execution date of December 3, 1956.

Whitney testified that he never represented Meat Co. and did not know of its existence until the time he was engaged to effect the said change of name. After the lease was signed, Whitney negotiated on behalf of Packing Co. for the purchase of certain fixtures from a certain Al Weikert (brother of the Weikert hereinbefore referred to). A conditional sales contract was entered into between said Al Weikert, as seller, and Packing Co., as purchaser. This contract was signed by Zaharis and White in their capacities as officers of Packing Co. Whitney testified that when he delivered the contract to Al Weikert it bore these signatures and Packing Co.'s seal. The terms of said contract provided for a down payment of $1,032.89, and a time balance of $14,787.08.

Pursuant to a permit for the issuance of stock, Zaharis became the sole shareholder of Packing Co. by the acquisition of 80 shares of its stock for which he paid $8,000. A certificate for said stock to Zaharis was issued on April 24, 1957. The officers and directors of Packing Co. were Zaharis, White and Frueh. Zaharis was elected its president. According 831*831 to the testimony of both Zaharis and Lafayette the latter was not in any way affiliated with Packing Co.

Schulman testified, further, that at the time said lease was being negotiated he was familiar with Meat Co.; that it had a good reputation and credit; and that he had not heard that a new company was being organized. He testified that he first heard of Packing Co. in November of 1958, and that prior to that time he did not know that there was a difference between Meat Co. and Packing Co., and that although he knew the lease was in Packing Co.'s name he did not know that this identified an organization separate from Meat Co. He also testified that he never saw a Packing Co. sign on the market premises.

Zaharis' total investment in Packing Co. was the $8,000 which he paid for the corporate stock. He withdrew $6,000 to $7,000 from Meat Co. These were personal funds and not company funds. Of the said sum of $8,000, the sum of $4,500 was used to pay the first month's rent and the lease deposit to appellant, the sum of $1,032.89 was used as a down payment on the fixtures, and the sum of $700 was paid as the first installment under the fixture conditional sale contract. When Packing Co. began business operations it had about $1,500 in cash. It had acquired on credit an opening inventory valued at between $2,000 and 3,000. The monthly rental was $1,500, the installment payment on the fixtures $700, and the weekly payroll was $893.67. The equipment in the shop belonged

12: ASSOCIATED VENDORS V OAKLAND MEAT

to the Trustee in Bankruptcy who permitted Packing Co. to use it pending the bankruptcy sale. The fixtures which were purchased for approximately $16,000 were valued by Zaharis at $60,000 in place, less than $50,000 if not installed. They were subsequently sold for $9,000.

About three months after the commencement of business Packing Co. was in need of funds. The sum of $3,500 was required to purchase the equipment from the trustee. Zaharis loaned $5,000 to the Packing Co. There are no minutes and no vote evidencing the transaction. A year later Zaharis needed the $5,000 for another venture. Packing Co. did not have the money to repay the loan, so a loan of $5,000 was made by Meat Co. to Packing Co. in order to repay Zaharis. This was the only loan ever made by Meat Co. to Packing Co. A chattel mortgage upon Packing Co.'s equity in the fixtures was executed on May 26, 1958, but was not recorded until December 17, 1958. This loan has not been repaid, nor has 832*832 Meat Co. made a demand for its payment. Zaharis did not make any other loans to Packing Co., nor did he pay any of its bills.

During Packing Co.'s business operations, Meat Co. advanced credit to Packing Co. Meat Co., however, was only one of several suppliers who continued to supply on credit. Packing Co.'s purchases amounted to approximately $25,000 per month. From 60 per cent to 70 per cent of such merchandise was procured from suppliers other than Meat Co. No price advantage was given or received by Meat Co. When Packing Co. vacated the leased premises it still owed Meat Co. about $15,000. This debt has not been paid nor have any arrangements been made for repayment. Zaharis testified: that this bill was not paid because the other creditors were paid in preference to Meat Co.; that he had guaranteed all other companies that there was no connection between the two companies; that he did not want to be responsible for owing any creditor any money; that he wanted to take the loss if any should arise; and that he wanted to protect his reputation. Lafayette testified: that Meat Co. did not intend to sue Packing Co. for this indebtedness because Packing Co. has no assets; that a suit would be worthless; and that the obligation would be merely written off. Packing Co. has paid all of its other obligations, bills and all of the rent up to the time it ceased doing business in January 1959.

Zaharis, White and Frueh rendered services to Packing Co. without compensation. They did, however, continue to receive their regular compensation from Meat Co. Zaharis testified that he devoted all of his time to Meat Co., and that his participation in the management of Packing Co. consisted of telephoning the manager of the market two or three times a day. Lafayette acted gratuitously as a business advisor and on occasion examined Packing Co.'s books. Lafayette testi-

12: ASSOCIATED VENDORS V OAKLAND MEAT

fied, however, that he did not do any work on Packing Co.'s books, nor did he sign any of its checks. On occasion Lafayette would pick up the cash from the retail market.

Other than its retail activities in the Housewives Market, Packing Co. did not maintain an office. Its books were kept at the Meat Co.'s address, and its book-keeper worked on Packing Co.'s books at the Meat Co.'s office. Most of Packing Co.'s mail was addressed to the retail premises, but on occasion some of it was addressed to the Meat Co.'s office. 833*833 On one occasion a letter was addressed to Meat Co., "attention Mr. Lafayette," concerning an employee of Packing Co. There was testimony that certain bills were addressed to Meat Co. for items properly concerning Packing Co. The Packing Co. had a separate tele-phone at the retail outlet but did not have a phone at the Meat Co. office. Mail arriving at the Meat Co.'s office would be opened by the same person, a Miss Duarte, whether addressed to Meat Co. or to Packing Co. Miss Duarte acted as bookkeeper for Packing Co. part of the time and for Meat Co. the rest of the time. There was testimony concerning the approval of bills received through the mail at Meat Co.'s office. Because some of the officers acted in an official capaci-ty for both companies the persons who would approve paying the bills were often the same regardless of which company paid the bill. Packing Co.'s bills were mailed from Meat Co.'s office, and all of said company's bills were paid from that office by said bookkeeper. All payments and all disbursements of Packing Co., including rent to appellant, were made upon its own checks and from its own bank accounts.

The licenses and permits permitting Packing Co. to operate a retail meat business bore the name "Oakland Meat Company." These licenses and permits were post-ed in a conspicuous place by the manager. City license notices were sent to "Oakland Meat Company, Housewives Market." The fees, however, were paid for by Packing Co. Zaharis testified that he had not seen the licenses and permits, and that the name "Oakland Meat" was put thereon without his permission. He also stated that this name was an abbreviation of Packing Co.'s name. The union contract covering Packing Co.'s retail employees only showed the name "Oakland Meat" as employer and was signed by Crowell, the manager of the retail depart-ment. Zaharis testified he had never seen a copy of this contract and that it should have shown Packing Co.'s name as the employer. A union representative testified that retail butcher complaints and wage claims were taken up with Lafayette. Separate workmen's compensation and fire policies were carried by Packing Co. in its own name, but the public liability and property damage insur-ance coverage for Packing Co. was added to Meat Co.'s policy. The insurance broker testified that this was done at the suggestion of the insurance company

12: ASSOCIATED VENDORS V OAKLAND MEAT

because the identity of the individuals exposed to liability, with the exception of Lafayette, 834*834 was the same; that it was more expedient to have the coverage with one company, and also that there would be a saving in premiums. On occasion Meat Co.'s automobiles were used by Packing Co. Zaharis stated that this was done as a favor.

Zaharis also testified as to his credit, stating he could get several thousand dollars worth of meat on the signature of an employee in the market. He stated further that the sum of $1,000 to $1,500 together with the cash intake of $25,000 per month was adequate to operate the market for a month. It was his testimony that the market had brought in about $25,000 per month prior to Packing Co. taking over, and that while Packing Co. was operating the retail market it brought in from $6,000 to $7,000 per week. Several wholesalers' representatives testified that credit was extended to Packing Co. because they relied on Zaharis' personal credit and integrity and upon the standing of Meat Co. in the meat industry.

A Mr. Pitcher testified that he sold and serviced equipment at the retail premises from time to time; that he billed Meat Co.; and was never informed that the bill was directed to the wrong company. He testified further that he was told by a butcher at the retail market to deliver the merchandise there, but to send the bill to the Meat Co. Pitcher stated that he didn't know there was any difference between Meat Co. and Packing Co., and that he didn't realize that they were two different companies. He stated further that he did work for both the Meat Co. and Packing Co. and testified that certain invoices for merchandise delivered to and work done at the retail market were paid for by Packing Co. checks.

Other testimony was adduced from several persons who dealt with Packing Co. showing that some confused the names of the two corporations. A Mr. Pariani testified that he charged meat delivered to the retail store to Packing Co. but invoiced it to "Oakland Meat." Pariani, however, testified that he knew of the existence of the two companies; that he dealt with both of them; and that each had a separate account number. Mr. Egland, a representative of Swift & Company, stated that meat delivered to Packing Co. was billed to "Oakland Meat Company," but he also testified Swift sold meat to both companies; that he was aware of the existence of the two companies at the different addresses, and the different nature of the two companies. A Joseph Thelen testified that the records of his company (Lewis & 835*835 McDermott, Inc.) listed the name of "Oakland Meat Co." rather than Oakland Meat & Packing Co., but that it was a result of laxity or brevity, stating: "We knew it wasn't the same company." Thelen testified further that his company dealt with both corporations; that he knew they were separate corporations; and that separate ledger sheets were kept

12: ASSOCIATED VENDORS V OAKLAND MEAT

for each. A Mr. Vignaux of Victor Meat Corporation dealt with both companies and maintained separate accounts, listing each company by its proper name. There was also testimony to the effect that when a Pierce Packing Company billed Meat Co. for Packing Co.'s meat, Meat Co. (through Mr. Frueh) objected to this procedure to Guidoni, the manager of the retail outlet. The record contains further evidence, mostly repetitious, which gives conflicting impressions on the unity or separateness of the two corporations. There was also evidence of billings properly made, and testimony that, irrespective of the manner of billing, the disbursements for Packing Co.'s bills were on Packing Co's checks.

There was also evidence presented that Packing Co. and Meat Co. kept separate bank accounts, separate sets of accounts, made separate disbursements, using checks bearing the individual company name; maintained separate payrolls; that the companies used different fiscal years for tax purposes; that they were represented by different counsel; and that they maintained separate minutes.

The Trial Court's Findings

[1a] There is substantial evidence contained in the record to uphold the findings of the trial court under the time honored rule that on appeal all conflicts in the evidence must be resolved in favor of the respondent, and that all legitimate and reasonable inferences will be indulged in to uphold the findings of the trial court. [2] It is an elementary principle of law that the power of the appellate court begins and ends with a determination as to whether there is any substantial evidence, contradicted or uncontradicted, which will support the conclusion reached by the trial judge. (Thayer v. Pacific Elec. Ry. Co., 55 Cal.2d 430, 438 [11 Cal.Rptr. 560, 360 P.2d 56]; Crawford v. Southern Pacific Co., 3 Cal.2d 427, 429 [45 P.2d 183]; Wade v. Campbell, 200 Cal.App.2d 54, 63 [19 Cal.Rptr. 173].) The appellant, in its briefs, acknowledges that any conflicts in the evidence must be resolved in favor of respondents and therefore states that it 836*836 sets forth only the undisputed testimony in its statement of facts because it feels that this undisputed testimony alone is sufficient to compel reversal of the judgment below. [3] What the appellant overlooks is that this "undisputed testimony" may not be considered to the utter disregard of disputed testimony which favors respondents. The appellant's statement of facts presents a case upon which a trial court might decide to pierce the corporate veil, but looking to all of the facts, which we have narrated above, it is another matter to say that under these facts the corporate veil must be pierced.

[1b] The essence of the trial court's findings is that Packing Co. is a separate and distinct entity from Meat Co.; that it was not organized by any of the respon-

12: ASSOCIATED VENDORS V OAKLAND MEAT

dents; that it has never been the alter ego of any of the respondents or used by them to operate any of their businesses under other than their own names; that there was no confusion between the two corporations and their affairs were conducted separately; that there was no commingling of Packing Co.'s funds with those of Meat Co. or the individual respondents; and that Packing Co. was adequately capitalized in relation to the reasonable requirements of its business and corporate purposes.

The appellant does not attack any specific finding of the trial court but contends not only that the uncontroverted evidence discloses factors which require that the corporate entity be disregarded, but that the two elements of unity of ownership and inequity are so conclusively present as to compel the disregard of such entity. The appellant further asserts that Packing Co. was under-capitalized as a matter of law and that this factor is sufficient in itself to warrant a disregard of the corporate entity. In attempting to sustain its position the appellant relies, generally, upon appellate decisions which have upheld judgments disregarding the corporate entity where the factual situation presented supplied factors which allowed the trial court to arrive at that conclusion.

Did the Trial Court Err in Refusing to Disregard the Corporate Entity?

[4] It is a fundamental rule that "[t]he conditions under which the corporate entity may be disregarded, or the corporation be regarded as the alter ego of the stockholders, 837*837 necessarily vary according to the circumstances in each case inasmuch as the doctrine is essentially an equitable one and for that reason is particularly within the province of the trial court. Only general rules may be laid down for guidance." (Stark v. Coker, 20 Cal.2d 839, 846 [129 P.2d 390]; H.A.S. Loan Service, Inc. v. McColgan, 21 Cal.2d 518, 523 [133 P.2d 391, 145 A.L.R. 349]; Automotriz etc. De California v. Resnick, 47 Cal.2d 792, 796 [306 P.2d 1].) [5] The basic rule stated by our Supreme Court as a guide in the application of this doctrine is as follows: The two requirements are (1) that there be such unity of interest and ownership that the separate personalities of the corporation and the individual no longer exist, and (2) that, if the acts are treated as those of the corporation alone, an inequitable result will follow. (Automotriz etc. De California v. Resnick, supra, 47 Cal.2d 792, 796; Stark v. Coker, supra, 20 Cal.2d 839, 846; Watson v. Commonwealth Ins. Co., 8 Cal.2d 61, 68 [63 P.2d 295]; Minifie v. Rowley, 187 Cal. 481, 487 [202 P. 673].) With respect to the second requirement, it is sufficient that it appear that recognition of the acts as those of a corporation only will produce inequitable results. (Stark v. Coker, supra, p. 846; Watson v. Commonwealth Ins. Co., supra, p. 68.) [6] The general rule is thus stated as follows: " 'Before a corporation's acts and obligations can be legally rec-

12: ASSOCIATED VENDORS V OAKLAND MEAT

ognized as those of a particular person, and vice versa, it must be made to appear that the corporation is not only influenced and governed by that person, but that there is such a unity of interest and ownership that the individuality, or separateness, of such person and corporation has ceased, and that the facts are such that an adherence to the fiction of the separate existence of the corporation would, under the particular circumstances, sanction a fraud or promote injustice.' " (Talbot v. Fresno-Pacific Corp., 181 Cal.App.2d 425, 431 [5 Cal.Rptr. 361]; Temple v. Bodega Bay Fisheries, Inc., 180 Cal.App.2d 279, 283 [4 Cal.Rptr. 300].)

The gist of the cases which have considered the doctrine is that both of these requirements must be found to exist before the corporate existence will be disregarded; that such determination is primarily one for the trial court and is not a question of law; and that the conclusion of the trier of fact will not be disturbed if it be supported by substantial evidence. (See also H.A.S. Loan Service, Inc. v. McColgan, supra, 21 Cal.2d 518, 524; Kasutoff v. Wahlstrom, 196 Cal.App.2d 65, 69 838*838 [16 Cal.Rptr. 207]; Talbot v. Fresno-Pacific Corp., supra, 181 Cal.App.2d 425, 432; Carlesimo v. Schwebel, 87 Cal.App.2d 482, 492 [197 P.2d 167].) [7] It should also be noted that, while the doctrine does not depend on the presence of actual fraud, it is designed to prevent what would be fraud or injustice, if accomplished. Accordingly, bad faith in one form or another is an underlying consideration and will be found in some form or another in those cases wherein the trial court was justified in disregarding the corporate entity. (See Talbot v. Fresno-Pacific Corp., supra, 181 Cal.App.2d 425, 431; Hollywood Cleaning & Pressing Co. v. Hollywood Laundry Service, Inc., 217 Cal. 124, 129 [17 P.2d 709]; Carlesimo v. Schwebel, supra, 87 Cal.App.2d 482, 491; Erkenbrecher v. Grant, 187 Cal. 7 [200 P. 641].)

A review of the cases which have discussed the problem discloses the consideration of a variety of factors which were pertinent to the trial court's determination under the particular circumstances of each case. Among these are the following: Commingling of funds and other assets, failure to segregate funds of the separate entities, and the unauthorized diversion of corporate funds or assets to other than corporate uses (Riddle v. Leuschner, 51 Cal.2d 574 [335 P.2d 107]; Talbot v. Fresno-Pacific Corp., supra, p. 431; Thomson v. L. C. Roney & Co., 112 Cal.App.2d 420 [246 P.2d 1017]; Asamen v. Thompson, 55 Cal.App.2d 661 [131 P.2d 841]; Goldberg v. Engelberg, 34 Cal.App.2d 10 [92 P.2d 935]; Sweet v. Watson's Nursery, 33 Cal.App.2d 699 [92 P.2d 812]); the treatment by an individual of the assets of the corporation as his own (Minton v. Cavaney, 56 Cal.2d 576 [15 Cal.Rptr. 641, 364 P.2d 473]; Thomson v. L. C. Roney & Co., supra; Riddle v. Leuschner, supra); the failure to obtain authority to issue stock or to

12: ASSOCIATED VENDORS V OAKLAND MEAT

subscribe to or issue the same (Automotriz etc. De California v. Resnick, supra, 47 Cal.2d 792; Wheeler v. Superior Mortgage Co., 196 Cal.App.2d 822 [17 Cal.Rptr. 291]; Marr v. Postal Union Life Ins. Co., 40 Cal.App.2d 673 [105 P.2d 649]; Claremont Press Pub. Co. v. Barksdale, 187 Cal.App.2d 813 [10 Cal.Rptr. 214]; Engineering etc. Corp. v. Longridge Inv Co., 153 Cal.App.2d 404 [314 P.2d 563]; Shafford v. Otto Sales Co., Inc., 149 Cal.App.2d 428 [308 P.2d 428]); the holding out by an individual that he is personally liable for the debts of the corporation (Stark v. Coker, supra, 20 Cal.2d 839; Shafford v. Otto Sales Co., Inc., supra); the failure to maintain minutes or adequate corporate records, and the confusion of the records of the separate entities 839*839 (Riddle v. Leuschner, supra, 51 Cal.2d 574; Stark v. Coker, supra; Temple v. Bodega Bay Fisheries, Inc., supra, 180 Cal.App.2d 279; Shafford v. Otto Sales Co., Inc., supra); the identical equitable ownership in the two entities; the identification of the equitable owners thereof with the domination and control of the two entities; identification of the directors and officers of the two entities in the responsible supervision and management; sole ownership of all of the stock in a corporation by one individual or the members of a family (Riddle v. Leuschner, supra; Stark v. Coker, supra; McCombs v. Rudman, 197 Cal.App.2d 46 [17 Cal.Rptr. 351]; Talbot v. Fresno-Pacific Corp., supra, 181 Cal.App.2d 425; Claremont Press Pub. Co. v. Barksdale, supra, 187 Cal.App.2d 813; Thomson v. L. C. Roney Co., supra, 112 Cal.App.2d 420; Asamen v. Thompson, supra, 55 Cal.App.2d 661; Sweet v. Watson's Nursery, supra, 33 Cal.App.2d 699; Goldberg v. Engleberg, supra, 34 Cal.App.2d 10; Gordon v. Aztec Brewing Co., 33 Cal.2d 514 [203 P.2d 522]; Pan Pacific Sash & Door Co. v. Greendale Park, Inc., 166 Cal.App.2d 652 [333 P.2d 802]; Shea v. Leonis, 14 Cal.2d 666 [96 P.2d 332]); the use of the same office or business location; the employment of the same employees and/or attorney (McCombs v. Rudman, supra; Talbot v. Fresno-Pacific Corp., supra; Thomson v. L. C. Roney Co., supra; Pan Pacific Sash & Door Co. v. Greendale Park, Inc., supra); the failure to adequately capitalize a corporation; the total absence of corporate assets, and undercapitalization (Minton v. Cavaney, supra, 56 Cal.2d 576; Automotriz etc. De California v. Resnick, supra, 47 Cal.2d 792; Stark v. Coker, supra, 20 Cal.2d 839; Talbot v. Fresno-Pacific Corp., supra, 181 Cal.App.2d 425; Temple v. Bodega Bay Fisheries, Inc., supra, 180 Cal.App.2d 279; Wheeler v. Superior Mortgage Co., supra, 196 Cal.App.2d 822; Claremont Press Pub. Co. v. Barksdale, supra, 187 Cal.App.2d 813; Engineering etc. Corp. v. Longridge Inv. Co., supra, 153 Cal.App.2d 404; Shafford v. Otto Sales Co., Inc., supra, 149 Cal.App.2d 428; Shea v. Leonis, supra, 14 Cal.2d 666; Pan Pacific Sash & Door Co. v. Greendale Park, Inc., supra, 166 Cal.App.2d 652); the use of a corporation as a mere shell, instrumentality or conduit for a single venture or the business of an individual or another corporation (McCombs v. Rudman, supra, 197

12: ASSOCIATED VENDORS V OAKLAND MEAT

Cal.App.2d 46; Asamen v. Thompson, supra, 55 Cal.App.2d 661; Engineering etc. Corp. v. Longridge Inv. Co., supra; Pan Pacific Sash & Door Co. v. Greendale Park, Inc., supra); the concealment and 840*840 misrepresentation of the identity of the responsible ownership, management and financial interest, or concealment of personal business activities (Riddle v. Leuschner, supra, 51 Cal.2d 574; Shafford v. Otto Sales Co., Inc., supra); the disregard of legal formalities and the failure to maintain arm's length relationships among related entities (Riddle v. Leuschner, supra, 51 Cal.2d 574; McCombs v. Rudman, supra; Wheeler v. Superior Mortgage Co., supra; Pan Pacific Sash & Door Co. v. Greendale Park, Inc., supra); the use of the corporate entity to procure labor, services or merchandise for another person or entity (Temple v. Bodega Bay Fisheries, Inc., supra; Pan Pacific Sash & Door Co. v. Greendale Park, Inc., supra; Engineering etc. Corp. v. Longridge Inv. Co., supra); the diversion of assets from a corporation by or to a stockholder or other person or entity, to the detriment of creditors, or the manipulation of assets and liabilities between entities so as to concentrate the assets in one and the liabilities in another (Riddle v. Leuschner, supra, 51 Cal.2d 574; Thomson v. L. C. Roney Co., supra, 112 Cal.App.2d 420; Sweet v. Watson's Nursery, supra, 33 Cal.App.2d 699; Talbot v. Fresno-Pacific Corp., supra, 181 Cal.App.2d 425); the contracting with another with intent to avoid performance by use of a corporate entity as a shield against personal liability, or the use of a corporation as a subterfuge of illegal transactions (Wheeler v. Superior Mortgage Co., supra, 196 Cal.App.2d 822; Claremont Press Pub. Co. v. Barksdale, supra, 187 Cal.App.2d 813; Shafford v. Otto Sales Co., Inc., supra, 149 Cal.App.2d 428; Asamen v. Thompson, supra, 55 Cal.App.2d 661); and the formation and use of a corporation to transfer to it the existing liability of another person or entity (Shea v. Leonis, supra, 14 Cal.2d 666; Engineering etc. Corp. v. Longridge Inv. Co., supra, 153 Cal.App.2d 404). A perusal of these cases reveals that in all instances several of the factors mentioned were present. It is particularly significant that while it was held, in each instance, that the trial court was warranted in disregarding the corporate entity, the factors considered by it were not deemed to be conclusive upon the trier of fact but were found to be supported by substantial evidence.

In the instant case the presence or absence of any of these factors, as well as the consideration of any other circumstances which would have warranted the trier of fact to disregard the corporate entity, were within the province of the trial court. [1c] There was ample evidence to support the inferences drawn by the lower court that there was not such a 841*841 unity of interest and ownership as between Packing Co. and Meat Co., or as between Packing Co. and the individual respondents, as to destroy the individuality of such corporations and the

12: ASSOCIATED VENDORS V OAKLAND MEAT

owner or owners of their stock. We need not repeat the evidence in detail, but a reiteration of the following facts supports the sufficiency of the trial court's findings, to wit: Zaharis' ownership of 26 per cent of Meat Co.'s stock and his ownership of 100 per cent of Packing Co.'s stock; the ownership by Lafayette of 26 per cent of Meat Co.'s stock and the fact that he was not a director or officer of Packing Co.; the ownership by White and Frueh of 24 per cent of Meat Co.'s stock each and their nonownership of Packing Co.'s stock; the separate incorporation of two corporations at different times; the employment of separate counsel by each corporation and the fact that the attorney for Packing Co. was not the attorney for any of the respondents; the issuance of stock by Packing Co. pursuant to permit and its compliance with the formalities required by the Division of Corporations; the keeping of separate minutes by Packing Co. and its holding of a number of meetings; the maintenance of separate records and bank accounts by Packing Co.; the fact that Packing Co. had its own employees and a separate payroll; the extent of the participation of Zaharis and the other individual respondents in the daily business affairs of Packing Co.; the making of disbursements by Packing Co. through its own checks; the absence of the commingling of funds; the fact that Meat Co. supplied Packing Co. from 30 per cent to 45 per cent of the meat sold by the latter, the remainder coming from other suppliers; the preparation of the lease by appellant's own attorney and the naming of Packing Co. as the lessee therein; and Zaharis' statement that he did not want any personal liability and that he would form a new corporation. Any conflict in the evidence with respect to any of these matters was, of course, for the trier of fact to resolve.

Considerable stress is laid by the appellant upon the claim of undercapitalization and its assertion that such appears in the instant case as a matter of law. Appellant has not cited any case in which an appellate court has held that a business was undercapitalized when the court made a contrary finding. In almost every instance where the trial court has found inadequate capitalization there are other factors present. (See cases above cited with reference to capitalization.) In some cases there were no assets or capitalization at all. [8] Evidence of inadequate capitalization is, at best, merely a factor to be 842*842 considered by the trial court in deciding whether or not to pierce the corporate veil. To be sure, it is an important factor, but no case has been cited, nor have any been found, where it has been held that this factor alone requires invoking the equitable doctrine prayed for in the instant case. In Carlesimo v. Schwebel, supra, 87 Cal.App.2d 482, a total capitalization of $1,221.82 was held not to be insufficient, as a matter of law, to operate a business engaged in the buying and selling of groceries. [9] Furthermore, we have testimony in the instant case, to the effect that the operating capital was adequate; that Packing Co. paid all of its bills for two years

12: ASSOCIATED VENDORS V OAKLAND MEAT

except for the money owed to Meat Co.; that the bills were paid promptly; and that the rent was paid until Packing Co. vacated the premises. There is also testimony by Zaharis that appellant's officer, Davidson, assured him that the capitalization would be adequate. This evidence, if believed by the trial court, would support its finding of adequate capitalization.

The appellant's assertion of inequitable result is predicated upon the argument that the respondents intentionally created a corporation without sufficient assets to meet daily business requirements. The thrust of this argument is the claim of undercapitalization and the contention that a creditor will remain unsatisfied if the corporate veil is not pierced. As we have pointed out above, the prerequisite of "inequitable result" must coexist with the other requirement of unity of interest and ownership, which the trial court has found not to exist in this case. Moreover, we have also indicated that the trial court was justified in its finding of adequate capitalization. [10] Certainly, it is not sufficient to merely show that a creditor will remain unsatisfied if the corporate veil is not pierced, and thus set up such an unhappy circumstance as proof of an "inequitable result." In almost every instance where a plaintiff has attempted to invoke the doctrine he is an unsatisfied creditor. [11] The purpose of the doctrine is not to protect every unsatisfied creditor, but rather to afford him protection, where some conduct amounting to bad faith makes it inequitable, under the applicable rule above cited, for the equitable owner of a corporation to hide behind its corporate veil.

The judgment is affirmed.

Bray, P. J., and Sullivan, J., concurred.

13: BAY PLASTICS V BT COMM.

In re BAY PLASTICS, INC., Debtor. BAY PLASTICS, INC., Plaintiff,

v.

BT COMMERCIAL CORP., et al., Defendants.

and related cross-actions.

Bankruptcy No. LA 90-01884 SB. Adv. No. LA 92-01359-SB.

United States Bankruptcy Court, C.D. California.

September 5, 1995.

316*316 317*317 318*318 319*319 George A. Juarez and Catherine A. Steiner of Pachulski, Stang, Ziehl & Young, P.C., Los Angeles, CA, for debtor.

320*320 Ronnie H. Walker, Orlando, FL, and Earl Hagen, Hagen Hagen & Hagen, Encino, CA, for defendants.

AMENDED MEMORANDUM OF DECISION ON SUMMARY JUDGMENT MOTION

SAMUEL L. BUFFORD, Bankruptcy Judge.

I. INTRODUCTION

The debtor has brought this adversary proceeding against the selling shareholders of a leveraged buyout ("LBO") to recover the funds that they received in the buy-out transaction. While the action was also brought against the bank that financed the transaction, the bank has settled. The Court grants summary judgment to the debtor on the undisputed facts.

The Court holds that the transaction may be avoided as a constructive fraudulent transfer under the California version of the Uniform Fraudulent Transfer Act ("UFTA"), on which the debtor relies pursuant to Bankruptcy Code § 544(b),[1] and that in consequence the debtor is entitled to recover against the selling shareholders. The Court finds that the transaction rendered the debtor insolvent, and that the sellers did not act in good faith.

II. FACTS

The Court finds that the following facts are undisputed. Defendants Bob Younger, Abner Smith and Paul Dodson ("the selling shareholders") formed debtor Bay Plastics, Inc. ("Bay Plastics") in 1979 to manufacture polyvinyl chloride ("PVC") plastic pipe for water well casings and turf irrigation. Bay Plastics filed this bank-

13: BAY PLASTICS V BT COMM.

ruptcy case on January 25, 1990.

A. The Buyout

Because they were nearing retirement, on October 31, 1988 (fifteen months before this bankruptcy filing) the selling shareholders sold their Bay Plastics stock to Milhous Corporation ("Milhous") for $3.5 million in cash plus $1.8 million in deferred payments.[2] Milhous did not acquire the Bay Plastics stock directly. Instead, it caused its subsidiary Nicole Plastics to form its own subsidiary, BPI Acquisition Corp. ("BPI"), to take ownership of the Bay Plastics stock. Formally, the parties to the stock sale transaction were ultimately BPI and the selling shareholders.

The sale was unexceptional. The difficulty lay in the financing of the purchase. Milhous put no money of its own, or even any money that it borrowed, into this transaction. Instead, it caused Bay Plastics to borrow approximately $3.95 million from defendant BT Commercial Corp.[3] ("BT") (a subsidiary of Bankers Trust), and then caused Bay Plastics to direct that $3.5 million of the loan be disbursed to BPI. BPI in turn directed that the $3.5 million be paid directly to the selling shareholders in substantial payment for their stock. Thus, at the closing, $3.5 million of the funds paid into escrow by BT went directly to the selling shareholders.

As security for its $3.95 million loan, BT received a first priority security interest in essentially all of the assets of Bay Plastics. In consequence, BT has received all of the proceeds of debtor's assets in this bankruptcy case, and nothing is left for unsecured or even for administrative creditors.

The financing also provided a revolving credit facility for working capital, in addition to the payment for the LBO, up to a total loan of $7 million.[4] A total of just over $4 million was owing to BT at the time of the bankruptcy filing, according to the debtor's 321*321 schedules. Thus most of the debt (all but approximately $500,000) owing to BT at the time of the filing resulted from the LBO.

The selling shareholders were not in the dark about the financing. On October 25, 1988 they and their attorney met with Milhous representatives in Los Angeles to finalize the deal. While the Milhous representatives provided rather little information about the Milhous finances, they did disclose the details of the BT secured loan to Bay Plastics to finance the stock purchase. In addition, the selling shareholders received a projected post-transaction balance sheet, which showed a balance of $250,000 in equity only because of the addition to the asset side of the ledger the sum of $2,259,270 in goodwill. Both the selling shareholders and their

13: BAY PLASTICS V BT COMM.

attorney were experienced in LBOs, and the selling shareholders discussed this feature of the transaction, and their exposure on a fraudulent transfer claim, with their attorney on that date. With this information in hand, Younger, Smith and Dodson approved the terms of the sale.

In contrast to the selling shareholders, the industry did not know about the LBO character of the transaction until a number of months later. Shintech Corp., a creditor at the time of the transaction (and continuously thereafter), did not learn of it until ten months later, in August, 1989.

B. The Shintech Debt

Some three months before the LBO, on July 22, 1988, Bay Plastics entered into a requirements contract with Shintech to supply PVC resin. Shintech agreed under the contract to supply up to 2.6 million pounds of PVC resin per month on payment terms of 30 days after shipment. To induce Shintech to enter into this contract, Bay Plastics granted Shintech a security interest in all its assets, and the shareholders gave personal guaranties. This arrangement stood in the way of the BT transaction.

In consequence, the selling shareholders, their attorney, and Milhous representatives met with Shintech in late October, 1988 (after Milhous had disclosed to the selling shareholders the terms of the LBO), to arrange a new deal with Shintech. The parties to the LBO persuaded Shintech of Milhous' good credit, and induced Shintech to release both its security interest and the guaranties.[5] However, they did not disclose the LBO character of the transaction, and Shintech did not learn of this until ten months later.

The impact of this transaction on the balance sheet of Bay Plastics was dramatic. Immediately after the transaction, its balance sheet showed tangible assets of approximately $7 million, and liabilities of approximately $9 million. Only the addition of almost $2.26 million in goodwill, which had not appeared on prior balance sheets, and for which no explanation has been provided, permitted the balance sheet to show a modest shareholder equity of $250,000. But for the newly discovered goodwill, there would have been a net deficiency of some $2 million. In contrast, immediately before the transaction Bay Plastics had assets of $6.7 million and liabilities of $5.6 million, and a net equity of $1.1 million.

Bay Plastics was unable to service this overload of debt, and filed its bankruptcy petition fifteen months later. According to the debtor's schedules, at the time of filing its two principal creditors were BT and Shintech: it owed approximately $4 million in secured debt to BT, and $3.5 million in unsecured debt to Shintech. No

13: BAY PLASTICS V BT COMM.

other creditor was owed more than $20,000.

III. DISCUSSION

The Bankruptcy Code gives a trustee the power to avoid a variety of kinds of prepetition transactions. Such transactions include preferential payments to creditors (§ 547), fraudulent transfers (§ 548), the fixing of statutory liens (§ 545), and setoffs (§ 553). A debtor in possession in a chapter 11 case has all of the rights (except the right to compensation) and the powers of a trustee under chapter 11. This includes the right to 322*322 exercise the avoiding powers. Bankruptcy Code § 1107(a).[6]

However, the debtor is unable to use the fraudulent transfer provision of the Bankruptcy Code (§ 548) in this case, because it is only applicable to transfers made or obligations incurred on or within one year before the date of the filing of the petition. 11 U.S.C.A. § 548(a) (West 1993). Where state law provides a similar avoiding power to a creditor, on the other hand, Bankruptcy Code § 544(b)[7] permits a trustee (or a debtor in possession) to stand in the shoes of the creditor and to assert the same cause of action. Kupetz v. Wolf, 845 F.2d 842, 845 (9th Cir.1988). Trustees and debtors in possession routinely utilize this provision to make fraudulent transfer claims under applicable state law, which typically provides a statute of limitations of four to seven years. See, e.g., Cal.Civ.Code § 3439.09 (West Supp. 1995). Thus the debtor has brought this adversary proceeding under § 544(b) and the UFTA as adopted in California.

A. Fraudulent Transfer Law

The purpose of fraudulent transfer law is to prevent a debtor from transferring away valuable assets in exchange for less than adequate value, if the transfer leaves insufficient assets to compensate honest creditors. See 4 Collier on Bankruptcy ¶ 548.01 at 548-4 through 548-24 (Lawrence P. King ed., 15th ed. 1995); Pajaro Dunes Rental Agency v. Spitters (In re Pajaro Dunes Rental Agency), 174 B.R. 557, 571 (Bankr.N.D.Cal.1994).

Modern fraudulent transfer law traces its origins to a statute of Elizabeth enacted in 1570. See 13 Eliz., ch. 5 (1570).[8] This statute provided that a conveyance made "to the End, Purpose and Intent to delay, hinder or defraud creditors" is voidable. Id., § 1. Courts often relied on circumstantial "badges of fraud" to presume fraudulent intent. See, e.g., Twyne's Case, 76 Eng.Rep. 809, 810-14 (1601). The English law of fraudulent conveyance passed into the common law in the United States. This law was revised and codified by the National Conference of Commissioners on Uniform State Laws ("NCCUSL") in 1918, when it promul-

13: BAY PLASTICS V BT COMM.

gated the Uniform Fraudulent Conveyance Act ("UFCA"). 7A U.L.A. 427, 428 (1985). The UFCA was adopted by California in 1939, and by a number of other states on various dates.

The NCCUSL rewrote the UFCA and promulgated it as the UFTA in 1984. Id., at 639. California adopted its version of the UFTA, which is applicable in this case, in 1986. See Cal.Civ.Code §§ 3439-3439.12 (West Supp.1995) (applicable to transfers made after January 1, 1987). Bankruptcy Code § 548 contains a similar fraudulent transfer provision.[9] See 11 U.S.C.A. § 548 (West 1993).

1. The Species of Fraudulent Transfer

A transfer or conveyance is fraudulent if it is (1) an intentional fraudulent transfer, i.e., a transfer made with the intent to defeat, hinder or delay creditors; or (2) a transfer that is constructively fraudulent because the debtor is in financial distress. There are three kinds of financial distress that make a transaction a fraudulent transfer: 323*323 (a) a transfer while a debtor is insolvent or that renders a debtor insolvent; (b) a transfer that leaves a debtor undercapitalized or nearly insolvent (i.e., with insufficient assets to carry on its business); (c) a transfer when the debtor intends to incur debts beyond its ability to pay. See UFTA §§ 4, 5; UFCA § 4; Bankruptcy Code § 548(a). Constructive fraudulent transfer law applies without regard to intent (except the intent to incur debts in the last alternative). See, e.g., Moody v. Security Pacific Business Credit, Inc., 971 F.2d 1056, 1063 (3d Cir.1992) (construing the UFCA).

In this adversary proceeding the debtor relies on the first two varieties of constructive fraudulent transfer, and is entitled to prevail if either cause of action is upheld. The Court addresses only the first (a transfer that renders the debtor insolvent), because it finds that the debtor is entitled to prevail on this cause of action.

2. Fraudulent Transfer Resulting in Insolvency

The UFTA, adopted in California effective for transactions after January 1, 1987, provides in relevant part:

A transfer made or obligation incurred by a debtor is fraudulent as to a creditor whose claim arose before the transfer was made or the obligation was incurred if the debtor made the transfer or incurred the obligation without receiving a reasonably equivalent value in exchange for the transfer or obligation and the debtor was insolvent at the time or the debtor became insolvent as a result of the transfer or obligation.

13: BAY PLASTICS V BT COMM.

Cal.Civ.Code § 3439.05 (West Supp.1995).[10]

3. Application of Fraudulent Transfer Law to LBOs

a. General

The basic structure of an LBO involves a transfer of corporate ownership financed primarily by the assets of the corporation itself.[11] Typically the corporation borrows the funds, secured by the assets of the corporation, and advances them to the purchasers, who use the funds to pay the purchase price to the selling shareholders. Kathryn V. Smyser, Going Private and Going Under: Leveraged Buyouts and the Fraudulent Conveyance Problem, 63 Ind.L.J. 781, 784-85 (1988). LBOs have two essential features:

First, the purchaser acquires the funds necessary for the acquisition through borrowings secured directly or indirectly by the assets of the company being acquired. Second, the lender who provides such funds is looking primarily to the future operating earnings of the acquired company and/or to the proceeds from future sales of assets of the company, rather than to any other assets of the purchasers, to repay the borrowings used to effect the acquisition.

Id., at 785. LBO investors thus generally consider cash flow, the money available for working capital and debt service, as the most important factor in assessing a potential buyout candidate. Id., at 785 n. 12.

The application of fraudulent transfer law to LBOs has generated considerable debate among courts and commentators.[12] LBOs 324*324 were a popular form of consensual corporate takeover in the 1980's. They fell into disuse at the end of that decade for economic reasons. However, the use of the LBO as an acquisition device has recently become popular again. See Laura Jereski, `Recaps' Are Secret Fuel for Leveraged Buyouts, Wall St.J., July 25, 1995, at C1.

The LBO dates back long before the 1980's. In earlier years, it was known as a "bootstrap acquisition." Some of these transactions were invalidated as fraudulent conveyances. See Steph v. Branch, 255 F.Supp. 526 (E.D.Okla.), aff'd, 389 F.2d 233 (10th Cir.1968); In re Process Manz Press, 236 F.Supp. 333 (N.D.Ill.1964), rev'd on juris. grounds 369 F.2d 513 (7th Cir.1966), cert. denied, 386 U.S. 957, 87 S.Ct. 1022, 18 L.Ed.2d 104 (1967); Diller v. Irving Trust Co. (In re College Chemists, Inc.), 62 F.2d 1058 (2d Cir.1933); Smyser, supra note 12, at 788 & n. 21.

b. Ninth Circuit Case Law

13: BAY PLASTICS V BT COMM.

The Ninth Circuit has had difficulties with the application of fraudulent transfer law to LBOs.[13] The Ninth Circuit case law is found in two opinions, Lippi v. City Bank, 955 F.2d 599 (9th Cir.1992), which arose under Hawaii common law, and Kupetz v. Wolf, 845 F.2d 842 (9th Cir.1988), which arose under the California version of the UFCA. The applicability of these precedents is complicated by the fact that each was based on a statute different from the California version of the UFTA involved in this case.

i. Lippi

Lippi involved the bankruptcy of Pacific Industrial Distributors, Inc. ("PID"), which originally was owned by three shareholders. At a time when the balance sheet showed that the stockholders' equity was $195,450, one of the shareholders bought out the other two for $500,000. Half of the financing was unexceptional: (1) the purchasing shareholder personally paid only $12,500 of the purchase price; (2) he, his holding corporation and his family borrowed $137,500 on an unsecured basis; (3) the selling shareholders financed $100,000, secured by a security interest in the stock.

The remaining half of the financing created the problem. In substance the remaining $250,000 of the financing came from a Small Business Administration loan (through City Bank) to PID, which was secured by a security interest in all of PID's assets. PID upstreamed the funds to theholding company to pay to the selling shareholders.

Although PID was directly liable for only $250,000 of the funds used to buy out the selling shareholders, in fact it paid out $667,000 in payments to City Bank and in dividends to the holding company to repay the entire purchase price (including the $12,500 paid by the purchasing shareholder). While all of the creditors who had lent money for the buyout had been paid in full, PID was left with unsecured debts of $485,000 at the time that the involuntary bankruptcy case was filed more than three years later.

Subsequent creditors challenged the LBO in Lippi pursuant to the Hawaiian common law of fraudulent conveyance,[14] which permitted subsequent creditors to attack a conveyance (a) that was made with intent to defraud creditors, (b) that was secret or concealed, or 325*325 (c) that was made with the intent to engage in a new or hazardous business, the risk of which would be placed on subsequent creditors. Lippi, at 607, citing Metzger v. Lalakea, 32 Haw. 706 (1933).

The defendants challenged the standing of the trustee, who represented only post-transaction creditors, to bring the action against them, on the grounds that they

13: BAY PLASTICS V BT COMM.

had no intent to defraud existing or future creditors of PID. The Ninth Circuit had "no quarrel" with the district court's limitation of the right of future creditors to challenge an LBO to cases where there was an actual intent to defraud or to conceal the transaction from public scrutiny. Lippi, at 606. The court found this consistent with Hawaii law, even though it omitted the third ground for attacking a fraudulent transfer, that the debtor intended to engage in a new and hazardous business, the risk of which would be placed on subsequent creditors.

The circuit court found that the district court erred, however, in making a defendant-bydefendant analysis of intent. The circuit court held that this determination must be based on the nature of the transaction:

Thus, the issue is whether future creditors were somehow precluded by actual fraud or concealment from discovering the nature of the transaction and the company's financial status at the time of their advances. Whether every defendant or transferee is in on the fraud or concealment is irrelevant.

Id. at 607 (emphasis in original). Because the trial court had found a triable issue of fact as to the intent of the purchasing shareholder, the circuit court found that summary judgment on standing as to the remaining defendants was improper.

In Lippi the circuit court also reversed the trial court's finding that the selling shareholders were within the safe harbor of Bankruptcy Code § 550(b)(1),[15] and thus entitled to keep the funds that they had received. Section 550(b)(1) protects third parties who receive transfers from the initial transferee of a fraudulent transfer.[16] The shareholders in Lippi contended that they were "immediate transferees" of the "initial transferee", the holding company established by the purchasing shareholder, and thus eligible to invoke the protection of the safe harbor provision.

The circuit court found that the selling shareholders in Lippi were not in substance initial transferees of the funds. It found that the funds were not transferred to the holding company "for the benefit" of these shareholders, as provided in § 550(a), because the funds were not passed on to them immediately. Id. at 611, citing In re Bullion Reserve of North America, 922 F.2d 544, 548-49 (9th Cir.1991). The court also found that the holding company did not act merely as a conduit, because it exercised full dominion and control over the dividends that it received before passing them on.

However, the circuit court found that the Lippi defendants had not shown that they satisfied the "good faith" requirement for the § 550(b)(1) safe harbor, and reversed and remanded on these grounds. The court held that, if the selling share-

13: BAY PLASTICS V BT COMM.

holders did not receive their transfers in good faith in an "above board" transaction, the transaction 326*326 may be collapsed and they may be treated as initial transferees ineligible for the safe harbor. Id., at 611-12; accord, United States v. Tabor Court Realty Corp., 803 F.2d 1288, 1302-03 (3d Cir.1986), cert. denied, 483 U.S. 1005, 107 S.Ct. 3229, 97 L.Ed.2d 735 (1987); Wieboldt Stores, Inc. v. Schottenstein, 94 B.R. 488, 500 (N.D.Ill.1988). This inquiry involves a consideration of the knowledge and intent of the selling shareholders, which must be undertaken on a case by case basis. Lippi, at 611-12.

The circuit court in Lippi found no direct evidence that the selling shareholders knew of any intent to defraud the debtor, knew that the buyout was leveraged, knew that the debtor was the borrower on the loan or were aware that they were to be paid from any source other than surplus of the debtor. Id. at 613. However, it found that they knew or should have known that the debtor was undercapitalized, that other entities controlled by the purchasing shareholder were in arrearage in payments to the debtor, that the debtor could legally only purchase its shares out of surplus, and that there was insufficient surplus to pay the purchase price. Id. It also found that the trial court had given inadequate consideration to what the selling shareholders should have known as corporate directors and officers who owed fiduciary duties to the corporation. Id.[17]

The court in Lippi found that it should respect the formal structure of the transaction only where it appeared to be a straight sale, in the eyes of the defendants. Id. at 612. On the other hand, if the selling shareholders either knew or should have known that the transaction would deplete the assets of the company, the court should collapse the interrelated transactions and look to the substance rather than the form. Id., citing Tabor Court Realty, 803 F.2d at 1302-03, and Wieboldt Stores, 94 B.R. at 500.

In Lippi the Ninth Circuit found conflicting evidence on whether the selling shareholders had knowledge of or reason to know of the leveraged character of the transaction. For this reason it reversed the summary judgment in favor of the selling shareholders. Lippi, at 613-14. The court let summary judgment stand, however, as to other defendants who undisputedly had no knowledge of or reason to know of the LBO feature of the transaction.

ii. Kupetz

Kupetz was a lawsuit by the trustee against the prior owners of Wolf & Vine, Inc., a corporation whose new shareholder had purchased the stock in an LBO. The purchaser formed a holding company to acquire the stock, partially in cash

13: BAY PLASTICS V BT COMM.

and partially with payments secured by letters of credit issued by Continental Illinois National Bank. The letters of credit in turn were secured by the assets of Wolf & Vine (as well as other assets). However, the selling shareholders did not know of the LBO character of the sale.

Because there were no pre-sale creditors in the ensuing corporate bankruptcy case, the trustee challenged the transaction as a constructive fraudulent transfer under § 5 of the UFCA, which provides:

Every conveyance made without fair consideration when the person making it is engaged or is about to engage in a business or transaction for which the property remaining in his hands after the conveyance is an unreasonably small capital, is fraudulent as to creditors and as to other persons who become creditors during the continuance of such business or transaction without regard to his actual intent.

California Civil Code § 3439.05 (repealed 1986). The trial court was particularly troubled by the application of constructive fraudulent conveyance law to this transaction for several reasons: there were no remaining pre-transaction creditors, the business was prosperous at the time of the sale, the purchaser was wealthy and well-connected with a major financial institution, and the sellers had no knowledge of the LBO feature of the transaction. Kupetz v. Continental Illinois National Bank & Trust Co., 77 B.R. 754, 760 (C.D.Cal.1987), aff'd, 845 F.2d 842 (9th Cir. 1989). In consequence, the trial court held 327*327 that § 5 could not be extended to the facts of this case.

The Ninth Circuit affirmed.[18] However, its reasoning is difficult to understand, and has been strongly criticized. See David R. Weinstein, From Kupetz to Lippi and Beyond: LBOs in the Ninth Circuit — Now What?, 21 Cal.Bankr.J. 169 (1993). In Lippi, however, the Ninth Circuit gave its authoritative interpretation of Kupetz, and mostly clarified the analytic difficulties.

In this interpretation, Kupetz established two propositions. First, subsequent creditors (and a bankruptcy trustee standing in the shoes of subsequent creditors) lack standing to challenge an LBO if it has been widely publicized at the time, absent actual intent to defraud. Lippi, 955 F.2d at 606-07. Second, an LBO transaction should not be collapsed for the benefit of subsequent creditors to deny the selling shareholders the safe harbor of § 550(b)(1) if the following four factors are present: (a) there is no evidence that the selling shareholders intended to defraud creditors; (b) the selling shareholders did not know that the purchaser intended to finance the purchase through an LBO; (c) there were no pre-transaction creditors;

13: BAY PLASTICS V BT COMM.

(d) the form of the transaction reflects a sale to an entity other than the issuer of the stock.[19] Id., at 612, quoting Kupetz, 845 F.2d at 847-48.

iii. Richmond Produce

There is one reported LBO case in the Ninth Circuit after Lippi, Kendall v. Sorani (In re Richmond Produce Co.), 151 B.R. 1012 (Bankr.N.D.Cal.1993), a decision by Judge Leslie Tchaikowski in the Northern District of California. The trustee prevailed in an attack on the LBO as a fraudulent transfer under Bankruptcy Code § 548,[20] the Bankruptcy Code analogue to UFTA § 4.

In Richmond Produce, Mechanics Bank lent $1.5 million to the debtor corporation, and took a security interest in all of its assets. The debtor used these funds to purchase a certificate of deposit at Bank of California ("BanCal"), which had issued a $1.5 million standby letter of credit as security for a portion of the purchase price of shares bought by the new shareholders. The certificate of deposit was used to secure the letter of credit. When the debtor eventually defaulted in paying property taxes, which was a default under the security agreement for the unpaid purchase price for the shares of stock, the selling shareholders called the letter of credit, and BanCal enforced its security interest in the certificate of deposit. In consequence, the selling shareholders and BanCal were paid. The trustee in Richmond Produce sued BanCal for the proceeds of the certificate of deposit.

In determining solvency, the court held that goodwill must be disregarded, even though it was calculated in a manner consistent with generally accepted accounting principles, because it could not be sold to satisfy creditors' claims. Id., at 1019. In addition, the court found extremely persuasive the fact that goodwill and organization expenses must be disregarded in a solvency determination for the purpose of determining whether a corporation may make a shareholder distribution. California Corporations Code § 500(b)(1) (West Supp.1995). After this adjustment, the court found that the LBO rendered the debtor insolvent.

The court found that BanCal was a second level transferee (immediate transferee of the initial transferee), and thus could assert a § 550(b)(1) defense. This required that the bank show that it gave value for the transfer, 328*328 in good faith, and without knowledge of the voidability of the transaction. The court found that BanCal gave value in good faith. However, the court found that BanCal knew sufficient suspicious facts to obligate it to inquire into the source of the funds that were used to purchase the certificate of deposit. This inquiry requirement defeated its § 550(b)(1) defense.

13: BAY PLASTICS V BT COMM.

B. Trustee's Prima Facie Case

After having explored the applicable statutes and governing case law, the Court is now in position to apply this law to the facts of the instant case.

The Court notes at the outset that this case is not determined by the Ninth Circuit case law as set forth in the Lippi and Kupetz cases. Those cases both involved a fraudulent transfer attack on behalf of subsequent creditors. This case, in contrast, is brought for the principal benefit of a creditor existing at the time of the transaction, which holds more than 99% of the outstanding unsecured debt.

We begin with the elements of the cause of action under the UFTA § 5, as adopted in California, for a constructive fraudulent transfer rendering the debtor insolvent. The elements of a cause of action under this statute are as follows: the debtor (1) made a transfer or incurred an obligation, (2) without receiving a reasonably equivalent value in exchange,[21] (3) which rendered the debtor insolvent (or the debtor was already insolvent),[22] and (4) which is attacked by a pretransaction creditor.

1. Transfer or Obligation

The selling shareholders do not dispute that, in making the BT loan, the debtor made a transfer or incurred an obligation. In fact, the debtor did both. The debtor undertook the $3.95 million obligation to BT, it transferred a security interest in essentially all of its assets to BT, and it transferred $3.5 million ultimately to the selling shareholders. Thus the first element of the cause of action is satisfied.

2. Lack of Reasonably Equivalent Value

The selling shareholders likewise do not contest whether the debtor received reasonably equivalent value for the BT loan. However, this element is not apparent on its face.

Nominally, BT's transaction was only with Bay Plastics. It lent the $3.95 million to the debtor, the debtor promised to repay the loan, and the debtor gave a first priority security interest in essentially all of its assets to secure the repayment. If this were the transaction, creditors likely would have no grounds for complaint, and it would not be vulnerable to fraudulent transfer attack.

However, the foregoing structure obscures the reality of the transaction. The selling 329*329 shareholders' transaction was formally with Milhous, and eventually with BPI, the new owner of Bay Plastics. BPI purchased their stock, and arranged

13: BAY PLASTICS V BT COMM.

for their payment with funds that Bay Plastics borrowed from BT. Before Bay Plastics received the funds, it directed that $3.5 million be transferred to its incoming parent, BPI, and BPI in turn directed that the funds be paid out for the stock purchase. Thus in substance $3.5 million of the funds that Bay Plastics borrowed from BT went to pay for the stock of the selling shareholders, rather than to Bay Plastics.

This raises the question whether the Court should collapse the various transactions in this case into one integrated transaction. Under Lippi this turns on whether, from the perspective of the selling shareholders, the transaction appeared to be a straight sale without an LBO. Lippi, 955 F.2d at 612. If, in contrast, there is evidence that the parties knew or should have known that the transaction would deplete the assets of the company, the Court should look beyond the formal structure. Id. In Kupetz the Ninth Circuit found it improper to collapse the transactions where the selling shareholders had no knowledge of the LBO character of the transaction, and there were no pre-transaction creditors.

In this case, in contrast, the selling shareholders had full knowledge that this was an LBO. The Milhous representatives informed them of this at the October 25 meeting before the transaction was finalized, and it was disclosed in the financial projections provided at that time. In addition, the selling shareholders discussed this feature with their legal counsel on October 25, and specifically discussed their exposure to a fraudulent transfer claim. Both the selling shareholders and their legal counsel were familiar with leveraged buyouts, because they had done others previously, and they knew the fraudulent transfer risks.

This knowledge of the selling shareholders distinguishes this case from both Kupetz (where the selling shareholders did not know or have reason to know of the LBO) and from Lippi (where the evidence was disputed). Instead, this case is like Richmond Produce, Wieboldt and Tabor Court Realty, where the transaction was collapsed because of the knowledge of the selling shareholders.

In addition, because Shintech qualifies as a pre-transaction creditor, the Court does not need to reach the issue of the knowledge of the LBO feature of the transaction by the selling shareholders: this is material to whether the transaction's various parts should be collapsed only when challenged by post-transaction creditors.

Thus, in this case the Court finds it appropriate to collapse the various pieces of this transaction into one integral transaction, in which the funds went to the selling shareholders, not to Bay Plastics or to its new parent BPI. The loan obliga-

13: BAY PLASTICS V BT COMM.

tion, in contrast, was undertaken by Bay Plastics, which also provided the security for the loan.

Bay Plastics received no reasonably equivalent value for the security interest in all of its assets that it gave to BT in exchange for BT's funding of the stock sale. Under California law, reasonable equivalence must be determined from the standpoint of creditors. Hansen v. Cramer, 39 Cal.2d 321, 245 P.2d 1059, 1061 (1952) (applying rule to "fair consideration" under predecessor statute); Patterson v. Missler, 238 Cal.App.2d 759, 48 Cal.Rptr. 215, 221 (1965) (same). The Ninth Circuit has adopted the same view in interpreting the California version of the UFTA. Roosevelt v. Ray (In re Roosevelt), 176 B.R. 200 (9th Cir. BAP 1994); Maddox v. Robertson (In re Prejean), 994 F.2d 706, 708 (9th Cir.1993); accord, Mellon Bank v. Metro Communications, Inc., 945 F.2d 635, 646 (3d Cir.1991); Nordberg v. Sanchez (In re Chase & Sanborn Corp.), 813 F.2d 1177, 1181 (11th Cir.1987); Pajaro Dunes Rental Agency v. Spitters (In re Pajaro Dunes Rental Agency), 174 B.R. 557, 578 (Bankr.N.D.Cal.1994); In re Consolidated Capital Equities Corp., 143 B.R. 80 (Bankr.N.D.Tex.1992). Payment of funds to a parent corporation prevents a transaction from satisfying the "reasonably equivalent value" requirement. Pajaro Dunes, supra, at 579. A financially healthy entity may give away its assets as it pleases so long as there remains enough to pay its debts. A financially distressed donor, however, 330*330 may not be so generous. Weinstein, supra note 12, at 176.

From the debtor's perspective, it is apparent that the $450,000 that Bay Plastics presumably received[23] (the $3.95 million loan less the $3.5 million paid to the selling shareholders) is not reasonably equivalent to the $3.95 million obligation that it undertook. Cf. Shape, Inc. v. Midwest Engineering (In re Shape, Inc.), 176 B.R. 1, 3 (Bankr.D.Me. 1994) (payment of $70,000 for stock worth more than $1.5 million lacks reasonably equivalent value). Thus Bay Plastics did not receive reasonably equivalent value for the loan obligation and security interest that it granted to BT.

3. Insolvency of the Debtor

The third element of the fraudulent transfer cause of action at issue in this litigation is that the transaction rendered the debtor insolvent, if it was not so already. In this case the Court finds the evidence undisputed that the LBO rendered the debtor insolvent.

Insolvency is defined in California Civil Code § 3439.02(a) (West Supp.1995): "A debtor is insolvent if, at fair valuations, the sum of the debtor's debts is greater

13: BAY PLASTICS V BT COMM.

than all of the debtor's assets." UFTA § 2(a) is essentially the same. These statutes adopt the balance sheet test for insolvency: a debtor is insolvent if the liabilities exceed the assets.

The usual starting point for determining the sufficiency of assets is the balance sheet, particularly if the balance sheet is prepared according to generally accepted accounting principles consistently applied. See Kendall v. Sorani (In re Richmond Produce Co.), 151 B.R. 1012, 1019 (Bankr.N.D.Cal. 1993); Ohio Corrugating Co. v. DPAC, Inc. (In re Ohio Corrugating Co.), 91 B.R. 430, 437-39 (Bankr.N.D.Ohio 1988). However, these principles do not control a court's decision regarding the solvency of an entity. Richmond Produce, 151 B.R. at 1019; Ohio Corrugating, 91 B.R. at 437-39; Foley v. Briden (In re Arrowhead Gardens, Inc.), 32 B.R. 296 (Bankr.D.Mass.1983).

The valuation of assets for insolvency purposes is based on "a fair valuation." This differs from a balance sheet, where most assets apart from publicly traded stocks and bonds are carried at historic cost, rather than current market value. The values of assets must be updated in light of subsequent use and market conditions: in accounting parlance, they must be "marked to market."

In addition, a balance sheet may include intangible assets such as goodwill[24] that may have no liquidation or going concern value, and which thus must be deleted in evaluating the solvency of an entity. Goodwill cannot be sold to satisfy a creditor's claim. Thus, in a liquidation bankruptcy case it must be disregarded in determining solvency of the debtor at the time of an LBO. Richmond Produce, 151 B.R. at 1019.

Nominally, Bay Plastic's corporate balance sheet showed the debtor to be solvent after the LBO. But this resulted only from the addition of $2.26 million of goodwill to the asset side of the balance sheet. Bay Plastics had not previously carried any goodwill on its balance sheets.

331*331 The parties to this litigation have accepted the debtor's balance sheet immediately after the LBO as a fair presentation of the debtor's financial status, with the exception of goodwill. Thus the Court is relieved of the burden of marking to market the debtor's assets. However, the trustee contends that the goodwill of $2.26 million that first appeared at that time must be deleted in determining the debtor's solvency.

The Court finds that the balance sheet must be adjusted by deleting the unamortized goodwill of $2.26 million. It was not carried on the balance sheet before the LBO, and in any case it could not be sold to satisfy a creditor's claim. Richmond

13: BAY PLASTICS V BT COMM.

Produce, 151 B.R. at 1019. This is a liquidation case, where goodwill has no other value. This downward adjustment left Bay Plastics with a negative net worth of approximately $2 million immediately after the LBO. For fraudulent transfer purposes, it was rendered insolvent by the transaction.

Indeed, this is exactly the type of transaction that poses the extreme risk of an LBO. No Milhous entity put any funds or assets at risk in the investment at all. In consequence of the structure of the transaction, all of the risks of the enterprise were placed on its creditors. Milhous retained only the right to reap the benefits if the business was sufficiently profitable to avoid bankruptcy.[25]

4. Attack by a Pre-Transaction Creditor

The final element of the cause of action for fraudulent transfer rendering a debtor insolvent is that the transaction must be attacked by a pre-transaction creditor.[26] This element is satisfied in this case.

Shintech, the principal unsecured creditor in this case, which holds more than 99% of the unsecured debt, is the pre-existing creditor. It was secured until this transaction, and in addition it held guaranties from each of the selling shareholders. In this transaction the selling shareholders and Milhous induced it to relinquish its security and guaranties to permit the transaction to be consummated. Although knowing the LBO character of the transaction, both the selling shareholders and Milhous failed to disclose this feature to Shintech.

The selling shareholders make three arguments against considering Shintech a qualifying pretransaction creditor. First, they argue that Shintech's account was current at the time of the LBO, and that in consequence all of its debt comes from a later date. Second, they argue that Shintech had an opportunity at the pre-closing meeting, where it agreed to release its security interest and guaranties, to ask any questions that it wanted, and it declared that it was satisfied with the information provided to it. Third, they claim that Nicole Plastic's purchase of Shintech's claim in settlement of a lawsuit by Shintech against Nicole and other Milhouse entities disqualifies this claim as a pre-transaction claim: in effect, the shareholders contend, the claim now belongs to the debtor itself. The Court finds all of these arguments unpersuasive.

a. Shintech as Creditor

First, the Court finds that Shintech is a pre-transaction creditor of Bay Plastics, even if the account was current at the time of the LBO. Just three months earlier Shintech had entered into a massive contract with Bay Plastics to provide all of its

13: BAY PLASTICS V BT COMM.

requirements of PVC, which were monumental — up to 2.6 million pounds (1300 tons) per month. Under this contract Bay Plastics owed a duty to Shintech to buy its PVC from Shintech for the duration of the contract, whether or not 332*332 the account was current on any particular day. The contract was in place on the day of the LBO, and remained in force until after the bankruptcy filing.

UFTA § 5 and California Civil Code § 3439.05 require a "creditor whose claim arose before . . . the obligation was incurred" to permit the court to set aside a transfer resulting in insolvency. UFTA § 1(c) and California Civil Code § 3439.01(c) define a "creditor" as "a person who has a claim." "Claim" is defined expansively in UFTA § 1(b) and California Civil Code § 3439.01(b) as follows:

a right to payment, whether or not the right is reduced to judgment, liquidated, unliquidated, fixed, contingent, matured, unmatured, disputed, undisputed, legal, equitable, secured, or unsecured.

Shintech's contract rights under its requirements contract to provide PVC were certainly not valueless, even if payments were current at the time of the LBO. If Bay Plastics had repudiated the contract on the day after the LBO, it would have owed massive damages to Shintech. If Bay Plastics had filed a bankruptcy case on that date and rejected the contract thereafter under Bankruptcy Code § 365, Shintech would have been entitled to an unsecured claim in the bankruptcy case. Bankruptcy Code § 364(g)(1).[27] The Court finds that this right satisfied the definitional requirements to make it a creditor holding a claim, as defined in UFTA § 1(b) and California Civil Code § 3439.01(b).

In Aluminum Mills Corp. v. Citicorp North America, Inc. (In re Aluminum Mills Corp.), 132 B.R. 869, 888-91 (Bankr.N.D.Ill. 1991), the court found that a complaint sufficiently alleged the existence of pre-transaction creditors where it claimed that there were agreements for open trade accounts in place at the time of the LBO and continuing until the bankruptcy was filed.[28] In this case there was more than an open account with Shintech: there was a massive requirements contract for all of the PVC that Bay Plastics needed.

The Court holds that this made Shintech a creditor of Bay Plastics at that time, and that Shintech maintained this status until the bankruptcy case was filed. Thus this element of the cause of action is met.

b. Investigation of the Transaction

Second, the selling shareholders argue that Shintech, the largest supplier of PVC resin in the industry, had every opportunity to investigate the nature of the LBO

13: BAY PLASTICS V BT COMM.

transaction, and cannot now be heard to complain about it. The Court finds this is irrelevant to the cause of action for a fraudulent transfer that renders a debtor insolvent.

Furthermore, at best, this evidence only shows that one supplier in the PVC pipe industry failed to discover the LBO. It does not establish, as required by Kupetz, that the entire industry knew or had reason to know that the stock purchase was a LBO. Kupetz, 845 F.2d at 849.

The shareholders assert that the sale notice sent to 25 suppliers of the debtor (presumably a bulk sale notice under UCC article 6) gave sufficient notice of the LBO. This notice, however, did not state that the transaction was an LBO or that the transaction would render the debtor insolvent. Furthermore, a public LBO only puts subsequent creditors on notice of possible financial problems. They may decide not to do business with the debtor, and avoid becoming creditors.[29] Existing creditors, on the other hand, 333*333 are already locked in, and subsequent notice does not do them any good.

Thus, the LBO acquisition of the debtor was a secret transaction in the PVC pipe industry. Fraudulent transfer law was designed from the outset (in 1570) to protect creditors from secret transactions. Kupetz, 845 F.2d at 849-50 n. 16. Indeed, the evidence is undisputed that the LBO feature of the purchase did not become well known in the industry until after the debtor filed its bankruptcy petition.

Shintech did change its position at the time of the transaction, in giving up its security and its guaranties. It apparently could have prevented the transaction from going forward if it had refused to make these concessions. However, the LBO feature of the transaction was hidden from it. Thus, the transaction was a secret transaction as to both Shintech and the industry, of the sort that the Ninth Circuit in Kupetz declared to be within the scope of a fraudulent transfer claim, even if brought only on behalf of subsequent creditors.

c. Settlement

Third, the Court finds that the Nicole Plastic's purchase of Shintech's claim in its settlement of Shintech's lawsuit against various Milhous entities does not moot Shintech's pre-LBO claim. Nicole Plastic's purchase of Shintech's claim does not eliminate the claim. While the selling shareholders contend that in effect Bay Plastics now owns this claim, this is not so. Nicole Plastics is a different entity, and not the debtor or the trustee. The claim is still pending against the Bay Plastics estate. It does not belong to the debtor, but to its parent corporation, which is a separate entity. Most important, the claim is clearly adverse to the sell-

13: BAY PLASTICS V BT COMM.

ing shareholders. It thus continues to support the debtor's fraudulent transfer claim against the selling shareholders.

C. Application of Fraudulent Transfer Law to LBOs

The Court finds it appropriate to apply fraudulent transfer law to an LBO. An LBO is different, not just in degree, but in character from the ordinary business and investment transactions engaged in by a corporation's management. An LBO is not a routine business transaction that should normally be given deference by the courts. It is not a corporate investment in a new venture, new equipment or property. Indeed, an LBO normally does not affect the business of the corporation at all: it only changes the ownership and adds a large layer of secured debt. Rather, an LBO is an investment of corporate assets, by borrowing against them, for the personal benefit of both old and new equity owners. Thus, the application of fraudulent transfer law to LBOs does not limit corporate entrepreneurial decisions.

Since an LBO reduces the availability of unencumbered assets, the buyout depletes estate assets available to pay creditors' claims. As the Ninth Circuit has stated:

Existing unsecured creditors are vulnerable in [an LBO]. From their perspective, a pledge of the company's assets as collateral to finance the purchase of the company reduces the assets to which they can look for repayment.

Kupetz, 845 F.2d at 846; accord, Moody v. Security Pacific Business Credit, Inc., 971 F.2d 1056, 1073 (3d Cir.1992). An LBO is attractive to the sellers, the buyers and the lender because it shifts most of the risk of loss to other creditors of the corporation. Mellon Bank v. Metro Communications, Inc., 945 F.2d 635 (3d Cir.1991). The acquired corporation receives little or nothing in exchange for the debt that it incurs.

From a creditor's point of view, an LBO is indistinguishable from a distribution or a gift to shareholders. The harm is quite like the harm imposed on creditors by donative transfers to third parties, which is one of the most traditional kinds of fraudulent transfers.[30] If the value of the security interest given by the corporation does not exceed the shareholders' equity as shown on the balance sheet (after suitable revisions to mark the assets to market and to eliminate intangible assets of dubious value), there is usually no 334*334 substantial harm to creditors. Indeed, typical corporate distribution statutes permit the payment of dividends in such circumstances, to the extent of the balance sheet equity. See, e.g., Cal.Corp.Code § 166 (West Supp. 1995). If the price paid to selling shareholders

13: BAY PLASTICS V BT COMM.

is higher, however, there may be insufficient assets remaining to satisfy creditors.

The vice of an LBO lies in the fact that the selling shareholders are paid indirectly with assets from the corporation itself, rather than by the purchasers. In effect, in an LBO the shareholders are paid with a corporate dividend or distribution. An LBO enables the selling shareholders to liquidate their equity interests, which are otherwise subordinate to general unsecured claims, without first paying creditors, which a normal liquidation would require. The selling shareholders in the transaction in effect disregard the status of the corporation as a separate entity for their benefit, but insist on respect of the corporation's separate status when it comes to creditors' claims (apart from those of the lender providing the funds for the transaction).

The possible detriment to creditors is exacerbated if the corporation's cash flow is not sufficient to service the loan. The bank eventually proceeds to foreclose on the corporation's assets and sells them at foreclosure prices, and leaves nothing for other creditors. Such foreclosure is frequently interrupted by the filing of a bankruptcy case. So it happened in this case.

Most courts that have considered the issue have decided that fraudulent transfer law should apply to LBOs. See, e.g., Moody v. Security Pacific Business Credit, 971 F.2d 1056 (3d Cir.1992); Lippi v. City Bank, 955 F.2d 599 (9th Cir.1992); Mellon Bank v. Metro Communications, Inc., 945 F.2d 635 (3d Cir.1991); O'Donnell v. Royal Business Group, Inc. (In re Oxford Homes, Inc.), 180 B.R. 1 (Bankr.D.Me.1995); In re Consolidated Capital Equities Corp., 143 B.R. 80 (Bankr.N.D.Tex.1992); Crowthers McCall Pattern, Inc. v. Lewis, 129 B.R. 992 (S.D.N.Y.1991); Vadnais Lumber Supply, Inc. v. Byrne (In re Vadnais Lumber Supply, Inc.), 100 B.R. 127 (Bankr.D.Mass.1989); Wieboldt Stores, Inc. v. Schottenstein, 94 B.R. 488 (N.D.Ill.1988). See generally, 4 Queenan, supra note 12, ch. 27; 3 Norton, supra note 12, ch. 58A. In fact, despite the reservations expressed in Kupetz, supra, and Credit Managers Ass'n of Southern California v. Federal Co., 629 F.Supp. 175 (C.D.Cal. 1985), there appears to be no published opinion to the contrary.[31]

It does not follow, however, that the fraudulent transfer analysis of an LBO will result in a recovery for the benefit of the bankruptcy estate. In both Moody and Mellon Bank the Third Circuit upheld the transactions at issue against the fraudulent transfer attack. In Lippi, similarly, the Ninth Circuit ruled in favor of some of the defendants, and remanded for further consideration as to the remainder.

Should all LBO's be exposed to fraudulent transfer challenge? Certainly not.

13: BAY PLASTICS V BT COMM.

Under this Court's analysis, two kinds of LBO's ordinarily escape fraudulent transfer attack. This includes many, if not most, LBOs.[32]

First, in a legitimate LBO,[33] in which the assets mortgaged by a corporation to support 335*335 an LBO do not exceed the net equity of the business (after appropriate adjustments), the transaction will not make the corporation insolvent, at least according to the balance sheet test.[34] If in addition it has sufficient pro-jected cash flow to pay its debts as they come due, the cash flow solvency test is met, also. This leaves an LBO exposed to fraudulent transfer attack only if the margin of equity is too thin to support the corporation's business.

A second kind of LBO also escapes fraudulent transfer attack, even though it leaves the subject corporation insolvent. If the cash flow is sufficient to make the debt payments, the transaction also is unassailable. This ordinarily turns on two factors: the degree of risk of default undertaken in the first instance, and the degree to which projected economic developments impacting the business are not overly optimistic. These LBOs escape fraudulent transfer attack either because of good financial projections or because of good luck: either factor is sufficient.

The Court's view of the proper application of fraudulent transfer law to LBO's does not make the selling shareholders the guarantors of the success of the LBO. A legitimate LBO, as described supra, shifts the risk of failure off their shoulders. As to subsequent creditors, they should not be required to shoulder the risk if the failure is caused by outside forces not reasonably foreseeable at the time of the transaction. Moody v. Security Pacific Business Credit, Inc., 971 F.2d 1056, 1073 (3d Cir.1992) (failure caused by increased competition rather than lack of capital); Credit Managers Association v. Federal Co., 629 F.Supp. 175, 186-87 (C.D.Cal.1985).

However, an LBO that is leveraged beyond the net worth of the business is a gamble.[35] A highly leveraged business is much less able to weather temporary financial storms, because debt demands are less flexible than equity interest. The risks of this gamble should rest on the shoulders of the shareholders (old and new), not those of the creditors: the shareholders enjoy the benefits if the gamble is successful, and they should bear the burdens if it is not. This, after all, is the role of equity owners of a corporation. The application of fraudulent transfer law to LBOs shifts the risks of an LBO transaction from the creditors, who are not parties to the transaction, back to the old and new shareholders who bring about such transactions. As Sherwin states:

These parties, who are directly involved as the principal engineers and beneficiar-

13: BAY PLASTICS V BT COMM.

ies of the buyout, should bear the risk of negative consequences if the transaction does not in fact comply with the standards for creditor protection set out in the fraudulent conveyance statutes. . . . They should be accountable to creditors for the benefits diverted from the corporation if they knew or should have known . . . of facts the court determines to establish a constructive fraud against creditors.

Sherwin, supra note 12, at 519.

How long should selling shareholders be exposed to the risk that an LBO will go bad? There is a traditional answer to this question: until the statute of limitations runs. Perhaps there should be a shorter statute of limitations for LBOs than the four to seven years that is common under the 336*336 UFTA. This is a decision for the legislature to make.

The Court perceives no unfairness in imposing the risks of an overleveraged LBO on the old and new shareholders who undertake the risks, rather on the creditors who do not intend to do so. Indeed, it is the selling shareholders who are ordinarily least worthy of sympathy in an LBO. As Epstein states:

In the beginning of the transaction they are below existing creditors. In the end, they "cash out" and march off over the heads of the existing creditors. It is a neat trick of legal magic that allow the shareholders to subordinate, unilaterally, the creditors' claims.

2 Epstein, supra note 12, at 74.

D. Good Faith Defense

The selling shareholders claim that they acted in good faith, and that this is a defense to the fraudulent transfer claim. From the earliest fraudulent transfer statutes, a good faith transferee for value has enjoyed an affirmative defense to the cause of action. See, e.g., 13 Stat.Eliz. ch. 5, § 6 (1570). However, this defense has been greatly restricted in recent statutes.

The UFTA, including California's version thereof, provides a complete defense to an intentional fraudulent transfer for a transferee who took "in good faith and for a reasonably equivalent value." UFTA § 8(a); Cal. Civ.Code § 3439.08(a) (West Supp.1995). This defense is not available for a constructive fraudulent conveyance, and thus is not applicable in this adversary proceeding.

A second good faith provision is contained in UFTA § 8(d) and the California Civil Code, which provide:

13: BAY PLASTICS V BT COMM.

Notwithstanding voidability of a transfer or an obligation under this chapter, a good faith transferee or obligee is entitled, to the extent of the value given the debtor for the transfer or obligation, to the following:

(1) A lien on or a right to retain any interest in the asset transferred.

(2) Enforcement of any obligation incurred.

(3) A reduction in the amount of the liability on the judgment.

UFCA § 8(d); Cal.Civ.Code § 3439.08(d) (West Supp.1995) (emphasis added).[36]

In this case the selling shareholders gave up their shares of stock in the debtor in exchange for their payment of $3.5 million. However, this provision is not applicable in this case, because the shareholders did not transfer their shares or give any other value to the debtor. The shares went to BPI, the new parent corporation of Bay Plastics, and from there to Milhous. The debtor itself received neither shares nor money. This did not constitute "value given the debtor", within the meaning of UFTA § 8(d) or California Civil Code § 3439.08(d). Thus the good faith defense fails. IV.

CONCLUSION

Having found no triable issue of material fact, the Court concludes that the trustee is entitled to a summary judgment setting aside the constructive fraudulent transfer in this case to the selling shareholders. After having collapsed the series of transactions into a single transaction, the Court finds that in substance the selling shareholders received payment for their shares that was secured by the assets of debtor, and that this transaction defrauded an existing creditor.

The payment to the selling shareholders is thus avoidable under UFTA § 5, as adopted in California in California Civil Code § 3439.05, which in turn is incorporated in Bankruptcy Code § 544(b).

[1] 11 U.S.C.A. § 544(b) (West 1993).

[2] Apparently the deferred payments have not been made. All but $100,000 of the deferred payments were designated as compensation for a non-competition agreement.

[3] The BT loan was structured to permit Nicole Plastics to make two acquisitions, the Bay Plastics purchase and the acquisition of Colby Plastic Converters, Inc. The Colby part of the transaction was separate from the Bay Plastics part, except as to the financing, and it is not involved in this litigation.

13: BAY PLASTICS V BT COMM.

[4] While working capital advances were authorized up to $3.35 million, the Court has received no evidence on whether such advances were actually made.

[5] In consequence of giving up its security and its guaranties, Shintech now holds more than 99% of the unsecured debt in this case.

[6] 11 U.S.C.A. § 1107(a) (West 1993).

[7] Section 544(b) provides:

The trustee may avoid any transfer of an interest of the debtor in property or any obligation incurred by the debtor that is voidable under applicable law by a creditor holding an unsecured claim. . . .

11 U.S.C.A. § 544(b) (West 1993).

[8] This statute is frequently referred to erroneously as the Statute of Elizabeth. In those times statutes were known according to the monarch under whom they were enacted. Thus every statute enacted during the reign of Queen Elizabeth I was a "statute of Elizabeth." The fraudulent conveyance statute was enacted during the thirteenth year of her reign (hence "13 Eliz."), and was the fifth statute enacted that year (hence "ch. 5"). A bankruptcy statute, England's second, was enacted the same year, and is found at 13 Eliz. ch. 7 (1570).

[9] The Bankruptcy Code and its predecessor the Bankruptcy Act of 1898 have traditionally included their own fraudulent transfer provisions, because a number of states did not adopt the UFCA, and some have not yet adopted the UFTA.

[10] These provisions are identical to the corresponding parts of UFTA § 5(a). 7A U.L.A. 652 (1985).

[11] While LBOs have frequently been used by management to buy out existing shareholders and take over the ownership of a business, management is not an essential party to an LBO. Indeed, in this case the purchaser was an outside third party.

[12] See, e.g., 4 James F. Queenan, Jr. et al., Chapter 11 Theory and Practice: A Guide to Reorganization ch. 27 (1994); 3 William L. Norton, Jr., Norton Bankruptcy Law and Practice ch. 58A (2d ed. 1994); David Weinstein, From Kupetz to Lippi and Beyond: LBOs in the Ninth Circuit — Now What?, 21 Cal.Bankr.J. 169, (1993); 2 David G. Epstein et al., Bankruptcy § 6-52 (1992); Emily L. Sherwin, Creditors' Rights Against Participants in a Leveraged Buyout, 72 Minn.L.Rev. 449 (1988); Kathryn V. Smyser, Going Private and Going Under:

13: BAY PLASTICS V BT COMM.

Leveraged Buyouts and the Fraudulent Conveyance Problem, 63 Ind.L.J. 781, 784-85 (1988); Kevin J. Liss, Note, Fraudulent Conveyance Law and Leveraged Buyouts, 87 Colum.L.Rev. 1491 (1987); Douglas G. Baird & Thomas H. Jackson, Fraudulent Conveyance Law and Its Proper Domain, 38 Vand.L.Rev. 829, 850-54 (1985).

[13] The Third Circuit views LBOs somewhat less skeptically than the Ninth. In Moody v. Security Pacific Business Credit, Inc., the court stated that, while LBO's are attractive to both the buyer and the seller, "failed LBO's merit close scrutiny under the fraudulent conveyance laws," because they have shifted the risk of loss to creditors. Moody, 971 F.2d 1056, 1073 (3d Cir.1992). In Mellon Bank v. Metro Communications, Inc., 945 F.2d 635 (3d Cir.1991), the court stated:

[A] thorough understanding of the typical LBO transaction reveals that there is a potential for abuse of the debtor's creditors, particularly those who are unsecured, when a company is purchased through an LBO.

Id., at 645. The court found in both Moody and Mellon Bank that the LBO at issue survived fraudulent transfer scrutiny. However, in United States v. Tabor Court Realty Corp., 803 F.2d 1288 (3d Cir.1986), cert. denied, 483 U.S. 1005, 107 S.Ct. 3229, 97 L.Ed.2d 735 (1987), the Third Circuit upheld a trial court's determination that an LBO was a fraudulent transfer.

[14] Hawaii never adopted the UFCA. Like California, it adopted the UFTA in 1985. However, the Lippi facts arose in 1981, before the UFTA was enacted. Id. at 602.

[15] Section 550(b) provides in relevant part:

The trustee may not recover under section (a)(2) of this section from —

(1) a transferee that takes for value, . . . in good faith, and without knowledge of the voidability of the transfer avoided. . . .

11 U.S.C.A. § 550(b) (West 1993). Section 550(a) provides in relevant part:

[T]o the extent that a transfer is avoided under section 544 . . . the trustee may recover, for the benefit of the estate, the property transferred, or, if the court so orders, the value of such property, from —

(1) the initial transferee of such transfer or the entity for whose benefit such transfer was made; or

13: BAY PLASTICS V BT COMM.

(2) any immediate or mediate transferee of such initial transferee.

11 U.S.C.A. § 550(a) (West 1993).

[16] The language of § 550 is difficult to parse. It contemplates that property subject to an avoidance action and recovery by the trustee may be transferred several times before the trustee catches up with it. The first to receive the property is the "initial transferee"; the second is the "immediate transferee" of the initial transferee; a subsequent transferee is a "mediate transferee".

[17] See also Sherwin, supra note 12, at 518.

[18] After prevailing in the Ninth Circuit, the Wolfs (but not the other shareholder) filed a malicious prosecution action against the chapter 7 trustee, his law firm, his attorneys and the financing bank. This Court granted summary judgment to all defendants, and granted substantial sanctions in their favor. See Wolf v. Kupetz (In re Wolf & Vine, Inc.), 118 B.R. 761 (Bankr.C.D.Cal.1990).

[19] In fact, Kupetz was a very narrow case: the Ninth Circuit itself stated in that case, "we should not be understood as insulating all LBOs from fraudulent conveyance laws. . . ." Kupetz, 845 F.2d at 850.

[20] 11 U.S.C.A. § 548 (West 1993). It is noteworthy that the court in Richmond Produce hardly mentioned Lippi and Kupetz: it referred to these cases only in footnotes, and then only to clarify their nonapplicability.

[21] In contrast, the UFCA makes a transfer fraudulent if it was made "without a fair consideration." UFCA § 4, 7A U.L.A. 474 (1985). "Fair consideration" is a defined term in the UFCA: § 3 provides:

Fair consideration is given for property, or obligation:

(a) When in exchange for such property, or obligation, as a fair equivalent therefor, and in good faith, property is conveyed or an antecedent debt is satisfied, or

(b) When such property, or obligation is received in good faith to secure a present advance or antecedent debt in amount not disproportionately small as compared with the value of the property, or obligation obtained.

UFCA § 3, 7A U.L.A. 448-49 (1985). The UFTA has no definition for "reasonably equivalent value."

Apart from this difference, the elements of a cause of action under the two

13: BAY PLASTICS V BT COMM.

statutes are the same. The elements of a cause of action for a fraudulent transfer rendering a debtor insolvent under Bankruptcy Code § 548 are the same as under the UFTA.

[22] The definitions of insolvency under the various fraudulent transfer statutes differ. The UFCA adopts the "equity" or "cash flow" test of insolvency, under which a debtor is insolvent if the present fair salable value of the debtor's assets is less than the amount required to pay existing debts as they become due. UFCA § 2(a). The Bankruptcy Code § 101(32)(A) adopts the balance sheet definition of insolvency, under which a debtor is insolvent if the debtor's liabilities exceed the debtor's assets. 11 U.S.C.A. § 101(32)(A) (West 1993). Under the UFTA, a debtor is insolvent if the debtor's liabilities exceed the debtor's assets (the balance sheet definition), and the debtor is presumed to be insolvent if the debtor is generally not paying his or her debts as they become due (the equity or cash flow test). UFTA § 2(a), (c).

[23] The record is silent on this point.

[24] Goodwill is generally understood to represent the value of intangible factors that are expected to translate into greater than normal earning power. In addition to the advantageous relationship that a business enjoys with its customers, goodwill also includes advantageous relationships with employees, suppliers, lenders and others. Commons, Industrial Goodwill 18- 26 (1919); see, also, Grace Bros. v. Commissioner, 173 F.2d 170 (9th Cir.1949); Vadnais Lumber Supply, Inc. v. Byrne (In re Vadnais Lumber Supply, Inc.), 100 B.R. 127, 135 (Bankr.D.Mass. 1989).

Because goodwill has no independent market or liquidation value, generally accepted accounting principles require that goodwill be written off over a period of time. In acquisition accounting, going concern value in excess of asset value is treated as goodwill. Dictionary of Finance & Investment Terms 157 (2d ed. 1987).

Goodwill frequently appears on a balance sheet after the sale of a business, where it represents the excess of the purchase price over the net value of the other assets purchased. See, e.g., Richmond Produce, 151 B.R. at 1019. It appears that this may be the explanation for the appearance of goodwill on the debtor's balance sheet in this case.

[25] In such a transaction there is a danger that the selling shareholders will be paid more than their stock is worth. With nothing at risk if the business is not sufficiently profitable, the purchaser has less incentive to make sure that the price

13: BAY PLASTICS V BT COMM.

is not excessive. Absent fraudulent transfer law, there is nothing to deter the buyers, sellers and bank from imposing all of the risks of loss on the creditors, as they did in this case.

[26] While the existence of a pre-transaction creditor is an element in the cause of action involved in this case, it was not an element in the causes of action involved in the Lippi and Kupetz cases. The Ninth Circuit treated this as a question of "standing" in those cases. Lippi, 955 F.2d at 606-08; Kupetz, 845 F.2d at 849 n. 16. It is not clear why it was an issue at all in those cases. See Weinstein, supra note 12, at 192.

[27] 11 U.S.C.A. § 365(g)(1) (West 1993) provides:

[T]he rejection of an executory contract . . . of the debtor constitutes a breach of such contract . . . —

(1) . . . immediately before the date of the filing of the petition. . . .

[28] Cf. Unsecured Creditors' Committee v. Banque Paribas (In re Heartland Chemicals, Inc.), 103 B.R. 1012, 1016 (Bankr.C.D.Ill.1989) (creditor does not qualify as a pre-transaction creditor if the indebtedness was paid off after the transaction and then extended new credit).

[29] The Court notes that this analysis only applies to voluntary creditors, such as those at issue in Kupetz and in this case. Involuntary creditors, on the other hand, such as tort claimants and taxing authorities, are generally no better able to avoid becoming creditors even if they know of an LBO, and the Kupetz analysis should not apply to them.

[30] David Epstein and his co-authors state: "[The creditors] are harmed just as much as if the debtor had given away the equity in its assets as a gift." Epstein, supra note 12, § 6-52 at 69.

[31] But see Kaiser Steel Corp. v. Pearl Brewing Co. (In re Kaiser Steel Corp.), 952 F.2d 1230 (10th Cir.1991), cert denied, 505 U.S. 1213, 112 S.Ct. 3015, 120 L.Ed.2d 887 (1992), where the court held that the trustee could not recover from selling shareholders of a publicly traded corporation because their payments constituted nonavoidable "settlement Bankruptcy Code § 546(e), 11 U.S.C.A. § 546(e) (West 1993). payments" under

[32] In Credit Managers Association v. Federal Co., 629 F.Supp. 175, 179 (C.D.Cal.1985), a district judge in this district stated, "it is not at all clear that fraudulent conveyance law is broadly applicable to [LBOs]." That court relied

13: BAY PLASTICS V BT COMM.

substantially on Baird & Jackson, supra note 12. Ten years of court decisions and scholarly commentary since that decision have helped to refine the application of fraudulent transfer law to LBOs. Even the Credit Managers court, however, apparently would permit pre-transaction creditors, such as exist in this case, to attack an LBO. Id., at 180-81.

[33] In Kupetz, 845 F.2d 842 (9th Cir.1988), the Ninth Circuit stated:

[W]e hesitate to utilize constructive [transfer law] to frustrate the purposes intended to be served by what appears to us to be a legitimate LBO. Nor do we think it appropriate to utilize constructive [fraudulent transfer law] to brand most, if not all, LBOs as illegitimate. We cannot believe that virtually all LBO's are designed to "hinder, delay, or defraud creditors."

Id., at 848. The Court is in agreement with this dictum. In this Court's analysis, however, the Wolf & Vine LBO at issue in Kupetz was not apparently a legitimate LBO. The selling shareholders escaped liability, as the Ninth Circuit held, because of their good faith defense based on their lack of knowledge or inquiry notice of the leveraged feature of the transaction, and because the publicity of the transaction in the industry prevented subsequent creditors from being defrauded.

[34] It makes sense to limit legitimate LBOs to transactions that do not leave a corporation insolvent. In a perfect world (as typically assumed by economists), an LBO would never run afoul of this rule, because the price paid for the stock would be the net equity in the firm. Baird & Jackson, supra note 12, at 851. Such an LBO would place the corporation on the verge of insolvency, but not beyond. In the real world, some LBOs leave corporations insolvent, perhaps because of imperfect information about the value of the corporation's stock.

[35] See 2 Epstein, supra note 12, § 6-52 at 69-70.

[36] Bankruptcy Code § 548(c) provides a transferee with a similar defense to a fraudulent conveyance claim to the extent of the value given to the debtor if such transferee acted in good faith. 11 U.S.C.A. § 548 (West 1993).

14: IN RE XONICS PHOTOCHEMICAL

In the Matter of XONICS PHOTOCHEMICAL, INC., Debtor.
Appeal of MITSUI AND COMPANY (U.S.A.), INC.

No. 87-2143.

United States Court of Appeals, Seventh Circuit.

Argued January 6, 1988.
Decided March 8, 1988.

199*199 Thomas D. Goldberg, Hughes Hubbard & Reed, Washington, D.C., for appellant.

Erick S. Rein, Schwartz, Cooper, Kolb & Gaynor, Chtd., Chicago, Ill., for appellee.

Before POSNER, COFFEY, and EASTERBROOK, Circuit Judges.

POSNER, Circuit Judge.

This bankruptcy case presents interesting questions concerning the status in bankruptcy of contingent liabilities and interaffiliate obligations. For background see Comment, Avoidability of Intercorporate Guarantees Under Sections 548(a)(2) and 544(b) of the Bankruptcy Code, 64 N.C.L.Rev. 1099 (1986). Xonics, Inc., now in Chapter 11 bankruptcy, has several wholly owned subsidiaries that are engaged in making medical equipment. The largest is Xonics Medical Systems, Inc.; one of the smallest is Xonics Photochemical, Inc., the debtor in the proceeding before us. In 1982 and 1983, a time of prosperity for the Xonics family, Xonics Medical Systems borrowed some $15 to $20 million from a bank, on a $25 million credit line. Xonics, Inc., the parent, caused Xonics Photochemical, Inc. (along with the other subsidiaries) to guarantee the loan; at the time Xonics Photochemical had gross assets of some $2.6 million and net assets of $1.7 million. Xonics, Inc. also caused Xonics Photochemical to become a co-maker with Xonics Medical Systems of a note to secure an additional loan of $3 million.

Shortly after these transactions, Mitsui & Co. (U.S.A.), Inc., a supplier to Xonics Photochemical, shipped it some chemicals, and invoiced it for the purchase price, which was (approximately) $124,000. Xonics Photochemical paid the invoice with two checks that cleared in January 1984. Fewer than 90 days later, Xonics Photochemical was in bankruptcy. Xonics Medical Systems had defaulted on its bank loan, triggering the guarantees of its affiliates. The total assets of the

Xonics family — all of which were pledged to the creditors of each member

14: IN RE XONICS PHOTOCHEMICAL

through guarantees similar to the one Xonics Photochemical had signed — were short of the total liabilities by many millions of dollars; so all the subsidiaries, as well as the parent, found themselves in Chapter 11. Xonics Photochemical, as debtor in possession (no trustee in bankruptcy had been appointed), brought an adversary proceeding against Mitsui to set aside the two payments as preferences voidable under 11 U.S.C. § 547(b). This provision makes transactions voidable by the trustee, but 11 U.S.C. § 1107(a) gives the debtor in possession the powers of a trustee. The dispositive issue was whether Xonics Photochemical had been insolvent when the payments to Mitsui were made; that is, did the fair value of its liabilities exceed the fair value of its assets (11 U.S.C. § 101(31)(A))? If so, the payments were indeed voidable preferences, see 11 U.S.C. § 547(b)(3), since the other conditions in section 547(b) had been met. The bankruptcy judge and the district judge thought Xonics Photochemical had been insolvent then; Mitsui disagrees and has appealed.

The startling feature of the case is the parties' apparent assent to the proposition that if the loan guarantee and the note that Xonics Photochemical had co-signed were valid obligations, Xonics Photochemical was insolvent as of the date the obligations were assumed, on the theory that they created liabilities greater than the company's net assets (much greater: $28 million in liabilities versus less than $2 million in net assets). The proposition is absurd; it would mean that every individual or firm that had contingent liabilities greater than his or its net assets was insolvent — something no one believes. Every firm that is being sued or that may be sued, every individual who has signed an accommodation note, every bank that has issued a letter of credit, has a contingent liability. Such liabilities are occasionally 200*200 listed on the firm's balance sheet, for example by earmarking a portion of surplus for contingent liabilities. (They are supposed to be listed "if the future event is likely to occur and if its amount can be reasonably estimated." Nikolai et al., Intermediate Accounting 611 (3d ed. 1985) (emphasis in original).) More often they are listed in a footnote, thus leaving the firm's stated net worth undisturbed. Often they are not listed at all, when they are remote or when they are too small to affect net worth substantially. On the proper accounting treatment of contingent liabilities see id. at 610-14; Faris, Accounting for Lawyers 362-64 (3d ed. 1975); Williams, Stanga & Holder, Intermediate Accounting 609-17 (1984); Meigs, Mosich & Johnson, Accounting: The Basis for Business Decisions 288 (3d ed. 1972); Financial Accounting Standards Board, FASB Statement of Standards No. 5 (1975).

There is a compelling reason not to value contingent liabilities on the balance sheet at their face amounts, even if that would be possible to do because the liability, despite being contingent, is for a specified amount (that is, even if there is

14: IN RE XONICS PHOTOCHEMICAL

no uncertainty about what the firm will owe if the contingency materializes). By definition, a contingent liability is not certain — and often is highly unlikely — ever to become an actual liability. To value the contingent liability it is necessary to discount it by the probability that the contingency will occur and the liability become real. Suppose that on the date the obligations were assumed there was a 1 percent chance that Xonics Photochemical would ever be called on to yield up its assets to creditors of Xonics Medical Systems (or other members of the Xonics family, since the system of guarantees had the effect of pooling their assets for the benefit of creditors of any member). Then the true measure of the liability created by these obligations on the date they were assumed would not be $28 million; it would be a paltry $17,000. For at worst Xonics Photochemical would have to yield up all of its assets (net of other liabilities), that is, $1.7 million, and the probability of this outcome is by assumption only 1 percent (we are ignoring intermediate possibilities — e.g., that Xonics Photochemical would be forced to cough up $1 million rather than $1.7 million). Discounted, the obligations would not make Xonics insolvent, and section 547(b) would not come into play unless events occurring between the assumption of the obligations in 1982 and 1983 and the bankruptcy in 1984 had altered the picture. We add that Xonics Photochemical did not in fact list these obligations as liabilities on its balance sheet.

The principle just outlined has long been recognized in cases dealing with the question whether a firm is insolvent within the meaning of the Bankruptcy Code (and this is such a case). It makes no difference whether the firm has a contingent asset or a contingent liability; the asset or liability must be reduced to its present, or expected, value before a determination can be made whether the firm's assets exceed its liabilities. See, e.g., Syracuse Engineering Co. v. Haight, 97 F.2d 573, 576 (2d Cir.1938) (L. Hand, J.); In re Ollag Construction Equipment Corp., 578 F.2d 904, 909 (2d Cir.1978); In re Fulghum Construction Co., 7 B.R. 629, 632-33 (Bankr.M.D.Tenn.1980), aff'd, 14 B.R. 293 (M.D.Tenn.1981); In re Hemphill, 18 B.R. 38, 48-49 (Bankr.S.D.Iowa 1982). The criticism of this position in the student Comment cited earlier, 64 N.C.L.Rev. at 1118-19, is perfunctory and unpersuasive.

Occasionally one finds the flat statement that "contingent or inchoate claims of the bankrupt are not included as part of the bankrupt's property." Allegaert v. Chemical Bank, 418 F.Supp. 690, 692 (E.D.N.Y.1976). This is the equally untenable opposite extreme from valuing them at their face amount. But the quoted language appears to be loose; what these cases actually mean is that if, but for a contingent claim unlikely to yield any cash in the near future, the firm would be deemed insolvent, the existence of a faint hope — cold comfort for creditors wait-

14: IN RE XONICS PHOTOCHEMICAL

ing to be paid — will not save it from bankruptcy. See Penn v. Grant, 244 F.2d 309 (9th Cir.1957) (per curiam); In re Bichel Optical Laboratories, Inc., 299 F.Supp. 545 (D.Minn.1969). 201*201 No more should the existence of remote contingencies, which do not seriously endanger the firm's ability to pay its debts, be deemed to make an otherwise solvent firm bankrupt. See In re Waters, 8 B.R. 163, 166 (Bankr.N.D.Ga.1981).

We have gone into this non-issue at such length only to avoid creating the unsettling impression that contingent liabilities must for purposes of determining solvency be treated as definite liabilities even though the contingency has not occurred. Mitsui has chosen not to make an issue of the contingent nature of the guarantee and of the co-signature of the note; maybe Xonics Medical Systems was really insolvent by the time Mitsui received the payments in issue from Xonics Photochemical, so that the contingent liability was no longer contingent. The only argument Mitsui makes against the finding that the payments to it were voidable preferences is that Xonics Photochemical was not insolvent when they were made because the transactions between it and its affiliates were (1) void under state law (the parties agree that the applicable state law is that of Illinois), or (2) voidable as fraudulent conveyances. If either contention is correct, the transactions created no liabilities on the part of Xonics Photochemical and therefore could not have made it insolvent, whatever the plight of Xonics Medical Systems; hence section 547(b) would not be triggered.

1. When a parent causes one of its subsidiaries to guarantee another's (or the parent's own) debts, there is an obvious danger — one indeed that has materialized in this case — that creditors of the guarantor, who normally are unaware of the contingent liability and may not even be aware of their debtor's affiliation with other corporations, will find themselves, without warning, dealing with a suddenly less solvent (not, as we have been at pains to stress, necessarily insolvent) debtor. The effect of the guarantee, especially where as here it is a part of a network of guarantees that have the effect of making the debts of each affiliate debts of all the other affiliates as well, is similar to that of a rule of law that treats the assets of affiliated corporations as a common pool available to the creditors of each affiliate. Such rules have sometimes been advocated, but the law has refused to adopt them, for just the reason stated; they make it harder for creditors of an affiliated corporation to assess their debtor's creditworthiness. If such rules were in force, "a sign of weakness in any member of a family of corporations would lead creditors to descend on each member, strong or weak, to claim their pound of flesh." In re Auto-Train Corp., Inc., 810 F.2d 270, 277 (D.C.Cir.1987). Hence there is no automatic "piercing of the corporate veil" in affiliation settings. The assets of affiliated corporations are not treated as a common pool available to the

14: IN RE XONICS PHOTOCHEMICAL

creditors of each affiliate unless unusual circumstances are present that would make it inequitable to allow the other affiliates to set up the principle of limited liability, the clearest such circumstance being that the creditors of all the affiliates had thought they were dealing with a unitary enterprise. For a thorough discussion see Cissell v. First Nat'l Bank of Cincinnati, 476 F.Supp. 474, 479-81 (S.D.Ohio 1979); see also Main Bank of Chicago v. Baker, 86 Ill.2d 188, 204-06, 56 Ill.Dec. 14, 427 N.E.2d 94, 101-02 (1981); Van Dorn Co. v. Future Chemical & Oil Corp., 753 F.2d 565, 569-70 (7th Cir.1985) (applying Illinois law); cf. In re Kaiser, 791 F.2d 73, 75 (7th Cir.1986).

But here the pooling was accomplished voluntarily, so the focus of analysis switches to the question whether the policy behind generally not piercing the corporate veil precludes ever enforcing a guarantee by one affiliate of another's debts. Courts have not thought so; a guarantee of an affiliate's debt is enforceable (see Telefest, Inc. v. Vu-TV, Inc., 591 F.Supp. 1368, 1377-81 (D.N.J.1984), and cases cited there) provided that the guarantor derives some benefit, even if indirect, see id. at 1379, from the guarantee. The benefit operates as a partial offset to the impairment in the prospects of the guarantor's creditors resulting from the debtor's assuming a contingent liability.

202*202 Whether Xonics Photochemical derived a benefit from its guarantees was a factual question, and we cannot say that the bankruptcy judge's resolution of it was clearly erroneous. Although the primary benefit of the loan accrued to the borrower, Xonics Medical Systems, that company's fortunes were entwined with those of Xonics Photochemical because the smaller company used its larger affiliate's distribution system to distribute its own products. The benefit may not have been great but neither was the cost. Xonics Photochemical was not paying any interest on the loan; it just was a guarantor, and all concerned assumed that the loan would be duly repaid and no guarantor would be out of pocket. The co-signed note was to secure a line of credit on which Xonics Photochemical as well as Xonics Medical Systems could draw; so again there was benefit.

2. Mitsui's second ground for invalidating the interaffiliate transactions is that they are fraudulent conveyances within the meaning of 11 U.S.C. §§ 544(b) or 548(a). These two provisions (well discussed in the student Comment cited at the beginning of this opinion) must be distinguished. Section 544(b) in effect allows the trustee to use the applicable state's law of fraudulent conveyances to set aside obligations incurred by the bankrupt. The action of a parent corporation in causing one of its wholly owned subsidiaries to guarantee the debts of another could in appropriate circumstances be deemed a fraud on the guarantor's own creditors, even if there was consideration for the guaranty — that is, even if the guarantor

14: IN RE XONICS PHOTOCHEMICAL

obtained some benefit from the transaction — so that it would not fail under ordinary contract law. Cf. Rubin v. Manufacturers Hanover Trust Co., 661 F.2d 979, 993 (2d Cir.1981). Nominal consideration is, in general, all that is needed to satisfy the requirements of the law of contracts (see 2 Blackstone, Commentaries on the Laws of England 440 (1766) ("peppercorn"); Farnsworth, Contracts §§ 2.11-.14 (1982)) — a requirement of adequate or commensurate consideration would gravely undermine freedom of contract — but a conveyance not supported by adequate consideration is "fraudulent" (that is, unenforceable) as against existing creditors of a debtor who gave up value in exchange for the inadequate consideration. See King v. Ionization International, Inc., 825 F.2d 1180, 1186 (7th Cir.1987). And, even if the consideration is adequate, the conveyance is fraudulent if made with intent to defraud creditors. See id.

Section 548(a) creates an alternative, federal concept of fraudulent conveyances — or rather two alternative federal concepts. If an obligation was incurred within one year before the filing of the petition for bankruptcy, and there was actual intent to defraud either an existing or a future creditor, the trustee can avoid the obligation. 11 U.S.C. § 548(a)(1). Alternatively, if the debtor "received less than a reasonably equivalent value in exchange for such ... obligation" and was insolvent on the date the obligation was incurred, the trustee again can avoid the obligation. 11 U.S.C. § 548(a)(2).

We shall not have to decide whether the obligations that Xonics Photochemical incurred by virtue of its guarantee of the loan to Xonics Medical Systems and of its becoming a co-maker with XMS of a note are vulnerable under either 544(b) or 548(a). The right to invoke these provisions belongs not to a particular unsecured creditor such as Mitsui but to the trustee (or debtor in possession) as the representative of all the unsecured creditors; and in this case the debtor in possession has not invoked either provision. It is not as if Mitsui itself had been a creditor harmed by the allegedly fraudulent conveyances; they preceded the payments in issue. Mitsui is seeking to stand in the shoes of creditors who may have been harmed, but only the trustee or debtor in possession can do that.

Since there is no trustee and the debtor in possession remains an affiliate of the firm whose debt the debtor had guaranteed, Mitsui is entitled to wonder whether the refusal by the debtor in possession to try to void the guarantee (and perhaps the co-signed note as well) was really made in good faith. But, if so, Mitsui could have sought the appointment of a trustee in bankruptcy, see 11 U.S.C. § 1104, and it 203*203 has never done so. Mitsui says it doesn't have enough at stake in this case to warrant bearing the expense of proving the need for the appointment of a trustee; yet it seems willing to supply the very same proof in order to per-

14: IN RE XONICS PHOTOCHEMICAL

suade us that it should be allowed to stand in the shoes of the debtor in possession and invoke fraudulent-conveyance law.

An alternative route possibly open to Mitsui, see In re Automated Business Systems, Inc., 642 F.2d 200 (6th Cir.1981); In re Jones, 37 B.R. 969 (Bankr.N.D.Tex.1984), was to ask the bankruptcy court to allow it to bring a form of derivative suit in the name of the debtor. But before it could do any such thing it would have to convince the court that the debtor was shirking his statutory responsibilities; and this Mitsui has never done. Cf. Fox Valley AMC/Jeep, Inc. v. AM Credit Corp., 836 F.2d 366 (7th Cir.1988), and cases cited there.

In these circumstances a better argument for Mitsui from sections 544(b) and 548(a), but one that Mitsui does not make, is that these provisions supply another reason for writing down the contingent liabilities upon which the finding of Xonics Photochemical's insolvency at the time of the preferential payments was (in part anyway) based. For if by virtue of fraudulent-conveyance law the liabilities might not be enforceable in the event of bankruptcy (depending of course on what a trustee in bankruptcy or debtor in possession might choose to do) — and indeed might be voided in an independent action before bankruptcy — this would be another reason for thinking that these liabilities should be drastically discounted in deciding whether they had made the debtor insolvent, and hence whether the payments to Mitsui are voidable under section 547(b). An unenforceable debt is not much of a liability.

Mitsui has presented no ground on which we are authorized to set aside the voiding of the payments made to it.

AFFIRMED.

15: BALDI V SAMUEL SON

Joseph A. BALDI, et al., Plaintiffs-Appellants,

v.

SAMUEL SON & COMPANY, LTD., et al., Defendants-Appellees.

Nos. 08-1022, 08-1136.

United States Court of Appeals, Seventh Circuit.

Argued September 24, 2008.
Decided November 24, 2008.

580*580 Jade R. Lambert, Perkins Coie, John M. Christian, (argued), Phelan, Cahill & Quinlan, Brian M. Graham, Smith Amundsen, 581*581 LLC, Chicago, IL, for Plaintiffs-Appellants.

Alexander D. Kerr, Jr. (argued), Tishler & Wald, Sean M. Sullivan, Daley, Mohan & Groble, Jodi Rosen Wine, Nixon Peabody LLP, Chicago, IL, for Defendants-Appellees.

Before POSNER, WOOD, and TINDER, Circuit Judges.

POSNER, Circuit Judge.

The trustee in bankruptcy (we simplify—actually there are two trustees) of a defunct firm named Longview Aluminum LLC filed adversary actions in bankruptcy court to recover for the debtor's estate several payments that Longview had made within four years before it declared bankruptcy. The principal basis for the claims and the only one we need discuss is 11 U.S.C. § 544(b), which allows a trustee in bankruptcy to avoid transfers made by the bankrupt that would be voidable under state law if made by an unsecured creditor. The Uniform Fraudulent Transfer Act, in force in Illinois, allows such avoidance if the debtor was insolvent on the date of the transfer and received less than a reasonably equivalent value in exchange. UFTA § 5(a); 740 ILCS 160/6(a). Only the first requirement is at issue. The corresponding provision of the Bankruptcy Code, 11 U.S.C. § 548(a)(1), is materially identical except that the federal provision allowed the trustee to reach back only one year (since raised to two years) before the declaration of bankruptcy, and that was too short a period to do anything for the trustee in this case.

Insolvency is defined by both statutes as having a balance sheet on which liabilities exceed assets. 11 U.S.C. § 101(32)(A); 740 ILCS 160/3(a). The bankruptcy judge found that Longview had not been insolvent during the period, running from February 26, 2001, to April 1, 2002, in which the transfers were made; and

15: BALDI V SAMUEL SON

the district judge affirmed. The trustee had tried only to show that Longview was insolvent on both the beginning and ending dates, on the assumption that if it was insolvent on both dates then probably it was insolvent on the dates of the actual transfers, which fell between those end points; there is nothing to counter this assumption, see Haynes & Hubbard, Inc. v. Stewart, 387 F.2d 906, 908 (5th Cir.1967), so we accept it. This approach is called the "rule of retrojection." In re Mama D'Angelo, Inc., 55 F.3d 552, 554 (10th Cir.1995); Briden v. Foley, 776 F.2d 379, 382-83 (1st Cir.1985). The question is whether Longview was insolvent at the beginning of the transfer period.

A company named Michigan Avenue Partners, LLC (we'll call it "MAP") decided to enter the aluminum industry, and did so by acquiring among other properties the Longview aluminum manufacturing plant, jointly owned by Alcoa and Reynolds Metals, in Washington state. A subsidiary of MAP had brought an antitrust suit against Alcoa and Reynolds that had eventuated in an order forcing the divestiture of the plant—a Pyrrhic victory for antitrust, for the result of the divestiture, as we are about to see, was a reduction in the output of aluminum.

MAP paid $140 million for Longview. But it did not have to dig into its own pockets for the money. The manufacture of aluminum requires large amounts of electricity; and Longview's electricity supplier, the Bonneville Power Administration (an agency within the Department of the Interior), desperate to be able to continue serving its most necessitous customers in a period of electricity shortage, paid Longview Aluminum LLC $226 million to cease buying electricity for the next 16 months. Longview planned to use the $226 million 582*582 not only to pay the purchase price of the plant but also to enable it to resume manufacturing aluminum at the end of this "curtailment" period, as the parties call it. Among the costs it would incur to resume would be some $33 million in union wage payments, and this was recorded as a liability on Longview's balance sheet when the company was formed on February 26, 2001. The balance sheet showed assets of $248 million and liabilities of $206 million.

Longview never did resume operations. By the end of the 16-month curtailment period, falling prices for aluminum and rising prices for electricity had made the production of aluminum from the plant uneconomical. The firm declared bankruptcy. (Its plant was ultimately dismantled.) But although it is a fair guess that Longview was insolvent before the curtailment period ended, the trustee's expert— and essentially his only source of evidence—Brooks D. Myhran (a business consultant who specializes in the valuation of companies), did not attempt to determine at what point during that period Longview became insolvent. The trustee pitched his entire case on showing that Longview had been insolvent from

15: BALDI V SAMUEL SON

the beginning, that is, from February 26, 2001.

Now it is very strange to suppose a start-up company bankrupt from the day of its formation. Especially this start-up. Why would experienced businessmen, which the principals of MAP were, pay $140 million for a firm that had negative value? There is no suggestion that Longview had significant liquidation value, should it never resume operations. So MAP must have thought that Longview would resume operations, or at least had a good enough chance of doing so to make the company worth at least $140 million. Of course many start-ups fail, but if a significant probability of failure sufficed to pronounce a start-up insolvent, how would any start-up finance its operations? Its trade creditors would fear being trapped by sections 544 or 548 of the Bankruptcy Code when they were paid by the start-up for supplies that they had furnished it. The trustee thinks it a killer point that Longview did not have any operating income when it started up. Well, of course not; no start-up starts with an income flow.

The pitfalls of hindsight are especially acute in dealing with a start-up. As we said, start-ups often fail. When one fails, it is easy enough to find an expert who will opine that it was certain to fail from the very start. Such facile proof should rarely be accepted, and it was rightly rejected in this case.

To establish Longview's insolvency at its starting date, Myhran jacked up its liabilities from the $206 million shown on the company's balance sheet to $367 million. He did this by adding contingent liabilities, including a contingent pension liability, contingent post-retirement benefit obligations, contingent severance payments, and the penalty provision in a take-or-pay contract with Bonneville. Contingent liabilities are—contingent. "By definition, a contingent liability is not certain—and often is highly unlikely—ever to become an actual liability. To value the contingent liability it is necessary to discount it by the probability that the contingency will occur and the liability become real." In re Xonics Photochemical, Inc., 841 F.2d 198, 199 (7th Cir.1988); see, e.g., Freeland v. Enodis Corp., 540 F.3d 721, 730 (7th Cir.2008); In re Chase & Sanborn Corp., 904 F.2d 588, 594 (11th Cir.1990). Myhran treated Longview's contingent liabilities as certainties. That invalidated his expert opinion. In re Wallace's Bookstores, Inc., 316 B.R. 254, 260-62 (Bkrtcy. E.D.Ky.2004); see FDIC v. Bell, 106 F.3d 258, 264-65 (8th Cir.1997).

583*583 The pension liability was not Longview's liability; it was the liability of companies affiliated with Longview. It would become Longview's liability only if the affiliates defaulted on their pension obligations, and Myhran offered no estimate of the probability of such an event. The take-or-pay provision required

15: BALDI V SAMUEL SON

Longview to pay some $20 million to Bonneville in the event that Longview did not reopen and therefore did not buy electricity from Bonneville after the curtailment period. Most of the other liabilities that Myhran treated as certain were similarly contingent on Longview's never resuming production. That was a risk, of course, but not a certainty; Myhran made no effort to discount the risk by the probability that it would materialize.

It is true, as explained in Covey v. Commercial National Bank, 960 F.2d 657, 660 (7th Cir.1992), that discounting a contingent liability can result in overstating a debtor's net assets. That is the case when the contingency is not whether there will be liability but whether the debtor will be able to pay it. If the debtor owed a creditor $1 million, but the probability of the creditor's being able to collect the debt was only 10 percent, the creditor's claim would be worth only $100,000 but the debtor's liability, for purposes of calculating its solvency when it assumed the debt, would still be $1 million. But that is not this case. The contingency was the probability that there would be a liability, not that it would be uncollectible. See In re Advanced Telecommunication Network, Inc., 490 F.3d 1325, 1334-36 (11th Cir.2007); Office & Professional Employees Int'l Union v. FDIC, 27 F.3d 598, 601-02 (D.C.Cir. 1994). "To decide whether a firm is insolvent within the meaning of § 548(a)(2)(B)(i), a court should ask: What would a buyer be willing to pay for the debtor's entire package of assets and liabilities? If the price is positive, the firm is solvent; if negative, insolvent." Covey v. Commercial National Bank, supra, 960 F.2d at 660. Longview's package of liabilities included some that might never materialize, so that to calculate the expected cost of the package Myhran would have had to estimate the probability that they would materialize.

In order to depress the appearance of Longview's solvency further, Myhran projected that electricity costs would increase (as in fact they did) and prevent the plant from resuming operations. There were of course pessimists who in February 2001 were predicting a continued rise in electricity prices, and Longview was taking a risk in guessing otherwise. But all businesses are at risk of future changes in supply or demand that cannot be predicted with any certainty; that does not make them insolvent.

We could go on whacking Myhran's evidence, but there is no need. It was radically unconvincing, as the bankruptcy judge, seconded by the district judge, found. Likewise unconvincing is the trustee's alternative ground for avoidance, which is that Longview was "undercapitalized." Undercapitalization is not a synonym for insolvency. Moody v. Security Pacific Business Credit, Inc., 971 F.2d 1056, 1069-71 (3d. Cir.1992). By way of an up-to-date example, suppose a bank is very heavily leveraged—that is, it has a very high ratio of borrowed money to equity. It

15: BALDI V SAMUEL SON

lends out the borrowed money, and as long as the borrowers pay on time it is fine. If many of them default, however, the present value of the bank's revenues may dip below what it owes its depositors and other lenders, and if so then without an adequate equity cushion the bank will go broke. But until the defaults reach the point at which its liabilities exceed its assets, the bank will be solvent. So "undercapitalization," 584*584 which should rather be termed excessive leverage, while it increases the risk of insolvency, is not insolvency and does not require separate consideration in a bankruptcy case.

This case is different from our bank hypothetical because there was not merely a risk but a certainty that there would be a period in which the firm's costs would exceed its revenues, and it needed a capital cushion to survive that period. Concretely, Longview had to have enough capital to be able to maintain the aluminum plant until the end of the curtailment period and then to reopen it and operate it until substantial revenue started flowing into its coffers. Its balance sheet indicated that it had enough capital for these purposes.

AFFIRMED.

16: FREELAND V ENODIS CORP

Daniel L. FREELAND, Trustee, Plaintiff-Appellee, Cross-Appellant,

v.

ENODIS CORPORATION and Welbilt Holding Company, Defendants Appellants, Cross-Appellees, and Marion H. Antonini, et al., Defendants, Cross-Appellees.

Nos. 06-4178, 06-4179, 06-4180, 06-4181.

United States Court of Appeals, Seventh Circuit.

Argued October 23, 2007.
Decided September 2, 2008.

726*726 Steven P. Handler (argued), David S. Rosenbloom, McDermott, Will & Emery, Chicago, IL, J. Joseph Bainton (argued), Bainton McCarthy, New York City, for Appellant.

Catherine L. Steege (argued), Jenner & Block, Chicago, IL, for Plaintiff-Appellee, Cross- Appellant.

Catherine L. Steege (argued), Jenner & Block, Chicago, IL, Gordon E. Gouveia, Shaw, Gussis, Fishman, Glantz, Wolfson & Towbin, Chicago, IL, Richard A. Kempf, Taft Stettinius & Hollister, Indianapolis, IN, for Daniel L. Freeland, Trustee-Appellee.

Before BAUER, CUDAHY and SYKES, Circuit Judges.

CUDAHY, Circuit Judge.

These appeals arise out of bankruptcy proceedings in which Daniel Freeland, Trustee for Consolidated Industries Corp. (Consolidated), sought to recover transfers made by Consolidated to Welbilt Corporation, a company now known as Enodis Corporation (Enodis). The bankruptcy court concluded that the Trustee could avoid over $30 million in transfers made by Consolidated between 1989 and 1998 and the district court affirmed. In addition, the district court, having withdrawn the reference on two of the Trustee's claims, found that the Trustee could avoid transfers made within one year of the filing of Consolidated's bankruptcy petition pursuant to 11 U.S.C. §§ 547 and 548. The defendants appeal these decisions. In his crossappeal, the Trustee challenges the lower courts' rejection of his alter ego/veil piercing claims against the corporate defendants, the district court's refusal to enter judgment against Welbilt Holding Company and the grant of summary judgment for the individual defendants. We conclude that the Trustee can avoid transfers 727*727 from Consolidated to Enodis between 1989

16: FREELAND V ENODIS CORP

and 1995 as fraudulent transfers but remand for further findings on the issue of Consolidated's solvency after 1995. We reverse and remand the district court's grant of summary judgment for the Trustee on his § 547 and § 548 claims. With respect to the Trustee's cross-appeal, we remand for further findings on the Trustee's alter ego/veil piercing claims but affirm the remainder of the district court's judgment.

I. Background

In the 1980s, Consolidated was a successful furnace manufacturer. It was a subsidiary of Welbilt Holding Company, which itself was a subsidiary of Enodis.[1] Enodis was a publiclytraded company and defendants David and Richard Hirsch and their friend Lawrence Gross were its primary shareholders. In 1988, the Wall Street leveraged buyout (LBO) firm Kohlberg & Co. acquired Enodis' stock through a company it formed, Churchill Acquisition Corporation (Churchill). After the leveraged buyout, Churchill owned 63.4% of Enodis' stock and the Hirsches and Gross owned 36.6%. The Hirsches and Gross became Consolidated's directors following the LBO. They were removed from the board in October 1990 and were succeeded by Marion Antonini and Daniel Yih.

Enodis directed Consolidated and its other subsidiaries to deposit its receivables in an account that Enodis controlled. Consolidated's deposits in the account were recorded as assets and Consolidated's assets were reduced by amounts that Enodis used to pay Consolidated's expenses. In February 1989, Enodis directed Consolidated to pay a cash dividend of $6.9 million. In addition, Enodis directed Consolidated to issue two dividend notes (the Notes) to Welbilt Holding. The first, a 10-year note with an interest rate of 13.75%, had a principal amount of $20 million. The second, a 10-year note with an interest rate of 13.75%, had a principal amount of $10 million.

Both dividend notes provided that:

The principal of this Note represents the payment of a dividend declared by the maker's board of directors and therefor is payable only out of funds legally available for the payment of a dividend. If this Note is not paid in full when due, the undersigned hereby agrees to pay all costs and expenses of collection, including reasonable attorneys' fees.

The Notes provided that if Consolidated failed to make an interest payment, they would "become immediately due and payable at the option of the payee." The Notes also stated that they were governed by Indiana law. Enodis collected the interest payments on the Notes by taking funds from Consolidated's deposits in

16: FREELAND V ENODIS CORP

Enodis' accounts and directing that Consolidated make the appropriate book entries. Between 1989 and the end of 1997, Enodis took $23,671,421.32 in interest payments from Consolidated.

Meanwhile, Consolidated began to design a new product line, a project dubbed "Project 92." In 1987, Congress set new standards affecting the furnace manufacturing industry that were to take effect in 1992, and Consolidated's management believed that the company would have to redesign its furnaces in order to comply with the new standards. To this end, Consolidated borrowed $7 million from Tippecanoe County in order to purchase new equipment that was required to manufacture the "Project 92" furnace. Enodis 728*728 guaranteed the loan. As it worked to get its new furnace line off the ground, Consolidated began to confront problems with its horizontal furnaces. A defect in the furnaces was causing fires and warranty claims were not covered by Consolidated's insurance. In 1990, North Carolina's Attorney General investigated Consolidated's furnaces and concluded that they were defective. In 1993, the Consumer Product Safety Commission (CPSC) began investigating another defect in Consolidated's furnaces. About this same time a group of consumers in California threatened to file a class action law suit, further threatening Consolidated's prospective financial health.

By 1994, Enodis had begun trying to sell Consolidated. In 1995, perhaps to make Consolidated more attractive to prospective purchasers, Enodis cancelled the $30 million in dividend notes. Enodis found an interested buyer in William Hall. Hall could not secure financing to purchase Consolidated, however, and the sale to Hall did not close. Consolidated's problems continued to grow. The California class action was certified and in 1997, the CPSC asked Consolidated to recall all of its furnaces in California. In January 1998, Hall, Welbilt Holding and Enodis entered into a Stock Purchase Agreement pursuant to which Welbilt Holding agreed to sell Hall the common stock of Consolidated. In connection with the transaction, Consolidated borrowed $7.5 million from Finova Capital Corporation (Finova) and granted Finova a lien on all of its assets. On January 5, 1998, Enodis loaned Consolidated $108,500 to purchase insurance. On January 6, 1998, the Hall sale closed. Consolidated directed Finova to wire $7,108,500 of the money it borrowed from Finova to Enodis. Seven million dollars corresponded to the purchase price of Consolidated's stock pursuant to the Stock Purchase Agreement. The rest represented repayment of Enodis' January 5 loan to Consolidated. On May 28, 1998, almost five months after the Hall transaction, Consolidated filed for bankruptcy under chapter 11 of the United States Bankruptcy Code.

16: FREELAND V ENODIS CORP

On May 10, 1999, Consolidated filed this lawsuit. A trustee was appointed and was substituted as the plaintiff. The bankruptcy case was subsequently converted to chapter 7. Section 544(b) of the Bankruptcy Code allows the Trustee to "avoid any transfer of an interest of the debtor in property . . . that is voidable under applicable law." 11 U.S.C. § 544(b). The Trustee sought to recover the $6.9 million cash dividend and the interest paid on the Notes, asserting a right to recover these sums under state and federal law governing fraudulent transfers, Indiana common and corporate law and the law of unjust enrichment. In addition, the Trustee brought breach of fiduciary duty claims against the Hirches, Gross, Antonini and Yih, asserted alter ego/veil piercing claims against Enodis and Welbilt Holding and argued that Enodis' claim should be disallowed or equitably subordinated. The Trustee also sought to recover the value of the transfers made in connection with the Hall transaction. The district court withdrew the reference as to Counts VIII and IX of the Trustee's Third Amended Complaint, which related to the Hall transaction.

Some of the Trustee's claims were disposed of on summary judgment. In October 2001, the bankruptcy court granted summary judgment for the Hirches and Gross on the Trustee's breach of fiduciary duty claims, finding that the claims were barred by the applicable statute of limitations. On December 9, 2002, the district court granted summary judgment against Enodis and Welbilt Holding on the Trustee's claims arising from the Hall transaction. The court concluded that 729*729 the Trustee could recover $7,369,559.35 as fraudulent transfers pursuant to 11 U.S.C. § 548. This amount represented $7 million that Consolidated directed Finova to transfer to Enodis on January 6, 1998 as well as $369,559.35 that Consolidated transferred to Enodis between May 28, 1997 and December 30, 1997. The district court also concluded that the Trustee could recover the $108,500 that Consolidated transferred to Enodis on January 6, 1998 as a preference under 11 U.S.C. § 547.

The bankruptcy court conducted a 22 day trial on the remaining counts. After hearing testimony from 19 witnesses and weighing the evidence, which included 457 exhibits, the court concluded that the Trustee was entitled to avoid $30,608,990.69 in transfers from Consolidated to Enodis between 1989 and 1998. This amount comprised the $6.9 million cash dividend as well as $23,671,421.32 in interest charged on the Notes between 1989 and 1998. The bankruptcy court found that the Trustee could recover the entire $30,608,990.69 under theories of actual fraud and unjust enrichment as well as under Indiana common law. The court also concluded that the Trustee could avoid $10,058,731 of those transfers as constructively fraudulent conveyances. In addition, the court disallowed Enodis' proof of claim. The court rejected the Trustee's alter ego/veil

16: FREELAND V ENODIS CORP

piercing claims against Enodis and Welbilt Holding on standing grounds. The court awarded the Trustee $12,780,302.10 in prejudgment interest for a total recovery of $43,389,292.79. Enodis appealed the bankruptcy court's decision and the Trustee filed a crossappeal. The district court affirmed the bankruptcy court's proposed findings of fact and conclusions of law in their entirety. Both parties appeal that decision. We have jurisdiction pursuant to 28 U.S.C. § 158(d).

II. Discussion

The parties raise many challenges to the conclusions of the courts below. We group the issues raised in these appeals as follows: (1) Enodis' appeal of the district court's avoidance of the 1989 $6.9 million cash dividend and the interest payments on the Notes; (2) Enodis' appeal of the district court's grant of summary judgment for the Trustee in connection with the Hall transaction; and (3) the Trustee's cross-appeal.

A. Avoidance of interest payments and the $6.9 million cash dividend

We review the bankruptcy court's factual findings for clear error and its legal conclusions de novo. In re Rivinius, Inc., 977 F.2d 1171, 1175 (7th Cir. 1992). "If the bankruptcy court's `account of the evidence is plausible in light of the record viewed in its entirety,' we will not reverse its factual findings even if we `would have weighed the evidence differently.'" In re Lifschultz Fast Freight, 132 F.3d 339, 343 (7th Cir.1997) (quoting Anderson v. City of Bessemer City, 470 U.S. 564, 573-74, 105 S.Ct. 1504, 84 L.Ed.2d 518 (1985)). Mixed questions of law and fact are subject to de novo review. Mungo v. Taylor, 355 F.3d 969, 974 (7th Cir.2004).

1. The Notes rendered Consolidated insolvent

Enodis' primary challenge to the avoidance of the interest payments and the cash dividend is that the courts below improperly valued the Notes, which led them to conclude that Consolidated was insolvent after the Notes were issued in 1989. The bankruptcy court's finding that Consolidated was insolvent from the time the Notes were issued to the date it filed its bankruptcy petition was central to its conclusion 730*730 that the Trustee can recover all transfers made by Consolidated to Enodis under each theory of recovery asserted by the Trustee. Enodis does not dispute that at the time the Notes were issued, the amounts of the principal of the Notes exceeded Consolidated's assets. Rather, the parties' dispute centers on how to value the Notes for the purposes of determining Consolidated's solvency between 1989 and the time the Notes were cancelled in 1995. The Trustee contends that the Notes represented liabilities in the amount of

16: FREELAND V ENODIS CORP

$30 million. For its part, Enodis argues that the restrictive language on the Notes prohibited Consolidated from paying any principal on the Notes if doing so would render Consolidated insolvent. Thus, Enodis contends, the fair value of the Notes could not be $30 million unless Consolidated had $30 million in funds available for a shareholder distribution, i.e., unless Consolidated could pay the full principal on the Notes and remain solvent. We review the interpretation of the Notes de novo. See Rizzo v. Pierce & Assocs., 351 F.3d 791, 793 (7th Cir.2003) ("Interpretation of an unambiguous contract is a question of law.").

Under Indiana and federal law, a debtor is insolvent if the fair value of its debts exceeds the fair value of its assets. IND.CODE § 32-18-2-12; 28 U.S.C. § 3302. Before the bankruptcy and district courts, Enodis contended that the Notes represented contingent liabilities. A contingent liability is "one that depends on a future event that may not even occur[ ] to fix either its existence or its amount." In re Knight, 55 F.3d 231, 236 (7th Cir.1995); see also In re Mazzeo, 131 F.3d 295, 303 (2d Cir.1997); In re Nicholes, 184 B.R. 82, 88 (9th Cir. BAP 1995); In re McGovern, 122 B.R. 712, 715 (Bankr.N.D.Ind.1989). Because an entity's liability on a contingent debt may never come into being, a contingent liability is not valued at its full amount when assessing the entity's solvency. Rather, a contingent liability is valued at its face amount multiplied by the probability that it will become due. In re Xonics Photochemical, Inc., 841 F.2d 198, 200 (7th Cir.1988).

We agree with the courts below that Consolidated's obligation on the Notes was not contingent. The creation of Consolidated's debt to Welbilt Holding did not depend on the occurrence of an extrinsic future event. Consolidated promised to pay a sum certain on a date certain. The only question was whether Consolidated would have the funds available to pay the amount due on the Notes. Enodis attempts to rely on Delphi Industries, Inc. v. Stroh Brewery Co., 945 F.2d 215 (7th Cir.1991), to support its argument that the Notes were conditional or contingent liabilities. That case involved several loans that, according to the parties' unwritten understanding, were to be paid out of the cash flow or proceeds from the sale of a company. We considered whether the loans could be breached if the funds from which they were to be paid did not exist and concluded that they could be breached. Id. at 217-18. Rather than bolstering Enodis' argument, Delphi Industries supports our conclusion that a limitation on the source from which an obligation can be paid does not render that obligation contingent.

On appeal, Enodis attempts to reframe the issue, asserting that the restrictive language on the Notes constitutes a condition precedent that, if unsatisfied, would have nullified Consolidated's obligation. This argument too is unavailing. "A condition precedent is either a condition which must be performed before the agree-

16: FREELAND V ENODIS CORP

ment of the parties becomes binding, or a condition which must be fulfilled before the duty to perform an existing contract arises." Barrington Mgmt. Co. v. 731*731 Paul E. Draper Family Ltd. P'ship, 695 N.E.2d 135, 141 (Ind.Ct.App.1998). In this case, Consolidated's obligation on the Notes arose when it executed and delivered them. By their terms, the Notes are unconditional promises to pay the principal amount on a date certain as well as interest accruing quarterly. The Notes provided that they would "become immediately due and payable at the option of the payee" upon the occurrence of certain specified events, including Consolidated's failure to make an interest payment. If the Notes were not paid in full when due, Consolidated was bound "to pay all costs and expenses of collection." Interpreting each Note as a whole, Beanstalk Group, Inc. v. AM Gen. Corp., 283 F.3d 856, 860 (7th Cir.2002), we agree with the courts below that the Notes created unconditional, noncontingent obligations on the part of Consolidated. Although we believe this conclusion emerges from the language of the Notes themselves, id. at 859, we note that Enodis charged Consolidated interest pursuant to the Notes and Consolidated performed its obligation to pay that interest, indicating that the parties themselves did not intend Consolidated's obligation on the Notes to be subject to the fulfillment of a condition at some future date.

Enodis also argues for the first time on appeal that the Notes were essentially declared but unpaid dividends and should be treated as other courts have treated stock redemption obligations or accrued but unpaid dividends. In general, arguments not raised before the district court are waived. Prymer v. Ogden, 29 F.3d 1208, 1215 (7th Cir.1994). Further, this case is distinguishable from the cases cited by Enodis because Consolidated delivered the Notes, which by their terms included express promises to pay the principal amount and interest, in payment of the dividends it declared. In addition, in one case on which Enodis seeks to rely, In re Joshua Slocum Ltd., 103 B.R. 610 (Bankr.E.D.Pa.1989), the court adopted the debtor's treatment of redeemable stock as stockholders' equity and concluded that the redemption value of the stock was not required to be treated as debt in determining solvency. Here, as in In re Joshua Slocum, the courts below accepted the parties' accounting treatment of the Notes as well as expert testimony as to how the Notes should be valued. In sum, we find that the courts below properly included the full value of the Notes as liabilities in their solvency analyses.

2. Consolidated's solvency after the Notes were cancelled

The Notes were cancelled in September 1995 and prior to their cancellation, they rendered Consolidated insolvent. We turn our attention to the bankruptcy court's solvency finding after the Notes were cancelled. In order to conclude that

16: FREELAND V ENODIS CORP

Consolidated was insolvent after the Notes were cancelled, the bankruptcy court had to find that the fair value of Consolidated's liabilities continued to exceed its assets. In its proposed findings of fact and conclusions of law, the bankruptcy court did not specifically value Consolidated's assets or liabilities after the Notes were cancelled. Rather, it stated simply that "[b]y the time the dividend notes were cancelled in 1995, the contingent claims had become so numerous, so potentially expensive and so severe that—even after being discounted for their contingent nature—they were sufficient to render Consolidated insolvent." Appellants' App. at 38.

On appeal, Enodis argues that the bankruptcy court erred by failing to estimate Consolidated's contingent liabilities—a catch-all term used by the court that includes product liability and warranty claims. In Xonics, we stated that it is 732*732 necessary to discount a contingent liability "by the probability that the contingency will occur and the liability become real." 841 F.2d at 200. It "must be reduced to its present, or expected, value before a determination can be made whether the firm's assets exceed its liabilities." Id. We reaffirmed the importance of discounting analysis in Covey v. Commercial Nat'l Bank of Peoria, 960 F.2d 657 (7th Cir. 1992), noting that "[d]iscounting a contingent liability by the probability of its occurrence is good economics and therefore good law." Id. at 660. While "[a]bsolute precision . . . is not required," a bankruptcy court must calculate an appropriately discounted value for contingent liabilities. In re Advanced Telecomm. Network, Inc., 490 F.3d 1325, 1336 (11th Cir.2007).

In the present case, the bankruptcy court did not value the contingent liabilities, merely comparing them to "an impending storm that initially looks small when it is on a distant horizon but grows ever darker and more dangerous as it approaches." Appellants' App. at 38. This description, although imaginative, does little to illuminate our understanding of the claims' value. The district court accepted the bankruptcy court's finding. Neither court placed a value on the claims, performed the required discounting analysis or indicated that it relied on any record evidence that purported to perform the required discounting.

The Trustee urges us to conclude that the bankruptcy court followed Xonics based on the court's statement that Consolidated's contingent liabilities rendered the company insolvent "even after being discounted for their contingent nature." Id. But Federal Rule of Civil Procedure 52(a), made applicable to bankruptcy proceedings by Bankruptcy Rule 7052, requires a bankruptcy court to make findings that supply a clear understanding of the grounds underlying the court's decision. See Andre v. Bendix Corp., 774 F.2d 786, 801 (7th Cir.1985) ("Rule 52(a) necessitates that the findings of fact on the merits include as many of the subsidiary

16: FREELAND V ENODIS CORP

facts as are necessary to disclose to the reviewing court the steps by which the trial court reached its ultimate conclusion on each factual issue.") (quoting Denofre v. Transp. Ins. Rating Bureau, 532 F.2d 43, 45 (7th Cir.1976) (per curiam)). Although Rule 52(a) does not require a court to discuss the relevance and importance of each piece of evidence, Mozee v. Jeffboat, Inc., 746 F.2d 365, 370 (7th Cir.1984), it does require a court to clearly state the factual basis for its ultimate conclusion. Kelley v. Everglades Drainage Dist., 319 U.S. 415, 422, 63 S.Ct. 1141, 87 L.Ed. 1485 (1943). In this case, the issue of solvency was highly contested by the parties and the absence of adequate subsidiary findings prevents us from being able to conduct a meaningful review as to whether the court's conclusion that Consolidated was insolvent after 1995 is clearly erroneous. The Trustee seeks to rely on the testimony of its expert and on Consolidated's internal financial statements to support the conclusion that Consolidated was insolvent after the Notes were cancelled, but it is not our station to weigh the evidence and make the findings that are necessary to support the decision. Mozee, 746 F.2d at 370; In re Cesari, 217 F.2d 424, 428 (7th Cir.1954). Remand is required for further subsidiary findings that indicate the factual basis for the bankruptcy court's solvency determination after the Notes were cancelled in 1995.

3. The transfers made prior to the cancellation of the Notes are recoverable as actual fraudulent transfers

The lower courts found that the Trustee could avoid all transfers made 733*733 pursuant to the Notes between 1988 and 1998 as well as the $6.9 million cash dividend under a theory of actual fraud.[2] A finding of fraudulent intent is a finding of fact that we review for clear error. See In re Acequia, Inc., 34 F.3d 800, 805 (9th Cir.1994); In re Jeffrey Bigelow Design Group, Inc., 956 F.2d 479, 481 (4th Cir. 1992); Springmann v. Gary State Bank, 124 F.2d 678, 681 (7th Cir.1941). It is not our station to review factual issues de novo, and we will reverse the findings of the bankruptcy court only if we are "left with the definite and firm conviction that a mistake has been committed." Anderson, 470 U.S. at 573, 105 S.Ct. 1504 (quoting United States v. United States Gypsum Co., 333 U.S. 364, 395, 68 S.Ct. 525, 92 L.Ed. 746 (1948)). "Where there are two permissible views of the evidence, the factfinder's choice between them cannot be clearly erroneous." Id. at 574, 105 S.Ct. 1504.

Under Indiana law, present and future creditors can avoid transfers that were made "with actual intent to hinder, delay, or defraud any creditor of the debtor." IND.CODE § 32-18-2-14. "Proof of fraudulent intent need not be made by direct evidence under Indiana law" and can be inferred from the presence of certain "badges of fraud." United States v. Denlinger, 982 F.2d 233, 236 (7th Cir. 1992).

16: FREELAND V ENODIS CORP

These badges include a transfer of property that renders the debtor insolvent or greatly diminishes his estate; a transaction whereby the debtor retains the benefit of the transferred property; a transfer that is made while litigation is pending; secret transactions outside the usual mode of business; a transfer conducted in a manner different from ordinary methods; and a transfer made in exchange for little or no consideration. Otte v. Otte, 655 N.E.2d 76, 81 (Ind.Ct.App.1995). Although "[n]o one badge of fraud constitutes a per se showing of fraudulent intent," Buffington v. Metcalf, 883 F.Supp. 1198, 1200 (S.D.Ind.1994), the presence of a number of badges of fraud "is said to `create . . . an overwhelming presumption of fraud' or to `raise . . . a strong inference of fraudulent intent.'" Denlinger, 982 F.2d at 236 (citations omitted). Once a Trustee establishes the presence of a number of badges of fraud, the burden shifts to the debtor to provide a legitimate purpose for the challenged transfers. In re Acequia, 34 F.3d at 806; Jones v. Cent. Nat'l Bank of St. Johns, 547 N.E.2d 887, 890-91 (Ind. Ct.App.1989), superseded by statute on other grounds as recognized by Gipperich v. State, 658 N.E.2d 946, 950 (Ind.Ct.App. 1995).

In this case, the bankruptcy court found the presence of several badges of fraud: the transfers were made to an insider; they occurred when Consolidated was being sued and threatened with suit; Consolidated did not receive reasonably equivalent value for the transfers; Consolidated was insolvent when the transfers were made; the transfers were made outside the normal mode of doing business; the transfers were secret; and Consolidated was left without the assets needed to pay its debts.

734*734 Enodis attacks the bankruptcy court's actual fraud conclusion on several grounds. First, it asserts that the court misapplied the badges of fraud. Enodis contends that the bankruptcy court erred in finding that the transfers made pursuant to the Notes were concealed and made outside the usual mode of doing business. Although we do not dispute Enodis' assertion that a dividend may be paid in the form of a note, the Notes in the present case were issued for value in excess of Consolidated's assets. See Litton Indus., Inc. v. Comm'r, 89 T.C. 1086, 1099, 1987 WL 46817 (Tax Ct.1987) (where company had earnings and profits in excess of $30 million, a $30 million distribution in the form of a note constituted a dividend). In addition, the bankruptcy court found that the $6.9 million dividend paid in February 1989 was never declared by Consolidated's board of directors. Enodis contends that this conclusion is clearly erroneous because a former director of Consolidated testified that the dividend was declared at a board meeting. But it is for the bankruptcy court to assess the credibility of witnesses and weigh evidence, and we will not second guess the court's resolution of conflicting evidence. See Anderson, 470 U.S. at 575, 105 S.Ct. 1504. Enodis also

16: FREELAND V ENODIS CORP

faults the bankruptcy court for stating that "the transfers were secret in the sense that they were discernable only by reviewing bookkeeping entries concerning inter-company transfers," arguing that Consolidated was privately-held and had no duty to publicly disclose its finances. Appellants' App. at 41. But the court also noted that creditors who inquired about Consolidated's "finances would have been given only financial information for [Enodis], which did not reflect any information concerning the transfers from Consolidated." Id. at 43. The bankruptcy court's findings thus support its conclusion that the transfers were secret and outside the usual mode of doing business.

Enodis also contends that there was insufficient evidence to support the conclusion that the transfers were made at a time when Consolidated was being sued or threatened with suit. Whether a transfer is fraudulent "must be judged by the circumstances existing at the time of the conveyance and not by subsequent events having no actual connection with the transaction." United States v. Smith, 950 F.Supp. 1394, 1404 (N.D.Ind.1996) (citing Stamper v. Stamper, 227 Ind. 15, 83 N.E.2d 184 (1949); Deming Hotel Co. v. Sisson, 216 Ind. 587, 24 N.E.2d 912 (1940)). Contrary to Enodis' assertions, the bankruptcy court did not base its finding of the litigation badge of fraud on the CPSC and California class action lawsuit, which occurred after 1992. The court heard testimony from Consolidated's former president, Richard Weber, that Consolidated began to see an increase in warranty and litigation claims in the mid-1980s and that he notified Consolidated's other directors about these claims. The court's reference to lawsuits against Consolidated by 1990 shows that the possible furnace-related claims against Consolidated that existed when the Notes and $6.9 million dividend were paid were more than the hypothetical lawsuits to which every corporation may be subject. It was reasonable for the court to infer from Consolidated's awareness of serious problems with its furnaces and the existence of lawsuits following fast on the heels of the Notes' being issued that Consolidated knew it faced significant furnace-related claims when it issued the Notes. As for Enodis' contention that the furnace-related liabilities were not viewed as a significant problem and that Consolidated had insurance to cover product liability claims, we decline Enodis' invitation to reweigh the 735*735 evidence and testimony on this point. See Anderson, 470 U.S. at 574-75, 105 S.Ct. 1504.[3]

We also reject Enodis' challenge to the bankruptcy court's finding that the transfers left Consolidated without assets to pay its debts. Enodis argues that any finding of actual fraud is negated by a good faith belief on the part of Consolidated's management as to the company's financial future. But the Trustee elicited testimony from Weber that Consolidated was unable to make expenditures that were crucial to its prospective economic stability because it transferred all of its cash to

16: FREELAND V ENODIS CORP

Enodis in the form of interest payments, undermining the claim that management believed in good faith that Consolidated would continue to be profitable into the 1990s.

Enodis argues that the lower courts' conclusion that Consolidated did not receive reasonably equivalent value in exchange for the interest paid on the Notes is inconsistent with their conclusion that the Notes rendered Consolidated insolvent. Under Indiana law, "[v]alue is given for a transfer or an obligation if, in exchange for the transfer or obligation, property is transferred or an antecedent debt is secured or satisfied." IND.CODE § 32-18-2-13(a). The bankruptcy court concluded that although in general interest paid on an obligation constitutes reasonably equivalent value, because the Notes were issued as dividends, and because dividends do not return value to the company, the Notes and the interest paid on the Notes lacked reasonably equivalent value. We agree with Enodis that there is inconsistency in the bankruptcy court's solvency and reasonably equivalent value conclusions. Since the court treated the Notes as contractual obligations of Consolidated, Consolidated was obligated to pay the interest that accrued on the Notes. Consolidated's payment of the accrued interest constituted "dollar-fordollar forgiveness of a contractual debt," which is "reasonably equivalent value." In re Carrozzella & Richardson, 286 B.R. 480, 491 (D.Conn. 2002).

Despite this inconsistency, we affirm the court's actual fraud finding based on the presence of the other badges of fraud. The transfers were to an insider at a time when Consolidated was insolvent and facing mounting furnace-related liabilities. They were concealed from creditors and were outside the normal mode of doing business. See, e.g., Brandon v. Anesthesia & Pain Mgmt. Assocs., Ltd., 419 F.3d 594, 600 (7th Cir.2005) (criticizing district court for concluding that five badges of fraud were insufficient to support liability); Denlinger, 982 F.2d at 236 (presence of four badges of fraud created presumption of fraudulent intent). The transfers occurred to ensure that Enodis received the bulk of Consolidated's cash during a time when Consolidated was likely going to be facing increasing warranty and liability claims related to its furnaces. Although another court might weigh the evidence differently, we cannot say that the bankruptcy court's finding of actual fraudulent intent is clearly erroneous.

Enodis raises several other challenges to the lower courts' actual fraud analysis, which we will address briefly. It argues that the courts below improperly based their rulings on Enodis' intent rather than on Consolidated's intent. But the bankruptcy 736*736 court's recognition of the sizable benefits Enodis derived from the transfers is insufficient to prove that the court failed to consider Consolidated's intent. Nor do we agree with Enodis that evidence adduced at trial

16: FREELAND V ENODIS CORP

shows the bankruptcy court's fraudulent intent finding to be implausible "in light of the record viewed in its entirety." Anderson, 470 U.S. at 574, 105 S.Ct. 1504; see also Malachinski v. Comm'r, 268 F.3d 497, 506 (7th Cir.2001). Enodis also contends that the lower courts' determination that Messrs. Antonini and Yih did not act recklessly or willfully in allowing the transfers to continue after they joined Consolidated's board of directors in 1990 and 1991 undermines the courts' actual fraud findings. It argues that because corporations can act only through individuals, the absence of intentional misconduct on the part of Antonini and Yih negates the possibility that Consolidated effected the transfers with fraudulent intent. But Antonini and Yih were not directors when the Notes were issued so the fact that they may have acted negligently, as the bankruptcy court suggested, in allowing Consolidated to continue making interest payments on the Notes does not negate the lower courts' determination that the Notes were devised as a scheme to hinder, delay or defraud Consolidated's creditors.

Finally, Enodis contends that the courts below misconstrued the purpose of the Notes, asserting that they represented a way for Consolidated to distribute money to its shareholder in a way that would result in tax savings. The fact that Consolidated saved $465,000 in state income taxes by making the distributions as interest payments does not negate the court's determination that Consolidated intended to hinder, delay or defraud its creditors by making the transfers. Further, the bankruptcy court found that Consolidated transferred $9.5 million more than was necessary to save on its state income taxes, a finding that Enodis does not dispute. We affirm the judgment of the courts below with respect to the $6.9 million cash dividend and transfers made pursuant to the Notes before the Notes were cancelled in 1995.[4]

B. Hall transaction

The Trustee sought to avoid transfers that Consolidated made to Enodis within one year of its bankruptcy filing under 11 U.S.C. §§ 547 and 548. The district court withdrew the reference on these claims. Under § 548, the Trustee sought to recover $7,000,000 that Consolidated transferred to Enodis in connection with Hall's purchase of Consolidated in January 1998.[5] 737*737 The Trustee also alleged that between May 28, 1997 and December 30, 1997, Consolidated transferred $15,815,582.36 into accounts controlled by Enodis. During this period, Enodis made transfers from its accounts on Consolidated's behalf, and the Trustee sought to recover $369,559.35, the difference between Consolidated's deposits and the amount Enodis spent on its behalf. In order to prevail on a fraudulent transfer claim under § 548(a), a trustee must establish that the debtor transferred an interest in property within one year of the petition date, that the

16: FREELAND V ENODIS CORP

debtor received less than reasonably equivalent value in exchange for the transfer and that the debtor was insolvent or was rendered insolvent as a result of the transfer. 11 U.S.C. § 548(a)(1)(B).

The Trustee also sought to avoid Consolidated's January 6, 1998 transfer of $108,500 to Enodis as a preference under § 547. A trustee may avoid a transfer under § 547 if it (1) was made to or for the benefit of a creditor, (2) was for or on account of an antecedent debt, (3) was made while the debtor was insolvent, (4) was made between ninety days and one year before the petition was filed and (5) allowed the creditor to receive more than it otherwise would have. 11 U.S.C. § 547(b).

Both parties moved for summary judgment on these claims and the court granted judgment for the Trustee. Summary judgment is appropriate where, viewing the evidence and construing all reasonable inferences in favor of the non-moving party, the court concludes that there is no genuine issue for trial. Jordan v. Summers, 205 F.3d 337, 341-42 (7th Cir.2000). "A genuine issue for trial exists only when a reasonable jury could find for the party opposing the motion based on the record as a whole." Roger v. Yellow Freight Sys., Inc., 21 F.3d 146, 149 (7th Cir.1994). We review the grant of summary judgment de novo. Moser v. Ind. Dep't of Corr., 406 F.3d 895, 900 (7th Cir.2005).

The district court concluded that when Consolidated transferred money to Enodis in connection with the Hall transaction several months before Consolidated filed for bankruptcy, it was insolvent. In re Consolidated Indus. Corp., 292 B.R. 354, 359-61 (N.D.Ind.2002). The court also concluded that Consolidated received no value as a result of the transaction. Id. at 359. Therefore, the court concluded, the Trustee could avoid the $7 million and the $369,559 amounts under § 548. The court also determined that the $108,500 transfer from Consolidated to Enodis in January 1998 was a voidable preference under § 547.

On appeal, Enodis challenges the court's determination that Consolidated was insolvent at the time of the transfers, claiming that the district court improperly weighed evidence in granting summary judgment for the Trustee. We agree. In concluding that Consolidated was insolvent, the court relied on Consolidated's internal financial statements. Id. at 360. In opposing summary judgment, Enodis proffered a draft audit as evidence that Consolidated was solvent prior to the Hall transaction. The district court rejected the audit's evidentiary value, stating that "[a]n uncompleted draft is not better evidence of the fair value than the statements prepared by Consolidated and sworn to by the highest manager of accounting of Consolidated." Id. at 361. Enodis also submitted a report by its

16: FREELAND V ENODIS CORP

expert, Keith Gardner. The court noted that inconsistencies existed between Gardner's deposition testimony and the conclusion he reached in his expert report and appears to have disregarded his report. Id. at 360.

738*738 On appeal, the Trustee defends the district court's solvency ruling, asserting that the draft audit had not been authenticated and was excludable as unreliable hearsay evidence. But the Trustee did not make this argument before the district court and thus has waived it. Zayre Corp. v. S.M. & R. Co., 882 F.2d 1145, 1150 (7th Cir.1989) ("An evidentiary objection not raised in the district court is waived on appeal . . . and this rule holds as true for a summary judgment proceeding as it does for a trial.") (internal citation omitted). The Trustee also argues that remand would be pointless because during the trial before the bankruptcy court, the author of the draft audit testified that if he had completed it, it would have shown that Consolidated was insolvent. When we review a district court's grant of summary judgment, our review is limited to the information that was before the court when it made its ruling. Hildebrandt v. Ill. Dep't of Natural Res., 347 F.3d 1014, 1024 (7th Cir.2003) (citing Harrods Ltd. v. Sixty Internet Domain Names, 302 F.3d 214, 242 (4th Cir.2002); Chapman v. AI Transp., 229 F.3d 1012, 1028 (11th Cir. 2000)). Thus, we will not consider the testimony that was elicited at trial. With respect to the district court's treatment of the defendant's expert's report, the court appears to have discredited his report in part because of inconsistencies with his deposition testimony. But credibility determinations are not a matter for summary judgment. Washington v. Haupert, 481 F.3d 543, 550 (7th Cir.2007). Viewing the evidence in the light most favorable to Enodis, as we must on summary judgment, we conclude that Enodis adduced evidence sufficient to raise a genuine issue of material fact as to Consolidated's solvency in the year prior to the filing of the bankruptcy petition.

Enodis contends that the district court should have entered summary judgment for Enodis on the fraudulent transfer issue because Consolidated received reasonably equivalent value in exchange for the challenged transfers and that we should enter judgment in its favor. Enodis faults the district court for failing to view Consolidated's transfers to Enodis and transfers made by Enodis as part of a single, integrated transaction in which Consolidated received reasonably equivalent value in exchange for the Hall transaction transfers. But Enodis did not make this argument before the district court and we will not consider it for the first time on appeal. See Republic Tobacco v. N. Atl. Trading Co., 381 F.3d 717, 728 (7th Cir. 2004); 10A WRIGHT, MILLER & KANE, FEDERAL PRACTICE AND PROCEDURE § 2716 (3d ed.1998). Moreover, the Trustee raised alternative theories of recovery, namely, that he could recover the transfers as preferences or as actual fraudulent transfers. The district court did not address these theories, precluding

16: FREELAND V ENODIS CORP

entry of summary judgment for Enodis. Chicago College of Osteopathic Med. v. George A. Fuller Co., 719 F.2d 1335, 1340-41 (7th Cir.1983). We reverse the court's entry of summary judgment for the Trustee and remand for trial as to the Trustee's preference and fraudulent transfer claims.[6]

C. Trustee's Cross-Appeal

1. Alter ego/veil piercing claims

The Trustee brought alter ego/veil piercing claims against Enodis and Welbilt 739*739 Holding, seeking a judgment that the Trustee could collect from Enodis and Welbilt Holding any amounts needed to satisfy Consolidated's creditors. The bankruptcy court concluded that the Trustee lacked standing under §§ 541(a) or 544(a) of the Bankruptcy Code to bring these claims. On appeal from the bankruptcy court, the district court concluded that the Trustee did in fact have standing to bring alter ego/veil piercing claims against Enodis and Welbilt Holding under § 541.[7] However, the court stated that it agreed with the bankruptcy court's "ultimate legal conclusion that the Trustee's claims fail under that section." Appellants' App. at 87. The Trustee contends that the district court erred in concluding that the Trustee was not entitled to judgment on his alter ego/veil piercing claims by purporting to adopt a ruling that the bankruptcy court never made and by failing to review de novo the merits of the Trustee's claims.

In order to prevail on an alter ego/veil piercing claim under Indiana law, a court will consider whether the plaintiff has adduced evidence showing:

(1) undercapitalization; (2) absence of corporate records; (3) fraudulent representation by the corporation's shareholders or directors; (4) use of the corporation to promote fraud, injustice, or illegal activities; (5) payment by the corporation of individual obligations; (6) commingling of assets or affairs; (7) failure to observe required formalities; or (8) other shareholder acts or conduct ignoring, controlling or manipulating the corporate form.

Nat'l Soffit & Escutcheons, Inc. v. Superior Sys., Inc., 98 F.3d 262, 265-66 (7th Cir.1996) (citing Aronson v. Price, 644 N.E.2d 864, 867 (Ind.1994)). As we have already noted, Rule 52(a) requires that the court in a bench trial set forth "findings, stated either in the court's opinion or separately, which are sufficient to indicate the factual basis for the ultimate conclusion." Rucker v. Higher Educ. Aids Bd., 669 F.2d 1179, 1183 (7th Cir.1982) (citation omitted). Doing so serves two purposes: "(1) to provide appellate courts with a clear understanding of the basis of the trial court's decision, and (2) to aid the trial court in considering and adjudicating the facts." Bartsh v. Nw. Airlines, Inc., 831 F.2d 1297, 1304 (7th

16: FREELAND V ENODIS CORP

Cir.1987).

In the present case, the district court's opinion does not indicate the factual basis for its conclusion that the Trustee has not presented evidence to support his alter ego/veil piercing claims. Although "findings on every issue presented in a case are unnecessary if the trial court has found such essential facts as lay a basis for the decision," In re Lemmons & Co., 742 F.2d 1064, 1070 (7th Cir.1984), in the present case, the courts below did not include any factual findings relating to the merits of the Trustee's alter ego/veil piercing claims. The decision to disregard the corporate form is a "highly fact-sensitive inquiry," Winkler v. V.G. Reed & Sons, Inc., 638 N.E.2d 1228, 1232 (Ind.1994), and in light of the district court's cursory treatment of the Trustee's claims, we are unable to discern the basis of the court's "ultimate conclusion on each factual issue." Denofre, 532 F.2d at 45. Thus, we vacate and remand with directions to the district court to comply with Rule 52(a).

2. Judgment against Welbilt Holding

The Trustee argues that the district court should have entered judgment 740*740 against Welbilt Holding under 11 U.S.C. § 550(a)(1), which allows a trustee to recover transfers that have been avoided "from the initial transferee of such transfers or the entity for whose benefit the transfers were made." The district court declined to enter judgment against Welbilt Holding on the grounds that judgment in the entire amount had been entered against Enodis and that 11 U.S.C. § 550(d) entitled the Trustee to only a single satisfaction of the judgment amount. Section 550(d) provides that "[t]he trustee is entitled to only a single satisfaction under subsection (a) of this section." The Trustee contends that the district court misconstrued § 550(d) and that although § 550(d) precludes the Trustee from collecting more than once, it does not prevent a court from entering judgment against more than one party. There is some support for the Trustee's position. As defined in the Bankruptcy Code, "or" is not exclusive. See 5 COLLIER ON BANKRUPTCY ¶ 550.02[4] at 550-16 (Alan N. Resnick et al., eds., 15th ed. rev.2007) (citing 11 U.S.C. § 102(5)). "Thus, the trustee can recover from any combination of the entities mentioned [in § 550] subject to the limitation of a single satisfaction." Id. Even if the district court erred, however, in order for the Trustee to be entitled to judgment against Welbilt Holding, he must establish that Welbilt Holding was an entity for whose benefit the transfers were made. The bankruptcy court found that "[t]he record does not indicate that any of Consolidated's money went to [Welbilt] Holding. . . . None of the transfers from Consolidated to [Enodis] were advantageous to [Welbilt] Holding." Appellants' App. at 50. The Trustee does not challenge that finding, arguing that because the transfers were actually owed to

16: FREELAND V ENODIS CORP

Welbilt Holding, it is an entity for whose benefit they were made.

Although a few courts have found that an entity need not actually obtain a benefit in order to be an entity for whose benefit a transfer was made, see, e.g., In re Richmond Produce Co., 118 B.R. 753 (Bankr.N.D.Cal.1990), requiring that the entity actually receive a benefit from the transfer is consistent with the "well-established rule that fraudulent transfer recovery is a form of disgorgement, so that no recovery can be had from parties who participated in a fraudulent transfer but did not benefit from it." In re McCook Metals, L.L.C., 319 B.R. 570, 591 (Bankr. N.D.Ill.2005); see also In re Meredith, 527 F.3d 372, 376 (4th Cir.2008) ("[A] person must actually receive a benefit from the transfer in order to be an `entity for whose benefit' the transfer was made."); In re Compton Corp., 831 F.2d 586, 595 (5th Cir.1987). Imposing liability on a nontransferee based on the debtor's intent to benefit him, without requiring proof that the nontransferee actually benefited from the transfer, "bears no relationship to the theory of cancellation that historically underlies avoidance remedies." Larry Chek & Vernon O. Teofan, The Identity and Liability of the Entity for Whose Benefit a Transfer Is Made under Section 550(a): An Alternative to the Rorschach Test, 4 J. BANKR.L. & PRAC. 145, 156 (1995). Because Welbilt Holding did not derive a benefit from the transfers, we affirm the district court's refusal to enter judgment against Welbilt Holding.

3. Hirsch defendants

The courts below concluded that the Trustee's claims against defendants Hirsch, Hirsch and Gross were barred by Indiana's two-year statute of limitations on breach of fiduciary duty claims and granted their motion for summary judgment. Under Indiana law, a claim for breach of fiduciary duty is subject to the two-year statute of limitations 741*741 that applies to tort claims for injury to personal property. Shriner v. Sheehan, 773 N.E.2d 833, 846 (Ind.Ct.App.2002). The Trustee filed this action on May 10, 1999. Although the filing date was almost nine years after the Hirsch defendants left Consolidated's board, the Trustee argues that the two-year limitations period should have been tolled under the adverse domination doctrine. The doctrine of adverse domination allows the tolling of the statute of limitations where the entity [to whom the cause of action belonged] is controlled by or dominated by wrongdoers. The statute of limitations begins to run again when the wrongdoers lose control of the entity. The rationale behind the adverse domination doctrine is premised upon the principle that officers and directors who have harmed the entity cannot be expected to take legal action against themselves.

16: FREELAND V ENODIS CORP

Resolution Trust Corp. v. O'Bear, Overholser, Smith & Huffer, 840 F.Supp. 1270, 1284 (N.D.Ind.1993) (citation omitted) (alteration in original).[8] The courts below concluded that Marion Antonini, who replaced Hirsch, Hirsch and Gross in October 1990, was "a disinterested outsider from the standpoint of any wrong which his predecessors may have committed." Appellants' App. at 90. Thus, any claim the Trustee had against the Hirsch defendants accrued in October 1990 and the applicable statute of limitations required Consolidated to bring its breach of fiduciary duty claims against the Hirsch defendants by October 1992.

When the Hirsch defendants moved for summary judgment, they asked the court to accept the facts in the Trustee's Third Amended Complaint as true. In the Third Amended Complaint, the Trustee alleged that Enodis controlled the composition of Consolidated's board of directors through January 1998. But this allegation is insufficient to create a genuine issue of material fact as to whether the Hirsches exerted any control over Consolidated after they left the board such that they would be in a position to prevent the company from suing them for breach of fiduciary duty. Celotex v. Catrett, 477 U.S. 317, 331, 106 S.Ct. 2548, 91 L.Ed.2d 265 (1986). We affirm the bankruptcy court's conclusion that the statute of limitations for the Trustee's claims against the Hirsch defendants began running in 1990 and had lapsed by the time the bankruptcy petition was filed in 1998.

III. Conclusion

To summarize, we affirm the district court's judgment allowing the Trustee to recover the $6.9 million dividend and transfers made pursuant to the Notes prior to the cancellation of the Notes in 1995. We remand for further findings on the court's solvency determination after the Notes were cancelled. We reverse and remand the court's entry of summary judgment for the Trustee on the transfers related to the Hall transaction. We vacate the judgment against the Trustee on his alter ego/veil piercing claims and remand for further proceedings consistent with this opinion. Finally, we affirm the district court's refusal to enter judgment 742*742 against Welbilt Holding and its entry of summary judgment for the Hirsch defendants. AFFIRMED in part, REVERSED in part, VACATED in part and REMANDED with directions. Each party shall bear its own costs of these appeals.

[1] We will refer to "Welbilt Corporation" as "Enodis" so as to avoid any confusion with Welbilt Holding Company, which will be referred to as "Welbilt Holding."

16: FREELAND V ENODIS CORP

[2] The Indiana and federal statutes provide that in the case of actual fraud, a cause of action does not begin to accrue until the transfer has been or could reasonably have been discovered. IND.CODE § 32-18-2-19(1)(B); 28 U.S.C. § 3306(b)(1). The bankruptcy court concluded that Consolidated's creditors could not have discovered the transfers when they occurred because the transfers only appeared on Consolidated's internal financial statements and in intercompany memoranda directing that the transfers be made. Thus, the bankruptcy court tolled the statute of limitations to allow the Trustee to recover all of the transfers made between 1989 and 1998.

[3] Enodis also contends that the courts below used improper hindsight analysis in making their fraudulent intent determinations. This argument reiterates Enodis' points relating to the litigation badge of fraud and we reject it for the same reasons we reject its challenges to the litigation badge of fraud.

[4] The lower courts concluded that the Trustee could avoid over $10 million in transfers as constructively fraudulent conveyances. Constructive fraud requires the trustee to show that the debtor transferred its property within the statutory look-back period, that it did not receive reasonably equivalent value in exchange for the transfer and that the debtor was insolvent at the time of or as a result of the transfer. IND.CODE. § 32-18-2-15; 28 U.S.C. § 3304. Our conclusion that the lower courts' solvency analysis is inconsistent with their conclusion that Consolidated did not receive reasonably equivalent value in exchange for the interest payments leads us to conclude that the courts below erred in finding that the Trustee could avoid the transfers as constructively fraudulent. This does not affect our conclusion that the Trustee can recover the transfers since they are recoverable as actually fraudulent transfers. Because we conclude that the transfers are recoverable as actually fraudulent, we need not discuss whether they could also be recovered under the law of unjust enrichment or Indiana common law, as the courts below held.

[5] The Trustee also argued in the alternative that the $7,000,000 transfer should be avoided as a preference under § 547. Because the court concluded that the transfer could be avoided pursuant to § 548, it never reached the Trustee's § 547 argument.

[6] We note that the district court purported to avoid the same $369,559.35 transfer twice— once in affirming the bankruptcy court's conclusion that the Trustee could avoid transfers made between 1989 and 1998, and once in granting summary judgment for the Trustee on his § 548 claims. The Trustee is entitled to recover this amount once and the district court should ensure that this amount is

16: FREELAND V ENODIS CORP

not awarded twice again following remand.

[7] The district court affirmed the bankruptcy court's ruling that the Trustee lacked standing to assert alter ego/veil piercing claims under § 544(a). The Trustee does not appeal this determination.

[8] It is unclear whether the adverse domination doctrine applies in Indiana, City of E. Chi. v. E. Chi. Second Century, Inc., 878 N.E.2d 358, 381 n. 22 (Ind.Ct.App.2007), although one court has assumed that it does. Resolution Trust Corp., 840 F.Supp. at 1284 (basing its decision on the "supposition" that an Indiana court would apply the adverse domination doctrine to toll the statute of limitations until the defendants no longer dominated the board of directors). We assume for the purposes of this discussion that the doctrine was available to the Trustee.

17: ROBLIN INDUSTRIES V FORD MOTOR

In re ROBLIN INDUSTRIES, INC., Debtor.

William E. LAWSON, Trustee, in Bankruptcy of Roblin Industries, Inc., Plaintiff-Appellee,

v.

FORD MOTOR COMPANY, Defendant-Appellant.

No. 588, Docket 95-5036.

United States Court of Appeals, Second Circuit.

Argued November 29, 1995.
Decided February 26, 1996.

31*31 32*32 33*33 Donald P. Sheldon, Buffalo, New York, for Plaintiff-Appellee.

Gabriel J. Ferber, Nesper, Ferber & DiGiacomo, L.L.P., Buffalo, New York, for Defendant- Appellant.

Before: McLAUGHLIN and LEVAL, Circuit Judges, and KOELTL,[*] District Judge.

KOELTL, District Judge:

This is an appeal by Ford Motor Company ("Ford") from an order of the United States District Court for the Western District of New York, Richard Arcara, District Judge, affirming a final judgment and order of the Bankruptcy Court, Beryl E. McGuire, Chief Judge. See Lawson v. Ford Motor Co. (In re Roblin Indus., Inc.), 127 B.R. 722 (Bankr. W.D.N.Y.1991). The underlying bankruptcy case was filed originally by the debtor Roblin Industries, Inc. ("Roblin") as a Chapter 11 petition on July 1, 1985, and later converted to a Chapter 7 liquidation in August 1987. The Chapter 7 trustee, William E. Lawson (the "Trustee") brought a complaint in this case against Ford to recover a payment made by Roblin to Ford on the basis that the payment was a preferential transfer recoverable under 11 U.S.C. § 547. Following a two day non-jury trial, judgment was entered for Roblin and the District Court affirmed.

On this appeal, Ford contends that the Bankruptcy Court erred in concluding that the Trustee proved that Roblin was insolvent when it made the preferential payment to Ford. Ford also contends that the transfer should not have been avoided in any event because the payment fell within the statutory exception under 11 U.S.C. § 547(c)(2) for certain specified payments made in the ordinary course of business.

17: ROBLIN INDUSTRIES V FORD MOTOR

Our review of an order of the district court acting as an appellate court in a bankruptcy proceeding is plenary. We review independently the factual findings of the bankruptcy court for clear error, while questions of law are reviewed de novo. Resolution Trust Corp. v. Best Prods. Co., Inc. (In re Best Prods. Co., Inc.), 68 F.3d 26, 29 (2d Cir.1995); United States Lines (S.A.), Inc. v. United States (In re McLean Indus., Inc.), 30 F.3d 385, 387 (2d Cir.1994), cert. denied, ___ U.S. ___, 115 S.Ct. 934, 130 L.Ed.2d 880 (1995); Gulf States Exploration Co. v. Manville Forest Prods. Corp. (In re Manville Forest Prods. Corp.), 896 F.2d 1384, 1388 (2d Cir.1990). We affirm.

I.

Roblin, a manufacturer of specialized steel, relied upon Ford for raw scrap metal. By September 1984, Roblin had accumulated a trade debt to Ford for purchases of scrap metal of about $745,000 and had fallen behind on its payments. Although Ford had made no effort to collect the overdue account, Roblin, out of concern for ensuring a steady source of supply, approached Ford to arrange a repayment plan for the outstanding balance and to negotiate terms for new purchases. After discussion, Ford and Roblin entered into an agreement whereby Roblin would pay off its debt to Ford at $50,000 per month plus interest at an annual rate of ten percent. Ford also agreed to continue selling scrap metal to Roblin with payment due on shipment. Over the following months, Roblin made its monthly payments to Ford pursuant to the agreement.

On July 1, 1985, Roblin filed its voluntary Chapter 11 petition. The payment that is the subject of this action was made by check dated March 29, 1985 and honored on April 34*34 2, 1985 in the amount of $53,320.78.[1] In the action brought before the Bankruptcy Court, the Trustee recovered this payment as a voidable preferential transfer.[2]

II.

To be recoverable as a preferential transfer, a payment must satisfy all of the requirements of 11 U.S.C. § 547(b); it must have been:

1. to or for the benefit of a creditor;
2. for or on account of an antecedent debt owed by the debtor before such transfer was made;
3. made while the debtor was insolvent;
4. on or within 90 days before the date of filing of the petition (providing that the payee is not an insider); and
5. enable the benefited creditor to receive more than such creditor would have

17: ROBLIN INDUSTRIES V FORD MOTOR

received had the case been a chapter 7 liquidation and the creditor not received the transfer.

See 11 U.S.C. § 547(b). The Trustee bears the burden of proving each of these elements by a

preponderance of the evidence. See 11 U.S.C. § 547(g); ABB Vecto Gray, Inc. v. First Nat'l Bank of Bethany, Oklahoma, 9 F.3d 871, 874 (10th Cir.1993) (citing 4 Collier on Bankruptcy ¶ 547.21[5], at 547-107 (15th ed. 1995)); Ralar Distribs., Inc. v. Rubbermaid, Inc. (In re Ralar Distribs., Inc.), 4 F.3d 62, 67 (1st Cir.1993).

Ford contests only the third element — whether the Trustee proved that the debtor was insolvent when the alleged preferential transfer was made. None of the other elements are disputed. For the purposes of the third element, the debtor is presumed insolvent during the ninety days preceding the filing of the petition. See 11 U.S.C. § 547(f); Riddervold v. Saratoga Hosp. (In re Riddervold), 647 F.2d 342, 344 (2d Cir.1981). This presumption is a rebuttable one. A creditor may rebut the presumption by introducing some evidence that the debtor was not in fact insolvent at the time of the transfer. If the creditor introduces such evidence, then the trustee must satisfy its burden of proof of insolvency by a preponderance of the evidence. See Clay v. Traders Bank of Kansas City, 708 F.2d 1347, 1351 (8th Cir.1983) (presumption affords initial benefit but ultimate burden remains on trustee to prove insolvency); Nugent v. First American Bank, No. 91-CV-1410, 1992 WL 200635, at *3 (N.D.N.Y. Aug. 12, 1992).

Ford argued to the Bankruptcy Court that it successfully rebutted the presumption by introducing the schedules of assets and liabilities prepared by Roblin in support of its Chapter 11 bankruptcy petition. The "Summary of Debts and Property" in the schedules listed total debts of $66,039,334.90 and total property of $69,757,243.30, resulting in an excess of assets over liabilities of a little more than $3.7 million. Ford also introduced the amendments to the schedules that reflected additional liabilities of $626,730.38, of which $540,000 was disputed. The amendments also added real property omitted from the original schedules at the $775,000 price for which the property was sold six months after the filing. Based on these amendments, Roblin's assets exceeded liabilities by nearly $3.9 million. The schedules were prepared by Roblin's counsel and verified by its president.

Ford also pointed to the fact that Marine Midland Bank and Chemical Bank, Roblin's primary lenders, had committed to provide $12 million in post-petition financing on the basis of the appraisals used to compile the 35*35 schedules.

17: ROBLIN INDUSTRIES V FORD MOTOR

Although this financing was withdrawn in December 1986, Ford maintains that the willingness of the banks to lend on the basis of the appraisals bolsters the accuracy of the appraisals and lends further support to the conclusion that Roblin was solvent at the time the payment to Ford was made in April 1985.

The Bankruptcy Court found that the presumption of insolvency was rebutted. The Trustee, however, offered evidence to establish that, indeed, the debtor was insolvent at the time of the transfer. Primarily, the Trustee relied on a February 1984 SEC Registration Statement amending the company's S-1 Registration Statement with respect to stock warrants. The Registration Statement included financial statements as well as descriptive text recounting Roblin's operations, financial performance, and industry conditions. The balance sheet, which valued most property at cost less depreciation, showed assets as of October 8, 1983, of $42,130,495 and liabilities of $51,528,323, resulting in a negative net worth of $9,397,828. The Registration Statement indicated continuing losses from operations for each year from 1979 through nearly all of 1983, including losses of $7,763,976 in 1982 and $3,763,305 for the first forty weeks of 1983.

The Registration Statement included assessments of Roblin's financial health in particular, and the condition of the steel industry generally. The picture painted was grim. The industry was described as operating during 1982 at severely depressed levels, and the survival of the company was described as depending on a substantial rebound in steel demand. The description from the Registration Statement of the adverse market conditions facing Roblin during the mid-1980s appears as an appendix to the Bankruptcy Court's opinion. See Roblin, 127 B.R. at 725-27.

Based principally on the information contained in the Registration Statement, combined with misgivings about the reliability of the schedules, the Bankruptcy Court found that Roblin was, in fact, insolvent at the time the payment was made to Ford. Id., 127 B.R. at 724. The Bankruptcy Court found that Roblin was a "failing business in a failing industry." Id. The Court indicated that it had considered the asset values from the schedules but determined that those values "could not be sustained in the crucible of reality." Id. The District Court affirmed, concluding that this result was not clearly erroneous. In re Roblin Indus., Inc., 91 CV 523A (W.D.N.Y. Mar. 29, 1995) (Roblin II).

Ford argues that the Bankruptcy Court's finding that Roblin was insolvent at the time the payment in question was made was clearly erroneous, particularly because the use of the balance sheet values from the Registration Statement was insufficient to sustain the Trustee's burden to show that the debtor was insolvent.

17: ROBLIN INDUSTRIES V FORD MOTOR

III.

The Bankruptcy Court has broad discretion when considering evidence to support a finding of insolvency. Insolvency is a question of fact, Klein v. Tabatchnick, 610 F.2d 1043, 1048 (2d Cir.1979); Join-In Int'l. (U.S.A.) Ltd. v. New York Wholesale Distribs. Corp. (In re Join-In Int'l (U.S.A.) Ltd.), 56 B.R. 555, 560 (Bankr.S.D.N.Y.1986), and the findings of the Bankruptcy Court in this regard will not be disturbed unless they are clearly erroneous. See Harvey v. Orix Credit Alliance, Inc., (In re Lamar Haddox Contractor, Inc.), 40 F.3d 118, 120 (5th Cir. 1994); Beldock v. Faberge, Inc. (In re S & W Exporters, Inc.), No. 88 Civ. 8780, 1990 WL 52300, at *4 (S.D.N.Y. Apr. 18, 1990) ("The question of insolvency is an issue of fact and a Bankruptcy Court's findings cannot be set aside unless they are clearly erroneous." (citing 1 Collier on Bankruptcy ¶ 1.19[5], at 130.12 (14th ed. 1974))).

"Insolvent" is defined by the Code as a "financial condition such that the sum of [the] entity's debts is greater than all of [the] entity's property, at a fair valuation...." 11 U.S.C. § 101(32). Fair value, in the context of a going concern, is determined by the fair market price of the debtor's assets that could be obtained if sold in a prudent manner within a reasonable period of time to pay the debtor's debts. See Rubin v. Manufacturers Hanover Trust Co., 661 F.2d 979, 995 (2d Cir.1981); Syracuse Engineering Co., Inc. v. 36*36 Haight, 110 F.2d 468, 471 (2d Cir.1940); Coated Sales, Inc. v. First Eastern Bank, N.A. (In re Coated Sales, Inc.), 144 B.R. 663, 666-67 (Bankr.S.D.N.Y.1992); see also Briden v. Foley, 776 F.2d 379, 382 (1st Cir.1985) (Timbers, J.) (fair valuation of assets should focus on fair market value "reduced by the value of the assets not readily susceptible to liquidation"); 2 Collier on Bankruptcy ¶ 101.32[5], at 101-116 to 101- 118 (15th ed. 1995).

Ford contends that the evidence of Roblin's insolvency was inadequate to sustain the Trustee's burden because the evidence consisted of asset values from the balance sheet in the Registration Statement, values based on the cost rather than the market value of those assets.

Ford is correct that many of the balance sheet figures in the Registration Statement used historical cost less accumulated depreciation, or "book value" for valuing most assets. It is also true that book values are not ordinarily an accurate reflection of the market value of an asset. See, e.g., United States Lines (S.A.), Inc. v. United States (In re McLean Indus., Inc.), 132 B.R. 247, 258 (Bankr.S.D.N.Y.1991) (cost or book value not presumptively equivalent to fair value), aff'd., 162 B.R. 410 (S.D.N.Y. 1993), rev'd. on other grounds, 30 F.3d

17: ROBLIN INDUSTRIES V FORD MOTOR

385 (2d Cir.1994), cert. denied, ___ U.S. ___, 115 S.Ct. 934, 130 L.Ed.2d 880 (1995); DeRosa v. Buildex Inc. (In re F & S Central Mfg. Corp.), 53 B.R. 842, 849 (Bankr.E.D.N.Y. 1985) ("Asset values carried on a balance sheet, even if derived in accordance with generally accepted accounting principles, do not necessarily reflect fair value."). "[T]he market value of particular property may of course differ substantially from its book value, and the market value of certain ... assets may [be] greater or less than their book value." Rubin, 661 F.2d at 995. Nevertheless, while book values alone may be inappropriate as a direct measure of the fair value of property, see Lamar Haddox, 40 F.3d at 121-22; Rubin, 661 F.2d at 995; Varon v. Trimble, Marshall & Goldman, P.C. (In re Euro-Swiss Int'l Corp.), 33 B.R. 872, 885 (Bankr.S.D.N.Y.1983), such figures are, in some circumstances, competent evidence from which inferences about a debtor's insolvency may be drawn. See Schlant v. Schueler (In re Buffalo Auto Glass), 187 B.R. 451, 453 (Bankr.W.D.N.Y.1995) (finding debtor insolvent based on negative retained earnings reported on tax return in absence of any other evidence); Coated Sales, 144 B.R. at 666-67 (using unaudited preliminary balance sheet as evidence of insolvency with respect to preference payment made several months after date of statement).

In any event, Ford is not correct that the only information derived from the SEC Registration Statement was the negative net worth figure of $9.4 million. Certainly this was part of the information on which the Bankruptcy Court relied in concluding that the Trustee had met its burden of proving that Roblin was insolvent at the time of the transfer. See Roblin, 127 B.R. at 724. But the figure itself is by no means the only relevant information found in the Registration Statement, as is evident from the fact that the Bankruptcy Court appended to its opinion a great deal more. The appendix to the Court's opinion includes many of the "High Risk Factors" from the Registration Statement. The first section entitled "Losses" discusses the severe losses Roblin sustained since 1979, including $6.8 million in 1980, $4.1 million in 1981, $7.8 million in 1982, and $3.8 million for the first forty weeks of 1983. The narrative reveals that Roblin's earnings had failed to cover fixed expenses since 1979. According to the Registration Statement, losses were expected to continue through 1983 and future profits would depend on a substantial increase in sales. See id., 127 B.R. at 725-27.

In another section discussing working capital and bank financing, the report indicates that Roblin was unable to pay the principal and interest on its bank debt for the latter half of 1982 and the first half of 1983. Yet another section describes market conditions in the steel industry as "Depression-era," comparing the capacity utilization rate of 49% in 1982 to that of the 1930s. The impact of such dismal demand on Roblin is called "severe." The report concludes that "[Roblin] is

17: ROBLIN INDUSTRIES V FORD MOTOR

dependent for survival upon a continued 37*37 recovery in steel demand." Id., 127 B.R. at 726.

Through the first half of 1985, when the payment to Ford was made, there was no evidence to suggest a recovery had occurred or that Roblin had recuperated. In fact, Roblin's vice president of finance, Gerald Roncolato, testified at trial that the market deterioration that caused the losses beginning in 1979 had continued with "increased intensity" thereafter. Roncolato further testified that he believed Roblin continued to lose money after October 1983, the date of the latest figures in the Registration Statement. In fact, Roncolato expressed the view that, had the banks withdrawn their postpetition financing in December 1985 instead of December 1986, he would have understood it.

In this case, it is appropriate to consider the financial statements included in the Registration Statement, as well as the accompanying descriptive text, to shed light on the schedules of property and debt values. Those schedules, prepared by the debtor, purported to show an excess of assets over liabilities of only about $3.9 million. Indications that the assets were overvalued in excess of $3.9 million would be affirmative evidence that the debtor was insolvent. There was in fact considerable evidence that the asset values in the schedules were overstated.

The schedules prepared in mid-1985 were based to a large extent on appraisals performed some time before, in some cases some real property appraisals dated to 1980. For personal property, appraisals from 1980, updated in 1982 to reflect inflation and market changes but not physical changes, were employed. The attorney who assembled the schedules testified that the schedules were prepared by extrapolating from the older appraisals, and the Bankruptcy Court, with the benefit of the live testimony of the witnesses and an intimate understanding of the case as a whole considered it "impossible to gauge how well founded those values [were]." Roblin, 127 B.R. at 724.

The vintage of the appraisals is not the only reason for a more critical view of the schedules. The largest single asset appearing on the schedules was an entry for the machinery and equipment at the plant in Dunkirk, New York. The testimony at trial indicated that this machinery consisted principally of the GFM rolling machine purchased at a cost of $25 million. Roncolato testified that the machine itself cost $7-8 million while the remaining $17-18 million represented the cost of special modifications to the building in order to house the highly sophisticated equipment. The appraisal of the GFM machine ultimately incorporated in the schedules prepared in mid-1985 indicated the value of this asset in place at $22-23 million. A still later appraisal in 1986 valued the same machine at $18 million.

17: ROBLIN INDUSTRIES V FORD MOTOR

Roncolato also testified that only a sale of the machine in place in the building could be expected to recover the value attributable to the building modifications; the value of the GFM machine alone would be approximately onethird as much.

Given the testimony, there is an ample basis to conclude an appraisal based on sale of the GFM machine in place may well have substantially overstated the fair valuation of the equipment. Moreover, the later 1986 appraisal of $18 million was evidence that the value of the GFM machine in April 1985, even if sold in place, would have been substantially less than the earlier appraisal of $22-23 million. See Coated Sales, 144 B.R. at 668 (court may consider information subsequent to date of payment to assure "valuation is based in reality"). The difference of $4-5 million is enough by itself to absorb entirely the slim margin of solvency on which Ford rests its argument.

Furthermore, the Bankruptcy Court received in evidence a "Summary of Value Conclusions" compiled by the debtor's appraisal firm, which appears to have been prepared in 1982. The summary presents both fair market and liquidation values for the real and personal property at each of six Roblin sites. Several of the fair market values for personal property are the same figures used to prepare the schedules. The summary indicates a $22.1 million difference between the fair market value of Roblin's assets of $63 million and the liquidation value of $40.9 million. The large variance between 38*38 the two appraisal values is significant in light of the evidence of Roblin's continued poor performance and significant losses, the foreign competitive pressures coming to bear, the unusually low demand for steel, and Roblin's precarious creditworthiness. According to the schedules as amended, Roblin was solvent by a mere $3.9 million, only about 5% of its total asset base. The variance in the two appraisals is over five times as much. In light of the other information about the conditions in the industry, Roblin's unstable financial condition, and its persistent losses through 1983, a year after the appraisal updates, we cannot say it is unreasonable to draw an inference that, in April 1985, Roblin could not have realized the values listed in the appraisals and was in fact insolvent.

This is not to suggest that the approach taken in this case is the ideal method of determining insolvency. Whenever possible, a determination of insolvency should be based on seasonable appraisals or expert testimony. See, e.g., Klein, 610 F.2d at 1048 (finding of insolvency often depends on expert testimony). Yet, appraisals are neither the exclusive nor dispositive means to make the determination.

[T]he matrix within which questions of solvency and valuation exist in bankruptcy demands that there be no rigid approach taken to the subject. Because the

17: ROBLIN INDUSTRIES V FORD MOTOR

value of property varies with time and circumstances, the finder of fact must be free to arrive at the "fair valuation" defined in § 101[(32)] by the most appropriate means.

Porter v. Yukon Nat'l. Bank, 866 F.2d 355, 357 (10th Cir.1989).

In light of the circumstances of this case, and our reading of the record and the Bankruptcy Court's opinion, we conclude that the finding that Roblin was insolvent at the time of the April 1985 payment is not clearly erroneous. Had the only basis for the Bankruptcy Court's finding been a negative net worth figure based on book values, we might reach a different conclusion, particularly because the schedules prepared by the debtor, on their face, indicate a thin margin of solvency. Here, however, there is more evidence in the record to support the finding of insolvency than merely the negative net worth figure based on the financial statements appearing in the SEC Registration Statement. The heavy losses sustained by Roblin in the years preceding April 1985, the lethargic demand for steel combined with burgeoning foreign competition, the tenuous state of Roblin's credit standing, the large portion of asset value attributable to the GFM machine and the dynamics of its valuation, the wide gap between fair market and liquidation value, the age of the appraisals, and all of the other factors discussed above, all combine to provide a reasonable basis to conclude that Roblin was insolvent in April 1985. In light of these considerations, we cannot say that the Bankruptcy Court's determination that the Trustee had met its burden of proving that Roblin was in fact insolvent at the time of the transfer was clearly erroneous. That determination is therefore affirmed. Consequently, the April 1985 payment to Ford was a preferential transfer voidable by the Trustee pursuant to 11 U.S.C. § 547(b).

IV.

Having concluded that the payment to Ford was indeed a preferential transfer, the remaining issue is Ford's asserted defense under 11 U.S.C. § 547(c)(2). This defense, commonly referred to as the ordinary course of business exception, provides a safe harbor from the trustee's avoidance powers for certain preferential payments. The exception under 11 U.S.C. § 547(c)(2) consists of three elements:

(c) The trustee may not avoid under this section a transfer
* * * * * *
(2) to the extent that such transfer was —
(A) in payment of a debt incurred by the debtor in the ordinary course of business or financial affairs of the debtor and the transferee;

17: ROBLIN INDUSTRIES V FORD MOTOR

(B) made in the ordinary course of business or financial affairs of the debtor and the transferee; and
(C) made according to ordinary business terms.

39*39 A creditor asserting the defense bears the burden of proving each of the three elements by a preponderance of the evidence. 11 U.S.C. § 547(g); see Advo-System, Inc. v. Maxway Corp., 37 F.3d 1044, 1047 (4th Cir. 1994); Sulmeyer v. Suzuki (In re Grand Chevrolet, Inc.), 25 F.3d 728, 732 (9th Cir. 1994); Jones v. United Sav. & Loan Ass'n. (In re U.S.A. Inns of Eureka Springs, Ark., Inc.), 9 F.3d 680, 682 (8th Cir.1993).

The Bankruptcy Court found that Ford was not entitled to the exception. Chief Judge McGuire held that:

Assuming that the agreement between the debtor and Ford to handle debtor's delinquent debt

may meet 2(A) and (B), the Court believes that there is no doubt but that it fails (C).

....

The notion that a delinquent debt, whether being repaid pursuant to formal agreement or not, could be viewed as being made according to ordinary business terms would stand preference theory on its head. The very genesis of the agreement is a failure to pay according to ordinary business terms. Thus, this transaction does not fall within the ordinary course exception.

Roblin, 127 B.R. at 725. The District Court affirmed, explaining that Ford had failed to establish that the payments were made according to ordinary business terms. Roblin II, slip op. at 13.

On appeal, Ford argues that the Bankruptcy Court's finding that the April payment was not protected by the ordinary course of business exception was clearly erroneous. The Trustee responds by arguing that the repayment agreement was a direct result of Roblin's default on its trade debt to Ford and that a restructured payment plan on a defaulted debt cannot be considered ordinary. In any event, the Trustee argues, Ford introduced no evidence to suggest that the repayment agreement was typical either as between Ford and Roblin or within the industry generally.

Bankruptcy courts in this Circuit have noted the absence of clear direction from this Court with respect to the interpretation of the elements of § 547(c)(2). See, e.g., McCord v. Venus Foods, Inc. (In re Lan Yik Foods Corp.), 185 B.R. 103,

17: ROBLIN INDUSTRIES V FORD MOTOR

114 (Bankr. E.D.N.Y.1995) (Duberstein, C.J.); Wallach v. Vulcan Steam Forging Co., Inc. (In re D.J. Management Group, Inc.), 164 B.R. 831, 833 (Bankr.W.D.N.Y.1994) (Kaplan, C.J.) ("Few issues in Bankruptcy Law are as unsettled in this Circuit as is the question of how one defines the `ordinary course of business' and `ordinary business terms' for purposes of 11 U.S.C. § 547(c)(2)...."). This case provides us the opportunity to join our colleagues in other circuits by setting forth the appropriate standard for § 547(c)(2)(C).

A.

With a single exception, each Circuit Court of Appeals to grapple with the meaning of "ordinary business terms" has come to the conclusion that the phrase refers broadly to customary terms and conditions used by other parties in the same industry facing the same or similar problems. See Advo-System, 37 F.3d at 1048; Grand Chevrolet, 25 F.3d at 733; Fiber Lite Corp. v. Molded Acoustical Prods., Inc. (In re Molded Acoustical Prods., Inc.), 18 F.3d 217, 223 (3d Cir. 1994); Clark v. Balcor Real Estate Finance, Inc. (In re Meridith Hoffman Partners), 12 F.3d 1549, 1553 (10th Cir.1993), cert. denied, ___ U.S. ___, 114 S.Ct. 2677, 129 L.Ed.2d 812 (1994); U.S.A. Inns, 9 F.3d at 683-84; In re Tolona Pizza Prods. Corp., 3 F.3d 1029, 1032-33 (7th Cir.1993); Logan v. Basic Distrib. Corp. (In re Fred Hawes Org., Inc.), 957 F.2d 239, 243-44 (6th Cir.1992). Only the Court of Appeals for the Eleventh Circuit has held that no evidence of industry practice beyond the conduct of the debtor and creditor in question is necessary to satisfy § 547(c)(2)(C). See Marathon Oil Co. v. Flatau (In re Craig Oil Co.), 785 F.2d 1563, 1566-67 (11th Cir.1986).

In In re Tolona Pizza Products Corp., 3 F.3d 1029 (7th Cir.1993), the Court of Appeals for the Seventh Circuit in an opinion by Judge Posner held that "ordinary business terms" refers to the general practices of similar industry members, and that "only dealings so idiosyncratic as to fall outside that broad range should be deemed extraordinary 40*40 and therefore outside the scope of subsection C." Id., 3 F.3d at 1033. Under this standard, a creditor must show that the business terms of the transaction in question were "within the outer limits of normal industry practices," id., in order to satisfy the third element of § 547(c)(2). The conduct of the debtor and creditor are considered objectively in light of industry practice.

The objective nature of the approach adopted in Tolona Pizza has been widely endorsed. The Courts of Appeals for the Third and Fourth Circuits have adopted a modified test by linking the extent to which the terms of a transaction may permissibly deviate from industry practice to the duration of the relationship

17: ROBLIN INDUSTRIES V FORD MOTOR

between debtor and creditor. See Advo-System, 37 F.3d at 1050; Molded Acoustical, 18 F.3d at 225. This embellishment aside, the thrust of § 547(c)(2)(C) under Tolona Pizza is clear. Assuming subsections (A) and (B) are satisfied, only when a payment is ordinary from the perspective of the industry will the ordinary course of business defense be available for an otherwise voidable preference. Defining the relevant industry is appropriately left to the bankruptcy courts to determine as questions of fact heavily dependent upon the circumstances of each individual case. See Molded Acoustical, 18 F.3d at 224; Tolona Pizza, 3 F.3d at 1033; Fred Hawes, 957 F.2d at 246; see also Transue & Williams Stamping Co. v. Cleveland Screw Prods. Inc. (In re Transue & Williams Stamping Co.), Nos. 93-60269, 95-6044, 1995 WL 646834, at *4 (Bankr.N.D.Ohio Sept. 19, 1995); Milwaukee Cheese Wisconsin, Inc. v. Straus (In re Milwaukee Cheese Wisconsin, Inc.), 191 B.R. 397 (Bankr.E.D.Wis.1995).

This formulation is the most reasonable interpretation of § 547(c)(2)(C) because it balances the competing interests involved with respect to voidable preferences. The trustee's power to avoid preferential transfers springs from a concern for the equitable treatment of all creditors as well as the desire to discourage creditors from hastily forcing troubled businesses into bankruptcy. As the legislative history indicates:

The purpose of the preference section is two-fold. First, by permitting the trustee to avoid prebankruptcy transfers that occur within a short period before bankruptcy, creditors are discouraged from racing to the courthouse to dismember the debtor during [its] slide into bankruptcy. The protection thus afforded the debtor often enables [it] to work [its] way out of a difficult financial situation through cooperation with all of [its] creditors. Second, and more important, the preference provisions facilitate the prime bankruptcy policy of equality of distribution among creditors of the debtor. Any creditor that received a greater payment than others of [its] class is required to disgorge so that all may share equally. The operation of the preference section to deter "the race of diligence" of creditors to dismember the debtor before bankruptcy furthers the second goal of the preference section — that of equality of distribution.

H.Rep. No. 595, 95th Cong., 1st Sess. 177-78 (1977), reprinted in 1978 U.S.Code Cong. & Admin.News 5963, 6138. Referring directly to this legislative history, the Supreme Court has explained that:

[T]he two policies are not entirely independent. On the one hand, any exception for a payment on account of an antecedent debt tends to favor the payee over other creditors and therefore may conflict with the policy of equal treatment. On

17: ROBLIN INDUSTRIES V FORD MOTOR

the other hand, the ordinary course of business exception may benefit all creditors by deterring the "race to the courthouse" and enabling the struggling debtor to continue operating its business.

Union Bank v. Wolas, 502 U.S. 151, 160-61, 112 S.Ct. 527, 532-33, 116 L.Ed.2d 514 (1991). Preferences are disfavored because they are often made on the basis of which creditor is the most demanding or most favored rather than on the basis of fairness to all. As the Court of Appeals for the Third Circuit explained:

The preference statute, by allowing the estate to recover in full — for the benefit of all the unsecured creditors — assets which a pushy unsecured creditor unilaterally plucked for itself or which a fawning debtor used in an irregular transaction to advantage a favored creditor, seeks to foreclose 41*41 these tragedy-of-the-common type responses to a struggling business.

Molded Acoustical, 18 F.3d at 223.

The ordinary course of business exception is consistent with the general thrust of preference law. The exception benefits all creditors by protecting payments received by those creditors who remain committed to a debtor during times of financial distress while at the same time affording a measure of flexibility to creditors in dealing with the debtor, provided that the steps taken are consistent with customary practice among industry participants. The approach taken by the court in Tolona Pizza flows naturally from the purpose of § 547(c)(2):

The purpose of this exception is to leave undisturbed normal financial relations, because it does not detract from the general policy of the preference section to discourage unusual action by either the debtor or [its] creditors during the debtor's slide into bankruptcy.

H.Rep. No. 595, 95th Cong., 1st Sess. 373 (1977), reprinted in 1978 U.S.Code Cong. & Admin.News 6329.

The alternative to the objective inquiry adopted in Tolona Pizza is to look to the conduct of the parties themselves to determine if the terms of a preferential transfer are ordinary. This was the approach taken by the Court of Appeals for the Eleventh Circuit in Craig Oil. See also Graphic Prods. Corp. v. WWF Paper Corp. (In re Graphic Prods. Corp.), 176 B.R. 65, 71-72 (Bankr.S.D.Fla.1994); Equipment Co. of America v. Production Supply Co. of Florida, Inc. (In re Equipment Co. of America), 135 B.R. 169, 173 (Bankr.S.D.Fla.1991). Under this approach, whether a payment is made according to ordinary business terms is examined solely in the context of the ordinary terms between the particular

17: ROBLIN INDUSTRIES V FORD MOTOR

debtor and creditor. But by treating both § 547(c)(2)(B) and (C) as subjective requirements and focusing entirely upon the conduct of the parties in question, the ordinary business terms requirement becomes surplusage. Congress could not have intended that one of the three separate requirements enacted to satisfy § 547(c)(2) was simply redundant. See, e.g., Tolona Pizza, 3 F.3d at 1032.

Moreover, a purely subjective approach which focuses solely on the prior dealings of the debtor and creditor does not adequately assure against inequitable treatment of those creditors not fortunate or prescient enough to establish a pattern of "ordinary" debt payments sufficiently in advance of an eventual bankruptcy. The court in Tolona Pizza alluded directly to this concern:

The second possible function of [subsection (C)] is to allay the concerns of creditors that one or more of their number may have worked out a special deal with the debtor, before the preference period, designed to put that creditor ahead of the others in the event of bankruptcy.

Tolona Pizza, 3 F.3d at 1032.

We agree with the reasoning of Tolona Pizza and hold that 11 U.S.C. § 547(c)(2)(C) requires a creditor to demonstrate that the terms of a payment for which it seeks the protection of the ordinary course of business exception fall within the bounds of ordinary practice of others similarly situated.

B.

Having determined the standard to be applied, we note that the Bankruptcy Court in this case did not engage in an objective analysis to determine whether Ford had demonstrated that the payment at issue comported with ordinary business terms in the industry. The Bankruptcy Court concluded, rather, that the terms could not possibly be ordinary because they arose from Roblin's failure to abide by the terms of its account with Ford. See Roblin, 127 B.R. at 725 (citing Craig Oil). We decline to adopt a rule that payments made pursuant to debt restructuring agreements, even when the debt is in default, can never be made according to ordinary business terms as a matter of law. That determination is a question of fact that depends on the nature of industry practice in each particular case, a factual inquiry that is appropriately left to the bankruptcy court. See Child World, Inc. v. Service Merchandise Co., Inc. (In re Child World, Inc.), 173 B.R. 473, 478 n. 4 (Bankr.S.D.N.Y.1994); Sapir v. Keener Lumber Co., Inc. (In re 42*42 Ajayem Lumber Corp.), 143 B.R. 347, 353 (Bankr.S.D.N.Y.1992). It is not difficult to imagine circumstances where frequent debt rescheduling is ordinary and usual practice within an industry, and creditors operating in such an environ-

17: ROBLIN INDUSTRIES V FORD MOTOR

ment should have the same opportunity to assert the ordinary course of business exception. See, e.g., U.S.A. Inns, 9 F.3d at 685 (regular practice in savings and loan industry to adopt payment plans for delinquent customers); Armstrong v. John Deere Co. (In re Gilbertson), 90 B.R. 1006, 1012 (Bankr.D.N.D.1988) (deferral agreements common in retail farm implement sales industry). Indeed, if the industry practice is to restructure defaulted debt, it would make little practical sense to require creditors to comply with any other standard in order to meet the requirement of § 547(c)(2)(C).

To apply properly the § 547(c)(2)(C) standard, "ordinary business terms" must include those terms employed by similarly situated debtors and creditors facing the same or similar problems. If the terms in question are ordinary for industry participants under financial distress, then that is ordinary for the industry. In this way, a creditor that agrees to restructure a debt in a manner consistent with industry practice in those circumstances does not lose the benefit of the exception. A creditor taking such steps should not be viewed as taking "unusual action" when it does no more than follow usual industry practice — precisely the kind of behavior the ordinary course of business exception was intended to protect. Restricting a creditor to courses of action typical in untroubled times leaves no room for realistic debt workouts and unfairly penalizes those creditors that take conventional steps to institute a repayment plan. See U.S.A. Inns, 9 F.3d at 682-86; but see Meridith Hoffman Partners, 12 F.3d at 1553-54.

C.

While the Bankruptcy Court did not perform the analysis dictated by the approach to § 547(c)(2)(C) we adopt today, the District Court did address both the subjective and objective aspects of the ordinary course of business exception, and it found no evidence of the industry standards that would have been required to support an ordinary course of business exception:

The Court finds that the evidence supports the bankruptcy court's conclusion that the payments were not made according to ordinary business terms. The record establishes that debtor contacted Ford and proposed the restructured payment agreement precisely because of its failure to pay the outstanding debt according to the original agreed upon terms. Moreover, the bankruptcy judge found the testimony of Roncolato established that the arrangement for payment of the delinquent debt was not part of an extension among all creditors, but was done in order to ensure debtor's continued supply of scrap material from Ford. No evidence was presented that the restructuring of the debt and the resultant payments were consistent with the prior course of dealing between the parties or in accor-

17: ROBLIN INDUSTRIES V FORD MOTOR

dance with customary business practice within the industry of which the parties are a part.

Roblin II, slip op. at 11-12 (citations omitted) (emphasis added).

Ford argues that the payments were made in accordance with ordinary business terms for several reasons. First, Ford argues that the repayment agreement itself had become the ordinary course of business for the two parties because for months prior to the bankruptcy, Roblin had made its payments when due without incident. Second, Ford contends that the ordinary course of business exception should apply because Ford took no unusual action to collect the debt from Roblin — no dunning calls were made, no collection letters sent, no litigation threatened. Third, Ford argues that the payments were made according to ordinary business terms because the repayment agreement was "inherently fair," imposing an interest rate below the prevailing prime rate. Finally, Ford argues that Roblin's own financial officer testified that similar arrangements were made with other suppliers, and that the terms of the agreement with Ford were consistent with the terms Roblin would have faced had it financed the debt with a third party. For all of these reasons, Ford argues that we should 43*43 reverse the Bankruptcy Court's finding that the payment did not comport with ordinary business terms.

None of these arguments remedies Ford's failure to introduce evidence of the ordinary practices of similarly situated firms. That failure of proof is fatal to Ford's position.

Ford's first two arguments concern solely the dealings between the creditor and debtor in this case and do not relate to the objective inquiry into industry practice that is required to satisfy § 547(c)(2)(C). Ford's third argument with respect to the prime interest rate does not solve Ford's failure of proof because there is no evidence of how the interest rate charged here compared with other rates generally charged on restructured delinquent debt in the industry. Finally, with respect to the arrangements Roblin made with others, there is also evidence that some creditors did not restructure their debt with Roblin. Ford's evidence did not establish ordinary business terms among Roblin's creditors, much less demonstrate an objective industry practice as required by § 547(c)(2)(C).

The evidence in this case is no more than the Court of Appeals for the Seventh Circuit found insufficient in In re Midway Airlines, Inc., 69 F.3d 792 (7th Cir.1995) (Ripple, J.). In that case a creditor appealed an adverse determination that certain payments would not be protected by the ordinary course of business exception because they were not made according to ordinary business terms. The

17: ROBLIN INDUSTRIES V FORD MOTOR

creditor had not offered any evidence of industry practice, relying instead on the conduct of the debtor both with respect to the creditor itself and the debtor's other suppliers. The Court affirmed, holding that "proof of the parties' own relationship is insufficient." Id., 69 F.3d at 799. The Court explained that "[r]eliance solely on the experience of the creditor renders ineffectual the important dichotomy between the subjective requirements of 11 U.S.C. § 547(c)(2)(A)-(B), which can be satisfied through proof of the parties' own dealings, and the objective requirement imposed by 11 U.S.C. § 547(c)(2)(C), which requires reference to some external datum." Id., 69 F.3d at 797-98.

The court in Midway Airlines relied, in turn, on another thoughtful decision on this point. In Logan v. Basic Distribution Corp. (In re Fred Hawes Organization, Inc.), 957 F.2d 239 (6th Cir.1992) (Rosen, J.), the Court of Appeals for the Sixth Circuit addressed the question of whether proof of industry standards was possible without examining practices beyond those of the parties in question. The Court acknowledged that:

[I]n looking at industry standards, a court may also refer to the manner in which the parties conduct their business with other, unrelated parties. This evidence alone, however, is insufficient to prove "ordinary business terms" by a preponderance of the evidence.

Id., 957 F.2d at 246 n. 7. The Court recognized that "courts do not look only at the manner in which one particular creditor interacted with other similarly situated debtors, but rather analyze whether the particular transaction in question comports with the standard conduct of business within the industry." Id., 957 F.2d at 246.

We agree with the proposition that the behavior of the parties cannot be sufficient in and of itself to sustain the creditor's burden of proof with respect to ordinary business terms in the industry. To permit a creditor to rely solely on such evidence would, in effect, shift the burden to the trustee to offer evidence that other industry participants behaved otherwise. The burden of proof to show industry practice, however, is on the creditor who seeks to retain a payment at the expense of the other creditors. See D.J. Management, 164 B.R. at 838 ("Other creditors who wait for payment are entitled to the benefit of the fact that it is the preferred creditor who must convince the Court that nothing 'idiosyncratic' was going on.").

Applying these principles to this case, we are convinced that Ford did not sustain its burden of proof at trial. No evidence of industry practice or custom apart from Roblin's own experience was introduced. In this case, because the record

17: ROBLIN INDUSTRIES V FORD MOTOR

before us yields no other result but the one reached below, the proper course is to affirm. See Molded Acoustical, 18 F.3d at 222 n. 7.

44*44 CONCLUSION

For the foregoing reasons, we affirm the order of the District Court affirming the judgment of the Bankruptcy Court in favor of the Trustee to recover Roblin's April 2, 1985 payment to Ford of $53,320.78 as a preferential transfer voidable under 11 U.S.C. § 547.

AFFIRMED.

[*] The Honorable John G. Koeltl, United States District Judge for the Southern District of New York, sitting by designation.

[1] The District Court correctly found, and the parties do not dispute, that for purposes of determining whether a transfer was made within the 90 day preference period, a transfer by check is deemed to occur on the date the check is honored rather than the date received by the payee. See Barnhill v. Johnson, 503 U.S. 393, 400, 112 S.Ct. 1386, 1390, 118 L.Ed.2d 39 (1992).

[2] Ford counterclaimed below for the return of two other payments made to Ford in May and June 1985 which Ford allegedly returned to Roblin by mistake. Having determined that the April 1985 payment was a preferential transfer, the Bankruptcy Court dismissed the counterclaims because the later payments were also preferential transfers. See Roblin, 127 B.R. at 725. The District Court affirmed. See In re Roblin Indus., Inc., 91 CV 523A, at 13 (W.D.N.Y. Mar. 29, 1995). For the same reasons that we affirm the judgment ordering the return of Roblin's April 1985 payment to Ford, we affirm the dismissal of Ford's counterclaims.

18: KLEIN V TABATCHNICK

Jerry B. KLEIN, as Trustee for the Liquidation of the Business of JNT Investors, Inc., Debtor, Plaintiff-Appellee and Cross-Appellant,

v.

Jay N. TABATCHNICK and S. Wolfe Emmer, Defendants-Appellants and Cross-Appellees.

Nos. 1075 to 1077, Dockets 78-7639, 79-7027 and 79-7074.

United States Court of Appeals, Second Circuit.

Argued June 13, 1979.
Decided November 26, 1979.

1044*1044 1045*1045 Kevin P. Hughes, New York City, Weil, Gotshal & Manges, New York City, for plaintiff-appellee and cross-appellant.

Lawrence Greenapple, New York City, Bobrow, Greenapple, Burton, Distler & Midler, New York City, for defendant-appellant and cross-appellee, Jay N. Tabatchnick.

Barbara Meiers, Los Angeles, Cal. (Gibson, Dunn & Crutcher, Steven A. Meiers, Los Angeles, Cal., Conboy, Hewitt, O'Brien & Boardman, Timothy C. Quinn, New York City, of counsel), for defendant-appellant and cross-appellee, S. W. Emmer.

1046*1046 Before VAN GRAAFEILAND and NEWMAN,[*] Circuit Judges, and BONSAL, District Judge.[**]

VAN GRAAFEILAND, Circuit Judge:

Jay N. Tabatchnick and S. Wolfe Emmer appeal from a $73,750 judgment recovered against them by Jerry B. Klein, trustee for the liquidation of the business of JNT Investors, Inc., under the Securities Investor Protection Act of 1970, 15 U.S.C. §§ 78aaa-78lll. Klein cross appeals from that portion of the judgment dismissing other claims for relief. The parties' differences have been much too extensively briefed and argued, both in this Court and in the court below. There are, however, several issues of substance that require discussion.

I

The Grant of Summary Judgment

JNT, a small securities broker and dealer with its office in New York City, was

18: KLEIN V TABATCHNICK

organized by defendant Tabatchnick in 1970. Tabatchnick was president of the company and owned 43 percent of its stock. Defendant Emmer owned 42 percent of the stock and maintained a trading account with the company. In October 1970 Tabatchnick obtained from the First National City Bank a personal loan of $50,000 payable on demand and secured by collateral owned by one Joseph Taub. Tabatchnick then loaned the $50,000 to JNT under a subordinated loan agreement maturing November 1, 1971.

When Tabatchnick decided to extend the subordinated loan for another year, Emmer supplied collateral for the bank loan to replace that of Mr. Taub. With Emmer's authorization, Tabatchnick used 7,000 shares of common stock of Commonwealth Silver Industries, Ltd., from Emmer's account at JNT for this purpose. To give Emmer some protection against loss, Tabatchnick delivered to him certain portfolio securities of JNT. The receipt signed by Emmer stated that the securities were "assigned to [Emmer] as additional collateral until which time your 7,000 shares of Commonwealth Silver Ind. common stock will no longer be needed as collateral for Mr. Tabatchnick's personal loan of $50,000 [from] First National City which was subordinated to JNT Investors, Inc."

On February 15, 1972, the United States District Court for the Southern District of New York determined that JNT's customers were in need of protection under 15 U.S.C. § 78eee and appointed plaintiff trustee for the liquidation of the company's business. This liquidation was to be conducted generally "in accordance with, and as though it were being conducted under," Chapter X of the Bankruptcy Act, 15 U.S.C. § 78fff(c)(1). Following his appointment, plaintiff contended that the transfer of JNT's portfolio securities to Emmer was a fraudulent conveyance under section 67(d) of the Bankruptcy Act, 11 U.S.C. § 107(d),[1] and demanded their return, which was refused. In the suit that ensued, the district court granted plaintiff's motion for summary judgment on the cause of action alleging a section 67(d) violation, reserving only the question of damages for jury determination. See Klein v. Tabatchnick, 418 F.Supp. 1368 (S.D.N.Y.1976). Damages subsequently were fixed by a jury at $73,750. For the following reasons, we believe that summary judgment should not have been granted.

In granting plaintiff's motion, the district court made several factual findings. He found (1) that the transfer of JNT securities to Emmer occurred on December 13, 1971, (2) that the transfer was without fair consideration to JNT, and (3) that JNT was 1047*1047 insolvent at the time of transfer. We believe that the making of these findings should have awaited trial.

(1)

18: KLEIN V TABATCHNICK

Fixing the date of transfer was important in this case because of the extreme fluctuations in the value of the volatile securities involved and because it was the date as of which insolvency had to be determined. Although the receipt for the transferred securities was dated December 13, 1971, there was strong indication in the motion papers that the transfer actually occurred in February 1972 and the receipt was either delivered before transfer or was back-dated by some unidentified person. JNT's inventory records show that the securities were in its vault as late as the end of January 1972, and there is deposition testimony that they were removed by Tabatchnick in early February. We have examined the voluminous affidavits submitted to the district court and are unable to determine when the transfer occurred. We conclude that the district judge erred in making that determination on plaintiff's application for summary judgment.

(2)

Fairness of consideration is generally a question of fact. McNellis v. Raymond, 287 F.Supp. 232, 238 (N.D.N.Y.1968), rev'd on other grounds, 420 F.2d 51 (2d Cir. 1970); see Roth v. Fabrikant Bros., Inc., 175 F.2d 665, 668 (2d Cir. 1949); Seligson v. New York Produce Exchange, 394 F.Supp. 125, 132-34 (S.D.N.Y.1975). The district court determined it as a question of law. See 418 F.Supp. at 1372. We do not believe the facts were so clearly established in plaintiff's favor that they warranted disposition in this manner.

The district judge focused on the fact that Emmer's written authorization for the use of his securities as replacement collateral was not executed until December 11, 1971, while the extension of Tabatchnick's subordinated loan agreement was executed on November 1st. From this, he concluded that the December 11 authorization was of no value to JNT. In so doing, the district judge overlooked Tabatchnick's sworn statement that he would not have extended the subordination agreement on November 1 if he had not obtained a prior commitment from Emmer that he would furnish replacement collateral.

Although the district judge was clearly correct in holding that transfers solely for the benefit of third parties do not furnish fair consideration under section 67(d)(2)(a), that statement may not be applicable to the transaction at issue. Benefit to a debtor need not be direct; it may come indirectly through benefit to a third person. See Williams v. Twin City Co., 251 F.2d 678, 681 (9th Cir. 1958); Mandel v. Scanlon, 426 F.Supp. 519, 523-24 (W.D.Pa.1977); McNellis v. Raymond, supra, 287 F.Supp. at 239; Hoflar v. Marion Lumber Co., 233 F.Supp. 540, 543 (E.D.S.C.1964). Tabatchnick was the majority shareholder of JNT, and everything he owned was in the firm. It appears from the motion papers that he

18: KLEIN V TABATCHNICK

operated the company as if it were his private domain. Emmer, the other substantial shareholder, denied that he participated in any way in company management. As he put it, "This whole company, JNT, was in fact Mr. Tabatchnick as far as I was concerned." The $50,000 that Tabatchnick borrowed from the bank was loaned to the company, and that loan, Tabatchnick says, would not have been renewed without the use of Emmer's collateral.

Construing the motion papers most favorably to the defendants, as we are required to do, Adickes v. S. H. Kress & Co., 398 U.S. 144, 157, 90 S.Ct. 1598, 26 L.Ed.2d 142 (1970), we cannot say that JNT received no benefit from Tabatchnick's use of Emmer's collateral. Whether this furnished fair consideration for the transfer of JNT's own securities to Emmer depended among other things on JNT's need for the $50,000, its availability from some source other than Tabatchnick, and the value of the securities transferred to Emmer. JNT was a new underwriting firm which started in business with little or no capital and no financial track record. The motion papers show that withdrawal of Tabatchnick's $50,000 would have created a severe cash and capital problem 1048*1048 in the company and that Emmer "provided a substantial benefit to JNT when he furnished the replacement collateral for the loan." Moreover, there was substantial dispute as to the value of the securities transferred to Emmer; Tabatchnick in particular placed a very low value upon them. Whether this value was fairly equivalent to the benefits received by JNT should not have been decided on motion papers.

(3)

Insolvency is also a factual question. Britt v. Damson, 334 F.2d 896, 902 (9th Cir. 1964), cert. denied, 379 U.S. 966, 85 S.Ct. 661, 13 L.Ed.2d 560 (1965); 1 Collier on Bankruptcy § 1.19 at 130.12 (14th ed. 1974); 4 Collier on Bankruptcy § 67.05 (14th ed. 1978). Moreover, a finding on the issue of insolvency often depends upon the factual inferences and conclusions of expert witnesses which, when controverted, do not lend themselves readily to summary judgment resolution. See United States v. Diebold, Inc., 369 U.S. 654, 82 S.Ct. 993, 8 L.Ed.2d 176 (1962); Seligson v. New York Produce Exchange, supra, 394 F.Supp. at 128-32.

In this case, the district court made a finding of insolvency on the basis of expert testimony by the trustee, whose accounting procedures and qualifications as an expert were challenged by defendants and who admittedly "made numerous subjective judgments concerning values of various assets." The district court erroneously assumed that defendants had deposed the trustee prior to the summary

18: KLEIN V TABATCHNICK

judgment application and emphasized that they had not sought out a certified public accountant to verify the accuracy of the trustee's conclusions. However, when Emmer moved for reconsideration of the district court's summary judgment order and produced the affidavit of a certified public accountant stating that JNT was solvent on both November 30, 1971, and December 31, 1971, the district court found that Emmer had presented no new evidence which would justify modification of its prior opinion. We conclude that this was error. Where, as here, intelligent adjudication requires more than the use of lay knowledge and the resolution of a disputed issue hinges in large measure upon conflicting opinions and judgments of expert witnesses, summary judgment is not appropriate. See Rains v. Cascade Industries, Inc., 402 F.2d 241, 247 (3d Cir. 1968); Cf. Vermont Structural Slate Co. v. Tatko Brothers Slate Co., 233 F.2d 9, 10 (2d Cir. 1956).

Because the grant of summary judgment was error, judgment for plaintiff on the second and fourth causes of action must be reversed.[2] The second cause of action is remanded for trial as against the defendant Tabatchnick,[3] the fourth cause of action as against the defendant Emmer.[4]

II

Dismissal of Plaintiff's Ninth Cause of Action

In February 1972, during discussions with the National Association of Securities Dealers (NASD), Tabatchnick agreed to cease conducting business with the public until 1049*1049 such time as JNT was able to comply with the Net Capital Rule. 17 C.F.R. § 240.15c3-1. Tabatchnick was instructed that he would have to raise $138,000 in order to bring JNT into capital compliance. Once again, he went to Emmer for help. Emmer instructed another brokerage firm, in which he maintained a substantial account, to give Tabatchnick a check of $100,000 payable to JNT, with the understanding that he would have his money back in 24 to 48 hours or else he would cancel the check.

Although Tabatchnick secured the check to placate the NASD, he apparently decided that his efforts to salvage JNT would be futile. He did not show the check to NASD officials, nor did he place it in the firm account. Tabatchnick informed the NASD staff supervisor that he had a check "which could be contributed to JNT but that the check was not going to be put into JNT." Instead, Tabatchnick tore the signature off the check and returned it to the brokerage firm which had issued it.

Plaintiff's ninth cause of action alleges that Tabatchnick's return of the check constituted a voidable preference under section 60 of the Bankruptcy Act, 11 U.S.C.

18: KLEIN V TABATCHNICK

§ 96, which defines a preference as a transfer of the debtor's property "to or for the benefit of a creditor for or on account of an antecedent debt". Id. § 96(a)(1). The district court held in the first instance that it was for the jury to determine whether Tabatchnick's return of the check constituted such a voidable preference. When the jury concluded that it did, the district judge reconsidered his earlier decision and directed that judgment notwithstanding the verdict be entered in favor of the defendants on the ninth cause of action. We believe that this latter determination was the correct one.

In order for the trustee to establish a preferential transfer, he had to show that the transferee was a creditor of the bankrupt, i. e., the owner of a demand or claim provable in bankruptcy. Richardson v. Shaw, 209 U.S. 365, 381, 28 S.Ct. 512, 52 L.Ed. 835 (1908); 11 U.S.C. § 1(11); 3 Collier on Bankruptcy § 60, at 834 (14th ed. 1977). For a debt to exist, something must be owed to the creditor. Zwick v. Freeman, 373 F.2d 110, 116 (2d Cir.), cert. denied, 389 U.S. 835, 88 S.Ct. 43, 19 L.Ed.2d 96 (1967). Moreover, the transferee must have become a creditor prior to the transfer, or it would not have been made "for or on account of an antecedent debt." 4 Remington on Bankruptcy § 1660, at 203 (5th ed. 1957). "Preference implies paying or securing a pre-existing debt of the person preferred." Dean v. Davis, 242 U.S. 438, 443, 37 S.Ct. 130, 131, 61 L.Ed. 419 (1917).

We agree with the district judge that JNT owed no antecedent debt to Emmer which he, as a creditor, could have proven in JNT's bankruptcy proceedings. The check itself was merely a request to the drawee bank to pay JNT $100,000; it did not operate as an assignment of these funds to JNT. Garden Check Cashing Service, Inc. v. First National City Bank, 25 A.D.2d 137, 141-42, 267 N.Y.S.2d 698, aff'd, 18 N.Y.2d 941, 277 N.Y.S.2d 141, 223 N.E.2d 566 (1966). Prior to the cashing of the check, there was simply no obligation owing to Emmer for which he could have had a recovery.

The judgment dismissing plaintiff's ninth cause of action is affirmed.

III

Damages and Setoff

Both defendants challenge the right of the district court to award damages against them. Emmer contends that plaintiff's sole remedy against him was the return of the JNT securities. Tabatchnick asserts that section 720 of the New York Business Corporation Law does not authorize the recovery of money damages.

Emmer also contends that he was entitled to recover damages from plaintiff for

18: KLEIN V TABATCHNICK

plaintiff's refusal to return securities owned by Emmer but in plaintiff's possession. Tabatchnick argues that he was entitled to a setoff against plaintiff's recovery of $50,000, the amount of his unrepaid loan to JNT.

(1)

Under the circumstances of this case, if the trustee is entitled to recover for
1050*1050 a fraudulent transfer of JNT securities to Emmer, that recovery is not
limited to a return of the securities. The remedial provisions of sections 67 and 70
of the Bankruptcy Act are somewhat ambiguous. Section 67(d)(6), 11 U.S.C. §
107(d)(6), provides that a fraudulent transfer "shall be null and void against the
trustee." Section 70(e)(2), 11 U.S.C. § 110(e)(2), on the other hand, provides that
the trustee "shall reclaim and recover such property or collect its value." We need
not decide whether these sections, read together, give the trustee the option in
every case to seek either recovery of the property or its value. But see Schainman
v. Dean, 24 F.2d 475, 476 (9th Cir. 1928). Where, as here, the transferee has
refused to return the securities upon the trustee's request and they have subsequently severely depreciated in value, if such refusal was wrongful, the district
court could permit monetary recovery.

(2)

Section 720 of the New York Business Corporation Law provides that an action
may be brought against a director to compel him to account for the violation of
his duties in the management and disposition of corporate assets. Relying upon
Ali Baba Creations, Inc. v. Congress Textile Printers, Inc., 41 A.D.2d 924, 343
N.Y.S.2d 712 (1973), Tabatchnick now contends, apparently for the first time,
that section 720 may not be used, as here, to obtain a money judgment in an
action at law for damages.

Because we are remanding for a new trial, this issue becomes largely academic.
Plaintiff is not seeking to recover any illgotten gains in the hands of Tabatchnick
but only the damages which JNT sustained as a result of Tabatchnick's allegedly
wrongful conduct. The New York Court of Appeals has held that section 720 "is
broad and covers every form of waste of assets and violation of duty whether as a
result of intention, negligence, or predatory acquisition." Rapoport v. Schneider,
29 N.Y.2d 396, 400, 328 N.Y.S.2d 431, 435, 278 N.E.2d 642, 645 (1972).
Whether pursuit of relief in the instant case is labeled as an action for an accounting or a suit for damages is of little consequence. Amending the ad damnum
clause in plaintiff's second cause of action to make it a demand that Tabatchnick
account for JNT's damages will cause no change of substance, nor will it preju-

18: KLEIN V TABATCHNICK

dice Tabatchnick in any manner. See Bush v. Masiello, 55 F.R.D. 72, 78, 79 (S.D. N.Y.1972). Such amendment may be had.

(3)

The question whether Emmer should be entitled to a monetary recovery for the trustee's allegedly wrongful withholding of stock owned by Emmer is an important one because of the securities' sharp decline in value. In his counterclaim, Emmer alleged that he owned certain securities which were held for his account by JNT and that the trustee had taken possession of them. These allegations were admitted by the trustee, who contended that section 57(g) of the Bankruptcy Act, 11 U.S.C. § 93(g), authorized him to retain possession.

Section 57(g) provides that the claim of a creditor who has received a voidable preference should not be allowed unless he surrenders the preference. Relying upon this provision, the district court held that the trustee could retain Emmer's stock until any judgment against Emmer was satisfied, at which time it would be returned. Although the facts were not fully developed on the trial, this holding may have been error.

Section 6(c)(2)(A)(iii) of the Securities Investors Protection Act, 15 U.S.C. 78fff(c)(2)(A)(iii), as it existed prior to the 1978 amendments, defined "cash customer" in much the same language as did its predecessor, section 60(e)(1) of the Bankruptcy Act, 11 U.S.C. § 96(e)(1), i. e., a customer entitled to immediate possession of his securities without the payment of any sum to the broker. Further tracking the language of section 60(e), the Securities Investors Protection Act provided that all property held by a stockbroker for the account of customers, except cash customers who were able to specifically identify their property, should constitute a separate fund for the benefit of the customers as a separate class of creditors. Section 6(c)(2)(B). The trustee was directed to return specifically identifiable property to the customers entitled thereto, section 6(c)(2)(C), and no provision 1051*1051 was made for an offset based upon a general indebtedness. The statute provided instead that one might be a cash customer as to certain securities and not to as to others. Section 6(c)(2)(A)(iii).

Our examination of section 60(e) and the Securities Investors Protection Act as originally enacted satisfies us that Congress did not intend in either statute for cash customers with specifically identifiable securities to be treated as creditors with regard to those securities. See Tepper v. Chichester, 285 F.2d 309, 312 (9th Cir. 1961); Cf. 15 U.S.C.A. § 78fff-2(c)(2) (Supp.1979). To the extent, if any, that Emmer was such a cash customer of JNT, he should not have been treated as a

18: KLEIN V TABATCHNICK

creditor subject to the provisions of section 57(g). Upon retrial, the district court should determine Emmer's rights and remedies on that basis. Other than as expressed herein, we have no present opinion on those issues.

(4)

If, on retrial, Tabatchnick is found to have breached his fiduciary duties to JNT through the transfer of its securities to Emmer, he will not be entitled to set off the $50,000 owed to him by the corporation. See Bayliss v. Rood, 424 F.2d 142, 147 (4th Cir. 1970); Ritter v. Mountain Camp Holding Corp., 252 A.D. 602, 604-5, 299 N.Y.S. 876 (1937); 4 Collier on Bankruptcy § 68.-04[2.1], at 872-77 (14th ed. 1978).

IV

Other Contentions of the Parties

The only other claim of the parties meriting comment is Emmer's claim that the trial court was without jurisdiction. The complaint alleged violations of the Securities Exchange Act and tortious conduct in New York State under the pendent state claims. The district court did not err in holding that jurisdiction existed. See 15 U.S.C. § 78aa; N.Y.Civ.Prac.Law and Rules § 302(a); Mariash v. Morrill, 496 F.2d 1138, 1142-43 (2d Cir. 1974); Neilson v. Sal Martorano, Inc., 36 A.D.2d 625, 626, 319 N.Y. S.2d 480 (1971); Francis I. DuPont & Co. v. Chelednik, 69 Misc.2d 362, 363, 330 N.Y.S.2d 149 (1971).

The judgment appealed from is affirmed in part and reversed and remanded in part in accordance with the foregoing provisions of this opinion. Tabatchnick and Emmer will be allowed fifty percent of their costs and disbursements on this appeal. This amount will adequately compensate them for the cost of presenting their nonfrivolous and nonrepetitive arguments to this Court.

NEWMAN, Circuit Judge, concurring in part and dissenting in part:

I agree with all of the Court's conclusions except the remand for trial of plaintiff's claim against Emmer for the value of the JNT portfolio securities alleged to have been fraudulently transferred from JNT to Emmer.

Emmer received the portfolio securities under the following circumstances. Tabatchnick borrowed $50,000 from Citibank secured by collateral that had been made available by Taub for one year. Tabatchnick loaned the $50,000 to JNT. In order to renew his loan to JNT, Tabatchnick needed to continue the bank's loan to him. Because the original collateral for Tabatchnick's loan had to be returned,

18: KLEIN V TABATCHNICK

new collateral was needed. Emmer supplied Tabatchnick $98,000 worth of Emmer's own securities to enable JNT to continue enjoying the proceeds of Tabatchnick's loan. Tabatchnick transferred to Emmer the JNT portfolio securities as security for return of Emmer's own securities.

Emmer lost every penny of the $98,000 worth of securities he furnished to keep JNT afloat. Now he is told he may also have to pay as damages the value of the portfolio securities he received to protect him against the risk that his own securities might not be returned. Can it be that someone who tries to help a financially troubled corporation is worse off when he receives security for his assistance than he would have been if he had received no security?

Under the second proviso of § 67(d)(6) of the Bankruptcy Act, 11 U.S.C. § 107(d)(6), "[a] lienor . . . who without actual fraudulent intent has given a consideration 1052*1052 less than fair . . . for such . . . lien . . . may retain the . . . lien . . . as security for repayment." Of course the lien does not extend beyond the amount of the consideration the lienor has extended. In re Peoria Braumeister Co., 138 F.2d 520 (7th Cir. 1943). While there is room for dispute in this case as to whether Emmer furnished fair consideration, there can be no dispute that he furnished for the benefit of JNT some consideration. He thus has a lien in the property transferred to him to the extent of his consideration. I do not believe the second proviso of § 67(d)(6) gives the lienor the right to retain his lien only at his peril of responding in damages for any decline in the market value of his security.

It may be that a trustee can seek the aid of the bankruptcy court to have a lienor's security sold and the lien transferred to the proceeds in order to guard against the risk of a decline in the value of the lienor's security. But the trustee here sought no such relief. I would dismiss the complaint as to Emmer.

[*] Judge Newman was United States District Judge for the District of Connecticut, sitting by designation, at the time of oral argument.

[**] Hon. Dudley B. Bonsal, Senior District Judge of the United States District Court for the Southern District of New York, sitting by designation.

[1] Section 67(d)(2)(a) provides that a transfer by a debtor within one year of filing for bankruptcy is fraudulent as to existing creditors if made without fair consideration and the debtor is or will thereby be rendered insolvent.

[2] Although the complaint contained nine causes of action, plaintiff waived six of them prior to trial and proceeded to trial only on the second, fourth, and ninth claims for relief.

18: KLEIN V TABATCHNICK

[3] The second cause of action alleges a claim under section 720 of the New York Business Corporation Law which authorizes actions against corporate directors for breach of their fiduciary duties. Because Emmer was not a director, plaintiff agreed at trial to limit this claim for relief to Tabatchnick. Although the judgment against Tabatchnick on the second cause of action resulted from a directed verdict at the close of trial, the directed verdict was based upon the prior grant of summary judgment on the fourth cause of action alleging a violation of section 67(d). Reversal of plaintiff's recovery under the fourth cause of action therefore requires reversal of his recovery under the second.

[4] The district court correctly held that Tabatchnick did not hold or receive JNT's transferred portfolio securities within the meaning of the bankruptcy law. 11 U.S.C. § 110(e)(2). See Jackson v. Star Sprinkler Corp., 575 F.2d 1223, 1234 (8th Cir. 1978); Elliott v. Glushon, 390 F.2d 514 (9th Cir. 1967). It did not err, therefore, in concluding that only Emmer might be held liable under the fourth cause of action alleging a violation of section 67(d).